Urban Warfare

Urban Warfare

Housing under the Empire of Finance

Raquel Rolnik

Foreword by David Harvey
Translation by Felipe Hirschhorn

VERSO

Work published with the support of the Brazilian Ministry
of Culture / National Library Foundation
Obra publicada com o apoio do Ministério da Cultura
do Brasil / Fundação Biblioteca Nacional

MINISTÉRIO DA CULTURA
Fundação BIBLIOTECA NACIONAL

First published in English by Verso 2019
First published as *Guerra dos lugares: a colonização
da terra e da moradia na era das finanças*
© Boitempo 2015
Translation © Felipe Hirschhorn 2019
Chapter 6 and afterword translation © Bianca Tavolari 2019
Foreword © David Harvey 2018

1 3 5 7 9 10 8 6 4 2

Verso
UK: 6 Meard Street, London W1F 0EG
US: 20 Jay Street, Suite 1010, Brooklyn, NY 11201

versobooks.com

Verso is the imprint of New Left Books

ISBN-13: 978-1-78873-160-7
ISBN-13: 978-1-78873-300-7 (HB)
ISBN-13: 978-1-78873-161-4 (US EBK)
ISBN-13: 978-1-78873-162-1 (UK EBK)

British Library Cataloguing in Publication Data
A catalogue record for this book is available from the British Library

Library of Congress Cataloging-in-Publication Data
A catalog record for this book is available from the Library of Congress

Typeset in Sabon by Biblichor Ltd, Edinburgh
Printed and bound by CPI Group (UK) Ltd, Croydon, CR0 4YY

For my mentors, Gabriel Bolaffi, Lúcio Kowarick,
Warren Dean and David Harvey

For Eugênia and Teresa, the two ends of the
ribbon of strength and love that unites us

Contents

Foreword

R aquel Rolnik has written a magisterial survey and analysis of what is fast becoming one of the most compelling global crises of our time: the seeming inability of our increasingly dominant free market economic and political system to furnish adequate, affordable housing for the mass of the world's population. While problems of housing provision have often been addressed in the context of the politics and policies of particular nation states, never before has such a broad global comparative work of the sort here presented been attempted.

Rolnik has been able to draw on a wealth of experience as an urbanist and urban planner. As director of the Planning Department of the city of São Paulo, she had to deal with the tumultuous problems of housing provision in one of the fastest-growing metropolitan areas of the world. As national secretary for Urban Programmes of the Brazilian Ministry of Cities in the first Lula Administration, she fought to put teeth into the clauses of the Brazilian constitution designed to protect the right to the city. But it was her years as UN special rapporteur that provided her with the basic raw materials to compile this remarkable study.

Her method of enquiry when she was UN rapporteur is worthy of note. Instead of basing her work on the words of government officials alone, she talked with those marginalised populations most affected by poor housing conditions and failing policies on the ground. This brought her into contact with social movement activists who furnished her with multiple grass roots perspectives on their vast and ongoing daily struggles to sustain and create adequate housing provision all too often under the most trying and sometimes even repressive circumstances.

While every city has its own rich and diverse particularities, what becomes apparent from Raquel's penetrating and moving accounts is that the dilemmas of adequate housing provision also have a universal dimension, thanks in part to the export of a particular model of housing provision under the aegis of inter-national institutions (such as the World Bank and the IMF, along with the Habitat Conferences sponsored by the UN).

The contemporary obsession with market provision, with land and property titling and the extension of private property arrangements, with home ownership and access to credit and finance, along with the so-called 'deepening' of financial arrange-ments to build a secondary mortgage market, is overwhelming. While often well-meaning and on occasion sufficiently robust to be judged successful (particularly with respect to the securing of social control), the main effect of these obsessions has been to open the path, as Raquel shows, to the exploitation of housing markets as vehicles for speculative gain for landholders, develop-ers and financiers.

Increasingly, the habit of shaping public policies to counter recessions and ward off depressions by 'building houses and fill-ing them with things' has given a macro-economic role to housing markets that is more about stabilizing capitalism than addressing deficits in housing for marginalized populations. The result has all too often been evictions and displacements of those popula-tions in the name of urban upgrading and renewals that disrupt supportive social networks, however fragile and tenuous. The neighborhood may improve but the needy people who once lived there have disappeared.

On some occasions, market reforms have allowed marginalized and impoverished populations to temporarily accumulate assets (through, for example, sub-prime lending and other forms of micro-finance) only to have those gains erased through subse-quent financial manipulations and crises. The most spectacular example is, of course, the foreclosure on more than 7 million households in the United States after 2007/8 and the loss of more than 70 per cent of the asset values held by low-income black populations. The endless accumulation of capital by financial institutions has largely occurred at the expense of the well-being of those populations that social policies were supposed to serve.

The political and social resistance to this system is everywhere in evidence, and Raquel's documentation of this widespread struggle from below to secure adequate housing rights and appropriate shelter is in many respects inspiring. Social movements fight and struggle to acquire or take back the right to a decent house in a decent living environment endowed with adequate life chances. The commodification of housing provision over the last forty years of neoliberal politics has not gone uncontested. While the well-to-do are furnished with abundant opportunities to indulge their fancies and their often bizarre tastes with multiple luxury mansions in a variety of privileged locations and climes, the mass of the world's population is either technically homeless or at best crammed together in insalubrious dwellings in fetid locations or, in the case of the swelling numbers of global refugees fleeing violence, war and environmental disasters, confined to tent cities in remote locations cut off from any kind of economic or social opportunities to re-establish a normal life. To these populations the idea that a decent house in a decent living environment with access to adequate life chances might be a basic human right must seem like a cruel utopian dream.

In clearing out my library recently I came across a booklet published by the New York Metropolitan Council on Housing in 1978. The title was *Housing in the Public Domain: The Only Solution*. In 1978, Raquel reminds us, the US Housing and Urban Development Department had a budget of $83 billion to help pursue that solution. Limited equity co-ops and even community land trusts were springing up in most major cities with municipal governmental support to offer non-market solutions. By 1983, with the Ronald Reagan neoliberal turn in full swing, the HUD budget for new construction had been reduced to $18 billion. In the Clinton years, a period of increasingly intensive neoliberal reforms, it was abolished entirely, along with almost any prospect of municipal support for non-market solutions. Forty years later, I find myself reflecting on the disastrous worldwide consequences of not taking up the obvious and the only solution. Forty years of demonizing that solution lies at the root of contemporary inadequacies. It is time to turn that around. Reading this excellent and inspiring book is a good place to start.

Introduction

'How dare this Brazilian woman come over here to evaluate UK housing policy?' These words summarise the reaction of members of the British Conservative government to my trip to the United Kingdom in 2013, as United Nations special rapporteur on adequate housing.

My visit to the UK coincided with a moment of political debate in the country. One of the proposed welfare reforms – part of the government's fiscal austerity programme – was being contested by the people affected. Under the pretext of opening up available stock to people in need of a home, the measure known as the 'bedroom tax' introduced cuts in housing benefits to individuals of working age who lived in public housing and had 'spare bedrooms'.[1] Those directly affected by the cuts were, by that time, organising local movements and building regional and national networks in protest. In addition, opposition party representatives and social movements fighting against the relentless dismantling of the British welfare state were endorsing the protests, alongside support from some sectors within the press.

Among those affected were individuals and families already living on the edge. These people were among the most vulnerable groups in public housing: the poorest of the poor, often coping with mental illnesses or physical disabilities. The new measures threatened to rob them of the stability, safety and guarantee of a dignified life that the public welfare system had promised them.

It was clear from the outset that council tenants with 'spare rooms' were going to be made to move to smaller houses or flats.

Furthermore, they were unlikely to be rehoused in the same neigh-bourhood, or even nearby. In sum, such a policy would forcibly uproot people from the communities in which they had built their lives. At the time of my arrival, a few months after the policy's implementation, most of the affected people were struggling to stay put, despite the cuts to their housing benefits and consequent deterioration of their living conditions.

Before my arrival, the UN rapporteur's visit to the UK was considered by the government as a mere diplomatic ritual, neces-sary to confirm the state's collaboration with the UN's human rights protocol. In the face of the unexpected outcry that erupted while I was there, the Conservative Party's reaction was to discredit the rapporteur – contesting the authority of the visit and attempting to characterise it as a politicisation of the UN's role by local opposition parties. This was done by undermining a rappor-teur who was unwise enough to listen to and believe the voices of those suffering as a result of the new policies.

However, the Conservatives' resentment was not merely against a UN rapporteur who criticised them. It was against a 'Brazilian woman', hailing from an 'underdeveloped' country marred by the existence of *favelas* and other degrading housing forms. One who, moreover, dared to state that the recent reforms in the British social housing system were a step backwards and a violation of the housing rights of the affected people. The campaign of disqual-ification that followed, spearheaded by the right-wing tabloids, only exposed the prejudices more clearly.

Firstly, a housing expert from the world's periphery should never leave their place of origin. They should focus on thoughts and actions directed towards overcoming what is defined by the Western North ('the centre of the world') as an incomplete modernising project. Subject to the geopolitics of the interna-tional division of labour and knowledge production, 'Third World' or 'underdeveloped world' intellectuals and policymak-ers should be restricted to their home contexts. For the dominant logic of developmentalism, those contexts are not considered singular social and political formations, but exam-ples of failed and incomplete projects of the nation states they are expected to reproduce.[2]

Secondly, in the geopolitics of the international system of human rights, European countries are identified as exemplary, assuring civil and political liberties along with reasonably universalised social security systems. In contrast, it is in the 'Third World' countries that the worst violations are concentrated. Especially violations of economic, social and cultural rights, which are denounced in the diplomatic arena mainly by developed countries.

Contrary to what the British Conservative Party believed, my visit to the UK was not motivated by the anti-bedroom tax campaign, but by a research hypothesis that evolved over the course of my six-year mandate as the UN rapporteur on housing rights. This hypothesis became the foundation for the construction of a large-scale narrative about a current global process: the radical transformation of the directions of housing policies worldwide, and its failure as an alternative to the provision of adequate housing for all.

In 2008, I had just started my mandate in the Human Rights Council (UNHRC) when the effects of the financial subprime mortgage crisis began to resonate around the world. Accounts arrived first from the US, then from Europe and other countries, of individuals and families who were losing their homes. The news spoke at the same time of the collapse of a globalised financial system, and indicated that this failure was highly connected and interwoven with the production of built spaces, especially housing.

Trying to understand the roots of the crisis, I started to research the origins of housing financialisation. I chose this theme as one of the main investigation and action axes of my mandate, striving to observe it through country missions, working visits and questionnaires addressed to countries. I presented my first report on this theme in 2009. In 2012, after completing country missions in the US, Kazakhstan, Croatia, Israel and in the World Bank, and following a visit to Spain, I presented my second report, observing the theme from different angles and locations.

These excursions reinforced the hypothesis that we are globally witnessing the impacts of the ideological and practical hegemony of a specific model of housing policy: one based on the promotion of home ownership through market purchase via credit loans – a model that spread around the world at the electronic speed of financial flows. Attempting to develop this hypothesis more deeply, in 2013 I chose the United Kingdom to be the last country mission of my mandate. It was appropriate, because the UK has been and continues to be one of the epicentres and laboratories of the theoretical formulation and practical transformation of housing into a financial asset.

Besides the financialisation of housing, throughout my mandate as a rapporteur I witnessed massive forced evictions, resulting as much from large-scale projects as from post-disaster reconstruction. A visit to Haiti, months after the 2010 earthquake, as well as missions to the Maldives and Indonesia, hit by the 2004 tsunami, allowed me closely to observe situations of extreme socio-environmental vulnerability, in which previous tenure arrangements were fundamental to define – or to block – rights. From these visits and three reports on the topic,[3] I formulated the hypothesis that the hegemony of registered individual freehold property over every other form of tenure relation is one of the most powerful mechanisms of the prevalent territorial exclusion. Within the contractual language of finance, territorial ties are reduced to the unidimensionality of their economic value and to the expectations of future revenue streams – conditional on the guarantee of perpetuity of individual property. Therefore, the expansion of the boundaries of land and housing financialisation goes hand in hand with the increased fragility of other forms of ties to the land, generating a machinery of dispossession.

Given the increasing connection between the organisation of sports mega-events and urban restructuring projects, this machinery becomes progressively more visible in the process of preparing the host cities. In the run-up to the FIFA World Cup in South Africa (2010) and the Beijing Olympic Games (2008), I received reports of forced eviction from individuals and organisations alike. Coincidentally, in 2007 Brazil was announced as the host of the 2014 World Cup and Rio de Janeiro as the host of the 2016 Summer Olympic Games. From then on, I focused on mega-events and the right to housing in a report presented to UNHRC in 2010, and started to chart this process in Brazil *in loco*. I visited host cities and talked to people affected or at risk of eviction, as well as to intellectuals and activists who that same year were beginning to organise the Brazilian World Cup Popular Committees.

Although the rapporteur's mandate was structured according to the grammar of human rights, it was impossible for me not to live this experience as a planner, housing policymaker and urban studies critical researcher. I also considered that, given my limitations in the juridical field, I should take advantage of my knowledge of city planning and housing to 'translate' the kind of information largely confined to human rights circles into the vocabularies of public policy and current critical urban thinking, thus striving to amplify the milieu in which this subject is debated.

Therefore, while the thematic and mission reports that I presented to the UN constitute the main basis for the empirical material and bibliographic references of this book, it is important to highlight that these documents were originally written in technical language, specific to human rights and with a predefined format. Here, the reports are free from diplomatic and formal constraints and serve as a stimulus for the arguments I will be presenting.

Real estate in general, and housing in particular, constitute one of the newest and most powerful of the expanding borders of financial capital. This expansion is based on the combination of two main elements. Firstly, the belief that markets can regulate the allocation of urban land and housing by generating the most rational distribution of resources. And secondly, the development of experimental and 'creative' financial products linking finance to built spaces.

This double movement led public policymakers to abandon the notion of housing as a social good and of cities as public artefacts. In the process, housing and urban policies renounced their role as redistributors of wealth. No longer was housing conceived as a common good that a society agrees to share, by providing for those with less resources. Instead it became a mechanism of rent extraction, financial gain and wealth accumulation. This process resulted in massive territorial dispossessions; the creation of 'placeless' poor urban populations; new processes of subjection structured around the mechanisms of debt; and a significant intensification of segregation in cities.

The reduction of the variety of possible ways of existing in a territory to one single recognised model – home ownership, a form itself completely colonised by disciplines of finance – has been conducted by and under the leadership of governments. In each one of the observed situations, the State produces its margins – subprime in the US, informal in 'Third World' cities – in order eventually to 'unlock' its territorial assets, expanding the market borders.

This book offers a global panorama of the process of urban land and housing colonisation by global finance in the past four decades. I identify its starting point in the 1980s, and its first high-magnitude international collapse in the 2007 financial crisis – caused by the burst of the US real-estate bubble. Following this track, the book shows the ties and connections between processes occurring simultaneously in cities of the global North, South, East and West.

The first and second parts correspond to the large-scale narrative to which I referred at the beginning of this text. It is a world map 'puzzle' of housing policies, that pieces together their relation with urban policies. Housing policies are at the same time part of a country's political economy and dislocated from it.[4]

In the first chapter, tracing the evolution of housing policies in various countries, I attempt to weave the lines of a net that defines the dominant paradigm: a model of privately owned homes bought via mortgage credit certificates. I also aim to present the specific forms and socio-political meanings that this new paradigm assumes in different contexts.

The second part of the book describes the processes of dispossession of the poorest and most vulnerable around the world. Using examples of post-disaster reconstruction projects and mega-event preparations, and referring to urban and land policies implemented in various countries, I attempt to relate the global crisis of tenure insecurity to the advance of the real-estate financial complex and its direct impact on housing rights.

In the third part, the same processes are reassessed in order to describe and interpret the Brazilian trajectory during the period 1980–2007. Land and housing colonisation by finance is treated in terms of the recent evolution of the country's housing and urban policy. The period studied also saw the return of democracy to Brazil, spawning a movement for urban reform in which the universalisation of housing rights was a key element. Institutional action increased as left-wing parties gained momentum at all levels of legislative and executive power. During the same period, the global movement that I describe in my first two chapters was also taking place in Brazil.

To some extent, the third part of the book revisits my own trajectory of activism, professional action and reflection upon Brazilian cities during that period, a time when I was in close contact with the country's housing and urban policy. I was part of the Movement for Urban Reform, I acted alongside parties and governments and I dreamed of the utopia of the right to the city for all. Therefore, the third part of the book is more than an essay on the theoretical-methodological application of the hypothesis developed in the two previous parts to Brazil's specific political economy context. Writing it was, for me, a way of mourning for those defeats, as well as an attempt to understand the complexity of the current Brazilian political and economic crisis. Once more, there is a displacement in the book: from a protagonist implicated in the construction of policies within Brazilian *realpolitik* to the intellectual honesty of a researcher and activist.

Lastly, the Afterword, written in 2018, offers a glimpse of the continuing process described in this work. Following the mortgage crisis of 2007, a new outbreak of financialisation – the seizure of residential rental markets by finance – has been raking over the ashes of the previous one, imposing a new circle of dispossession over the same, racialised and deprived bodies. In the Brazilian case, the eruption of protests in 2013 announced the beginning of a political crisis that led to the impeachment of President Dilma Roussef and the capture of the Brazilian government by a liberal conservative coalition.

In the Afterword I also point out the porosities and resistances within the global processes that I have described, revisiting the scenes of protest and resistance that open each chapter of the book. This is the urban warfare announced by the book's title, which simultaneously questions the prevalent policies and prefigures other possible urban worlds.

It was a privilege to observe the world for six years from the vantage point of a UN special rapporteur on adequate housing. I have no doubt that this experience was fundamental in spurring me to break away from the methodological parochialism and nationalism in which we intellectuals from the 'global South' are often ensnared – we urban researchers situated on the margins of the world's intellectual production, forever urged to reflect within the confines of the 'national' – or, at best, regional – universe.[5]

If further reason were needed, my photo in the *Daily Mail* (the reliably xenophobic tabloid that once supported the British Union of Fascists), presented as the image of a sorceress, a practitioner of African rituals from the putrid Brazilian *favelas*, fortified my resolve. I knew that after concluding my work as a UN rapporteur, this book would immediately be written.

PART I

1

The Global Financialisation of Housing

Scenes from the beginning of the twenty-first century, September 2010.

It was a cold and windy morning in Astana, the futuristic capital of Kazakhstan. After crossing a sort of plateau ablaze with the shiny creations of fashionable big-name architects, we finally arrived in a large tent to meet the hunger strikers. Lying on hammocks surrounded by signs written in Kazakh and Russian, Asian-looking elderly people were mixed with red-haired white women and middle-aged couples, taking shifts in beds and chairs. Having paid the instalments for apartments they had acquired off-plan, they were victims of construction companies that had gone bankrupt and disappeared, leaving the buildings' skeletons unfinished and families with neither home nor money.

Astana's hunger strikers were just the most daring among the 16,000 borrowers affected by the bankruptcy of – mainly Turkish – construction companies that had already halted 450 projects.[1] In addition to the hunger strikers, there were also those affected by foreclosures in Almaty, the country's historic capital and economic centre. During the years of credit boom, Kazakh banks and their clients contracted debts in both US dollars and euros, and were now struggling to pay their obligations.

In Astana and Almaty, the victims of the economic crisis, many now homeless, told us that they had been strongly encouraged by the government to buy apartments via mortgage credit certificates. (The president, Nursultan Nazarbayev, led the Communist Party during the USSR era and has been head of the government since Independence.) They also reported that the public institutions in which many of them used to work had even sponsored the sales of apartments to their employees. The group of strikers in Almaty, mostly made up of women, received me in a small apartment decorated with a banner that read: 'Government, help your people'.[2]

May 2012

We climbed the highest hill of Puente Alto, in Santiago de Chile's metropolitan region, in order to look across the Bajos de Mena area. It is one of the neighbourhoods in which thousands of social housing projects built by private companies are concentrated. They were commercialised via an association of mortgage credit certificates and governmental subsidies to low-income borrowers. These estates have been built in Chile since the beginning of the 1980s. The view is impressive: a sea of houses and four- or five-storey buildings as far as you can see.

The housing rights activists who accompanied me pointed to Volcán II, a housing estate in the process of being demolished. They explained that this neighbourhood has become one of the metropolitan region's most problematic areas from a social point of view: drug addiction and trafficking, domestic violence and social vulnerability.[3]

They also showed me a 1983 document, written at the moment of the launch of Chile's housing program. It was signed by the then minister of housing and urbanism, a man from the Chilean Chamber of Construction. In the document, he declared that the need for housing is 'an element of social order that is translated and expressed in square metres' and that the demand for housing is 'a factor of economic order that is materialised in monetary quantities'.[4]

Autumn 2009

The streets of Pacoima, a few kilometres away from Los Angeles, California, looked like a ghost town. In the suburban landscape of front yards reaching to the streets, signs of abandonment were everywhere: mountains of forgotten rubble; dozens of 'For Sale' and 'For Rent' signs next to mailboxes; doors and windows sealed with wood or bricks. The minister of a local church, who accompanied me in the visit, told sad stories of families who'd had to leave their homes because they could not afford the repayments on their loans. He evoked the difficulties of those who remained in the neighbourhood, struggling to survive in a town that, having lost its fiscal base, could not keep basic services running.

At the end of a street, in an old SUV transformed into a home, Roger, Mary and their young children were cooking pasta on an improvised stove: 'We've lost our house and we simply have nowhere to go.'

November 2012

As morning broke in a neighbourhood of Bilbao in the Basque Country, cash machines and bank headquarters were covered in graffiti: '*murderers*'. It was the day after fifty-three-year-old Amaia Egaña's suicide. She jumped from the window of her fourth-floor apartment, moments before being evicted. She had failed to pay the instalments for the bank loan that she had taken out to buy the apartment. This was the second death in similar circumstances in less than one month.[5] Bilbao was not the only – nor the most seriously – affected city in terms of foreclosures. According to data from the Spanish judicial system, between 2007 and the third trimester of 2011, 349,438 home foreclosures were initiated in Spain. According to the same source, on each day of 2011, 212 new foreclosure processes were opened.[6]

1 March 2012

In Barcelona, one of the cities most rocked by the crisis, I attend an assembly of the *Plataforma de Afectados por la Hipoteca* (Platform for People Affected by Mortgages). Since 2009, this social movement has worked to organise the people concerned in order to make the crisis visible, establishing support networks and lobbying for the promotion of public policies to address this situation. I listen to dozens of testimonies during the meetings: Latin American migrants who lost their jobs and could no longer pay the instalments; pensioners who, as guarantors of their children's loans, now must hand over their own home to banks; couples who lost their home and still have huge debts . . . All this because, in Spain, with the drop in property prices after the bubble burst, the value that banks obtain from the sale of a house does not cover the entirety of the debt.

Moreover, if no buyer is present at the auction of the confiscated house (which happens in 90 per cent of cases), the law stipulates that the value of the property covers only 60 per cent of the total loan.[7] As a result, in addition to losing their homes, people remain mired in debt.

Summer 2011

At dawn in Tel Aviv, one of the city's most important arteries, Dizengoff Street, is filled by tents. The occupation of public spaces was part of the strategy of thousands of demonstrators – mostly young people – against the lack of accessible housing. The decade-long spiralling rise of real-estate prices had reached its peak. The lack of rental options and public housing in areas in which economic opportunities are concentrated had put housing policy at the centre of Israel's political agenda that summer.

August 2013

When I entered the nineteenth-century hall of an old factory, now converted into a culture and events centre in Manchester, I remembered Friedrich Engels's writings and thought: 'The saga started here'.[8]

We arrived just as the first part of the meeting was about to finish. On the walls, signs written in marker spelt out strategies and schedules for the following months. It was one of the regional meetings for the campaign against the bedroom tax – one of the coalition government's recently implemented fiscal austerity measures that most severely affected residents of British housing estates. Our presence was announced, and anyone who felt comfortable sharing their experience was invited through to another room.

Around thirty people gathered next door. There was hesitation at first. Many of them had known each other for months, having participated together in preparatory mobilisations and meetings; however, they had never talked about their personal dramas. A middle-aged lady stood up and said that she was a professional nurse, a widow, and that she used the extra bedroom in her house to occasionally host her two granddaughters. Her daughter, addicted to cocaine, was unable to look after the children in moments of relapse. Losing the two-bedroom house would mean inability to provide this support to her daughter and granddaughters.

Another woman said she suffered from depression and, having lived for thirty years on the same estate, could count on a network of friendly neighbours to help her keep stable. Therefore, she said, she chose not to move out, despite having to pay a penalty to live alone in a two-bedroom apartment. Ashamed, she admitted that now she could hardly afford to buy food, so that, as well as resorting to food banks,[9] she had often looked for left-overs in the estate's bins.

Other accounts followed, but the most touching moment – at least for me – was when a young man, in an electric wheelchair and showing clear signs of a learning disability, said that he could never move away from the estate where he lived, alone, in a two-bedroom apartment. For him, daily life required a herculean effort to remain autonomous and dignified despite his extremely fragile physical and mental situation. His life was entirely based on his existence – and permanence – in that community.

October 2010

After walking for seventy kilometres, a forty-year-old Indian carpenter suffers a fatal heart attack. The goal of his walk was to borrow money from friends who lived in a different town, in order to pay his micro-credit debts. A report from the Indian government stated that his death was 'due to pressure put by the micro-finance institutions for repayment'. In 2002, the carpenter had borrowed US$350 from a micro-credit institution in order to build a room in his house. His wife, working in a tobacco factory, had already borrowed US$1,100 from her employers. In 2008, he was persuaded by another micro-credit agent to borrow an additional US$330 in order to cover the previous debts. When he died, the payment of all three loans was more than twenty weeks late. This was not the first nor the last death related to micro-credit debts occurring that year in the state of Andhra Pradesh.[10]

The scenes I have described – in places as diverse as Europe, the US, Latin America, the Middle East and Asia – are the expression and result of a long process of deconstruction of housing as a social good and its transformation into a commodity and a financial asset, which began in the first decade of the twenty-first century.

The extent and impact of this process go far beyond the financial subprime mortgage crisis that, spreading from the US since 2007, contaminated the international financial system. It is, in fact, the takeover of the housing sector by finance – the structural element of contemporary capitalism. We live under the empire of finance and fictitious capital hegemony, an era of increasing dominance of rent extraction over productive capital.[11] The international literature on political economy of housing has termed this process 'financialisation', that is, 'the increasing dominance of financial actors, markets, practices, measurements and narratives, at various scales, resulting in a structural transformation of economies, firms (including financial institutions), states and households'.[12]

The promotion of the ideology of homeownership,[13] already deeply rooted in some societies and more recently introduced in others, has been a central element of the new paradigm of housing. Together with the 'socialisation of credit', it supported a double movement: on one hand, the inclusion of middle- and low-income consumers into financial circuits; on the other, the takeover of the housing sector by global finance. This process opened a new frontier for capital accumulation, allowing the free circulation of funds throughout almost all urbanised land.[14]

Between 1980 and 2010, the value of the world's financial assets – stocks, debentures, private and government bonds, bank investments – increased by a factor of 16.2, while the world's GDP increased by less than a factor of five in the same period.[15] This pool of super-accumulation resulted not only from the profits earned by large corporations, but also from the emergence of economies such as China. This 'wall of money'[16] increasingly sought new fields of application, transforming whole sectors (such as commodities, education financing and health care) into assets to feed the hunger for new vectors of profitable investment. The imbalance between the size of the available financial capital and the domestic markets from which they originated resulted – mainly from the 1990s – in the search for internationalisation of investments. This environment was responsible for creating a structural scarcity of high-quality collateral. There was a wall of money as if airborne, seeking a 'spatial fix' (David Harvey's concept), a place to land.[17]

The creation, reform and strengthening of housing financial systems became one of these new fields for surplus investment, both for macroeconomics and domestic finance and for this new flux of international capital. The creation of a subprime mortgage market was one of the main vehicles used to connect domestic systems of housing finance to global markets. However, other non-bank financial instruments, as well as interbank loans, allowed local banks and other intermediaries to increase their leverage, enlarging credit availability.[18] The entrance of global surpluses of capital allowed credit to grow beyond internal markets' sizes and capacities, creating and inflating real-estate bubbles.

The takeover of the housing sector by finance does not represent the mere opening of another field of investment for capital. It is, in fact, a peculiar form of value storage, as it directly relates macroeconomics to individuals and families, and allows, through financing mechanisms, the interconnection of many central actors of the global financial system – such as pension funds, investment banks, shadow banking, credit institutions and public institutions.[19]

In highly dynamic economies, including some EU countries and the US, homeownership, because of its capacity to feed growth via credit, was also responsible for propelling the rise in household consumption in a context of wage reduction and limited employment growth.[20]

On the other hand, the public or semi-public nature of housing institutions and financial policies defines this sector as one of high political relevance.[21] No setting-up of housing financing systems – regardless of its degree of connection to global finance – can happen without state action. Government intervention is needed not only to regulate finance, but also to build the political hegemony of the notion of home as a commodity and financial asset. Therefore, in every context that I have observed in different nation states, this movement also had significant political effects by creating and consolidating a conservative popular base, in which citizens are replaced by consumers and players in capital markets. It is in this sense that we may affirm, with Fernandez and Aalbers, that 'This housing-finance elixir acts like a political drug.'[22]

Finally, we must flag up the huge impact that changes in housing provision formats have over cities' structures. Through land markets and urban regulation, the new political economy of housing also involved a new political economy of urbanisation, restructuring cities. It is not only a new housing policy, but also a redesign of cities by the expansion of an urban, real-estate/financial complex.[23]

Thousands of mortgaged lives, the subprime victims of a decade-long credit supply boom; empty neighbourhoods, desolate cities; demonstrators occupying streets and public spaces for months; a hunger strike of proprietors deprived of their promised apartments. Some of the scenes described at the beginning of this chapter took place in the immediate wake of the 2007 US subprime mortgage crisis. After the bubble burst, the crisis quickly spread across the world, at the speed of financial products and with the intensity of the globalisation of markets to which the mortgage market was connected. It is not surprising that the first sector affected by the crisis was housing. Supplied by pension funds, hedge funds, private equities and other 'fictional products', housing became a fictional product itself when it was taken over by finance.[24]

The intensity of this change can be described as a movement that transformed a 'sleeping beauty' – the hitherto inert, immobile and illiquid housing from the Bretton Woods period – into a neoliberal 'fantastic ballet', in which assets leap from hand to hand through fast and constant transactions.[25]

That movement led to a change in the paradigm of housing policy in almost every nation on the planet. Formulated in Wall Street and in the City of London, rolled out for the first time by North American and British neoliberal politicians at the end of the 1970s and beginning of the 1980s, the change in the economic role of housing was further powered by the fall of the Berlin Wall and the free market hegemony that followed. Adopted by governments or imposed as a conditionality to access loans by multilateral financial institutions – such as the World Bank and the International Monetary Fund (IMF) – the new paradigm is based mainly on the implementation of policies that create stronger and bigger housing financial markets, drawing in the low- and middle-income consumers previously excluded from them.

At the end of the 1970s and throughout the 1980s, in response to economic and fiscal crises, a series of policies began to dismantle the basic institutional components that sustained the welfare state systems. Among the roots of these crises, especially relevant were the drop of Fordist sectors' profitability, the intensification of international competition, the exacerbation of deindustrialisation and mass unemployment, and the suspension of the Bretton Woods monetary system. The set of policies adopted by states after the crisis of Fordist development was generically named 'neoliberalism'.[26]

Despite being a general tendency, neoliberal restructuring strategies are applied to specific institutional configurations, particular socio-political power constellations, and pre-existing spatial configurations. In other words, since neoliberalism is an eminently unequal process, any perspective that ignores each country's political and economic context has little explanatory strength.

The importance of contexts becomes clear when we examine the reforms of housing systems in different countries in that period. In general terms, there is a move to dismantle social and public housing policies, destabilise security of tenure – including rental arrangements – and convert the home into a financial asset. However, this process is path-dependent: the institutional scenarios inherited by each country are fundamental for the construction of the emergent neoliberal strategies. Neoliberal policies must be understood as an amalgam between these two moments: it is a process of *partial* destruction of what exists and of *trend* creation of new structures.

In countries such as Britain or the Netherlands, with their strong welfare state systems, the new watchword was privatisation – or even destruction – of public housing stocks, and drastic reduction of public funding for social housing. Instead, the creation of a mortgage-based financial system was stimulated in order to encourage the purchase of homes in the private market.

Moreover, subsidies began to be redirected towards supply rather than demand.

This budget reduction and the demolition of public housing units also occurred in the US. However, there are significant differences. Firstly, the idea of a welfare state system was never fully implanted there. Moreover, the support for homeowner-ship based on mortgage credit certificates has been the guiding principle of US housing policy since the 1930s. Throughout the 1980s, the building of public housing units by the state was gradually replaced by a policy of mass stimulation of home purchase via subprime credit. Everywhere, the presence of these credit certificates and the deregulation of the rental market were designed to dismantle existing options of access to hous-ing, and stimulate home-purchase as the only pathway to a roof over one's head. Spain is one of the paradigmatic examples of this route.

Twenty years ago, an influential World Bank report – *Housing: Enabling Markets to Work* – summarised this new line of thought on housing policy.[27] This document contains not only arguments about how important the housing sector would be to the econ-omy, but also directives to governments on how best to formulate their policies. Since the 1990s, housing financing grew radically in developed economies. In the US, UK, Denmark, Australia and Japan, for example, residential mortgage markets represent between 50 and 100 per cent of GDP.[28]

According to another World Bank document, intended to promote mortgage markets in emergent economies, other coun-tries have also seen an increase in housing financialisation, although at a slower pace. Residential mortgage markets in South Korea, South Africa, Malaysia, Chile, and the Baltic countries accounted for 20 to 35 per cent of their GDPs. More recently, this phenomenon arrived in other countries (China, Thailand, Mexico, the majority of EU new members, Morocco, Jordan, Brazil, Turkey, Peru, Kazakhstan and Ukraine), where residential mortgage markets represent between 6 and 17 per cent of GDP. According to the World Bank, this 'progress' can also be observed in some less developed countries such as Indonesia, Egypt, Pakistan, Senegal, Uganda, Mali, Mongolia and Bangladesh, 'but not on a large-enough scale to address some of the chronic housing issues they face'.[29]

From the old Central Asian and Eastern European Soviet Bloc all the way to Latin America, and from Africa to Asia, the take-over of the housing sector by finance has been a massive and hegemonic tendency. So much so, that a World Bank publication crowed – one decade after the launch of the housing private market manifesto referred to previously – that 'the genie is out of the bottle.'[30]

The mercantilisation of housing – as well as the increased use of housing as an asset integrated into a globalised financial market – deeply undermined the right to adequate housing around the world. The belief that markets could regulate the allocation of housing, combined with the development of experimental and 'creative' financial products, led to the abandonment of public policies that regarded housing as part of the social commons. In the new political economy, centred around housing as a means of access to wealth, the home becomes a fixed capital asset whose value resides in its expectation of generating more value in the future, depending on the oscillations of the (always assumed) rise of real-estate prices.[31]

Like other social spheres, housing was affected by the disman-tlement of basic welfare institutions and by the mobilisation of a series of policies aiming to expand market discipline, competition and commodification.[32] These new ideas confronted the welfare systems and economic-political coalitions around housing that had previously existed in each country.

In former socialist countries, in the US and in many European countries, the privatisation of public housing and drastic cuts in state investment in social housing were combined with reductions in welfare programs and rental subsidies. These measures were accompanied by the deregulation of financial markets and by a new urban strategy, allowing domestic capital mobilisation and international capital recycling. The new tendencies had a smaller impact in less developed countries, where welfare housing systems had never existed, or were small and marginal compared to the housing needs. The global imposition of neoliberalism has been highly unequal – both socially and geographically – and its institutional forms and socio-political consequences vary significantly around the world. In each context, much depends on specific interactions between inherited regulatory landscapes and emerging market-oriented restructuration projects.[33]

By considering the World Bank's first document as a starting point and the 2007 subprime mortgage crisis as the first large international trigger, this first chapter of the book has mapped some of the key elements of the neoliberal perspective on housing and its impact on the right to housing in different contexts.[34]

Through observing different countries' housing trajectories during my mandate as the UN special rapporteur on adequate housing, I detected three forms that the process of financialisation of housing can assume, which differ from each other not only in their origin, but also in the kind of impact they have on economies, cities and people's lives. They are: mortgage-based systems; systems based on the association of financial credit with direct governmental subsidies linked to the purchase of market-produced units; and micro-finance schemes.

As with every generalisation, these are for the most part models abstracted from the specificity of concrete situations, and not a rigorous classification. However, they allow us to understand the patterns of financialisation governing the takeover of the housing sector – in all its diversity – by the financial sector.[35]

In the US and the majority of European countries – which had previous experience of public housing provision, and enjoyed significant economic development in the Fordist period – the development of a residential mortgage financial market was the main mechanism for the promotion of homeownership. It increasingly replaced rental systems – however regulated, provisioned or subsidised by the state – as the dominant form. It is these countries' experience that I will analyse in the next pages.

2

The Mortgage System

In the late nineteenth and early twentieth centuries, when the extreme poverty of the majority of the urban population began to be revealed by social reformers in Europe and North America, governments began to provide housing assistance to people and families, as well as directly supplying homes.[1]

Public housing provision gained prominence and intensity at the beginning of the twentieth century and, in some countries, between the first and second world wars. However, it was after WWII – particularly during the 1950s and 1960s – that public housing provision became one of the structural pillars of Europe's social welfare policy, a redistributive pact between capital and labour that sustained decades of growth.[2]

Nevertheless, if we consider all European countries, few could boast, at any given moment of their history, a stock of social housing that was significant in relation to the total amount of existing homes. We may classify the European countries into three large groups in terms of social housing provision.

The first group is composed of countries whose public or semi-public social housing production has historically been non-existent, or where housing auto-construction or auto-promotion prevailed. This group includes Greece, Portugal and Spain, among others. The second group is formed, among others, by Belgium, Germany, Ireland and Italy. In these countries, social housing has never been significant in terms of its participation in the general composition of households. And the third group is composed of countries whose social housing stock has been – and still is – significant. Countries such as Austria, Czech Republic, Denmark, Finland, France, Holland, Poland, Sweden and the United Kingdom are part of this group. Together they concentrate almost 80 per cent of Europe's social housing stock today.[3] Public or semi-public housing projects, generally intended for rental, are defined differently within the strategies of each country. Variations depend on forms of financing; the nature of promoters and 'owners'; the definition of demand; and forms of administration.

In some countries, especially in Germany, the inexistence of a significant public stock of social housing does not mean that housing is absent from their welfare policies. Both the regulation of private rental and the direct aid provided to lower-income families for rent payment can be considered forms of state intervention in housing, with the aim to universalise social rights. Still today, Germany and Switzerland are two of the European countries where rented homes – promoted by a highly regulated private sector – are the predominant form of tenure.[4]

Countries which built large stocks of public housing experienced a peak in construction between the late 1960s and the early 1970s. At that point, the consensus and the political-economic macro-conditions from which the policy originated began to fade. The 1970s economic-financial crisis caused the longest international recession since the 1930s. From that moment on, a transformation of the government's role was mooted in both theoretical and practical terms: from housing providers they became 'facilitators', whose mission was to make way for and support the expansion of private markets. The above-mentioned 1993 World Bank document summarises this thinking: 'Governments should be encouraged to adopt policies that enable housing markets to work . . . and [to] avoid distorting [them]'.[5] Their role was henceforth to create the conditions, institutions and regulatory models that would promote housing financial systems capable of enabling home purchase.[6]

In some countries, this happened through the sale of the public social housing stock to their residents – boosting homeownership and reducing state expenditure.[7] This privatisation process was further encouraged by the stigmatisation and residualisation of social housing, which started to be identified with poverty and marginality.[8] In Europe and North America, the privatisation of public housing stocks occurred in various forms: the sale of units to long-term tenants through Right to Buy in the UK;[9] the transfer of properties to not-for-profit organisations in the Netherlands;[10] and in some cases, the transfer of properties to for-profit companies, as in the US. In various countries, such as Spain, the 'advantages' of the creation of a home-purchase market also included the reform of rental legislation, reducing protection and increasing insecurity of tenure for tenants. In almost every country – mainly via tax exemptions and subsidised interest – housing commodification was promoted through the adoption of incentives to purchase.

Throughout the 1990s, the majority of former socialist and communist countries also embarked on large-scale public housing privatisation projects, through right-to-buy programmes. In some places, this policy resulted in the near eradication of public housing stocks. In various former communist countries, private homes now represent the great bulk of the housing stock – 96 per cent in Estonia, 77 per cent in Slovenia and more than 80 per cent in China, for example.[11]

Even where the privatisation of public stocks was not drastic, the ideological transferral of the responsibility for housing provision to private markets was hegemonic. The paradigm of 'homeownership' became virtually the only housing policy model. This process eclipsed other well-established forms of tenure, such as (public and private) rental and forms of cooperative and collective properties.[12]

As a result, the rates of homeownership have grown continuously:[13] in the mid-2000s, they reached more than 50 per cent in all member states of the Organisation for Economic Cooperation and Development (OECD), except Germany and Switzerland. Spain and Ireland led the ranking with 83.2 per cent and 81.4 per cent, respectively.[14]

The increase of private housing property and its mobilisation as a form of wealth coincided with the ageing of populations and with the huge pressure that this represented for public retirement systems. One of the responses to this pressure was the migration of retirement systems from public funds to individuals and families. Homeownership performed a fundamental role in this migration as it became an asset-based welfare.[15]

The use of homeownership as wealth stock, its valorisation over time and possible monetisation worked, in practical terms, as potential substitutes for public pension and retirement systems. The basic difference in relation to the previous system is that the risks, too, migrate from collective institutions – and, ultimately, from the state – to individuals and families.[16] This change also transformed housing – in the words of American economist Nouriel Roubini – into a sort of ATM machine. The new system makes housing capable of functioning as security for loans. It is intended to fund consumption in a period (from the 1980s on) of decline of the participation of wages in total global wealth. Across the world, this percentage declined from 63 per cent in the 1980s to 54 per cent in 2011.[17]

In order for privately owned homes to perform this role, the continuous rise of real-estate prices was a necessary condition. While this rise lasted, it made economic growth viable despite a significant wage drop – especially in countries such as the US, UK and Spain. It was a type of 'privatised Keynesianism'.[18]

This process occurs simultaneously with the globalisation of finance, creating an international capital market with large freedom of movement, as previously existing barriers to the free circulation of financial capital have been knocked down. Thus, capital surplus – converted into financial capital – was able to penetrate both the promotion of residential real estate and the financing of its consumption. These elements contributed to comprehensively inflate real-estate market prices. As an example, between 1997 and 2004, the average cost of home purchase rose by 149 per cent in Spain, 139 per cent in the UK, 187 per cent in Ireland, 112 per cent in Australia and 65 per cent in the US.[19] The increase in real-estate prices yielded more wealth for proprietors. Nevertheless, it is, in fact, a wealth-disguised debt, as a significant part of this stock corresponds only to the mortgage debts of property-owning families. In some countries, such as the UK, Spain, South Korea, the US and Canada, this participation is superior to government debt.

Through the finance of private home purchase, global capital market expansion was based on private indebtedness, establishing an intimate link between individuals' biological lives and the global process of income extraction and speculation. Therefore, the channelling of capital surplus flows into residential property also has a lived dimension: mortgaged lives, namely the generation of men and women in debt – a new subjectivity produced by the disciplinary mechanisms that subject life itself to debt servicing.[20] This became evident when the real-estate bubble burst, and all risk and onus fell on those who had borrowed. It was they who, having exposed their lives to the risky oscillations of fictitious commodities' speculative game, suffered the real consequences of the crisis: they were turned into indebted, often homeless people overnight.

It is important to note that it would not have been possible to expand the mortgage market on this enormous scale had other housing access options not been blocked or rolled back to a residual level. The crisis of access to housing that followed the bubble was aggravated by the erosion, abandonment or liberalisation of non-mercantile mechanisms for the allocation of housing resources. Even countries with a long tradition of social rental housing redesigned their systems in favour of homeownership, 'free markets' and competition. A significant reduction in construction of adequate public housing for the poorest and most vulnerable occurred alongside the reduction of national budgets and public funds for social housing. In the US, for example, the Department of Housing and Urban Development (HUD) budget was reduced from $83 billion in 1978 to $18 billion in 1983. Between 1996 and 2001, the budget earmarked for public housing construction was nil.[21] The steady reduction of the housing supply resulted in long waiting lists, while lack of maintenance led to the deterioration of the existing public stock and, consequently, to a large number of people living in squalid conditions.[22]

Even in former USSR countries – which, following mass privatisation of the housing stock, did not experience housing scarcity in the short term – low-income families soon faced a huge problem in terms of access to housing.[23] The decrease of state investment in social housing, alongside the rising focus on homeownership – shrinking the private rental market[24] – made access to housing finance vital for low-income families. They were left with no option but to sign up to credit schemes – where and when such credit was available, and under conditions established by the real-estate and financial markets.[25]

The role of states went beyond that of a mere 'facilitator'. States actively deconstructed housing and urban policies and deregulated monetary and financial markets – a destruction of the previous order. At the same time, they actively promoted the new alternatives. The above-mentioned trajectory can be better understood by observing concrete national experiences. It is no coincidence that I will start with the UK and the US, the two epicentres of this theoretical and practical model.

Pioneers: The United Kingdom

Access to adequate housing for all has marked the history of UK public policy. Over many generations, Britain forged the notion that a dignified life should include access to fair and decent housing, irrespective of personal wealth or any other status. This notion was translated into a combination of land, housing and territorial planning policies designed to provide adequate housing and to deal with the existing housing stock's deficiencies. Moreover, housing benefits were included in the British welfare system.

The first housing policies were established in the UK at the end of the nineteenth century. Later, in 1909, the first national Housing and Planning Act introduced public subsidies for the construction of residential units and granted local authorities the power to define development plans, which included housing needs. During and after World War I, housing policies remained at the top of the public agenda. The 1915 Glasgow strikes against high rents led to the government's first recognition of affordability in housing, which entailed the creation of laws restricting the rise of rental prices, while the 1918 Tudor Walters Report set the standard for social housing construction. During the interwar period, around 4 million social housing units were built.[26]

After World War II, houses were built to remedy bomb damage and the precarious housing conditions previously existent. At that time, there was a consensus around public investment in adequate housing and the allocation of public lands for this purpose. Another measure in that direction was the 1947 Town and Country Planning Act, that demanded the formulation of local development plans by every UK council. These plans were to allocate land for residential use and define each municipality's requirements for infrastructure, transportation and access to employment.

The same Act also determined the nature of private entrepreneurs' participation in the provision of public land and infrastructure, through instruments such as *betterment* and *planning gains*.[27] Over time, this law has been amended many times. In 1990, specific planning obligations were introduced, commonly known as *Section 106 agreements and planning gains*. Since then, these agreements have contributed to the provision of accessible housing in the UK in two ways: firstly, with proportions of new development projects being allocated for social housing; secondly, with road infrastructure and/or public equipment being built with private contribution.[28]

Housing also became one of the pillars of the welfare state after WWII. In 1942, a report from the Inter-Departmental Committee on Social Insurance and Allied Services proposed a series of measures to deal with extreme poverty. It argued that it was the state's duty to provide adequate housing to widows and sick, unemployed or retired people. This report was the blueprint for the National Assistance Act 1948, establishing the base for the British social security network, which included aid for adequate housing. Local authorities were instructed to house those who could not house themselves. More than one million new homes, half of which were council houses, were constructed within five years after WWII. This rhythm was sustained during the following two decades, with peaks of more than 300,000 units per year in the early 1950s and late 1960s.[29] Even in times of economic constraint, expanding the social housing stock was a priority.

Between the mid-1940s and late 1970s, council housing was the main housing provision for middle- and low-income working-class households. In some regions, council estates worked as a social equaliser, guaranteeing income-diverse neighbourhoods, even in 'high value' central urban areas. This was possible thanks to the use of public land for the provision of social housing, especially in the post-war period. On the other hand, large council estates were constructed in peripheral zones and not all public facilities were of a high quality.

By the end of the 1970s and beginning of the 1980s, with Margaret Thatcher's reforms, there was a considerable change of paradigm. Policies and institutions were created in order to deregulate housing finance systems, privatise council housing and reduce public expenditures – except those related to fiscal benefits and other forms of subsidy for homeownership.[30] The Housing Act passed in 1980, aiming 'to provide security of tenure', introduced 'Right to Buy' as a central element of this new approach.[31] Essentially, the Right to Buy system gave to long-standing tenants the opportunity to buy their council house at a large discount – between 33 per cent and 55 per cent of their market price – based on various criteria, such as length of occupation and sum of rents already paid. Around 2 million social housing units were sold between 1980 and 2013 – most of them in the 1980s. Of those, 1.8 million were council housing units.[32] With sales exceeding new construction, social housing participation fell to 17.3 per cent of the total housing stock between 1987 and 1998.[33]

The Right to Buy system, with its attractive discounts, was a major factor in the creation of a new political base for the Conservative Party, capturing a sizeable part of the Labour Party's traditional base. Local authorities, for their part, lost a proportion of their housing stocks while becoming hard-pressed to maintain the remaining units, as subsidies and transfers from the central government were drastically reduced. At the time, local authorities received half of the total revenues from the sales; however, rigid capital control was imposed, making it practically impossible to replace the units that had been sold.

What remained of the public housing stock was transferred either to housing associations or to social landlords, who became providers of below-market-rate housing. Since the mid-1970s, cooperatives, not-for-profit organisations, philanthropic associations and other social landlords – but not local authorities – have received government aid to cover the portion of capital costs of their housing activities that were not covered by rent payments. Until the end of the 1980s, such aid would generally reimburse 80 per cent (and often reach 100 per cent) of the building costs of new housing units.[34] This rate – as we will see – has deteriorated throughout the 1990s and more so in the 2000s.

While UK public housing stock was privatised, housing credit was promoted via systems such as the Mortgage Interest Relief at Source (MIRAS), which ran from 1969 to 2000. MIRAS offered fiscal incentives corresponding to the payment of mortgage interest, which alleviated the impact of the instalments for new buyers.[35] Credit for home purchase became the main housing policy tool, progressively connecting housing to finance. Behind this policy lay the assumption that the residential private market would guarantee access to adequate housing for everyone, so long as a juridical and institutional support system was put in place. Homeownership was highly subsidised by the state, both through right-to-buy discounts and MIRAS.

Homeownership and housing financialisation shaped the role of housing in the UK, transforming it from a social good into a financial asset.[36] An 'asset-based welfare' has put down roots since the 1990s, acting as an incentive to keep prices high. At the base of this policy is the notion that the welfare state has changed: before, it was a system centred on state provision of welfare; gradually, it became a system in which individuals would take more responsibility for their own social well-being and security, as consumers of financial assets that would provide income in old age.[37] In this context, homeowners rely on the valorisation of their homes and support the policies that promote it.

Consequently, the structural composition of housing tenure forms has changed. In 1971, owner-occupiers represented 52 per cent of England's housing stock; in 2007, this rate was close to 70 per cent.[38] Social rental housing corresponded to around 30 per cent of the housing stock in 1970; in 2007, it was less than 18 per cent. The private rental sector has been steadily growing since 2000.[39] Similar changes occurred in Scotland: in 1981, less than 40 per cent of the housing stock was in the hands of owner-occupants. In the mid-2000s, this rate had risen to 62 per cent.[40]

Nevertheless, the long-term rise in price and the short-term volatility – alongside the drop in salaries and the rise in unemployment – reduced the economic viability for middle- and low-income households of purchasing residential real estate. Some borrowers became exposed to increasing risks. From 1997 to 2012, the average price of real estate in England rose by 200 per cent, while the average full-time salary rose only by 54 per cent.[41] It is possible to say that today there is a housing crisis in the UK in terms of availability, economic viability and access to adequate housing – particularly in regions such as Greater London and eastern England.

The gap between supply and demand must not be underestimated. In 2012, for an estimated demand of 250,000 housing units in England,[42] only around 115,0000 units were built – 89,000 of which, by private entrepreneurs.[43] Many years of underproduction[44] and low availability of urbanised land for housing are cited by the government as justification for this situation.

However, these overall figures mask a worsening inequality. In reality, highly priced homes abound, while social housing is desperately scarce. The waiting lists for renting a public unit are growing, as is the homeless population. The private rental sector has swelled to the point of becoming the only option for many people, despite its conditions of extreme insecurity of tenure – such as six-month contracts. Moreover, there has been a deterioration of housing conditions amid the pressures of overcrowding. In April 2012, faced with a waiting list that had grown by 81 per cent since 1997,[45] English authorities realised that it would be necessary to resort to units previously destined for private rental – particularly to provide emergency accommodation. However, 1.4 million units – 35 per cent of the private rental sector – do not comply with the Decent Homes Standard.[46]

The problem lies in the priorities that were established for the allocation of resources. In 1975, around 80 per cent of public investment in housing was channelled through direct grants to local governments to build new council housing or to maintain their existing stock. In 2000, however, the bulk of public expenditure on housing was directed towards housing benefits, or rental subsidies for those who could not afford it. More recently, a significant proportion of this amount has been going to private landlords.[47] In addition, housing stocks are no longer seen as public resources that should be preserved for several generations. The Barker Review of Housing Supply, commissioned by the British government in 2004, warned of the negative impacts of residential market volatility, in which elevated prices tend to favour older generations over younger: 'The wealth gap between home owners and others is widening.'[48] Today, one in every five households in the UK cannot afford their housing costs and require government support.

There are more than 1.8 million families registered for social housing and more than 650,000 living in overcrowded conditions, while the cost of private rent rose by 37 per cent in the last five years.[49] The Barker Review highlighted the necessity of resuming the provision of social housing. Nonetheless, the directive that was in fact incorporated into housing policy was that of promoting the construction of 120,000 houses or flats per year – regardless of who would live in them. This measure aimed to reduce the average increase of real prices that had been observed within the market over the previous thirty years. The attempt was to reduce it from 2.4 per cent to 1.1 per cent per year, in line with the average of other European countries.[50]

The 2007 financial mortgage crisis had its peculiarities in the UK. Although residential real-estate prices had dropped in some areas – as an immediate result of the crisis – they had already recovered by 2010. The main effect of the crisis in the UK was a decrease in the number of transactions, loans and constructions. According to Mary Robertson,

> the housing crisis in the UK has taken the form of a crisis of supply and affordability: as tighter credit conditions have reduced the pool of those able to access mortgages, fewer people have been able to afford a suitable property to purchase.[51]

A combination of measures taken by the government, the Bank of England and mortgage creditors restricted the number of foreclosures during the financial crisis. These measures included: Support for Mortgage Interest, a regime of capitalisation for

mortgage bailouts that was aimed at helping homeowners to stay
in their homes as tenants, instead of being evicted; low basic bank
fees; increased transparency about loan modifications; greater
tolerance of arrears; and the Funding for Lending Scheme, to
support the renegotiation of debtors with private institutions.
However, some of these measures are temporary. Northern
Ireland – and especially Belfast – witnessed the largest number of
mortgage defaults and bank foreclosures, partly because of a more
difficult economic situation, with greater unemployment levels.[52]

The private rental sector has been continuously growing:
between 1981 and 2012, the number of households in this sector
doubled – from 1.9 to 3.8 million.[53] Families of differing compo-
sitions are renting in the private sector, including a growing
number of families with children and young people. The general
rule is fragile security of tenure, with contracts typically lasting
for twelve months – but also including cases of six-month
contracts – and subsequent eviction of tenants if they cannot
afford rent hikes. Today, 26 per cent of the homeless population
are of no fixed abode because of evictions due to defaulting on
private rents.

Private rental sector regulation varies in the UK. In England, the
government believes that regulation could lead to disinvestment
by landlords, reducing the supply of houses for rent. There is a
range of regulations for landlords – safety rules related to gas
installations and fire prevention, for example – but they are
difficult to enforce, as tenants fear retaliatory evictions if they
complain.[54]

For many, private rental is the only option. However, in addition to insecurity of tenure, discrimination against specific
groups – particularly migrants – aggravates the rental market
situation.[55] These problems are more serious in areas of high
demand, such as London.[56]

In England, the planning system has also undergone reforms
that, according to the government, purported to remove obstacles
that discourage or paralyse urban development, such as excessive
environmental controls. These reforms included a new National
Planning Policy Framework in 2012, amendments to its Section
106 in 2013, and measures introduced by the Localism Act

2011.[57] These measures were intended to eliminate the regional strategies demanded since 2004, seen as a centralised, bureaucratic and anti-democratic approach to development. Their goal was also to transfer power to the central government and local communities. Local planning authorities are now encouraged to draw up a local pro-growth plan. They are also expected to propose a supply of residential land plots for the next five years and speedily grant planning permissions, in the absence of significant negative impacts.

It is possible to view these measures as aiming to expand the availability of land for residential real estate. Nevertheless, easier access to licences – if not followed by any type of sanction for the speculative retention of land – can, instead, lead to more land financialisation. This practice stimulates entrepreneurs to apply for licences and then use the licensed land as collateral, without building on it in the short term.[58]

Other initiatives, too, sought to boost the housing market. One of them was the release of public lands, based on the estimate that around 40 per cent of the locations suitable for urban development are public-sector-owned.[59] The land marked for release will be sold for the highest bid to private entrepreneurs, who will build residential units. Once the land is released, local planning authorities will negotiate the type of residence that should be built. There is no conditionality or priority towards social or even 'affordable' housing.

A package of economic measures was launched through governmental incentives to stimulate the residential market and the economy. In order to help people access mortgage finance, the UK government introduced three schemes – the New Buy Guarantee, liquid asset loans and the Help to Buy program – which introduced mortgage guarantees for all UK borrowers.[60] In the absence of any finance ceiling and conditionality, these measures are liable to feed the real-estate bubble, undermining the government's goal of expanding access to housing, especially for those on lower incomes.

The Right to Buy programmes (for council housing, housing associations and social landlords) are still in force, allowing the sale of social housing units to their tenants. In England, since

2012, discounts for the purchase of council housing can reach up to £75,000 pounds. Since 2013 in London, they can reach up to £100,000.

In July 2013, the Scottish government announced its intention to cancel the Right to Buy programme for new social housing tenants as of 2017, as part of its new Housing Act of 2014. In November 2013, when approving the new Act, Scottish ministers argued that

> while the RTB [Right to Buy] has provided new options for households over the last thirty years, the costs of this policy will now fall on future generations. The transfer of hundreds of thousands of properties out of the social housing sector has decreased our social housing stock, and placed increasing pressures on councils and housing associations. It has also had a profound and detrimental effect on some communities, with less desirable areas now even more marginalised. At the same time, many of those who exercised their right to buy have struggled to meet the costs of home ownership.[61]

Parallel to these measures, England cut social housing finance by two-thirds. Housing associations must fight the cuts to subsidies by searching for financial resources in capital markets. In order to pay the interest, social landlords will have to raise rent for new tenants. They are now authorised to raise rents up to 80 per cent of market rates. Although the government considers this an incentive for landlords to invest in housing, the approach can potentially create new problems, including the reduction of affordability. Moreover, some measures impact the security of tenure for new social tenants (or existing ones who move house) in England: instead of perpetual rental – previously the rule for public rental stock – social landlords can now offer contracts for as little as two years.

The 2012 Welfare Reform Law, adopted by Westminster as part of their fiscal austerity program, contains measures that directly infringe the right to adequate housing. These reforms occur in a context already marked by: lack of social housing for low- and middle-income sectors; increasing numbers of homeless people;

rising unemployment; and salary squeeze. According to a 2013 Oxfam forecast, total UK public expenditure would face a cut of 11.5 per cent between 2010 and 2014. Public sector salaries had been frozen, and between 2010 and 2018, 1.1 million public jobs would be eliminated – two-thirds of which are today held by women. The estimate is that real wages fell 3.2 per cent, reaching the level of 2003, representing a lost decade for the average worker.[62] It is even more concerning that in 2012, around 13 million people lived in poverty in the UK; of those, more than half (6.7 million) were members of working families.[63]

One of the cuts to housing benefits applied by this law was the 'end of the spare room subsidy', which came into force in April 2013. It is also known as the 'under-occupancy penalty' and, popularly, as the 'bedroom tax'. This measure reduces the housing benefits received by social housing tenants of economically active age, based on the number of bedrooms in the home and on family composition. According to the new regulation, a social housing tenant has the right to occupy a house or flat containing one bedroom for each couple or single adult. It is expected that a child will share a bedroom with another child of the same sex until the age of sixteen, and regardless of their sex until the age of ten. Additional considerations come into play for individuals with special needs, people who require external carers during the night, or in cases of provisional child carers (a service provided by the state).[64]

For a family who have one bedroom above the limit, housing benefit can be reduced by 14 per cent. For two or more extra bedrooms, the reduction can reach 25 per cent. In Scotland, the government estimated that this reform would cost, on average, £50 more per month for the 82,000 potentially affected families. Eighty per cent of these households include an adult with special needs and 15,500 of them are families with children.[65] For this reason, the Scottish Parliament decided not to apply the bedroom tax and to bear the onus before the British Treasury.

Alongside the austerity argument, the government justifies the reduction of housing benefits as a 'fairness' measure. Firstly, it is aimed at reducing the current imbalance between overcrowding and under-occupancy. Secondly, it would introduce parity with tenants from the private rental sector, whose housing benefits are proportional to the number of bedrooms in the unit. Since the beginning of the implementation of the measure, the National Housing Federation (NHF) has expressed concern. The shortage of smaller houses and flats in existing housing estates reduces the options for tenants seeking to move so as to avoid benefit cuts.[66]

Some reports have already shown a rise in rent arrears since April 2013, as people struggle to remain in the homes where they have spent much of their lives.[67] Although the new policy does not oblige them to move out, most will obviously have no alternative, as many are workers with no savings. Faced with impossible choices between paying for either food, heating or rent, and with the imminence of expulsion from an entire socio-affective network, many people are driven to despair.

In addition to the bedroom tax, other austerity measures directly hit the poorest. Among these were the elimination of benefits to support payment of council tax (municipal tax paid by individuals, not proprietors alone) and the reduction of the Local Housing Allowance (LHA) – monetary aid for the payment of rents in the private sector. These cuts coincided neatly with a rise in rental costs: between May 2005 and May 2013, private rents rose by 8.4 per cent in England. The biggest increases were in London (11 per cent) and in East England (8.3 per cent) and the smallest ones in the East Midlands (5.3 per cent).[68]

Specific groups are particularly affected by the cumulative impact of these various policies and reforms. Among them, we can highlight lower-income sectors, people with special needs and the young. A research paper from Liverpool shows that pressures of living costs and cuts in social benefits lead low-income households to increase the use of payday loans (short-term loans with high interest rates) to cover essential expenses such as rent and energy.[69] Even a relatively slight change to their income, or a delay in benefits payments, quickly compounds poorer people's fragility, given their narrow margins of financial survival.

Poverty also contributes to rent arrears and occasionally, when these build up, to evictions. According to NHF, more than 14,000 households started to fall behind with their rent in Merseyside (one of England's poorest regions) a mere four weeks after the bedroom tax came into force. There are not enough smaller social housing units, or reasonably priced alternatives in the private sector. As a result many people hang on in their 'under-occupied' homes, forced to manage on less at a time of rising living costs and public service prices.[70]

According to research carried out in 2012 by the National Housing Federation in eastern England, the number of homeless people in the region grew by 44 per cent in only two years. NFH cites the scarcity of housing and the rise of residential real-estate prices and rents as contributing factors. Young families are the most affected group. In 2010, the average price of housing was around £195,000, almost 7.5 times bigger than the regional average income.[71]

For people with special needs or chronic diseases, adequate housing means living in homes adapted to their specific needs, close to health facilities that are part of their daily routine, as well as to friends and relatives and the community at large. This is essential for them to live an independent and dignified life. Too often, the scarcity of adapted and economically accessible housing alongside other changes in the social welfare system has left people with special needs 'between a rock and a hard place': they must choose between further limiting their living conditions or delaying rent payments and risking eviction.

Young people face more barriers than ever in terms of access to housing, due to their low income, high unemployment or under-employment rates within this age group and greater difficulty in obtaining a mortgage. This is a generation whose parents had far greater access to homeownership, mainly through subsidised privatisation of the public housing stock and tax exemptions.

It is important to emphasise that the British process of consti-tuting a generation of homeowners corresponded to a political-ideological dismantlement of the welfare system, with a wide base of social support. Deliberately marginalised and residu-alised, social housing became – both in the political-social imaginary and in practical terms – the place of the weak, those depending on social handouts, incapable of managing financial assets. Social housing thus became stigmatised. It is not a coinci-dence that recent austerity measures target social tenants and welfare recipients above all. Nevertheless, the current housing crisis in the UK is a victim of the success of the strategy that has been implemented over decades: real-estate prices cannot drop, because this would mean eroding the political-social base and their asset-based welfare. Public social housing cannot be promoted, because this would symbolise regression to a state of dependency. Therefore, British people – especially the youngest and poorest – simply have nowhere to live.

The British experience epitomises the political, ideological and economic dismantling of social housing and its takeover by the sphere of finance. It also shows how this shift led to the reduction of the right to housing for the poorest and most vulnerable, and to the regression of housing conditions for current generations. Comprehension of the North American trajectory, which I will present next, is fundamental to understand the – theoretical and practical – origin of one of the most powerful models of housing financialisation: the mortgage.

Pioneers: The United States

In the US, modern housing policy began during the Great Depression, when the National Housing Act of 1934 created the Federal Housing Administration (FHA) to register and insure mortgages and to provide security for creditors in cases of default. The US government also created the Federal National Mortgage Association (better known as Fannie Mae) to buy mortgages from creditors, increasing their liquidity and thus allowing them to offer further loans to buyers.

These measures came in response to the first large-scale financial-mortgage crisis, which occurred after 1929 in the US. The Federal Reserve Act, in 1913, permitted commercial banks to offer loans for real-estate purchase, generating a mortgage market. The bubble's burst led to more than 250,000 residential foreclosures per year in the worst years of the Great Depression.[72]

Another measure adopted after the 1929 crisis was the Housing Act of 1937 (Wagner-Steagall Act), which introduced federal intervention on social housing, authorising the government to fund, construct and become the landlord of rental units for the lower-income population. In a context of deep recession, this measure was justified as a way to improve conditions in urban 'slums' – areas of tenement housing – and to create jobs in the construction sector.[73]

The 1934 and 1937 Housing Acts inaugurated a dual housing system: on the one hand, the construction of public rental housing projects, with direct aid for low-income families. On the other, subsidised credit – mainly via tax exemptions – to promote home-ownership among middle-class families. This dual housing policy was also responsible for creating a new urban landscape: the housing projects were largely located in inner-city areas, while the majority of the private houses built via FHA credit were concentrated in exclusively residential suburbs with low population densities.

Under the new 1937 legislation, FHA built, in 260 localities, more than 170,000 units – principally in apartment towers organised into superblocks. Eighty-nine per cent of them were built in areas already dominated by tenements and other forms of low-income habitat, which were demolished to make way for the new buildings.[74]

In the 1940s and 1950s, residents of housing projects were essentially the working poor who could pay rent. However, this demographic changed from the 1960s on, with the large migration movement from the Southern states and the suburbanisation of a new generation of white workers. Originally, racial minorities represented between 26 and 39 per cent of public housing tenants, but this rate exceeded 60 per cent in 1978.[75] At the same time, between 1950 and 1970 tenants' average income fell from 64 to 37 per cent of the national average.[76]

Between the 1960s and 1970s, under the pressure of the civil rights movement, a second batch of housing projects was constructed, this time more clearly identified as a welfare scheme – or as a solution for those in need.[77] The majority of the new residents were black and/or poor:[78] the projects became ethnically, geographically and socially defined.

The purchase of private homes by the (predominantly white) middle class was vigorously supported by federal funding: more than half of the suburban houses built in the US during the

1950s and 1960s were funded by the government. This increased the proportion of homeowners from 30 per cent in 1930 to more than 60 per cent in the 1960s.

The social and ethnic geography of suburbs and inner cities was largely due to discriminatory practices by the banks. The Homeowners Loan Corporation, a company created to refinance mortgages and rescue debtors in the 1930s, developed a broad system of credit-acquirement evaluation, incorporating the culture and practice of real-estate agents. According to this system, areas to which it was possible and desirable to loan money were classified as green or yellow; by contrast, areas with a concentration of vulnerable populations were 'redlined', or marked in red, considered excessively risky for the banks.[79] Most loans were therefore not accessible to black people, and entire neighbourhoods occupied by African Americans and groups of impoverished migrants saw no new residential real estate projects for decades. White people received 98 per cent of federal-approved loans between 1934 and 1968, when redlining became forbidden by the Fair Housing Act.

The public housing stock numbered 1.4 million units at the end of the 1970s. The programme had been implemented by the federal government in order to provide decent and safe rentals to low-income families, elderly people and individuals with special needs. However, the model of housing projects came under scrutiny as they were increasingly stigmatised as sites of extreme poverty, crime and social marginalisation. The perception of a decline in quality of public housing came both from the buildings' physical deterioration – due to their age and lack of maintenance – and from official inaction around the wider issue of racial and economic segregation in some cities.[80]

The Housing and Community Act of 1974 decreed the end of federal funding for the construction of public housing projects. It also introduced the Housing Choice Voucher Program (commonly known as Section 8), granting subsidies to private-sector tenants and to real-estate developers who agreed to reserve some of their units for rent-controlled contracts. In the first case, tenants can choose a housing unit owned by a private landlord who accepts the vouchers. Tenants pay part of the rent – based on their income and generally corresponding to no more than 30 per cent of their total household income – and the rest is covered by federal resources. The Section 8 programme marked an important change in public housing policy, as it moved funds from public housing authorities – historically in charge of building and managing housing projects – to the private sector. The justification for its creation was

> to avoid concentrations of low-income people . . . However, it faced resistance from tenants and buildings in middle-income neighbourhoods and in some cities 'the concentration of [Section 8] buildings and tenants has been blamed, just like public housing, for community decline'.[81]

A decade later, the Tax Reform Act of 1986 created the Low-Income Housing Tax Credit, a new mechanism designed to generate capital for housing construction. Subsidised fiscal credit certificates (Project-Based Assistance) were directed to builders of pre-approved projects, to increase local supply of housing at prices slightly below market rate. These certificates have generated approximately 2 million affordable rental units.

Therefore, since the 1970s, public resources earmarked for the construction and maintenance of public housing stocks have been

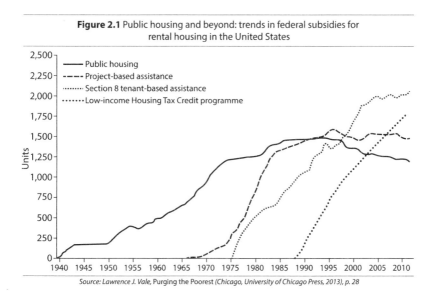

Figure 2.1 Public housing and beyond: trends in federal subsidies for rental housing in the United States

Source: Lawrence J. Vale, Purging the Poorest (Chicago, University of Chicago Press, 2013), p. 28

progressively reduced. This process was aggravated by President Reagan's fiscal restructuring measures. Concurrently, public subsidies for home-purchase grew, as well as programmes supporting private rental, such as Section 8 and Project-Based Assistance.

In the 1980s, budget cuts resulted in the gradual erosion and lack of maintenance of the public housing system. By the beginning of the 1990s, hundreds of thousands of public housing units were dilapidated. In the 2000s, there was a liquid loss of 170,000 public housing units due to deterioration. Today, most of the stock stands in need of substantial repair and restoration. Notwithstanding, public housing annual resources dropped 25 per cent between 1999 and 2006.

As federal resources began to be reduced, becoming progressively insufficient, housing agencies found themselves obliged to slash their own expenses. Measures included the transfer of units to more affluent tenants, able to pay higher rents, and cuts to areas such as security and maintenance.[82]

In 1989, Congress created the National Commission on Severely Distressed Public Housing in order to evaluate the situation. The commission concluded that, although the majority of the 1.4 million public housing units were well maintained and managed, a small proportion of them – 86,000, or 6 per cent – were in 'the most distressed and notorious urban developments in the nation, where crime, poverty, unemployment, and dependency were solidly entrenched'.[83] In 1992, based on the commission's recommendations, the HOPE VI programme (Housing Opportunities for People Everywhere) was created.

HOPE VI goals included: the revitalisation of public housing; the dispersal of low-income families; and the creation of sustainable communities through the demolition, restoration, reconfiguration or substitution of a large number of public housing units by mixed-income projects – that is, housing units intended for different income groups.[84] The programme provided resources for local agencies to demolish degraded or obsolete public housing projects and to replace them with mixed-income projects, generally in collaboration with private developers. Between 1991 and 2006, HOPE VI invested US$6.1 billion of federal resources in 235 projects. A total 96,200 public housing units were demolished and 107,800 were built or renovated – of which 56,800 were affordable units. Moreover, 78,000 housing vouchers have been issued.[85] Lower-density and mixed-income projects have been built to replace the old project towers, generally as a combination of public housing units, affordable units and units at market rate. Under this model, the responsibility for the provision of subsidised housing was transferred from the federal government to local authorities and the private sector.

In addition to the fact that many of the demolished units have been replaced by market-rated homes, many of the 'affordable' ones are too expensive for most public-housing tenants. It is undeniable that HOPE VI has improved the quality of the public housing stock. However, it has also reduced the number of accessible housing units for poor families and permanently displaced many residents of the demolished projects. In principle, non-rebuilt units were replaced by housing vouchers, but this procedure was not consistently followed through. Moreover, this policy transferred to the users the responsibility of finding a home in the private market. In practice, the choices that are actually available to voucher-holders are often limited, as, in certain neighbourhoods, there are no units available or no landlords willing to be part of the programme.

Units have been demolished despite insufficient mechanisms being in place for their tenants to find similar housing options. Often, displaced residents have had to move to other subsidised units in neighbourhoods as degraded as the original ones; often, too, they suffered discrimination in their new neighbourhoods. The demolition of the old housing projects and the construction of the new ones took much longer than originally planned. Also, the efforts to track down former residents in order to offer them the renovated units were insufficient. In fact, less than 12 per cent of the former public housing residents ultimately remained in the renovated communities. In general, fewer units were reconstructed than were demolished.

An example is the Cabrini Green community, in Chicago. Originally it consisted of 3,114 public housing apartments, of which 2,700 were demolished. Since the demolition, only 305 public housing units have been built in mixed-income neighbourhoods. As a result, many residents have been displaced and are unable to return.[86]

On the one hand, this federal housing policy resulted in an even higher number of homeowners – reaching approximately 69 per cent. On the other, it reduced the supply of public housing (which numbered 1 million units in 2010) through demolishing or closing more than 300,000 units without replacement. This loss was accompanied by the government's gradual exit from the housing sector.

In terms of homeownership promotion, important changes also occurred in the domain of housing finance. A movement to incorporate lower-income sectors was accompanied by the amplification of ties to the financial market *sensu stricto*. These changes resulted from two interconnected processes: firstly, the Community Reinvestment Act of 1977 and the consequent appearance of subprime loans; secondly, the growth of securitisation. The 1977 Act required banks to allocate part of their mortgage portfolios for the neighbourhoods from which their depositors came. Banks had therefore to modify their usual risk definitions, transforming what was, until then, 'redline' into a specific mortgage product: *subprime* – or very high-cost credit certificates, offered mainly to families composed of minorities or other groups who, historically, had no access to credit, as they were considered high-risk.[87]

Large and small banks began to push subprime loans, especially after the deregulation of the banking system by the Depository Institutions Deregulatory and Monetary Control Act of 1980. Another incentive was the successful launch of subprime mortgage products, such as 'teaser rates' (two years' repayments at very low interest rates and twenty-eight years at high interest rates) and ARM (Adjustable Rate Mortgages, or variable interest rates, allowing the re-establishment of high rates after a few years). From 8.9 per cent of the market in 2001, these loans reached 20 per cent of the total in 2006. Almost 90 per cent of subprime loans were ARM-type.[88]

Another significant deregulation was the permission for banks and non-bank investment institutions to securitise mortgages – in addition to Fannie Mae and Freddie Mac, which were government-created securitisers. This meant that institutions could buy portfolios created by banks with subprime loans, pack them together with other financial products and sell them on as residential mortgage-backed securities (RMBS) in the capital market. Financial instruments such as collateralised debt obligations, collateralised loan obligations and credit default swaps – derivatives based on mortgage-guaranteed debts – could be freely exchanged between financial operators, themselves protected from the new products' risks.

Securitisation allowed the operators to 'clean' credit institutions' balances through the selling of those derivatives to banks or investment funds. Moreover, as in an assembly line, they could produce, compile and synthesise financial products created from a mix of real-estate credit certificates. The workers on this assembly line were: real-estate credit certificates brokers – responsible for direct contact with consumers; intermediaries – who bought those certificates wholesale in order to later redistribute them according to the specifications of financial institutions and hedge funds; and, finally, rating agencies, who determined whether the composition of these asset-portfolios satisfied the quality standards or not.[89]

The federal government did everything it could to encourage this secondary market, which became one of the biggest sources of credit leverage – also for the financing of home-purchase.[90] Securitisation also included subprime loans. In 2007, the subprime business accounted for US$1.5 trillion within the global financial market. Wall Street banks and investment funds created special divisions to operate in the subprime mortgage market and earned high commissions for every transaction in the global market.

The growth of available resources for residential real-estate financing and the development of 'innovative' mortgage products allowed buyers to acquire more expensive properties, which also contributed to the elevation of real-estate prices. So long as prices kept growing, buyers with any kind of difficulty in paying instalments could refinance their homes through new loans. But when the real-estate bubble burst, prices levelled out or dropped, and ARM plans began to bill larger instalments. So the debacle began: debts piled up, leading to foreclosures and loss of homes.

A HUD report from 2009 stated: 'The extent of the housing and economic crisis is now painfully apparent ... approximately 3.7 million borrowers began the foreclosure process in 2007 and 2008.'[91] RealtyTrac (the leading provider of foreclosed homes) reported an increase of 32 per cent in the number of foreclosure processes between April 2008 and April 2009.[92]

The crisis affected not only indebted homeowners, but also tenants of mortgaged houses and buildings: 'At least 20 per cent of foreclosed properties are not owner-occupied, and in many parts of the country (such as New England, New York City, and Minneapolis), half or more of households living in foreclosed buildings are renters.'[93] When creditors foreclose rented properties, tenants are often evicted, despite having regularly paid rent.

Rent-control legislation is one of the tools used by some cities in the US to provide accessible housing. This legislation was introduced by the federal government during World War II, when President Franklin D. Roosevelt signed the Emergency Price Control Act of 1942. Subsequently, various states and local jurisdictions instituted rent-control measures, many of which still exist today.[94] This rental stock faces growing pressure from real-estate markets and, more recently, threats from predatory capital.

Predatory capital arose and gained strength during the recent real-estate market bubble: an investor buys a building with stabilised rents through a securitised mortgage that is repeatedly sold over a short period for ever larger sums. As mortgage instalments grow with every sale, the existing rents become insufficient to cover the costs. As a result, landlords adopt aggressive tactics to evict current residents and find new tenants who will pay higher rents. Therefore, the building is no longer within the stabilised-rent system. With the real-estate market retraction, some investors simply departed, leaving the building to the bank and an uncertain future for the tenants. In New York alone, a civil society organisation identified more than 90,000 rent-controlled units that are subjected to predatory capital.[95]

The housing crisis for low-income families and individuals was further exacerbated as a result of other types of pressure on the housing stock. In the 1960s, the federal government established a partnership with private construction companies to supply accessible housing for a twenty- to forty-year period. Depending on the nature of each subsidy, the owners of these buildings had different options for making a profit: they could pay off their entire mortgage, to then start charging market prices, and/or refuse to renew expired contracts.[96] Either way, the stock of rent-controlled accommodation would shed that status. Many contracts expired without being renewed. Thousands of units have already been lost and a report estimates that another 300,000 contracts will expire within the next five years.[97]

Housing vouchers became the country's largest scheme for low-income housing assistance, benefiting more than 2 million families in the extreme low-income bracket. Even so, the majority of municipalities have long waiting lists for new vouchers – generally five years. Under the current budget, federal programs can only serve one quarter of the low-income families who are entitled to assistance according to their profile and income.[98] The budgetary cuts caused an additional loss of 150,000 vouchers between 2005 and 2007. According to a 2008 study from the United States Conference of Mayors, due to excess demand, many cities closed their waiting lists for Section 8/Housing Choice Vouchers and for public housing.[99]

The effects of the political choices taken with regard to housing since the late 1970s are patent in the country's current housing crisis. The number of homeless families, the costs of renting, and the waiting lists for social housing and vouchers are soaring in unison. In 2007, around 22 per cent of the 36.9 million tenant families in the US were spending more than half of their income on rent.[100] The number of households facing serious housing-cost problems grew by 33 per cent between 2000 and 2007. Around two-thirds of them were families with children, elderly people or people with special needs.[101] In the USA, around 12.7 million children – more than one-sixth of all American children – belong to families who spend more than half of their income on housing.[102]

The drastic curtailment of social housing resources and programmes was supposedly based on two neoliberal imperatives: to reduce public expenditure and to withdraw the state from areas in which the market can act. Nevertheless, the evolution of US housing policy allows us to present a very different narrative. Firstly, the argument of reducing public expenditure is fallacious. In the US, although the HUD budget has dropped, between 1976 and 2004 public expenditure on housing did not stop growing; only it was, instead, directed to higher-income sectors through tax exemptions for home purchase, as shown in Figure 2.2.

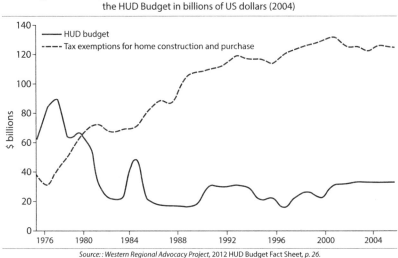

Figure 2.2 Comparison between Federal Tax Exemptions for Home Purchase and the HUD Budget in billions of US dollars (2004)

Source: : *Western Regional Advocacy Project*, 2012 HUD Budget Fact Sheet, *p. 26.*

Secondly, the subprime mortgage crisis was not the product of an unsuccessful attempt to amplify the private housing market to embrace the poorest, reducing their dependency on public funds and on the state. Instead it resulted from a clear and aggressive policy of destruction of the existing alternatives of housing access for the poorest. Such a policy intended to facilitate, precisely within the lower-income housing sector, a new form of income extraction: income moved from mortgage markets and indebted homeowners to financial investors.[103]

The Model in Western Europe

In 2008, a decision made by the European Commission restricted the provision of government-subsidised social housing. For all member countries, only the socially underprivileged – those whose income is not sufficient to afford housing market prices – would have access to this type of benefit. This decision was intended to guarantee freedom of competition and to reduce state intervention in sectors where the market also acts. It defined housing as a 'service of general economic interest' (SGEI) within the terms of Article 36 of the Charter of Fundamental Rights, adopted at the formal creation of the European Union (EU).

This interpretation clearly challenged the universalist policy of social housing provision previously accepted in Europe, especially in the Netherlands and Denmark. In these countries, the public or semi-public housing stock was still available at controlled prices – below market rates – to all citizens, regardless of income. In the Netherlands, the implementation of this decision made social housing inaccessible to 400,000 families who were now classed as high-income. In 2011 in Sweden, housing was simply excluded from the list of sectors considered as SGEI. In France, the National Union of Real-Estate Proprietors denounced the French government to the European Commission for establishing excessively high upper-income limits for access to public social housing, which, according to them, represented unfair competition.[104]

The 2008 European Commission's decision is merely one more juridical-political move within the ongoing process of transforming housing policy across Europe, even in countries where social housing represented up to 40 per cent of the total units – such as the Netherlands, the Nordic countries and the United Kingdom. This process means the focalisation and residualisation of housing policy, breaking with its universalist nature to make way for mercantilisation and financialisation.

Indeed, the takeover of the housing sector by finance in Europe goes beyond the pressure to restrict access to public and semi-public housing only to the very poor. Even social landlords have begun to rely on market-financing mechanisms to continue producing and/or managing their stocks. Moreover, even in countries where social housing still has a significant presence, the processes of home-purchase via mortgage, securitisation of the mortgage market and growth of household debt have been galloping forward.

The Netherlands (the European country with the current largest proportion of social housing, at 35 per cent) is an instructive example of the above. From the 1920s, Dutch municipalities and private organisations built large housing estates, especially between 1945 and 1990. Rent-controlled housing units – produced

by non-profit private organisations, the *Woningcorporaties* –
expanded the social housing sector participation from 23 per cent
of all households in 1960 to 38 per cent in 1985, involving both
low- and middle-income sectors.[105] This expansion was possible
thanks to the increase of public subsidies – multiplied six-fold
between 1970 and 1987[106] – and to rent-control legislation that
limited prices and readjustments, for the private rental sector as
well. In cities such as Amsterdam, this policy was complemented
by a system of territorial planning and public ownership of land,
designed to mitigate the impact of land prices on total housing
costs. It was thus possible to provide high-quality social housing
all over the city, configuring one of the least segregated European
cities in socio-spatial terms.[107]

Since 1974, the Dutch government has provided financial aid to
tenants (both in social housing and in the private sector) in the
form of rent assistance. This measure allowed an initial readjustment of rental prices both in *Woningcorporaties*' units and in the
private rental sector. However, the large subventions for
Woningcorporaties were gradually terminated from 1995 on,
significantly reducing the supply of new stocks. The existing facilities were maintained, mainly through the sale of units, the
elevation of rents and the emergence of new mechanisms used by
social landlords to raise and manage funds via capital markets.[108]

It is not a coincidence that from the 1990s on, homeownership
began to grow apace amid a flourishing mortgage market. Two
factors influenced this trend: firstly, the government played an
active role by offering fiscal incentives to buyers and encouraging
building proprietors to sell their apartments. Secondly, monetary
policy reforms kept interest rates low and encouraged banks to
incur larger risks, increasing credit limits.[109]

In the late 1990s and early 2000s, the combination of these
measures resulted in an exorbitant rise in housing costs, both rent
and purchase. The Dutch Bank estimated that, by the end of the
1990s, half of the country's economic growth was a function of
rising home equity, rather than genuine growth.[110]

The result was a restructuration of Dutch cities' housing stocks,
with an expansion of the supply of market-priced units and a
reduction of the supply of affordable housing. In this context,

lower-income individuals and families – especially young people –
are hard-pressed to find a roof: Amsterdam is on the brink of a
new segregation between income groups.[111]

Sweden offers another example of momentous changes in a
country where social housing was a universalist policy. On the
whole, the Swedish welfare system resisted the neoliberal wave
better than those of other European countries. The exception was
housing. The 'Swedish model' of housing was once considered one
of the most radical among the European social-democracies:
universalist and tenure-type-neutral, this state-funded model
offered both subsidies for the production of social housing and
direct aid to tenants. It also established strict regulations and
incentives for home-buyers and investors.

Planned in the 1930s and 1940s, this model reached its peak in
terms of social housing availability, quality and accessibility in
1975, after the implementation of a scheme for the construction
of 'one million houses' (1964–75). However, the model underwent
a profound liberalisation over the last two decades, with the
demolition or sale of housing complexes and the residualisation of
social housing. Faced with an economic crisis and losing advantage within the global economy, Sweden held its welfare system
responsible. Housing was one of the first departments to be
reformed.[112]

Popularly oriented publications such as *A Market for Housing
for All* (Andersson et al. 1990) and *Power Over the Home*
(Meyerson, Ståhl, and Wickman 1990), drawing on inspiration
from neoliberal policies in the United Kingdom and the United
States, called for an end to existing housing policies, laying out a
road map for neoliberal reforms. One of the first things the
Conservative government did after coming to power in 1991 –
the first government in Sweden led by a Conservative prime
minister (Carl Bildt) since 1930 – was to close the Department of
Housing.[113]

In 1993, a new model, the so-called Danell system for housing
finance, drastically reduced subsidies and housing aid. The return
of the Social Democrats to power in 1994 did not signal a rupture

of this policy, and the neoliberal programme advanced. Reforms clearly prioritised homeowners over tenants: the latter suffered large rises in rent, which generated great income concentration on a national scale.

The production of new housing units plummeted, increasing conditions of overcrowding. Municipal public companies that had not been shut down and which still owned housing stocks began to operate with an eye to profit, further constraining lower-income people's access to housing – especially in good locations with decent infrastructure. At the same time, social housing estates in areas that were appealing to the market were renovated, which attracted higher-income residents. The result was, mainly in big cities, a notable segmentation, polarisation and segregation of the housing market.[114]

Both in the Netherlands and in Sweden, social housing and protected rents were overlooked in favour of homeownership via mortgage finance. This process is similar to the pioneering British model. In all three countries, beyond the elimination of social housing from the economic and social landscape, a deep transformation in its socio-cultural and political meaning is manifest. Clearly, actors involved in the production and consumption of social housing lost out to the rise of not only homeowners but, above all, real estate developers and financial intermediaries. Not by coincidence, in all three countries the housing reforms were accompanied by reforms in planning and land policy. These reforms limited public control over and intervention in the organisation of the territory, and made regulations more flexible in order to attract private developers. As indicated earlier, reforms in the banking and financial systems expanded the field of action for financial intermediaries, thereby increasing their political influence.

In no European country was this clearer than in Spain. Combining the deregulation of both credit market and tenancy laws with reform of the planning system and entrance into the European Community, Spain enjoyed two decades of a 'real-estate party'. It embarked on frantic construction of residential developments in extended peripheries, accompanied by exponential growth of real-estate mortgage credit to buyers – including the low-income population.

Unlike the three European countries that we previously discussed, Spain has never had a significant social housing policy, and public or not-for-profit subsidised housing facilities never surpassed 2 per cent of total homes.[115]

The country's housing history was marked by self-builds and, mainly in big cities, by a significant percentage of private rental housing. In 1960, owner-occupiers represented 51.9 per cent and tenants 41 per cent of the housing market.[116] Ever since General Franco's dictatorship, central governments have been keen to foster homeownership, using incentives and tax breaks. At the launch of his housing plan in 1957, José Luis de Arrese, Franco's minister of housing, declared: 'We want a country of homeowners, not of proletarians [*de propietarios, no de proletarios*].'[117]

From an economic perspective, Franco's dictatorship relied heavily on the promotion of the real-estate industry, with two main goals: to dynamise the economy and, simultaneously, to enhance social control through the deactivation of potential revolutionary impetus, for 'those who own a property have something to lose, concrete interests to defend and little time to conspire'.[118] Especially in the 1960s and 1970s, during the so-called *desarrollo* [development] period, credit and tax exemptions were given to real-estate developers for the promotion of what they named 'protected housing'. These measures significantly boosted real-estate activity and home-purchase by the middle class. Owner-occupied units went from 45 per cent of the total in 1950 to 57 per cent in 1970, reaching 78 per cent in 1991.[119]

Nevertheless, the movement observed in the 1990s and especially in the 2000s was of a different nature. In 1985, the Boyer Decree reformed the Urban Tenancy Act: it liberalised the rental market, abolished the cap on upward readjustment and limited the duration of contracts to five years, making rental tenure more insecure.[120]

From 1991 on, a new law allowed private agents to enter mortgage markets – which had, until then, been restricted to banks and public funds. This law also allowed the rise of the mortgaged proportion within the total value of a unit. In 1992, the secondary mortgage market was regulated. In 1998, on the other hand, a revision of national planning regulations declared that 'all

non-urbanized land can be incorporated into real-estate development', which opened up the whole territory for new developments.
What is more, the regulation of land-use control was decentralised, now falling to local authorities.[121]

At the start of the 2000s, this measure coincided with the
increase of local administrations' financial deficits. As their
responsibilities and competences grew, they depended more and
more on taxes from real-estate transactions.

Between 1997 and 2007, 6.6 million new housing units were
built – almost twice the number of new households in the same
period.[122] In a context of great liquidity and falling interest rates,
deregulation and mortgage market securitisation – as well as the
country's adoption of the euro – contributed to two important
movements. First, the multiplication of the housing supply by the
private market and an unprecedented urban expansion. Second,
the rise of real-estate prices, generating a bubble.

Tax exemptions for housing savings-accounts and the reduction
of taxes on sales and purchases of residential buildings – even for
second or third homes – stimulated home-purchase and price
appreciation. This occurred because consumers could afford to
purchase dearer properties, knowing they would be reimbursed by
the annual tax return. At the same time, banks and other financial
institutions could finance 100 per cent of the units' value, which
allowed the sale of progressively more expensive houses even to
people who did not have enough savings to buy them.[123]

This process was widely encouraged via the media, including
messages from the government itself claiming that houses were a
safe investment, one that would never lose value. It was also stimulated by the launch of ever more 'creative' financial products,
such as 'young mortgage', 'free mortgage', 'open mortgage',
'de-mortgage'.[124] The country was fomenting a policy of reckless
private borrowing. Debts jumped from 55 to 130 per cent of families' disposable income between 1997 and 2007. For every €3 of
debt, €2 corresponded to mortgage debts. Contrary to the media
messages, the policy of easy credit was crucial in elevating prices,
which meant that families had to multiply their efforts to keep up
with their debts. In 1997, in order to buy an apartment, a family
needed, on average, 3.8 gross annual salaries; in 2007, this rose to

7.6 salaries. Measured another way, the percentage of income necessary to pay the house instalments rose from 37.6 per cent of a family's monthly income to 51.2 per cent in those ten years.[125]

In 2007, when the bubble burst and financial and economic crisis ensued, soaring unemployment added to the difficulties of mortgage-holders. In 2008, the number of Spaniards defaulting on their mortgage credit certificates grew by 310 per cent and 2.7 million people finished the year unable to pay their debts. In 2009, defaults reached 850,000 – a number that was repeated in 2010.[126]

According to Spain's judicial system, between 2007 and the first trimester of 2011 almost 350,000 foreclosures were initiated. Although some second homes and buy-to-let investments were involved, 85 per cent of those affected owned only their mortgaged home. Moreover, as loan guarantors are included in foreclosure processes, their properties too were affected and could be seized by the bank. Research estimates from 2013 indicate that 2 million people were affected by foreclosures.[127] At the same time, according to the 2011 census, there are approximately 3.5 million empty residential units in Spain – the greatest stock of unoccupied houses and apartments in the European Union.[128]

Spain's case is one of the most extreme examples of the impact of housing financialisation as part of a 'credit socialisation' movement via the inclusion of low- and middle-income sectors into credit markets. It also shows the effects of the financial real-estate complex on people's lives. In Spain, the euphoria of the expansion of credit for home-purchase fed a real-estate orgy – the rapid and massive proliferation of residential construction was one of the central pillars of the country's political economy for over a decade.

Literally millions of residential units were produced by this system. Although they have the materiality of cement, brick and concrete – and are implanted in cities, transforming their landscape and ways of functioning – these objects are, at the same time, abstractions, fractions of units of value circulating in the financial sphere. Alongside other fractions, they flow through the financial web, whose speed itself was accelerated by digital communication networks. Therefore, housing – in the real, concrete world – is connected to an abstract network in which values circulate, via loans and their anticipated recuperation with interest over time by the investors who bet on it. This web of debt that unfolds around the world originates with one group of people, the debt 'holders', who work hard to pay loans back. For the investors, housing is one bet among many others, a mix of future forecast and asset that is called speculation – inherent to the financial logic of winners and losers. For the inhabitant of the mortgaged house or apartment, it has other dimensions and meanings. For those who are indebted beyond their current worth and wealth, in particular, one of those meanings had been the expectation of future income growth via the appreciation of the mortgaged property. However, this hope fades away when one has nowhere else to live and it is no longer possible to be part of the 'game'.

At the end of the day, debt – this abstract currency that travels around the world – is the responsibility of those who agreed to pay for it. In the case of Spain, the loss is not restricted to the property that, undervalued after the bubble burst, goes back to the bank; it involves too the payment of the entire original property value. During the 2007 debacle, after the homeownership orgy, Spain was left with empty homes and, at the same time, homeless indebted people. People who are only too real, flesh and blood, abused by the speculative mechanisms and games of chance of the financial world.

3

Exporting the Model

This paper articulates the housing policy of the World Bank as it has evolved during the 1980s and early 1990s and proposes a number of important new policy directions for both the Bank and its borrowers. It advocates the reform of government policies, institutions, and regulations to enable housing markets to work more efficiently, and a move away from the limited, project-based support of public agencies engaged in the production and financing of housing. Governments are advised to abandon their earlier role as producers of housing and to adopt an enabling role of managing the housing sector as a whole. This fundamental shift is necessary if housing problems are to be addressed at a scale commensurate with their magnitude – to improve substantially the housing conditions of the poor – and if the housing sector is to be managed as a major economic sector.[1]

The paragraph quoted above, written in 1993 by Stephen Mayo and Shlomo Angel (experts at the World Bank's Urban Development Division, Transport, Water, and Urban Development Department) announces the new consensus in terms of housing policy. According to this, governments should renounce their role as providers of affordable housing in order to become facilitators.

Various World Bank documents claimed that this change in the direction of housing policy – widely followed by other multilateral banks, such as the Inter-American Development Bank (IDB) – was a result of a reassessment of the Bank's action within the sector. They began to consider the previous system as markedly limited in scope and lacking the capacity to recover costs.[2] That system was the rule in the 1970s: loans to governments for projects that promoted access to land for the poorest – thus offering low 'investment' return. With this model, urban land was directly provided by the state, aiming to enable the gradual construction of homes by the beneficiaries themselves or to launch slum-upgrading projects. During this period, Sites and Services and slum-upgrading pilot-projects were financed mostly in Latin America (above all in Peru, El Salvador and Venezuela) and Asia (especially in Indonesia and the Philippines), but also – on a smaller scale – in Sub-Saharan Africa. In the 1970s, these projects were implemented in fifty-five countries, involving around US$2 billion.[3]

The change that started in the 1980s led the World Bank to progressively redirect its policy towards loaning to financial institutions – resulting in the virtually complete disappearance of loans for Sites and Services and the urbanisation of informal settlements in the 1990s. One of the arguments for the shift was these pilot projects' low potential for replication. However, the Bank's entrance into the restructuring of countries' housing finance systems meant, in reality, an opportunity for the institution to get involved with larger processes of economic readjustment in indebted countries – particularly those affected by the debt crisis. According to the World Bank, a 'well-functioning' housing finance system would contribute to wider financial goals, such as capital mobilisation and fiscal adjustment. Public expenditure would be applied through more transparent and focalised subsidies and private capital could be mobilised.[4]

The initial goal was to create autonomous financial institutions in the countries, capable of offering long-term mortgage loans to low- and middle-income families, enabling a reduction of the 1980s World Bank housing subsidies. In the 1990s, however, the policy evolved towards the creation of a 'housing sector that serves the needs of consumers, producers, financiers, and local and central governments; and that enhances economic development'.[5]

With the World Bank's progressive abandonment of major urban infrastructure projects, loans integrated into larger structural adjustment programs in indebted countries grew within the

Bank. These new loans were not necessarily associated to loans for investment and subsidies within the housing sector and operations of technical assistance. This change amplified both the amount of resources available and the participation of housing finance in the Bank's total loans: in the 1980s, more than US$4 billion were involved in these operations; in the 1990s, it almost reached US$7 billion. At the time, this value represented more than half of the total loans from the Bank's infrastructure and urban development sector – in which housing is allocated.[6]

This change also represented a significant transformation in the profile of countries which receive 'help' from the World Bank: after the fall of the USSR, former Communist Eastern European and Central Asian countries became important World Bank clients. Together, they have received almost 20 per cent of all housing loans – US$900 million in the 1990s.[7]

Alongside the decisive presence of commodification and financialisation in World Bank structural adjustment programmes, the institution played a key role in the dissemination of the model of market-oriented housing policy. It did so not only through direct loans to countries (Latin America continued being an important client, as we will see, as well as countries in the north of Africa and in the Middle East), but, more importantly, through its influence over the theoretical and practical development of the model. In organisations such as the World Bank, the European Central Bank and other multilateral banks and institutions, loans are sometimes non-repayable and almost always accompanied by a package of economic measures and technical assistance. This assistance is performed by consultants who base their analysis on reports produced inside the institution itself and follow its directives. Experts and consultants also take part in international forums and events that gather ministers, mayors and housing programme managers. In these ways, the banks' action transforms each loan into a laboratory for technical-political experiments, which has been further consolidated into a sort of 'recipe' and disseminated by the banks themselves.

The recipe was formulated back in 1993, in the previously mentioned *Housing: Enabling Markets to Work*. According to this World Bank policy paper, governments have seven instruments at their disposal to facilitate the action of housing markets: three to tackle obstacles to the growth of demand, three to augment supply, and one to improve the sector's performance as whole. The three instruments to make the demand viable are: first, enforcement of the right to property, in order to guarantee the establishment and legal enforcement of a system of free trade in housing – achievable through the implementation of a land and property registration system and the regularisation of insecure forms of tenure; second, development of a housing finance system through the creation of healthy and competitive mortgage credit institutions and the development of innovative products, capable of extending home-purchase to the poorest; and third, the rationalisation of subsidies, to ensure that they are focalised and accessible, measurable, transparent and adequately scaled, avoiding the distortion of residential markets.

The three instruments for supply expansion are: provision of infrastructure for urbanisation; reform of urban and buildings regulation systems, aiming to balance the costs and benefits of norms that impact land and residential markets and removing laws that unnecessarily hinder the supply of housing; lastly, organisation of the civil construction industry to foster competition and eliminate commercial obstacles and barriers to input.

The seventh instrument is institutional strengthening of the housing sector, in order to monitor and manage its performance as a whole.[8]

According to the same document, these seven instruments are applicable to all World Bank clients, but the priority for the mobilisation of one or another should vary from country to country. For countries classified as 'low-income', the priority is the reform of tenure through the development of market-oriented systems of property rights, as well as investment in infrastructure and in the construction industry. In countries holding large debts, the priority is fiscal and financial reform, especially the reduction of public expenditure on housing and the implementation of housing finance systems. In former Communist countries, the priorities are: to reform property rights, housing finance systems, land and construction subsidies and regulations; to improve the real-estate development sector; and to further the production and distribution of building materials. In other countries, classified as 'middle-income', the priorities should be the reform of land and building-use regulation – enabling a transition to more responsive systems of housing supply – and the development of a mortgage market.[9]

Alongside the World Bank's direct loans to governmental institutions, the International Finance Corporation (IFC, the Bank's private arm), associated to its Capital Market Department, also played a decisive role in the success of this overhaul of housing policy. The IFC helped create mortgage credit companies in Bolivia, Botswana, Colombia, Indonesia, Lebanon and Senegal, and instigated the Housing Development Finance Corporation in India. It also worked in the private sector, to create mortgage credit institutions capable of competing with the public sector. And it contributed to the reform of finance systems, easing the development of prime and subprime mortgage markets.[10]

The above exposition of the World Bank's engagement in the spread of the housing financialisation model does not purport to be an evaluation of the Bank's strategies and outcomes. The intention here is to reveal another mechanism of dissemination of the theoretical and practical models that led to the takeover of the housing sector by finance. In each country's concrete experience, the Bank's involvement in the reforms may have been greater or lesser, both in volume of resources and in political influence. Regardless of this variable, agents from the international market interfered with the countries' political economy in many ways – including their participation in strategies of cooperation via multilateral banks or cooperation agencies.

Indeed, the World Bank's own documents recognise an important effect of this new – and allegedly successful – housing policy focus: the gradual stifling of support for social housing for lower-income populations. In the 1970s, this type of support represented 90 per cent of the World Bank's loans to the housing sector; since the mid-1990s, this rate has dropped to less than 10 per cent. The Bank also admits a reduction in the number of less developed countries on the institution's client list: from 40 per cent in the 1970s to 20 per cent in 2006.[11] Therefore, as in the experiences that I have previously described, financialisation policies were more useful for the expansion of financial markets themselves than for increasing access to housing for the poorest and most vulnerable.[12]

In later chapters of this book, I will analyse more deeply the reforms of property systems, as well as the impact of the above-mentioned policy of focalised subsidies on the World Bank's 'revenues'. Certainly, the application of these 'revenues' depends on the specific national context. As we have seen, the so-called 'transition economies' – countries that abandoned Communism and reformed their economic, political and financial systems in the 1990s – were an important laboratory for the new housing policy paradigms so clearly laid out in the Bank's documents. By way of several examples – with particular attention to Croatia and Kazakhstan – I will examine how this process occurred, and the consequences it had for former Communist countries.

Lost in Translation: The Housing Trajectory of Former Communist Countries

> Until very recently, housing policy in South Eastern Europe was predominantly concerned with the reconstruction of properties damaged during conflict, and with the privatization of the publicly owned stock. By now, most of the damaged or lost properties have been rebuilt and it would seem timely to pursue the next critical stages of a post-privatization housing policy agenda ... to develop the legal and regulatory conditions to enable new private homeowners ... to maintain and use this asset efficiently; [and] to pave the way for an emerging housing finance market [which] is an important segment of the financial sector of any country and contributes to its economic growth.

With these words, the president of the Council of Europe Development Bank and the World Bank vice president for Europe and Central Asia presented the result of the Ministerial Housing Conference for South Eastern Europe, held in Paris in 2003.[13]

In Communist countries, housing provision was an obligation of the state and was universally guaranteed to all as part of the non-monetised living conditions, salaries excepted.[14] Despite their apparent homogeneity, the models and systems for housing provision varied among the countries. Even inside a region or bloc of countries, differences prevailed – such as among the former members of the USSR (in Eastern Europe and Central Asia), Yugoslavia, South Eastern Europe or the Asian countries under the influence of China.[15]

The predominant model was the construction of a public housing stock by central governments, municipalities, cooperatives or state companies and its subsidised letting to residents. However, some countries (such as Hungary, Bulgaria, Poland and former Yugoslavia) also ran public banks and agencies that issued cheap loans for people to build their own residences. In Yugoslavia, for example, subsidies for home purchase became part of housing policy in the 1960s, while in Hungary, self-builds were common in the suburbs of big cities. In any case, in socialist countries, the predominance of state organisations for home finance and construction made housing a state duty – even in the case of home purchase. Public banks offered long-term mortgage loans with fixed repayments and low interest rates. These loans were allocated according to lists from syndicates, municipalities or the Communist Party. In further urbanised countries, such as Poland, the German Democratic Republic and Czechoslovakia, cooperatives mobilising previous collective savings became gradually more prevalent.[16]

In the case of public rental housing – the predominant modality in socialist countries – tenants enjoyed extraordinary security: they could not only remain in the building, but also move apartments.[17] Rent and utilities (such as electricity and water) were extremely cheap, amounting to an average 2–3 per cent of the family budget.

Despite many different situations from country to country, at the end of the 1990s the number of homeless people was minimal in most of them. This is not to say that public housing projects were of a high standard, well located or fairly allocated among those in need. Large housing complexes were usually built using low-cost prefabricated technology of very poor quality. Moreover, many families and individuals had no option but to share overcrowded and precarious apartments and houses. Often these complexes were residential-only, with no social, sports or cultural facilities, and inadequately maintained. Privileged allocation of the better apartments to party or union leaders was also a common practice.

At the beginning of the 1990s in Europe, and at the end of the same decade in Asia, the majority of former Communist countries embarked on projects of privatisation of their large-scale public housing stock, which resulted, in many cases, in its complete suppression. These countries adopted right-to-buy schemes – the possibility for tenants to buy the units where they lived with large discounts (and sometimes at no cost). Only Poland and the Czech Republic did not introduce national legislation on the theme, letting municipalities decide what should be done with their stocks.

An example of this is Slovakia. Between 1948 and 1990 – when the country was still part of Czechoslovakia – 1.3 million rental housing units were built (for a population of 5 million people by the end of that period). This number dropped after the transition from a planned economy to a market economy, in 1989. From 1991 to 2000, three-quarters of the public housing stock was lost. However, the main characteristic of the transition was the change in the property regime: public rentals shrank drastically in comparison to residential private property. Nowadays, state rental units represent only 2.7 per cent of the country's housing stock. Slovakia implemented a slightly different version of the right-to-buy system, as it kept a proportion of its housing stock as controlled-rent units.[18]

Another example is Slovenia, which, between 1991 and 1993, privatised its entire housing stock. By the end of this period, 88 per cent of all housing units were privately owned. By the end of 2000, 11 per cent of the total stock was state-owned and used for social housing.[19] In Estonia, before the 1989 reforms, 25.8 per cent of all residential buildings belonged to the central government, 34.7 per cent to local governments, 5 per cent to housing cooperatives and 34.5 per cent to private owners. After the Privatisation Law, the Population and Housing Census of 2000 indicated the following percentages: the public sector (mostly in the form of local governments) owned 6 per cent of all residential buildings, while the rest were privately owned. Later statistics show that privatisation kept growing: in 2005, only 4 per cent of all residential buildings were state-owned.[20]

As part of the privatisation of some Russian and Bulgarian companies, production complexes that comprised workers' accommodation were transferred to new (private) proprietors, housing and tenants included. Thus, former state-owned companies that were privatised became large landlords of residential complexes.

In addition, many countries – such as the Czech Republic, Estonia, Slovenia and Albania – returned buildings to former owners (or their descendants) who had been expropriated by the Communist regimes. Some countries – such as Russia and Bulgaria – did not implement property-return policies, while others – Hungary, for example – preferred to financially compensate former proprietors.[21]

Despite the variety of internal socio-political configurations and options chosen during the transition, former socialist countries radically transformed their housing tenure structure during the 1990s, with clear predominance of homeownership over tenancy.

In Europe, all former Communist countries have homeownership percentages above 80 per cent of their residential stock – in some cases, above 90 per cent, such as in Slovakia, Lithuania, Albania and Romania. This rate is superior to the European average, currently around 70 per cent.[22] In Central Asia and China, homeownership rates also exceed 80 per cent.[23] Privatisation was accompanied – again in different proportions and timings – by the introduction of housing finance systems. As indicated previously, the World Bank and international cooperation agencies had participated intensely in this process, especially in European countries.[24]

The transformation of housing, from a public and social good entirely under the state's responsibility into a product available on the market, has already impacted on access to housing in the above-mentioned countries, affecting mainly the poorest layers. On the one hand, most households enjoyed a first moment of tenure security and, especially in the former Soviet countries, there has been no large short-term housing deficit. On the other, however, the issue of affordability soon emerged as a problem. Families who bought the apartments where they lived had never borne their costs before – nor their management and maintenance expenses. Given the low quality of many of these units and in the absence of a policy to tackle the issue, their physical condition quickly deteriorated.[25] At the same time, companies that had become landlords of large housing complexes began to raise the rent – which had rarely reached 5 per cent of the household income before – above many residents' capacity to pay.

Moreover, the privatisation of the housing stock was accompanied by the privatisation of public utilities (electricity, water and gas), entailing an immediate rise in housing costs as a whole. In most cases, renovation expenses also followed the general rise of previously subsidised prices.[26]

Another important consequence was the virtual paralysis of the construction sector, due to the interruption of public production and the nonexistence of a replacement private supply.[27] The only housing solution for new families or young people was therefore through the private rental sector, which, in urban areas, could tie up more than half of their income.[28]

The rise of housing prices and overcrowding in large urban centres also relates to other processes: the growth of internal migration (which was previously controlled), the influx of foreign investment and the opening of land and real-estate markets to the speculative movements of financial capital. One country where this phenomenon stands out is China.

China started its reform towards housing commodification in 1998. The new policy ended the system of housing allocation, following the plan of Special Economic Zones (SEZs) that intended to set up a new system based on subsidised purchase in some parts of the country. The basis of the previous system for housing registration, or *hukou* – implemented by Mao Zedong in rural zones in the 1950s – was not eliminated. This system relates access to public services, including housing, to the place where an individual is registered. Nevertheless, as substantial migration flows followed the jobs from rural areas into cities, there was a meteoric development of residential real-estate markets and a house-price boom.[29]

In the absence of housing supply for these 'illegal' migrants, the new paradigm has been simply incapable of providing access to housing for lower-income sectors, leading to increased segregation and situations of precariousness and informality in urban areas.

The surplus rural population, estimated at 150 million people in 2013, is expected to steadily fuel the migration movement. Such migrants, *hukou*-blocked where housing is concerned, represent approximately half of the poor urban population.[30]

Within this overheated residential market, the solutions found to absorb such contingents are in the informal field. An example is 'group rental' (*qunzu*), in which middle- or even high-income apartments are divided into small cells and sublet to various individuals or families.[31]

It is not only in China that informal housing markets have grown in order to accommodate an increasing demand that had no other alternative. Non-regulated or non-authorised settlements are a trademark of affordable housing in various former socialist countries. For example, in Kazakhstan – which I will analyse later – more than half of the population live in precarious settlements. This rate reaches 30 per cent in Moldova and 19 per cent in Romania, Bosnia-Herzegovina, Croatia and Macedonia.[32]

Many countries created, reformed or liberalised their housing finance systems during what came to be called the 'second phase' of the transition process. This occurred for the most part after the 1996 economic-financial crisis in Eastern Europe, when newly privatised banking systems in countries such as Bulgaria, Bosnia and Albania collapsed. In the post-crisis period, most banks – which had been sold to foreign investors – resumed their activities.[33] Banking internationalisation and the increased availability of surplus European capital at the start of the 2000s expanded mortgage loans. This happened especially in Croatia, Hungary and Kazakhstan. In Hungary, more potential clients had their activities connected to the informal sector and the competition between mortgage credit institutions became fiercer. As a result, banks began to relax their criteria for guarantees and proof of income and to offer loans with variable repayment rates.[34]

Moreover, a significant proportion of the region's mortgage loan contracts were in a foreign currency. In 2010, 5 per cent of the population of the European Union's emergent countries had a mortgage – and 42 per cent of these contracts were in foreign currency.[35]

Mortgages in Swiss francs – a currency considered stable – were common in Eastern European countries, such as Hungary, Poland, Romania, the Czech Republic and Croatia, before the 2008 crash. With the crisis, the appreciation of the Swiss franc in relation to local currencies obliged mortgage borrowers to face rising instalment prices. The same process boosted mortgage prices, which largely exceeded the value of the houses and apartments concerned. In some countries, the construction sector was one of the first to suffer the consequences of the crisis, and many construction companies went bankrupt, leaving unfinished projects and indebted and homeless proprietors, as we will see in the case of Kazakhstan. The result was that mortgage borrowers were worse hit by the crisis than non-indebted people in Eastern Europe. However, in a completely unregulated and buoyant rental market, it was tenants rather than buyers who allocated the most substantial part of their income to housing.[36]

To sum up, former Communist countries which reformed their housing systems in the direction of commodification are experiencing an affordability crisis in the sector, as well as related problems of supply, access and quality of housing.

The specific trajectory of Kazakhstan, which I will survey next, introduces new elements to this narrative. By analysing specific scenarios, we can understand the evolution of housing policy beyond the binary contraposition between state-produced housing and market-produced housing, in order to understand the political economy of housing in each context.

Kazakhstan

In 1995, when the government of newly independent Kazakhstan decided to move the country's capital from Almaty to Astana, the latter barely existed. It was merely a cluster of old Soviet housing complexes in the middle of a vast, frozen steppe in the north of the country – a region called Akmola. However, after ten years of economic growth at an annual rate of 10 per cent – essentially based on the exportation of oil and gas – Astana ('capital' in Kazakh) became a hotbed of experimental 'brand' architecture, attracting the likes of Norman Foster and Manfredi Nicoletti to design state buildings, commercial towers, shopping centres and luxury hotels. The Khan Shatyr centre ('queen of tents' in Kazakh), in the shape of a mammoth tent, was inaugurated in 2010 on the occasion of President Nursultan Nazarbayev's seventieth birthday. It accommodates up to 10,000 people, who can shop international brands such as GAP and Timberland, watch 3-D films and relax on a 'tropical beach' whose sand was imported from the Maldives. Another landmark is a residential tower complex that hosts a shopping centre and a five-star hotel. Built by Aldar Properties, the largest Abu Dhabi real-estate developer, the complex cost US$1.6 billion and was financed by the city's government and private UAE investors.

Kazakhstan's rapid economic growth and the central government's decisive action turned Astana into a magnet for international investment. The construction of the new capital was one element of an aggressive strategy to open the local banking system, attract foreign investment into the real-estate market and construction industry, and increase credit availability – particularly for consumers of residential units. According to the government, this strategy aimed to transform the construction industry into the engine of national development, improving current living conditions and housing standards, generating jobs and stimulating the construction industry chain.

The government of Kazakhstan drastically changed its housing policy after independence, concentrating all efforts on promoting the construction and sale of individual properties via the market. To that end, it provided well-located urban land to new development companies and courted private investors. The predominant model was the sale of off-plan apartments via shareholding participation (*dolevoeuchastie* in Kazakh). Aspiring homeowners contribute to the financing with their own savings – partially upfront and partially through monthly instalments. The contracts hold developers to deliver the finished product within two years.

This system was also strategic for President Nazarbayev's government to consolidate the territory under Kazakh control as an independent country, strengthening his – and his clique's – power over the direction of politics and the economy. During the Soviet era, this territory, thinly populated by nomad tribes, was occupied for the exploitation of its mineral resources, leading to mass immigration from Russia and other USSR republics. In 1989, only 6.5 million of its 16.5 million inhabitants were of Kazakh origin.[37]

In 1984, still under the Soviet regime, Nursultan Nazarbayev, a Kazakh metallurgic engineer, had already served as prime minister and, still before the country's independence, as first secretary of the Communist Party of Kazakhstan. By declaring independence in 1990, he became its first president. In 1995, a referendum 're-elected' him for another five-year term and, ever since then, he has continued to be re-elected every five years, standing as the sole candidate and always gaining more than 90 per cent of the votes. In 2007, a constitutional amendment guaranteed that he will be allowed an unlimited number of mandates.

Beyond his total control over the political apparatus, President Nazarbayev promotes a monarchic cult of personality. An example is Bayterek Tower (known as 'the lollipop' by the local population). This monument is at the centre of a monumental complex that includes the presidential palace, itself an emulation of the White House. In the large glass sphere that tops the Bayterek, a bronze mould of the president's right hand is dramatically positioned at the very centre of the highest room, granting the population the experience of touching the president's hand. Nazarbayev himself drafted the design and, defining himself as a contemporary Louis XIV, compared Astana to Versailles.

This political economy of real-estate *stravaganza* helps to affirm both the president's power and the Kazakh nationality, working in a double sense: on one side, it radically throws open the freezing steppes as experimental fields for global financial circuits; on the other, it consolidates an authoritarian and centralised power founded on a contemporary cult of personality constituted through the construction of monuments to consumption.[38]

'These cities smell of money', was the frequent comment by visitors from other Central Asian republics when describing the urban boom at Astana and Almaty (the country's previous capital and main economic centre). In 2007, Kazakhstan boasted the highest level of foreign investment per capita among all Central Asian republics, and its banking system was considered the most developed of all 'transition' economies.[39] A significant part of the investment in the construction sector had come from international financial institutions as loans to commercial banks, which in turn lent to final consumers under the form of mortgage credit certificates. The majority of them represented short- and mid-term credit supplied through the mortgage market.[40]

Nevertheless, with the financial crisis – as we will see – the volatile capital that had landed on Astana and other Kazakh cities quickly vanished, leaving a desert of half-constructed buildings and thousands of people with neither savings nor homes.

Astana's large-scale programmes of urban renovation and city embellishment attracted internal migrants, who moved into the new capital seeking the job opportunities within the construction sector and a better standard of living. According to the census of 2009, Astana's population grew from 328,341 to 613,006 inhabitants between 1999 and 2009. Almaty, with a population of 1,365,632, remains the largest city in Kazakhstan. Like Astana, Almaty attracted high numbers of migrant workers after the economic crisis that followed the USSR's collapse. According to official estimates, more than 300,000 people per year internally migrate from rural to urban areas.

Thanks to its economic performance, Kazakhstan became a favoured destination for migrant workers from other Central Asian countries and from China. According to official estimates once more, Kazakhstan hosts between 500,000 and a million foreign workers, but other sources consider a number between 2 and 3 million migrants more plausible. A considerable proportion of these migrants are employed within the construction sector.[41]

Mass migration of low-income workers, combined with the absence of housing policies for this population, led to the proliferation of informal settlements and shanties around the peripheries of both Astana and Almaty. Due to their unofficial nature there are no reliable statistics about the number of people living in these settlements, which tend to be located in environmentally protected zones, flood-prone areas, or places facing a high risk of destruction by earthquake.

Most of these informal dwellings lack kitchens, sanitation, electricity and running water, and their residents are constantly at risk of forced eviction by public authorities. The absence of a legal address prevents them from registering their place of residence, yet this is a legal requirement – in force since the Communist era – for families and individuals if they are to qualify for various state services, including social housing.

Eligible citizens can only apply for social housing in the municipality where they are registered. Towns and cities keep separate lists for the following eligible categories: people with special needs and war veterans; low-income and socially protected families; certain categories of public functionaries; and people who live in severely dilapidated accommodation. While social housing units are allocated based on these lists, people with special needs and war veterans take precedence over the other categories.

Local authorities also use their budget to provide housing benefit to struggling families whose housing expenditures exceed 10 or 15 per cent of total family income. This aid is used for rent, housing maintenance or public services. And yet, none of these programmes serve the thousands of migrants who flocked to cities after the country's economic liberalisation.

Kazakhstan was seriously affected by the international financial crisis because of the radical deregulation of the country's financial system. Due to the expansion of access to mortgage credit – even for families with little capacity to pay – and the attraction of short- and mid-term international investment, the financial crisis provoked the collapse of the banking system as a whole. According to the World Bank, the annual growth rate plummeted from almost 10 per cent between 2000 and 2007 to 3.3 per cent in 2008, and 1.2 per cent in 2009.

The construction sector was one of the first to suffer the adverse effects of the global economic decline. Many construction companies were forced to shut down, leaving 450 unfinished projects. According to the government, more than 62,000 borrowers were negatively affected by the crisis. Around 16,000 of them were deceived by private construction companies – the majority from

Turkey – who left the country without completing their projects. Other individuals were unable to pay their loan instalments, and banks started foreclosure proceedings against them. Following the extrajudicial sale of their property by banks and other financial institutions, many individuals and families became homeless or were forced to move into low-quality dwellings.[42]

The hunger strike staged by those 'deceived by construction companies' was the scenario in 2010: an expression of the housing crisis after the financial euphoria.

4

Post-Crisis Measures:
More of the Same?

The burst of the bubble, the credit crisis that swept the international financial system and the state of housing emergency that ensued in some countries did not change the paradigm. Instead, governmental responses assumed three basic forms: bailouts – massive injections of public resources into private banks and credit institutions to save them from bankruptcy; the introduction of some regulatory measures in order to increase loan transparency and control; and ... a new batch of incentives for private-sector housing production, with units sold via mortgage credit to galvanise the economy. Housing – one of the most dynamic new frontiers of late neoliberalism during the decades of economic boom – switched to being one of the main Keynesian recuperation strategies after the bust. According to Manuel Aalbers, 'neoliberalism is like that: it can further its agenda both during economic booms and economic busts.'[1]

The most immediate post-crisis responses were interventions from the Federal Reserve (the central banking system of the United States), the European Central Bank and other national central banks, which bought US$2.5 trillion of public debts and toxic assets from commercial banks, configuring the largest liquidity operation of credit markets in history. The US and France also recapitalised their central banks by more than US$1 trillion, buying preferred stocks from the biggest banks. The injection of money into those banks involved with the mortgage web had the declared objective of putting them back to work, allowing not only the refinancing of mortgages, but also the provision of new loans. In Spain, for example, since 2008, almost €170 million have been spent to rescue financial institutions, with no conditions attached.[2] Without the imposition of any strings, the new resources injected by central banks followed financial logic and, rather than being funnelled into the recuperation of local housing markets, sought investments in more lucrative areas in emergent markets, notably China.[3]

Stimulus packages such as the American Recovery and Reinvestment Act (ARRA), enacted soon after President Obama's inauguration in 2009, strove to energise certain fields of activity (infrastructure, health science, etc.) through tax incentives, while increasing the resources for unemployment benefits and other social expenditures.[4]

In the same year, the American federal government also launched the Making Home Affordable programme, one of whose aims was to prevent foreclosures. Through partnerships with the private sector, this programme offered loan refinancing and better contract terms.[5] From the start, there were doubts about its capacity to reduce the wave of foreclosures. The critiques were based on the small number of banks and investment funds signing up to a scheme whose success relied entirely on the creditors' will to take part, and on the modest number of proprietors actually benefiting from it. Moreover, most loans reviewed via the scheme were temporary, valid for an experimental period of no more than five months, with only a small proportion of them becoming permanent.[6]

In Kazakhstan, the bank rescue operation cost the government US$4 billion (approximately 4 per cent of the country's GDP). As well as bailing out the largest banks, the government announced a stimulus package that put US$3 billion into the real-estate market – US$1 billion of which was directed towards mortgage refinancing – and US$3 billion for the economic revitalisation of industrial, agricultural and infrastructural sectors. The US$3 billion earmarked for the real-estate market were used for the purchase of unfinished constructions and for the refinancing of the debts of borrowers who had no other properties and whose homes measured less than 120 square metres. The purchase of unfinished constructions was managed through the creation of a real-estate fund linked to the country's sovereign wealth fund (the Samruk-Kazyna). Resources were poured into construction companies to ensure the completion of projects which had been slowed down or paralysed by the financial crisis. In total, US$1.1 billion of public resources were allocated to this fund.

In some countries, post-crisis measures also included a tighter regulation of loan types. This led financial institutions to increase their anti-risk precautions, upping interest rates and reducing loan maturity – and, consequently, restricting the loans.[7] These restrictions, combined with a general scenario of recession and economic crisis, further reduced the supply of credit for home-purchase, even in contexts of real-estate price drop and huge vacancy rates, as in Spain. In countries such as the United Kingdom, where prices did not fall and the supply of new residential units has been limited for decades, one of the main measures adopted in the face of the crisis was a programme to stimulate house-building and sales via subsidised mortgage credit.

The 2007 mortgage crisis had its peculiarities in the UK. Although house prices dipped in some areas – as an immediate result of the financial crisis – they had already recovered by 2010. In fact, the main characteristic of the credit crunch was a drop in financial transactions, loans and constructions.[8] The UK government then launched a stimulus package for the residential market and the wider economy, through governmental guarantees for mortgage equities – the liquid value of properties, discounting the debt. In order to help people to access mortgage financing, the government introduced three schemes, with different types of subsidies: the New Buy Guarantee Scheme (guarantees for home-purchase), the Help to Buy Equity Loans (subsidised loans for home-purchase) and the Help to Buy Mortgage Guarantees (mortgage guarantees for home-purchase).[9]

Many other countries also redoubled incentives and subsidies for home-purchase mortgage credit as a remedy for the mortgage crisis. This is the case of Montenegro, which, in 2010, launched a mortgage plan for low-income sectors called 1000+ *Stanova* [1000+ Homes]. Besides its ambition to reduce the country's housing deficit, this programme was a direct response to the effects of the 2008 crisis. The policy is earmarked for low-income individuals or families who cannot afford housing at market rates. The project has an estimated value of €50 million, half covered by a €25 million loan from the European Bank for Reconstruction and Development; the other half was financed by Montenegrin commercial banks. Beneficiaries receive government subsidies for the payment of interest on commercial mortgages. The proposition was to build 1,000 units to kickstart the civil construction and banking sectors – which were both in crisis.[10]

In Andorra, as a response to the 2008 crisis, Law n. 31/2008 raised the limit of foreign investment in the real-estate market, and shortened the statutory notice period before the rescission of rental contracts.[11] This law reapplies, after the crisis, measures widely used in other countries to dismantle older housing alternatives – in this case, protected rents – and stimulate the entrance of global financial circuits into the residential real-estate market.

Overall, then, among the measures taken after a crisis caused by the financialisation of housing, the most common response has been none other than increased finance for housing. The crisis did not inspire the slightest reinforcement of programmes or policies of non-commodified social housing, nor did it encourage the implementation of new models of housing provision and management.[12]

In the US, despite housing being at the heart of the economic crisis, the HUD continues to be starved of resources and public housing agencies are excluded from stimulus packages. More dismaying still, the fiscal adjustment measures passed by Congress in 2011 further reduced the resources available for the payment of vouchers and for the maintenance, renovation and construction of public housing units.[13]

In the UK, austerity measures slashed funding for council and social housing. At the same time, welfare reforms meant hardship for low-income households, as described in the previous section.

Abetted by international organisations, fiscal austerity measures – as part of economic recovery plans – led to cuts in the few programmes of social housing support that still existed in some countries. Sometimes they resulted in the wholesale extinction of these programmes, as in Greece and Portugal, for example.

In Greece, until 2012, the main organisation in charge of housing projects for the low-income population was the Workers'
Housing Organisation (OEK), created in 1954. Beneficiaries
included private-sector workers (whether Greek or legal migrants)
who contributed to OEK; public functionaries who contributed to
OEK; and pensioners who had previously belonged to one of the
above categories. The OEK was part of the Ministry of Labour
and Social Security, but enjoyed financial autonomy. Its projects
were financed through workers' and employees' contributions – 1
per cent of the workers' salaries and 0.75 per cent of the public
employees' salaries. Units were sold at cost price and beneficiaries
could pay for them in twenty to twenty-five years with no interest.
Pensioners, single people or low-income families had the option of
using a rental subsidy. Benefits were conditional on family income
and non-repayable. A Special Solidarity Fund existed to pay the
debts of families under severe financial pressure. It had been
expressly crafted for cases of illness or long-term unemployment
and could support families for six to twelve months. Over its fifty-
eight years of operation, 700,000 families gained access to housing
through OEK.

The organisation was legally abolished in 2012, as part of the
austerity package imposed on Greece in the wake of the financial
crisis.[14]

Many other countries saw the deterioration of a range of
housing-related indicators: increased homelessness; a rise in the
number of overcrowded units; soaring housing expenses; and
higher participation of private rental within the housing market.
This transformed the subprime and mortgage crisis into new
business opportunities for financial investors. The portion of the
housing stock that is undervalued and empty – due to unsold
projects, foreclosures or 'remnants' of public stocks that were not
sold during the privatisation tornado – becomes a new destination
for the spatial fix of financial circuits.

At the beginning of this chapter I already observed that, because
of overaccumulation, the market's territorial and sectorial expansion permitted the absorption of surplus capital by transforming
housing into a commodity and financial asset in many parts of
the world. This, in turn, generated a boom and a new cycle of

overaccumulation under the control of financial agents. When the market became collateral-saturated, the investors' quick entrance immediately devalued the stock, creating a new rental market and thus constituting a new frontier for financial accumulation.

This is one of the contradictions of capitalism: the fact that it requires physical space to work. At certain moments in history, capitalism destroys the space – and, consequently, devalues most of the capital invested therein. In the following moment, it generates a new spatial fix, through the opening of new territories for a new cycle of accumulation.[15]

A detail, nonetheless, eclipses the seemingly splendid trajectory of financial capital's powers of reinvention: in the cycle that concerns us, it left behind indebted people who lost everything they possessed – including their only home – and now have nowhere to go.

5

The Demand-Side Subsidies Model

An important component of the expansion of housing finance systems, also present in the mortgage systems that I have previously analysed, is the provision of public resources in the form of subsidies – that is, resources directed straight to house-buyers. The reasoning behind demand-side subsidy programmes is that with large financial contributions by the state, even lower-income families should be able to mobilise their savings and finance their housing through the market. The main types of demand-side subsidies are:

- Direct subsidies to buyers – either under the form of a one-off grant added to the required deposit, contract costs or insurance price, or subsidies added in monthly instalments;
- Subsidies tied to savings programmes;
- Subsidies embedded in interest rates or in the payment of interest;
- Tax exemptions linked to the payment of mortgages or to real-estate taxes.[1]

As well as representing the possibility of market expansion, subsidies also establish a connection between the state and individuals and families, through a gesture offered and interpreted as 'help' for those who adhere to the proposed model. Most countries employ a combination of the types of subsidies listed above. In Europe, the US, Canada and Australia, programmes of demand-side subsidies usually take the form of tax exemptions, interest-rate subsidies or savings-account bonuses.² In France, there is a mix of subsidies, including savings-account bonuses for home purchase or renovation, as well as loans for first-time buyers.³

One of the most common housing subsidies in Germany, France and other European countries is the system of contract savings. Savers who honour their contracts are candidates for mortgage loans with below-market interest rates. This model spread to many other countries, especially post-Communist European states. Besides stimulating the marketplace, it encourages saving, guaranteeing the commitment of individuals and families to the financial system and rewarding those who put something aside – a fundamental element of the biopolitics of life financialisation. Paraphrasing a definition of 'subsidy' attributed to the United States Congress in 1969, the World Bank characterises it as: 'an incentive provided by government to enable and persuade a certain class of producers or consumers to do something they would not otherwise do, by lowering the opportunity cost or otherwise increasing the potential benefit of doing so'.⁴

Tax exemptions, subsidised interest rates and savings bonuses usually benefit the middle class, or groups with the ability to save and/or with a balance to pay in their annual tax return.⁵ In most countries, it is a regressive expenditure, mobilising a large amount of public resources without benefiting those who most depend on them to access adequate housing. In the Philippines, for example, interest-rate subsidies account for 90 per cent of all housing subsidies. And yet 77 per cent of the country's population cannot afford loans in the formal sector – not even at subsidised interest rates.⁶ In the US, as we have seen, public spending on tax breaks for the middle and upper classes has historically outstripped any investment on housing for the poorest. In Spain, tax exemptions for the purchase of property made up half of total public expenditure in the early 1990s, and reached a rate of 80 per cent in 2003.⁷

These forms of subsidy already existed in the Keynesian phase of capitalism, in both developed and less developed countries. As analysed in the first chapter of this book, in many countries a policy of subsidies existed alongside a social housing system, as part of the welfare apparatus. However, in the 1960s and 70s, in

Spain, Greece, Portugal, Brazil and Mexico, subsidies were the only housing policy.

Nevertheless, grant subsidies are more common in developing countries, especially in Latin America. There, the low income of most individuals and families excludes them from real-estate markets, and during the Fordist period, self-built housing was predominant.[8]

In many countries, neoliberal processes of housing policy reform interact with traditional forms of housing provision such as self-construction of homes and neighbourhoods. Typically, industrialisation attracted thousands of migrants, mainly from the countryside, without offering any structures for their integration into the city by means of land and housing policies. In part two of this book, I will consider in detail the nature, role and fate of these settlements in the last decades.

First, however, I will analyse the housing policy in Chile, rolled out in the late 1970s under the logic of neoliberalism, and constituting the main laboratory for the elaboration of a market-oriented housing policy that might be applicable in other emergent countries where informal settlements were predominant. The Chilean model became a benchmark for other countries.[9] This model emphasises: the transferral of the responsibility for housing provision from the government to the private sector; the award of a single grant to subsidise the purchase and, simultaneously, the cut of all indirect subsidies; and mechanisms of qualification of beneficiaries through a transparent points system based on the family's income and saving capacity.

These programmes aim to improve people's economic chances to access housing, through cash grants that cover a proportion of the price of a housing unit formally built and marketed by private companies. Grants can also be combined with mortgages.

The Chilean model has been promoted as 'best practice' due to its transparency, the transferral of the supply of housing to the private market (considered more efficient than governments at dealing with very diverse demands for housing) and its focus on poor populations.[10] It has been widely reproduced in Latin America (Brazil, Colombia, Costa Rica, Ecuador, El Salvador, Guatemala, Mexico, Panama, Peru and Venezuela).[11] Outside of

Latin America, this model of grant subsidies has been extensively implemented in South Africa since 1994.[12]

The Chilean Laboratory

In 1973, a military coup d'état led by General Augusto Pinochet overthrew President Salvador Allende and inaugurated what some writers call a 'neoliberal revolution'.[13] Indeed, long before the IMF and multilateral banks started to promote so-called structural adjustment in developed countries, the Chilean government – under the technocratic wing of the 'Chicago Boys'[14] – radically took on the role of social-policy subsidiary, executing reforms in education, health, pensions and housing.

At the time of the coup, the political context of housing was one of vigorous mobilisation and pressure from campaigners. Since the mid-1960s, *comités sin casa* [homeless committees] had begun to occupy empty lots and to organise *campamentos* [settlements] as a form of pressure on the Christian-Democratic government of Eduardo Frei, demanding the fulfilment of his housing construction promises. *Campamentos* also became part of the foundation for the growth of left-wing parties, contributing to the victory of Allende's Unidad Popular coalition in 1970. There were more than 300 occupations in Santiago between 1968 and 1970, and they started multiplying. In 1972, more than 500,000 Chileans – 400,000 in Santiago alone – lived in *campamentos*.[15]

In 1978, Pinochet introduced reforms that reversed policies from Allende's socialist run. He decreed the liberalisation of prices, the return of nationalised companies to their former owners, the privatisation of all state companies, the elimination of customs barriers, and the liberalisation of the financial market and its opening to international capital. In this context, the Ministry of Housing designed an instrument to underwrite the massive and sustained production of housing units by the private market – a system that remains in place today.[16] Essentially, this policy consisted of: transferring housing finance and construction to the private sector; classifying the demand via a unified points system (called *ficha CAS*) on the basis of income, savings and other criteria; and awarding grant subsidies, tied to families' savings.

The financing of this model occurred through families' savings and through a complex system of mortgage-linked deeds commercialised in the subprime mortgage market.[17]

In practical terms, according to a 1979 flyer from the Ministry of Housing, homes are goods acquired through family savings efforts, 'with State contributions via subsidy. Beneficiaries and State share the responsibilities in order to respond to the home-ownership dream.' In its role of subsidiary and 'in the name of all Chilean citizens, the state assists with home-purchase and the search for a solution to homelessness – in cash. That way, you gain the human dignity that you so greatly deserve through the honour of your work. This is not paternalism. It is social justice.'[18] The requirements for applying for a subsidy included being the head of a family, not being a homeowner, never having obtained a home via state policies and maintaining a savings account – whether in a bank or in a savings and loan association. Initially, the requirements also included owning land and being able to spend 20 per cent of one's income on mortgage repayments.

In mid-1984, when a leader of the Chilean Chamber of Construction became head of the Housing Ministry, the system was tweaked to increase the subsidies for lower-income families who could not access bank loans. The scope of the housing market was thereby expanded and the construction sector, then in crisis, was reactivated. The same year, Pinochet approved a decree (Decree 168, 17 October 1984) that technically defined social housing, establishing a ceiling of 400 UF (Unidad de Fomento, an abstract unit-of-account used by the Chilean credit industry) for the cost of constructions, and defining the architectonic and urbanistic characteristics of the so-called '*viviendas económicas*'.[19]

In terms of supply, social housing would no longer be produced by the state, but offered by the market. Instead of building what the public sector determines, builders should compete to produce what consumers 'desire'. According to this model, construction companies must deliver a product cheaper than that historically supplied by the state, giving poor people a 'choice' of housing, which is made accessible through state contributions. To ensure that prices fell, the government deregulated the sector, reducing construction standards (such as the minimum size of housing units and plots of land) and reforming the land market.

In 1979, all restrictions to the development and expansion of the metropolitan area – dating from the 1960 Metropolitan Plan – were abolished, and Santiago's buildable surface leaped from 36,000 to 64,000 hectares.[20] The housing and planning reform clearly had a political slant: between 1979 and 1985, a complete eradication of *campamentos* was accompanied by a politico-administrative decentralisation of the metropolitan area, which divided the former seventeen districts into thirty-four, and trans-ferred residents en masse from central *campamentos* to recently created peripheral districts (many in former rural zones). More than 28,000 families were evicted.[21] The most dramatic instance was La Pintana, a *comuna* in Santiago Province whose population grew by 90 per cent in two years (1982–84) as almost 30 per cent of the displaced persons were resettled there.[22]

This action – whose declared goal was to terminate unregulated settlements – directly impinged on a territory of high real-estate value that had been structured by lower-class organisations and inhabited by their militants. At the same time, many of the old *campamentos* located in outlying districts were upgraded and regularised and endowed with sanitation and infrastructure. For people who lived in more central *campamentos*, there was no voluntary application for subsidies. Instead there was compulsory displacement – carried out with army support – to new peripheral housing projects, composed of 25-square-metre units in plots of 100 square metres.[23]

Combined with massive voluntary market supply, evictions from *campamentos* represented the production of a vast territory occupied mostly by lower-income housing units, offering scant facilities and services and lacking social heterogeneity and diver-sity of uses. In its competitive search for the lowest prices, the private market had chosen the best-value land as its *locus* for producing low-income housing – in peripheral areas that had not previously been urbanised. It signified a restructuring of the metropolitan area, intensifying socio-spatial segregation.[24]

More than 2 million new residential units were produced between 1980 and 2000, of which more than 500,000 were '*viviendas económicas*'. This drastically reduced the country's housing deficit, and ostensibly 'solved' the 'housing problem'. Nevertheless, many studies carried out since the end of the 1990s show the opposite: the new-built stock did not mean a solution, but the creation of a fresh problem. If 'families without roofs over their heads' was the great housing problem in the 1970s and 1980s, the great socio-housing problem in Santiago in the 2000s became 'families with roofs over their heads'. Almost all of the Chilean poor own low-quality houses or apartments, and precarious settlements now represent less than 4 per cent of the total housing stock.

However, within Santiago's socio-spatial dynamics, these new homes and their environments produce a new place associated with poverty and marginality in the city. A survey performed in 2002 by SUR (a Chilean research centre) revealed that 64.5 per cent of residents in these areas want to 'leave their *vivienda*'. The reasons included problems with neighbours and perceptions about lack of safety and drug-related activities. Among those who wanted to leave, 90 per cent were scared and ashamed of living there. In order to understand such attitudes, researchers cross-checked the georeferenced information from '*vivienda económica*' complexes with the locations of violence reported in the city. The result demonstrated that a higher level of inter-family violence occurs in areas in which lower-income housing stocks are concentrated. Stigma, spatial confinement and institutional framing work together to define these places as authentic ghettos.[25]

For many of those evicted from *campamentos*, the resettlement meant the loss of their jobs, increased expenses (especially on transportation), difficult access to education and health services and, above all, the dismantlement of their informal social networks and the disappearance of community organisations.[26]

In 2006, two large social housing complexes – one comprising 900 units and the other 1,500 – were demolished. Six years after the publication of the first paper criticising Chilean social housing policy,[27] the government admitted that this programme was essentially about setting up a machine for the production of cheap homes. Its main objectives were the invigoration of the construction industry and the penetration of finance into the social housing sector, regardless that it generated a new housing and urban problem: the ghettos of *los con techo* – poor people 'with roofs over their heads'.[28]

The supposed advantages of this approach – freedom of choice and affirmation of the consumers' desires – represent, in fact, the most shameless lack of choice: the government uses public resources to commercialise products of appalling quality, which would never be bought if people had money and real freedom of choice. Within the higher-income housing market, the supply must be sensitive to the requirements of the demand and, so, to the triad product/price/location, as it operates in a competitive context. Conversely, operators supplying social housing have captive demand – especially when this demand is highly subsidised.

In a context of housing deficit, receivers of subsidies will simply 'buy' whatever is available and attainable at that moment. Social housing suppliers can, thus, be less sensitive to the preferences of their demand, or simply ignore them, as there is no competition.[29]

The 'success' of the Chilean experience was rapidly incorporated into the agenda of housing policy reforms in developing countries by bilateral or multilateral agencies, particularly the IDB. In 1988, one of the 'inventors' of the Chilean model became part of the IDB's staff. From then on, almost all loans involving the housing sector included the Chilean model of subsidies. The IDB also sent Chilean social housing policymakers to several Latin American countries to present their policy's fundaments and mechanisms. From 1995 on, when IDB's Executive Council decided to officially enshrine the formal production of housing units as a strategy to combat poverty, the model was definitively incorporated in all of the Bank's operations.[30]

For readers who might have noticed similarities with the Brazilian programme *Minha Casa Minha Vida* [My Home My Life], it is not a mere coincidence. In the third part of this book, I will analyse in detail the trajectory of that programme. The list of Latin American countries that have implemented versions of the model does not stop growing: Mexico, Guatemala, Bolivia,

Ecuador, Brazil, El Salvador, Colombia, Venezuela. As well as the
IDB, the United States Agency for International Development
(USAID) was highly instrumental in the promotion and diffusion
of this policy, by sponsoring debates, seminars and meetings
between the countries' Construction Chambers and housing
policymakers.

The influence of this model moved beyond the borders of Latin
America. In 1992, for example, one of the main World Bank
researchers presented the Chilean policy to South Africa, which
had recently abandoned apartheid. In 1994, a World Bank mission
in the country proposed a programme of subsidies significantly
influenced by Chile's experience.[31]

The example of Chilean programmes designed to provide mass
housing via the market is not, then, an isolated one. Chile's
pioneering experience has been replicated across Latin America,
Africa and Asia.

In countries where the model has been in operation for some
years, the socio-territorial effects are clear. In the case of Mexico,
it is already possible to chart the increase of urban sprawl, the
reduction of population density and the proliferation of acres of
standardised, extremely small houses.[32] Moreover, the complexes
are badly integrated, as they are disconnected from the cities and
do not offer basic infrastructure, public services or job opportunities.[33] These drawbacks led many people who had acquired
mortgage credit certificates to return to the city, opting to rent out
the purchased home.[34] Another problem is vacancy: almost 5
million new houses were simply abandoned.[35] The press reports
that some of the empty units have been occupied by drug traffick-
ers and that banks have a hard time foreclosing these abandoned
assets, whose instalments have not been paid by the people who
bought them.[36]

Subsidy schemes in South Africa, Mexico and – as we will see
in part three of this book – Brazil, have been criticised for replac-
ing informal dwellings scattered around cities by shoddy,
stigmatised units that have concentrated lower-income families in
one place. This process has reinforced – when not generated –
social and urban segregation, disparity in access to urban services,

worsening local living conditions, environmental degradation and ever more urban security problems.

These programmes have also neglected habitability. The developments are not only badly located, they are often too small or built with low-quality materials, offering scant possibilities of improvement. As an example, the basic state-subsidised housing unit in Santiago in 1990 measured a mere 33–34 square metres. Despite an increase of the average size during the 1990s, in 1998 each family had at their disposal only 9.3 square metres per occupant. Initially, the average space in South Africa was only 25 square metres and the houses had no subdivisions.[37]

Despite being intended for the poorest and most vulnerable, grant subsidy programmes found difficulties in reaching the lowest-income families, mainly because these still could not afford the down payment or the instalments defined by the market.[38] In some cases, subsidies were so low that it was impossible to buy a home without previous savings or substantial additional credit. Many proprietors, even when capable of meeting the credit or savings requirements, had nothing left over for maintaining their homes or paying the bills, and were ultimately forced to sell up.[39]

Attempting to complement the available resources, some governments encouraged private banks and NGOs to supply microcredit to low-income families, on top of the already awarded state subsidies. The Swedish cooperation agency, SIDA, was particularly generous with projects of this kind in Central America. Such schemes act as institutional intermediaries between families and the state, helping the former to bridge the gap in order to become eligible for subsidies. Nevertheless, surveys conducted in South Africa, Pakistan and other countries where these mechanisms have been tried show that the combination of microfinance with subsidies was not successful.[40]

Despite appreciable state budgetary investment and an explicit focus on low-income families, grant subsidies have promoted, in part, only the economic-financial aspect of the right to adequate housing. They privileged the substantial reduction of the housing deficit in some developing countries over wider aspects of this right, such as habitability, location, availability of services and infrastructure.

6

Microfinance: The Last Frontier

It is necessary to take the money from where it is: with the poorest. Granted, they do not have much, but they are so many!

Alphonse Allais

In her book *Poverty Capital*, Ananya Roy recounts that when Muhammad Yunus and the Bangladeshi Grameen Bank were the Nobel Peace Prize laureates in 2006, Grameen's microfinance model gained international legitimacy, after a long trajectory of growth within poverty combat circles. Elizabeth Littlefield, CEO of the Consultative Group to Assist the Poor (CGAP, a donor forum based in the World Bank that advocates a market-based approach to development), considered that: 'Yunus was one of the early visionaries who believed in the idea of poor people as viable, worthy, attractive clients for loans.'[1]

The majority of the planet's urban poor live in unplanned and not previously urbanised settlements, where residents gradually produce their own homes, mobilising their own material and financial resources. Until the 1980s, slum-dwellers and poor urban populations were not considered a market for financial services.[2] The reasons were: low- and middle-income families' inability to afford housing-finance debt; the incompatibility of the formal requirements for the concession of financial loans (collateral and payment capacity) with such households' profile (low or irregular income, often obtained through informal work, and lack of security of housing tenure); and little interest from financial institutions in lending to the poorest, as the latter generally borrow small sums, involving high transaction costs and high default risks. As a result, low- and middle-income families have historically adopted 'informal' financial strategies, based on individual savings, family loans or remittances, loan-specialised companies or pawnbrokers and moneylenders.[3]

Nevertheless, in the 1980s, a new finance paradigm emerged. Apparently, the poorest might be served by the extension of small, informal and income-generating credit: microfinance. Private investors became convinced of microfinance's profitability and started to regard even the most deprived as 'bankable'.[4] Since then, there has been an intense expansion of the flow of private investment capital (supported by donors, multilateral banks and international organisations) to the microfinance sector. Initially aimed at financing the entrepreneurship of the poorest – one of the ideological and economic bases of the expansion of neoliberal policies – microfinance recently included lines of credit specifically to support progressive self-build projects. In the last decade, this initiative was incorporated as a programme by the UN and the World Bank, through the creation of the Cities Alliance and UN-Habitat's Slum Upgrading Facility.[5]

In Grameen Bank's pioneering experience, in Bangladesh, microfinance adopted the language of human rights or 'the right to credit'. Microfinance was framed as a non-profitable loan to combat poverty and empower women. Individuals donated resources to a revolving fund. After small amounts were lent to women from villages and impoverished shanties, the money would be returned through a process that also involved the apprentice-ship of market discipline and, initially, the constitution of solidarity groups and community co-responsibility.

Of course, the poverty combat concept that animates this model is centred on the promotion of entrepreneurship, not on the redistribution of income, the multiplication of opportunities or any principle of equality. The model of poverty mitigation is, thus, at the same time, centred on poor people and opposed to welfare systems. Yunus has repeatedly affirmed that self-employment – and not formal salaried employment – is Grameen Bank's goal.[6]

Microfinance quickly ceased to be restricted to non-profit organisations such as the Grameen Bank and penetrated commercial banks and the capital market. The increasing presence of large Western banking groups in developing countries, like these consortia's interest in microfinance (of housing among others), reflects the idea that the 'bottom of the pyramid' represents a large and untapped market.[7]

New models of microfinance institute rigid financial sustainability rules and emphasise profit rather than human development, hoping that the 'bottom billion' – the world's poorest – will act as a 'frontier market', opening up new horizons of capital accumulation.[8] The age of microfinance is part of a larger transformation of capitalism itself, termed 'creative capitalism' by Bill Gates. This gentler capitalism envisages 'eradicating poverty through profits'.[9]

In the last ten years, the number of housing-related microfinance programmes has been growing. These offer loans of between US$300 and $8,000 to homeowners, with the possibility of top-ups, and amortisation deadlines of one to fifteen years. Compared to microfinance for entrepreneurs, housing microloans generally involve much higher values and are conceded for longer periods. But compared to mortgage loans, microloans involve significantly lower values, are conceded for shorter periods and target people who are not served by formal financial institutions, private or public.[10] Due to their limited scope, housing microloans are mainly used to fund home improvements (such as the construction of sanitation facilities) or extensions.[11]

Today, housing microfinance is offered by a large variety of institutions, including microfinance agencies such as Grameen and Accion, with their affiliated bodies. It is also offered by commercial banks and institutions, such as HDFC Bank in India, and Cemex in Mexico (through the Patrimony Today scheme). In addition, microfinance is offered by intergovernmental organisations and NGOs specialised in housing supply, such as the Rural Housing Loan Fund in South Africa, and Habitat for Humanity.[12]

The World Bank, USAID and UN-Habitat have been enthusiastic promoters of this kind of action. Directly financing, or publishing information on the theme, they have played a fundamental role in pushing back the geographical frontiers of such initiatives. According to the World Bank,

If ever supplied at a larger scale, HMF [housing microfinance] could play an important role in helping to provide an answer to the 'qualitative' housing deficits, and complement conventional mortgage markets that remain bordered by an 'access frontier' – as developed by D. Porteous and FinMark ... The potential reach of HMF may be found among those who do not qualify under current banking criteria but would pay for a higher credit rate for a HMF loan.[13]

When launching its Slum Upgrading Facility (SUF), UN-Habitat understood that the problem is one of finance. Hence the need to ensure slum residents' access to finance in order to improve their living conditions. This should be achieved thanks to the saving efforts and discipline of the poorest, combined with private finance resources inside the market sphere. There is no mention of social redistribution – the state's role is to provide the optimum conditions for the market to operate.[14] The starting point of UN-Habitat's perspective is, thus, the identification of a 'finance gap': 'the stark reality that combined public and private investment and official development assistance meets only 5 per cent to 10 per cent of the financing required for improvements in housing and basic services in Sub-Saharan Africa, South Asia and Southeast Asia'.[15] SUF proposed to demonstrate that projects for slum upgrading – which can range from 'area improvement' to house construction and improvements – can be achieved via financial-commercial investment. This principle is encapsulated in the term 'bankable'.[16]

Most housing microfinance initiatives are situated in developing countries and emergent markets. Latin America holds the world's largest housing microfinance portfolio, in institutions such as MiBanco, in Peru; BancoSol, in Bolivia; Banco Solidario, in Ecuador; Banco Ademi, in the Dominican Republic; Calpiá (now ProCredit), in El Salvador; and Génesis Empresarial, in Guatemala.[17] This type of finance is also significantly growing in Asia and, at a slower pace, in Africa.[18] Examples include the Kuyasa Fund (South Africa), the Jamil Bora Trust (Kenya), the Kixi-Casa (Angola), the Pride (Tanzania), the BRI (Indonesia), and the Card (Philippines).[19] The scale of some housing microfinance programmes can be significant. Grameen Bank, for example, has issued more than 650,000 housing loans.[20]

Nevertheless, housing microfinance options around the world remain scarce in relation to global GDP and to microfinance activities in general.[21] It is still a service primarily for people who are already clients of microfinance institutions. Within a typical microfinance scheme, the size of the 'housing' portfolio varies between 4 and 8 per cent.

Microfinance institutions employ more diverse and flexible guarantee strategies than traditional mortgage schemes. They can include co-signers, future income assessment, deductions from wages, other financial assets (such as life insurance) and the 'social guarantee' (the borrower's reputation, or an analysis of the social circles to which they belong).[22] Some microfinance agencies attempt to minimise the necessity of guarantee by assessing the client's history.[23] Many of them – mainly in Asia and Africa – require the existence of savings that serve both to evaluate the borrower's payment capacity and as a source of funds.[24]

Although microfinance agencies' interest rates are typically lower than those of informal moneylenders, they are much higher than those charged by formal financial institutions, with much shorter repayment schedules. In most cases, rates vary between 20 per cent and 50 per cent.[25] For example: MiBanco, in Peru, charges an annual interest rate of 37 per cent[26] and Compartamos Banco, in Mexico, charges almost 70 per cent interest on its housing microfinance programme.[27] The poorer the client, the more likely it is that the microfinance agency will try to offset the default risk by reducing both the loan duration and the amount lent.[28] In some cases, the small loan is not sufficient and must be complemented by additional borrowing from external sources, which also charge very high interest and expose families to higher risks. Variable interest rates are commonly used and tend to rise over time, sometimes doubling the original.[29] High interest rates deepen the clients' indebtedness and aggravate the vicious circle poverty/probability of default.[30] In order to keep up with payments, families may need to sell traditional assets (such as equipment or land) or divert money from other income sources (such as remittances or pensions). These 'last-resort' strategies explain microfinance's generally high amortisation rates. Nonetheless, they reduce equity within families, their power of economic recovery and their economic access to housing. As is generally the case for high-risk mortgage loans, housing micro-finance clients are punished for their 'low profitability' and are forced to pay more because of it.

For all these reasons, microfinance schemes represent another highly exploitative form of subprime loan. Moreover, the nature and small scale of most stop these programmes from addressing issues such as security of tenure, location and availability of infra-structure and services. On the one hand, the provision of financial services for the extension and/or upgrade of constructions is a relatively straightforward and manageable activity. On the other, however, the process of land acquisition and infrastructure supply is complex in juridical, financial and political terms. It demands institutional and financial capabilities, as well as legal clout – which is usually only available to organisations within local and national governments. The focus on house enlargement or upgrade can, in some cases, promote better habitability and help slum resi-dents to improve their homes, but does little in terms of wider aspects of the right to housing. While housing microfinance certainly expands economic access to housing, it also generates new difficulties, as borrowers substantially increase their housing expenditures and, even after an upgrade, remain underserved in terms of health, sanitation and education services. What is more, lacking security of tenure they risk eviction from their renovated homes – without compensation or relocation.

There is, too, an increasing awareness of the industry's failure to reach the poorest. Due to their financial orientation, many housing microfinance programmes seem to focus more on the higher-income poor urban population (whose income is 120–150 per cent above the national poverty line); families on poverty's borderline (whose income is 50 per cent above the national poverty line);[31] 'economically active poor people' (sometimes holding formal jobs); and, finally, those who rely on diverse strat-egies for their livelihoods. The ultra-poor (under the 15 per cent threshold of income distribution), who are often spread over rural areas and represent high costs for credit and infrastructure

services, will not be considered by microfinance.[32] In some micro-
credit programmes, the demand of security of tenure may further
restrict potential clients to those who are poor but in relatively
'better' economic conditions.

Within the vast universe of NGOs and financial institutions,
many groups have their roots in cooperative practices for the creation of self-managed community trusts. They are particularly
present in Africa and Asia. These trusts work with group loans
and/or savings, aiming to help communities in the regularisation
or acquisition of land, the implementation of infrastructure and
services, and the upgrade of their homes. They offer, for example,
technical and financial support for the acquisition of land and
infrastructure (roads, drainage, water supply, etc.) in partnership
with other actors, such as the government and the original landowners. These groups originated from collective processes of
mobilisation and organisation.[33] Some organisations (such as the
National Cooperative Housing Union, in Kenya) offer microcredit
both to individuals and to community groups or cooperatives.[34]
'Umbrella-type' international organisations were created to facilitate the operation of community-based organisations that sprang
from social housing movements, such as Slum Dwellers
International or the Society for the Promotion of Area Resource
Centres, in India.[35]

Community trusts such as Baan Mankong, in Thailand, and
the Community Mortgage Programme, in the Philippines, show
great capacity for expansion of their coverage and execution of
complex housing and infrastructure projects involving national
and local governments, landowners and various communities.
The Baan Mankong programme, created in 2003 by the Thai
government and implemented by a non-governmental agency (the
Community Organisations Development Institute), had a target
to improve the living conditions of 300,000 families before 2008.
Its strategy for offering housing to low-income families was to
channel resources to community-based organisations, which
planned and executed the work.[36] This programme became a
benchmark for slum upgrade schemes involving community
support, despite being carried out on a rather smaller scale than
originally planned.[37]

Such programmes have developed in parallel to the evolution of housing microfinance. However, they embody a significantly different approach, which emphasises collective property and mobilisation and works on behalf of wider aspects of adequate housing, such as location, access to infrastructure and services and security of tenure.[38] As community trusts are less governed by financial considerations, loan interest rates are generally lower than those of housing microfinance. Moreover, repayment deadlines are generally longer, reaching up to twenty-five years.[39] Such trusts require resources to be available with no expectation of profit and the intense involvement of both local and national governments at every stage to achieve the necessary scale, sustainability and technical assistance. At the same time, they are closely tied to – and have often originated from – organisations and social movements fighting for the right to housing, whose action often exceeds the microfinance operation *per se*.

It is still too early to evaluate the impact of these community trusts on access to housing for the poorest people within their radius; more systematic and long-term surveys would be needed. However, financial sustainability has already emerged as a problem. Due to their ample scale and their dependence on multiple factors, community trusts largely depend on financial donations and technical support. Moreover, research indicates that they experience low amortisation rates and high default rates. Of equal concern is the fact that these loans lead to power conflicts and imbalances within participating communities, due to differing payment capacities among families and individuals.[40]

Finally, in the universe of microfinance, many institutions began their activities as self-management community trusts and 'evolved' towards financialisation. Microfinance, in turn, walks towards securitisation. The first initiative of securitising a microfinance portfolio was launched in 2006, to lend approximately US$180 million to the Bangladesh Rehabilitation Assistance Committee (BRAC, one of the world's largest NGOs for social assistance and anti-poverty action). Structured by RSA Capital, Citigroup, Netherlands Development Finance Company and the development bank KFW, this business 'involves a securitisation of receivables arising from the microcredits extended by BRAC ... and the creation of a special purpose trust which purchases the receivables from BRAC and issues certificates to investors representing beneficial interest in such receivables.'[41]

Fazle Abed, founder and president of BRAC, celebrated securitisation as 'a landmark for the micro finance industry ... We have brought the global financial markets to the doorsteps of nearly 1.2mn households in Bangladesh.'[42] In 2008, ASA International – a London-based global holding that administers trusts for microfinance institutions operating in China, Cambodia, Ghana, India, Indonesia, Nigeria, Pakistan, the Philippines and Sri Lanka – insured US$125 million in stocks of Catalyst Microfinance Investors (a private equity fund co-managed by ASA International itself and Sequoia, a corporate investment company). These securitisations aim to generate access to cheap capital for microfinance institutions and, therefore, as stated by BRAC, to reduce 'dependency on volatile donor financing.'[43]

It is worthwhile to mention a report from the Consultative Group to Assist the Poor, a global partnership between the main European, North American and multilateral cooperation agencies with company foundations, advocating the financial inclusion of the poorest. According to this report, 'microfinance institutions (MFIs) have emerged relatively unscathed from the financial crises of the past few decades', which proves the resilience of these portfolios. Further, 'assets of the top 10 microfinance investment funds grew by 32 percent in 2008', meaning that 'microfinance is one of the few asset classes with a positive return in 2008.' The links between 'micro entrepreneurs and international capital markets' are celebrated, and microfinance is seen as a market 'where arbitrage possibilities remain to be exploited'.[44]

There are two things that must be understood about housing microfinance, in terms of financialisation: one, it is a model that establishes links between slum residents and national capital markets – and, more recently, international ones as well. Two, it is a model that presupposes a financial view on life, in which a home is regarded as an asset to be invested in exchanged or used as collateral to leverage additional financing in aid of consumption, welfare or entrepreneurship activities.[45]

Microfinance seems to be the new subprime frontier for capitalism, in which capital destined for the promotion of development and financial capital merge and work together, identifying new development subjects and opening/consolidating new investment territories. Whether in the North American subprime mortgage market or the Spanish 'creative' mortgage market, microfinance transforms neglected territories and stigmatised populations – discriminated against on grounds of race, class, gender or form of tenure – into objects for financial colonisation and exploitation, all in the name of inclusion.

According to Ananya Roy, the subprime logic is the same as that of microfinance,

> for it allows the poor access to credit but on terms that are significantly different from those enjoyed by 'prime' consumers – be they the high interest rates of Compartamos or the intimate discipline enacted by the Grameen Bank. In other words, the subprime marks the limits of the democratization of capital.[46]

In other words, microfinance marks the expansion of capital towards its last urban frontier: the slums of capitalism's peripheries. It is the end of the road for a long strategy of deconstruction of housing as a right and its transformation into financial asset – in the name of the fight against poverty.

PART II

7

Tenure Insecurity

Cambodia, 2008
Mao Sein, thirty-four-year-old widow and scavenger, is sitting with her three children under a straw sleeping mat in her shack, waiting for the seemingly endless monsoon rains to stop. Two years ago, the police raided the settlement where she lived in Phnom Penh, the capital of Cambodia. She was then relocated by the government to an empty field almost twenty kilometres away from the capital. The precariousness of Andong – where she lives now – and its shacks reminds her of the refugee camp that sheltered her grandfather thirty years ago, when he was forced to flee the city by the brutal Communist Khmer Rouge. Like thousands of people in the country, Andong residents are victims of the rural and urban land grabs that have been causing evictions and forcing people to live in the streets. Economic growth is leading to a massive transfer of land towards agriculture, mining, tourism, fisheries and real-estate development. The evictions and official seizures can be violent, including late-night raids by the police and military. 'They arrived at 2 a.m. with electric batons,' said Ku Srey, another inhabitant of the settlement. 'They pushed us into trucks, they threw all our stuff into trucks and they brought us here.' In a report published in February 2008, Amnesty International estimated that 150,000 people were at risk of forced evictions in Cambodia because of land disputes, land seizures and new development projects. If these people have indeed been forced to move, it will have been the biggest displacement of Cambodian people

since the days of the Khmer Rouge. In 1975, the regime began the evacuation of Phnom Penh, herding thousands into the country-side and emptying the city. In 1979, the Khmer Rouge were overthrown by a Vietnamese invasion, driving hundreds of thou-sands of Cambodians to seek refuge in Thailand.

Many of the refugees returned to the country in the 1990s and set up huge squatter colonies in Phnom Penh. Mao Sein remem-bers the *pakdivat* – revolution – that made her family lose everything, and laments that it is all happening again, this time because of *akdivat* – development. The Cambodian economy grew almost 9 per cent in 2007 and the sprouting of towers and shopping malls is quickly transforming Phnom Penh's landscape. In Andong, on the other hand, people slowly build their own houses by hand and there is just one, partially paved road. But Mao Sein suspects that this might be another temporary home. The suburbs of Phnom Penh are only a few kilometres away and, if the city keeps expanding, she and her neighbours will soon be forced to move again.[1]

Jakarta, June 2013

When I approach the old train station, the scene is devastating: debris on the floor, scrap metal, pieces of wood, cement, strewn clothes, plastic basins. As I get closer, women and children surround me. They literally grab me, crying and shouting Indonesian words that I can't understand. I quickly look around, searching for one of the translators who is accompanying me on the mission. He joins me and, with his help, I try to calm the women down so that they can tell me their stories. We then learn that the land we are on belongs to the Indonesia State Railroad Company, whose lines and stations have not been active for years.

The women tell me that they used to pay rent to the company for the space in which they set up their market stalls. This area is in the very centre of the city and thousands pass through it every day. They also tell us that some families, besides using the space for trade, have been living there for many years. In addition, according to a new government policy, empty plots of land must be sold to construction companies for the highest bid. Because of the new legislation, Indonesia State Railroad Company had, that morning, instructed the police to remove the area's current inhabitants. Their desperate questions echoed: what now? Where shall we go? What will happen to us? While I try to note down the information and explain who I am and what I am doing there, I realise that the translator is crying too. On the way back to the car, he explains why: he misses his village, in the most far-flung island of the vast archipelago that makes up the country. With the land reform – which turned the clans' collective properties into the individual property of families – his family's entire heritage in the village was sold against his will. After that, he had to leave his home and his island, migrating to Jakarta, where he started working as a missionary for the Pentecostal Church. He explains that accompanying me on visits to those who have been uprooted and resettled would continuously rekindle his memory of that moment and reinforce the certainty that his own departure, although not violently imposed by the police, was also a forced eviction.

Haiti, June 2011

A year and a half after the earthquake that devastated Port-au-Prince, I arrive in a city with more than 1,000 camps of internally displaced persons (IDPs), harbouring almost 800,000 people waiting for housing solutions. Threats to clear part of these camps were a daily occurrence, especially against those who, since January 2010, had squatted in privately owned areas. According to Camp Coordination and Camp Management Cluster – the organisations responsible for the establishment and management of the camps – in January 2011, more than 220,000 people were threatened with eviction in 179 camps in Port-au-Prince. Humanitarian and reconstruction agencies are in despair before the lack of prospects and any viable responses to the situation. They are accustomed to the logic of rapid rebuilding on the same land where the affected people lived before the disaster, a procedure for which they have a legal mandate and an organised apparatus. This time, they are facing a completely different situation.

Most of the camps' population are refugees from the huge informal settlements of the city. This means that, first, the land on which their houses should be rebuilt is not their legal property, which immediately blocks the reconstruction. Moreover, these plots do not even have a legal existence, as they were not the result of urban development, with the previous opening of streets and lots, public and private. On the other hand, even if the buildings were to be reconstructed, the situation remains paradoxical: in those same settlements, people who have not been affected by the earthquake live no less precariously than those in the IDPs' camps. Indeed, there are advantages to the camps, since at least they provide water, bathrooms and, in some cases, schools and health clinics. Despite the millions poured into Haiti by humanitarian aid, the situation in June 2011 is, literally, one of paralysis.

Maldives, January 2009

As suggested by the government, I visit one of the islands that was chosen to host a major reconstruction project, destined to shelter communities who lived in numerous small islands before the devastating tsunami in 2004. The government proudly shows me the quality of the constructions: the water desalination plants, the schools, the health clinics, the refuse recycling centres, the large houses with three bedrooms, American-suburban-style.

I decided to request a visit to one of the islands that had been devastated. I had to be insistent, as this was not part of the initial plan and 'there's nothing to see, as everything has been destroyed', according to my interlocutors from the government and from the United Nations Development Programme (UNDP), who had helped to organise this visit. Finally, they agreed that our boat could make a brief stop on the 'destroyed' island. On landing, I realised, to my surprise, that all the houses were standing, merely lacking doors, roofs and window frames – basically, everything that can be removed. The mosque (Maldivians are predominantly Muslim) was absolutely intact. During the following days, I began to understand the situation better. Over a decade ago, the government of the Maldives – with 300,000 inhabitants spread over more than 500 islands – had launched the strategy of 'consolidating' the population onto only a few islands, with the goal of easing the provision of public services. After that, the vacated islands could be leased to tourist resorts – a procedure already in place and proving a great success, thanks to the paradisiac characteristics of the archipelago-country. Local communities reacted against the proposal, refusing to move and to merge with other communities. The tsunami was the opportunity to implement the strategy: the islands hit by the catastrophe were declared 'uninhabitable' and international aid enabled construction of some of the consolidation points.

Buenos Aires, April 2011

We roamed the alleys of one of the oldest informal settlements in the Argentinian capital, Villa 31, situated at a strategic point and inhabited by thousands of people. It was one of the few *villas* to resist the mass eviction policy of the dictatorship, which, between 1976 and 1983, removed more than 200,000 people from Argentinian inner cities. As though in a scene from a 1960s Italian neorealist film, as we walked, more and more people joined us, all talking loudly at once, tripping on dogs and chickens, jumping over open-air sewage ditches. The whole cortege was followed by indigenous boys holding cameras – the Villa 31 radio and TV crew. At last we arrived at some kind of central football pitch. By then there were already more than 300 of us. A megaphone appeared and was immediately fought over by a councilwoman and two community leaders (one of whom I later learned worked in a congressman's office). One speaker succeeded another, voicing complaints about the programmes that were never implemented, or never completely – in a corner, I saw a half-built playground. The history of that place was coming together in my mind in fragments. The city council had approved a law determining that Villa 31 would be definitively urbanised and that a *mesa de concertación*, formed by community members and public authorities, would undertake and manage the process step by step. Additionally, a project developed by Buenos Aires University had already been presented. However, there was no sign of anything happening. As a Bolivian lady next to me said, after listening attentively to the speakers: '*Señorita*, it's a law, not reality!'

Rio de Janeiro, April 2012

The Engineering Club auditorium was full when I arrived. I had been invited by the People's Committee for the World Cup and Olympic Games in Rio de Janeiro to present the dossier

'Mega-Events and the Violation of Human Rights in Rio de Janeiro'. Sitting next to me on the debating panel was Altair Guimarães, then president of Vila do Autódromo's Residents Association, one of the communities that resisted (and still resists!) the eviction. All those present at the table spoke about rights and reported abuses, in something akin to a 'counter-voice' against the consensus celebrating the arrival of an urban 'revolution'. This revolution would be thanks to the city's 'conquest' of the role as next host of the Olympic Games (2016) and the World Cup (2014). When it was Altair's turn to speak, he calmly started to tell his story: 'I spent my life being volleyed around like a shuttle-cock – from here to there, from there to here.' In 1967, when he was fourteen and lived in a community called Ilha dos Caiçaras, on the banks of Lagoa Rodrigo de Freitas, he and those who lived in the other favelas bordering the lake were evicted and relocated to the infamous Cidade de Deus housing project – well known thanks to the film *City of God*, a recent blockbuster in movie theatres around the world. He went on:

> 'What governor Carlos Lacerda said to justify the eviction was that my community dirtied the lake and killed the fish. Nowadays we see that this was a huge lie because the fish keep on dying. What they actually wanted was to conduct social cleansing, to bring in pedalos, to embellish the city. I stayed in Cidade de Deus from my fourteenth until my thirty-fifth year. It was supposed to be a model city, but it became an arsenal of war. Do you know what it means to me, a married man, to be forced to lie on the floor next to my daughters because of tracer bullets? And then one day, we were again taken by surprise with eviction, this time because of Linha Amarela [Yellow Line, the express roadway built in the 1990s, connecting the International Airport with Zona Sul – the upper-class area of the city]. I was there, in the way, and had to leave. Again.'

With no other alternative, Altair went to Vila do Autódromo, an old fishing community that became a neighbourhood in 1975, when the workers building the municipal motor racing circuit – *autódromo* – settled there. In the 1990s, the area was 'legalised', obtaining from the State of Rio, the owner of the land, a '*concessão do direito real de uso*', authorising the inhabitants to live there for ninety-nine years. However, since 1996, the municipal government have been trying to evict the community, employing many different arguments: environmental reasons, high-risk area, building works for the Pan-American Games and, now, the Olympics . . . The community – well organised – fought both in court and in the streets for their right to stay put. 'We are in Jacarepaguá, right in the eye of the construction companies' hurricane. They want to evict us and build luxury residential condos here. But this time, we won't leave!'[2]

A global insecurity of tenure crisis blights the lives of millions on the planet. They are individuals and families who have had their lives mortgaged or have lost the possibility of remaining in their home neighbourhoods because of the real-estate price boom in international markets,[3] as described in part one of this work.

Moreover, millions were forcibly expelled from where they lived, displaced by land grabs, large infrastructure urban renewal projects, natural disasters and armed conflicts.

The international tenure crisis manifests itself in many forms and contexts. Forced evictions are its most visible and shocking signs. In the absence of global and comprehensive statistics on forced evictions, the estimation of cases reported by humanitarian organisations – as well as the reports received by the UN special rapporteur on adequate housing – confirms that forced evictions happen all over the world and affect millions every year.

COHRE (Centre on Housing Rights and Evictions), for example, estimated that more than 18 million people were affected by this kind of displacements between 1998 and 2008.[4] The negative impacts of the evictions are tremendous: they deepen poverty and destroy communities, leaving millions in an extremely vulnerable position.

Many people are displaced because of large infrastructure projects or economic exploitation, such as the expansion of mining sites and agribusiness. According to a former World Bank consultant, such projects affected 15 million people every year between 2001 and 2010.[5] Urban projects in preparation for mega-events have also been sources of tenure insecurity and forced evictions.[6]

Conflicts and natural disasters – including those aggravated by current climate change phenomena – also cause displacements and can undermine tenure security. More than 26 million people were internally displaced by the end of 2011 because of armed conflicts, violence or human rights violations. Another 15 million were displaced due to natural disasters.[7]

An earthquake or of a great flood – like the project of a hydroelectric power plant or of a large sports facility within an inhabited territory – has stronger impacts on areas in which tenure status can be contested at any moment by authorities or private agents. In cities, many words are used to designate this situation: favelas, unregulated settlements, informal settlements, slums. As we will see later on, the choice of these terms is not innocent: the intention is to define a situation of otherness in relation to the predominant urban-juridical order, representing a multiplicity of very distinct situations. Nevertheless, it is possible to affirm, at least in the urban world, that these spaces can be defined by housing precariousness and tenure-related ambiguities. This is the predicament of more than half of the inhabitants of cities in the Global South,[8] but it is also present in cities of the developed world, where Roma, Bedouins and other ethnic minorities also live in a permanent state of transience.

Unfortunately, there are no global data about the number, nature or exact circumstances of the communities who live in these conditions. The very nature of tenure relations, of permanence or transience, is to some degree a matter of perception and experience, strongly rooted in the political, economic, juridical and cultural context of each region and nation, making it difficult to accurately depict this universe.[9]

UN-Habitat provides data on 'slums' – the word they adopted to define these urban settlements, characterised by 'the most intolerable of urban housing conditions, which frequently include: insecurity of tenure; lack of basic services, especially water and sanitation; inadequate and sometimes unsafe building structures; overcrowding; and location on hazardous land'.[10] In one study, the agency estimated that in 2001, 924 million people lived in slums.[11] A later estimate (2010) calculated the number at approximately 828 million.[12] However, considering that in 2010 the agency's surveys did not take tenure security into account, this figure provides just a small insight into the current extent of tenure insecurity in urban areas.[13]

These so called slums – or favelas in Brazil – are by no means the only example of insecure tenure. In fact, a large range of individuals and groups can be in an insecure position: refugees and internally displaced persons, affected by conflicts, natural disasters and climate change, or at risk of these elements; people affected by or in land for development projects; occupants of valuable lands; tenants with or without legal title, in informal settlements or under formal agreements, in urban and rural areas; internal and international migrants; minorities; nomad communities; groups affected by caste or other discrimination; poor, landless and homeless people; leaseholders; workers in a regime of servitude; other marginalised groups, such as disabled people or people living with HIV; indigenous people; groups with consuetudinary rights to the land; and even owners of mortgaged houses. Although no one is completely protected against insecure tenure, the poorest and most vulnerable bear the largest share of the burden resulting from this situation.

Fundamentally, insecure tenure is a matter of political economy: laws, institutions and processes of decision-making related to the access and use of housing and land are conditioned by the power structures that exist in society. Consequently, both urban planning strategies and forms of land management bear strongly on the possibilities of granting – or blocking – access to urban land to lower-income residents.[14] It is inside this juridical-administrative web that the mechanisms of inclusion/exclusion in the city are embedded.

Likewise, land administration and management reform programmes potentially impact on tenure security/insecurity. They may resolve or aggravate land conflicts, reinforce or undermine tenure security. They, too, are contingent on political decisions: who will determine the agenda for the land governance reform? Who will receive the benefits distributed by the reform?[15] These questions cannot be ignored, especially in a context of increasing interest in land and of a contentious juridical pluralism.[16]

In these times of financialised capitalism – when rent extraction supersedes productive capital surplus value[17] – urban and rural lands have become highly disputed assets. The consequences have been dramatic, especially – but not exclusively – for emergent economies. The dynamics that follow land market liberalisation are increasing market pressures on territories controlled by low-income communities, in a global context in which urban land is not available to the poorest groups. Thus, communities remain under the constant risk of their territorial assets being despoiled.

Although central and local authorities hold primary account-ability for ensuring that land and housing policies respect the right to adequate housing, humanitarian and development agencies also perform a significant role: they may either be diligent, taking care to avoid involuntary complicity with human rights violations or – allied with urban real-estate development companies, inves-tors and national and international financial institutions – they may have a deleterious effect on the rights of the poorest urban populations and other groups, becoming accomplices in cases of forced evictions and land grabbing.

Policies of land planning, administration and management, including of public lands, have an enormous impact on the construction of the security/insecurity matrix. However – as in the case of housing policies – programmes of land reform and administration around the world have instituted the hegemony of individual private property over all other forms of tenure. Because they focus on bestowing individual private property titles on non-disputed users or owners, the majority of these projects have failed to recognise and protect all forms of tenure and, in particu-lar, to shield the poorest.[18]

Therefore, land reform programmes, including title-granting programmes, often contribute to dispossess the poorest of their territorial assets, capturing a reserve of land for the expansion of the frontiers of capital. In the next chapter I will try to unveil this process, revealing the strategies, policies and mechanisms through which spaces of ambiguity are constructed (and destroyed) in the contemporary urban world.

8

From Enclosures to Foreclosures

In the nineteenth century, the monstrous reality of England's cities, so well depicted by Charles Dickens, transformed one idea into common sense: that cities contain a spare 'other' – the horde of poor people who are unemployed or working under informal regimes, subsisting in a situation of housing precariousness. This vision then spread ad nauseam. By this account, cities grow faster than they should, unable to absorb all who migrate to them, thus generating 'bloat' rather than orderly growth. The migratory movement from the country or smaller towns to major cities should be avoided at all costs, to stem the creation of these monsters.

I have participated in hundreds of debates and symposiums in the last thirty-five years and none have lacked an individual who expressed this position. The idea has underpinned theoretical positions and structured public policies throughout history. Its influence is present everywhere, from the theory of marginality popular in 1950s Latin America (the view that self-built working-class settlements symbolised the persistence of an archaic, traditional, rural-based society, resistant to the modernity represented by cities),[1] to the migratory control policies implemented by communist countries in the twentieth century, many of which are still in force – one being the *hukou* system in China.[2]

All these theories, policies and perceptions have aspects in common: first, a kind of implicit revulsion at the presence of vast contingents of poor people in cities; second, the construction of a concept that links a certain spatiality – marked by scarce material resources – with a socio-political status: the outcast or the outsider. The very origin of the word 'slum' – largely used in international literature – reveals the perversity of this amalgam. According to Mike Davis,

> The first published definition reportedly occurs in the convict writer James Hardy Vaux's 1812 *Vocabulary of the Flash Language*, where it is synonymous with 'racket' or 'criminal trade'. By the cholera years of the 1830s and 1840s, however, the poor were living in slums rather than practicing them. Cardinal Wiseman, in his writings on urban reform, is sometimes given credit for trans-forming 'slum' ('room in which low goings-on occurred') from street slang into a term comfortably used by genteel writers. By mid-century slums were identified in France, America, and India, and were generally recognised as an international phenomenon.[3]

The couching of theories and policies concerning informal settle-ments did not dismantle the territorial stigma: still today, in cities of the developed, emerging or impoverished world, a discrimina-tory hegemonic discourse persists, employing ethnic, economic, juridical and spatial elements in order to designate this tenacious 'place of urban outcasts'.[4]

The theory of marginality and its dualistic conception were strongly contested by a branch of Marxist-based literature produced in Latin America in the 1970s. According to Francisco de Oliveira and Lúcio Kowarick, it is not a question of a dualistic system that opposes archaism to modernity.[5] Rather, it is a periph-eral model of capitalist accumulation. This model requires and reproduces a 'spare' labour force: it does not incorporate these extra workers into the active labour force, nor does it altogether guarantee their reproductive conditions, replicating forms of work and production linked to minimal conditions of survival. The presence of this population – and its 'informal' activities – would respond to a double necessity of the accumulation process in peripheral capitalism: keeping labour-force reproduction costs down, and ensuring a permanent 'industrial reserve army'. The existence of a large population of poor people and people without ownership of the means of production in cities would hence enable the maintenance of low wage levels. This is a *sine qua non* condition for the productivity of companies that operate on the periphery of capital, as they cannot rely on economies of scale and agglomeration or on technology, as their rivals in the central countries do. Moreover, consumer products that are essential to survival – including housing – are offered in a non-monetary way or at a reasonably low price. This too keeps wages below the vital minimum. Therefore, self-built houses represent the super-exploitation of the labour force through overwork and urban spoliation.

In the concrete experience of countries in the Global South that went through import substitution industrialisation in the mid-twentieth century, intensive migration and the formation of sprawling self-constructed settlements were their own peculiar formula of 'capitalist revolution'. It constituted a *locus* of labour-force reproduction under extreme conditions of inequality and low wages. Understood in these terms, the current dynamics of urbanisation in the Global South appears to replicate the precedent set by Europe and North America in the nineteenth and beginning of the twentieth centuries. At that time, the migration of thousands of peasants was the motor of industrialisation in cities like Manchester, Berlin and Chicago. Cities like São Paulo and Pusan in the mid-twentieth century, and Ciudad Juárez, Bangalore and the Chinese megalopoli today, all follow roughly that same trajectory. However, in Davis's words:

> Most cities of the South, however, more closely resemble Victorian Dublin, which, as historian Emmet Larkin has stressed, was unique amongst 'all the slums produced in the western world in the nineteenth century ... [because] its slums were not a product of the industrial revolution. Dublin, in fact, suffered more from the problems of de-industrialization than industrialization between 1800 and 1850'.[6]

The galloping urbanisation currently under way in Sub-Saharan Africa and in parts of Asia has little to do with processes of industrialisation, employment growth and economic development. Kinshasa, Khartoum, Dar es Salaam and Dhaka grew irrepressibly during the difficult years of the 1980s and beginning of the 1990s, despite the ruin of import-substitution manufacturing, the drop in real wages, the increase in prices and the upsurge of urban unemployment.[7]

Since the debt crisis of the early 1980s, programmes of economic restructuration were implemented globally through the efforts of the US and other G7 members. Banks and multilateral institutions urged fiscal adjustments and austerity programmes.[8] In many southern countries, these policies strongly interacted with the 'traditional' pattern of housing provision for the poorest – the self-built settlements – deepening and transforming the conditions of poverty and exclusion.

Particularly in countries that had undergone intensive urbanisation in the 1960s and 1970s – such as Brazil and other Latin American countries – the cuts to public spending interrupted fragile attempts to introduce social welfare systems. Moreover, the economic crisis also restricted the earning possibilities of those working sectors already established in cities. In Latin America, social housing provision programmes, limited as they were, suffered significant cuts. For example, between 1990 and 2000, the region's 'housing deficit' grew from 38 million to 52 million units, even in regions already marked by the so-called demographic transition (the decline of birth and fertility rates for all income levels). The result was the worsening of poverty and quality-of-life indicators among the urban lower classes.[9] Informal settlements had been the prevalent housing solution for Latin American workers during the decades of industrialisation and urban expansion. However, it was in the 1990s and the beginning of the 2000s that *favelas* exploded – even in cities like São Paulo, where they had not been the predominant form of housing.

According to Davis,

> This perverse urban boom surprised most experts and contradicted orthodox economic models that predicted that the negative feedback of urban recession would slow or even reverse migration from the countryside ... The situation in Africa was particularly paradoxical: How could cities in Côte d'Ivoire, Tanzania, Congo-Kinshasa, Gabon, Angola and elsewhere – where economies were

contracting by 2 to 5 percent per year – still support annual population growth of 4 to 8 percent?[10]

Part of the secret, of course, was that policies of agricultural deregulation and financial discipline enforced by the IMF and World Bank continued to generate an exodus of surplus rural labour to urban slums even as cities ceased to be job machines.[11]

The global forces 'pushing' people from the countryside – mechanization of agriculture in Java and India, food imports in Mexico, Haiti, and Kenya, civil war and drought throughout Africa, and everywhere the consolidation of small holdings into large ones and the competition of industrial-scale agribusiness – seem to sustain urbanization even when the 'pull' of the city is drastically weakened by debt and economic depression. As a result, rapid urban growth in the context of structural adjustment, currency devaluation, and state retrenchment has been an inevitable recipe for the mass production of slums.[12]

Although countryside transformation under the impact of the global commodities market – agricultural or mining – has heightened the scale of migration towards cities, this process has been known since the origins of capitalism, when the 'enclosure of the commons' withdrew access to land from former servants, driving them to proletarianisation in cities.[13] In these terms, can one say that we are again witnessing a cycle of territorial expansion and dispossession, which once more expands the frontiers of capital in its imperative to find a new spatial fix?

The situations described below suggest that we are not seeing a new cycle of capitalist occupation of space, but a new relationship between capital and space. This relationship takes place under the hegemony of financial and rentier capital: land, more than a means of production, is a powerful store of value. Expulsion and dispossession are no longer a machine for the production of proletarians. They are a kind of collateral effect of a new geography, based on the control of assets: 'a capitalised property title and its value is set in anticipation of either some future stream of revenue or some future state of scarcity.'[14]

The land seizure movement observed in rural zones on several continents may indeed indicate this dimension of future scarcity.

This became clear between 2007 and 2008, when companies, investment funds and sovereign funds rushed to buy up large tracts of land in Africa, Asia and Latin America, with the declared purpose of expanding food production. However, according to José Graziano, the director general of FAO (the UN Food and Agriculture Organisation), after five years only 10 to 15 per cent of the acquired land in Africa is being cultivated.[15]

As analysed in part one of this book, since the end of the 1970s, capital invested in land and in the real-estate market has gained new importance. It offered a guarantee capable of both leveraging more credit and feeding the hunger for compound growth (the necessity of exponential remuneration for financial capital) with growing remunerations.[16]

According to Fernandez and Aalbers:

> The growing role of housing wealth is also illustrated in Thomas Piketty's bestseller *Capital in the Twenty-First Century*, in what he describes as the 'metamorphosis of capital'. His data show that the ratio of the capital stock to income followed a U-shaped curve in the period from the 18th to the 21st century in different economies. A stable capital stock in the range of 600 per cent of income throughout the 18th and 19th centuries was largely based on agricultural land and increasingly from colonial investment outlets. After WWI the ratio of capital to income declined dramatically, only to return from the 1970s onwards. This return towards a large stock of capital to income was largely propelled by real estate (housing) . . . In this longue-durée exposé of the transforming composition of capital, Piketty shows that the present-day value of real estate in relation to the overall stock of capital and of national income is truly of historic proportions.[17]

The movement of land seizure by financialised capital has taken numerous forms. One of them is purchase – starting with the 'regularisation' of the property and its register as private, as we will analyse later. However, it also happens through 'land concessions', or state-remunerated grants of land for exploration and cultivation by private companies.

In Indonesia, for example, forests belonging to traditional communities were conceded for mining and babassu oil (biofuel) plantations. This provoked conflicts and displaced entire groups to Jakarta and other major cities. The country's land legislation is based on colonial norms and practices, over which post-colonial reforms have been superposed. All of the country's land must fit into one of two possible categories: Forest Estate (approximately 70 per cent of the territory) and Non-Forest Estate (the remaining 30 per cent). Forest Estates are under the responsibility of the Ministry of Forestry and are regulated by the 1967 Forest Law. Non-Forest Estates are managed and administered by a state agency (BPN – National Land Agency), in accord with the 1960 Basic Agrarian Law. Thus, land is administered through a dual system, managed by two distinct organisations. On top of this are the colonial inheritance and the *adat* – the non-integrated traditional communities' consuetudinary rights.[18] The Basic Agrarian Law recognises private property, but reserves control of all non-registered land for the state. According to BPN, only 30 per cent of Non-Forest Estates are formally registered,[19] and some 60 million land plots are not certified.

Since 2006, the Indonesian government has had a land tenure certification programme for the lower-income population and those living in rural and remote areas, The People's Service of Real-Estate Certification [*Layanan Rakyat untuk Tanah Sertifikat* – LARASITA]. The programme offers free mobile registration services.[20] However, extra fees charged to cover more complex registrations and the lack of necessary administrative information exclude a large part of the population from the land registering system – especially those who live in remote villages. In the last few years, BPN registered an average of approximately one million plots per year.

The Basic Agrarian Law recognises the permanent validity of rights resulting from the *adat* (consuetudinary or customary) law. Nonetheless, the possessor of the right cannot register it or have it permanently recognised by the state before they obtain BPN's certificate, confirming that the land is not owned by the state. *Adat* lands can only be registered and certified after having been slotted into one of the seven land rights of private law recognised in Article 16 of the Basic Agrarian Law. Thus, although in many cases the rights of land occupants are rooted in *adat* law – predating the creation of the Indonesian state in 1945 – BPN officials work on the premise that all non-registered land belongs to the state until the contrary is proven. Moreover, *Hak ulayat* (which can be translated as 'communal right to allocation') cannot be registered. This prevents communities from demanding a collective register.

The Basic Forest Law and Mining Law (both 1967) designated all forest lands as state property and eliminated *adat* rights of local communities, recast as illegal 'occupations'. According to the Ministry of Forestry, however, only 14 per cent of the forest lands were legally defined (gazetted). Unrecognised rights – including to *adat* communal lands – still generate conflicts, as there are about 33,000 villages (circa 48 million people) located in Forest Estates and their environs. They have been inhabited for generations – even centuries – without their existence or their lands being recognised by the state.[21]

From 2004 to 2009, the Ministry of Forestry allocated 1.2 million hectares of forests to mining activities; it plans to allocate another 2.2 million between 2010 and 2020. Land was also granted in forest areas for the production of babassu oil, as Indonesia controls 14.3 per cent of the world market in vegetable oil. It is estimated that 66 per cent of all current babassu plantations in the country are in these areas.

Land conflicts are frequent: between 2004 and 2010, there were approximately 2,000 of them, involving 600,000 families and a total 10 million hectares of forest lands.[22] The country does not hold a complete inventory of reliably georeferenced plots of land – forest or non-forest. And since there is no one authority in charge of resolving land disputes, such issues are negotiated via formal or informal agreements. Juridical procedures involving land litigation are slow, and often too expensive for the poor. Furthermore, quality legal advice is rarely available for lower-income families and there is no transparent or accessible information about the land. Large-scale land litigations are commonly resolved through political channels, as the parties do not trust any civil recourse.[23]

In a 2012 report, Oxfam dubbed the movement described above in Indonesia as a 'global land rush'.[24] It is a clear reference to the North American 'gold rush' of the turn of the nineteenth century – a savage appropriation of indigenous lands (the Wild West). The current encroachment is under way in contexts in which large parts of the terrains occupied by rural communities are not formally recognised as such. Where they are, they belong to a 'parallel' category of tenure, not integrated into a single register or management system.

> In 2002, it was estimated that only 1–3 per cent of territories in West African States were occupied through the acquisition of registered property. 'Modern' land law was inherited from the colonial administration and used to define customary lands as state property in order to cede them to colonial companies immediately after. Therefore, the law was always perceived as 'foreign' by the majority of African rural populations, unfamiliar with the cultural perceptions and social relations related to land ownership. Registered property titles, meanwhile, are inaccessible to most of the rural communities.[25]

The situation described above constitutes a basic factor in the weakening of community land rights, making them an easy target for land usurpation.

Nevertheless, as pointed out in the beginning of this section, it is not another movement of border expansion, but a movement that occurs at a specific moment of the capitalist advance, defined by two conditions: the growth of rentier capital and a context marked by the scarcity of natural resources and land.

The food crisis of the late 2000s and concurrent demographic growth – due to the medical advances that extended longevity and decreased infant mortality – highlighted Malthus's catastrophic predictions about the impossibility of feeding every human being. At the same time, the process of the planet's territorial occupation – initiated in the fifteenth century with the 'discovery' of America in the mercantilist phase of capitalism – was accelerated in the 1990s, after the fall of the Berlin Wall and the opening of the last territories previously 'blocked' to the free flow of capital. Thus, the movement we are now watching represents a final border expansion, as capitalism will soon run out of wild wests to 'conquer'.

According to David Richard – building on Malthus – capital will end when land and natural resources become so scarce that all revenues will be absorbed either by the wages needed to cover the high price of food, or by the increasing rents charged by an unproductive, albeit powerful, rentier class. In his time, Malthus's prediction of scarcity was contradicted by other economists, who pointed out the new perspectives brought by the advance of mechanisation in agriculture, which increased work productivity. Many years later, Keynes predicted the euthanasia of the rentier class and the construction of a state-conducted regime of growth – which was partially implemented in the post-1945 period.[26]

However, in the current post-Keynesian era (initiated at the end of the 1970s) the growing power of financial capital – exactly the unproductive rentier capital evoked by Richard – is staggering. Its assets were transmuted into stocks and shares, currency futures, credit default swaps, CDOs and other financial instruments. These were initially created to spread risk but, in fact, serve to transform the volatility of short-term trading into an enormous field for speculative profits.[27] In this context, land revenues regained a central position.

Land speculation – as well as large-scale land acquisition in rural zones – undermines tenure rights and local subsistence forms.[28] Combined with drought and other climate-related changes, these activities are huge propellers of migration from rural to urban areas. There, land and adequate housing are not usually available to new arrivals – especially the poorest. As a result, people live in settlements and homes under insecure tenure deals. These are the mechanisms that combine to produce the expansion of vast urban areas defined by ambiguity and insecure tenure.[29]

Nevertheless, in addition to justifying urbanisation without economic growth, the processes we are witnessing point to new dynamics and a new role for land occupied by the poorest, in both urban and rural areas.

The only recognised type of tenure – in country and city – is titled and registered individual property. All land acquired in other ways assumes a new role in the financialised and rentier phase of capitalism: it functions as a reserve, ready to be occupied at any moment by any arm of financial capital, driven by the insatiable appetite for new collaterals for its assets. Thus, from the *locus* of an industrial reserve army, informal settlements around the world become new land reserves for rent extraction, under the hegemony of the real-estate–financial complex.[30]

In the next chapters, I will approach the mechanisms, policies and strategies through which these processes occur in cities today, focusing on urban unnamed territories, the favelas and informal settlements of the urban world. To this end, I will analyse two fundamental elements: territorial stigma and the construction of permanent transience.

9

Informal, Illegal, Ambiguous

My name is Flavia. I live in Rio de Janeiro, the most beautiful city in the world. I am seventeen as I finish this diary, and I am a trespasser ... I was nine when this happened, and I was in the house, 200 metres away from the battlefield. But I can still tell this story because my uncle and my grandfather repeated it in conversations on the porch of our home ... The men in uniforms crossed the steep and slippery trail in a line. They were military police, with helmets, truncheons, shields, tear gas and stun grenades and, of course, firearms. The resistance movement had locked the solid iron gates with chains and padlocks and made a barricade with tree logs at every entrance ... As they got closer to the entrance, the police were confronted by a human wall, arm hooked with arm, row after row, blocking all the space between the river and the ravine ... The squad entered in formation and marched up to the barrier, beating their truncheons on their shields: then, as no one moved, they stopped face to face with the first row ... In front of them, around 200 people: men, women, adults, young, elderly, white and black people. Not one gun, not one menacing person. No one moving. Someone began chanting the national anthem and soon everyone was singing ... The riot police warned: 'We are coming in.' Among the people, many started praying. All held position. Then, like a wedge aimed at a specific point of the human wall, the squad surged. With the barrier broken, the battle began. Truncheons span and hit, people ran everywhere ... A sixty-year-old lady fell and passed out, with blood spurting from her head ... a military policeman received a flying kick in the chest and fell rolling over – his helmet went into the river. In the dust, people fell and stood back up . . . [they] ran away but came back if they were not too badly hurt . . . Then, almost instantaneously, everything ended. Two congressmen had arrived, a lawyer had called a prosecutor and so came the order to suspend the action. The police regrouped, the dust settled. The more seriously injured were taken away – an ambulance was parked outside – the barricade was removed and the gate was opened. The resistance had won: despite the brutal assault, the target had been protected.

My great-great-grandfather came here in the beginning of the last century, when Horto didn't have anything – there were just bushes and ponds. After him, my great-grandfather and my grandfather – both born here – also worked in IBDF [Brazilian Institute of Forestry Development], IBAMA [Brazilian Institute of Environment and Natural Renewable Resources] and the Botanical Garden: they all had a licence to build their houses in plots close to the Botanical Garden, where my family still live today . . . During my grandfather's time, this was still far from the city, but people started looking at this area. Governor Carlos Lacerda wanted to build a cemetery, he had even chosen the name: Santa Catarina de Siena – beautiful, isn't it? But the land's residents stopped it. In the dictatorship years, an act was decreed donating this land to BNH [Brazilian National Housing Bank] for the construction of a housing project of sixty-five apartment blocks. However, the residents of the surrounding areas and Botanical Garden employees rejected the project, so it was abandoned. From the 1970s on, things started moving faster. Rede Globo [the country's main media group] had installed their head-quarters nearby . . . A luxury residential condo was built on the higher plots, behind the hill, for truly rich people – bankers, industrial owners, etc. The bigger the city grew, the more desirable Horto became . . . There have been attempts to evict former employees and original residents' families to 'best utilise the land' . . . All of this happened long before I started writing this diary, but the story must be properly explained in order to understand this kind of complicated situation: actually, I did not become a trespasser. I was already a trespasser before I was born.[1]

Flavia's testimony (reproduced here with her consent) reveals the complex web that defines the place of informal settlements in cities: that of ambiguity, contradictory signs, laws and decrees that come and go. The residents of Horto – some of whose ancestors were there before the construction of the botanical garden in 1808 – were 'incorporated' into the park as workers, obtaining a 'licence to live there'. Until this point, it is not possible to anticipate any illegal acts or transgressions. Nonetheless, this 'licence' was probably granted as a type of concession from the employer. Therefore, it did not represent a definitive transfer of the plots' ownership to their residents. The area has since been fought over and claimed for different uses, even within the governmental machine. A combination of resistance from residents and interests around the preservation of the park managed to prevent the eviction. Like other similar city territories, the neighbourhood grew to encompass houses for descendants, family friends and tenants.

Although eviction attempts were unsuccessful, the 'state of non-definition' of the area's ownership remained. So much so, that, in 2005, the neighbourhood was the object of a repossession action accompanied by heavy-handed repression. The residents once more resisted, this time joining violent battle.

In her testimony, Flavia questions why her 'people' were being treated as 'thugs', as 'enemies'. Whose enemy? In her view, the 'rich', 'powerful', Rede Globo-type incomers who had bought property nearby could not tolerate their presence in a locality so highly valued by the market. In addition, the eco and heritage discourse in defence of the park – that stopped its transformation into a cemetery or a housing project in the 1960s – is now used to frame Horto's inhabitants as vandals and trouble-makers.

This testimony manifests the basic elements of which this and similar places are composed: permanent transience and territorial stigma. Despite being born there, like her father, grandfather and great-grandfather, Flavia is a trespasser and hence a transgressor. However, the law and its apparatus are not completely absent from this place. On the contrary, it was formed by layers of legality permeated by tensions of every type. In the words of Vera Telles:

A number of practices and situations engrained in society's political life (and democratic normality), in their contemporary
configurations, in fact extend a zone of indetermination between
law and non-law, territories of uncertain and continuously
moving borders where every single person becomes dispensable,
a *homo sacer*.[2]

Situations like these are hardly confined to Brazil or even Latin
America. Lisa Björkman reports a similar case in a study of water
supply problems in Mumbai, India. In 1975, Prime Minister
Indira Ghandi declared a state of emergency in the country.
Shivajinagar-Baiganwadi, a housing venture launched by the
municipality to ressetle the residents, became a 'slum, illegal
area'. At that time, the Indian National Congress (Indira Gandhi's
party) governed the state of Maharashtra and the city of Mumbai.
In a bid to modernise the city – and at the same time as a response
to the precariousness of mass settlements – the government
undertook a mega-registration operation, enumerating 1,680
neighbourhoods considered to be in violation of the zoning or
density norms of the 1967 Development Plan and Control
Regulations. These areas' residents (2.8 million people – almost
half of the city's population at the time) were photographed in
front of their homes and received a photo pass. It was a document associating a particular family with a particular house in
the settlement, ensuring 'some kind of security of tenure', as well
as a guarantee of compensation in the event of demolition or
displacement. Simultaneously, the government – empowered by
the state of emergency – promoted large-scale demolition of
houses that stood in the path of large infrastructure and upgrade
projects. In this context, a municipal colony for resettled people
was created on the edge of a rubbish dump in 1976: Shivajinagar-
Baiganwadi. There, 10 x 15-foot plots – grouped in rows of
sixteen within ninety-four blocks – sheltered people who were to
pay a small monthly fee as 'indemnity' for occupying lands
belonging to the municipality.

However, many of the families who were resettled into this
'district' never lived there. First of all, the majority of these families had social networks and businesses where they lived before, so

they simply returned. Moreover, reports of the 'district's' early
years portrayed a squalid place, close to a dump and a mosqui-
to-infested swamp. Many families sold, sublet or abandoned their
plots. What came next – the neighbourhood growing and becoming one of the densest areas of the city – has 'deleted' the memory
of the settlement as a planned district. Today, this locality epitomises the city's 'illegal' production of homes and services. In the
words of an engineer from the Hydraulic Engineer Department of
the Municipal Corporation of Greater Mumbai (MCGM):
'Shivajinagar is an illegal area which is not part of the city plan.
They occupied it illegally and keep illegally building; moreover,
they steal water with illegal connections.'[3]

In this case, as in that of Horto – where residents fight to
remain where they are – the same basic elements are present. Both
exemplify territories with shifting definitions of the legal and the
illegal, constructed from an amalgam of different types of pressure, political mediation and several layers of legality. Here, too,
territorial stigma transforms residents into criminals or violators
of the urban order. However, Mumbai's case also reveals some
new elements. As in many other cases, the 'crime' in Mumbai is
non-compliance with planning, although it is precisely planning
that defines the permitted – or prohibited – forms of occupying
space. Finally, in this case, the market relationships are clear. The
plots of land are sold, bought and rented. It is, thus, a powerful
land and housing market, inside and on the margins of the city.

According to Mike Davis,

> There are probably more than 200,000 slums on Earth, ranging
> in population from a few hundred to more than a million people.
> The five great metropolises of South Asia (Karachi, Mumbai,
> Delhi, Kolkata, and Dhaka) alone contain about 15,000 distinct
> slum communities whose total population exceeds 20 million.[4]

An even larger slum population covers the fast-urbanising coast
of West Africa, while other immense and deprived conurbations
are spreading through the highlands of Anatolia and Ethiopia;
their reach embraces the foothills of the Andes and the Himalayas;
they explode away from the skyscraper cores of Mexico City,

Johannesburg, Manila and São Paulo; and, of course, they border the Amazon, Niger, Congo, Nile, Tigris, Ganges, Irrawaddy and Mekong rivers.

Nevertheless, Kolkata's *bustees*, Mumbai's *chawls* and *zopadpattis*, Karachi's *katchi abadis*, Jakarta's and Surabaya's *kampung*, Manila's *iskwaters*, Khartoum's *shammasas*, Durban's *umjondolos*, Rabat's *intra-murios*, Abidjan's *bidonvilles*, Cairo's *baladis*, Ankara and Istanbul's *gecekondus*, Quito's *conventillos*, Brazil's *favelas*, Buenos Aires's *villas miseria*, Caracas's *barrios* and Mexico City's *colonias populares* are not just different names for the same configuration. Because they are deeply rooted in local political economies, their configurations are unique, as are their trajectories in time.[5]

It is possible to affirm, though, that they all occupy a zone of indetermination between legal/illegal, planned/not planned, formal/informal, inside/outside the market, presence/absence of the state. Such indeterminations are the mechanisms through which a situation of permanent transience is constructed – the existence of a large reserve territory, ready to be captured 'at the right moment'. These are the mechanisms that will be examined in the following sections.

Legal/Illegal: Superpositions, Pluralisms and . . . Irresolutions

In the informal settlements of cities around the world, the category 'illegal' should not – must not – be treated as an absolute. In many cases, the majority of their inhabitants live in tenure systems that can be considered parallel to legality, semi-legal or almost legal. Tolerated or legitimised by consuetudinary laws or simply by use or tradition, they may be either recognised or ignored by the authorities.[6] In the first place, the formation of these neighbourhoods has not necessarily originated from a legal infringement. When aspiring residents occupy vacant land without its owner's consent, they are, in principle, violating the law and might be liable to sanction. However, in many cases the 'owner' does not exist in formal terms, or perhaps the land is an object of dispute between various parties. Thus, even within a

situation that would seem clearly illegal, the presence of the occupiers cannot be immediately contested, which may lead to the
consolidation of the occupation. The term 'slum', defined as the
squatting of land belonging to others, was chosen by Mike Davis
to designate this 'other' space of many names. However, a 'slum'
is not necessarily the origin of the majority of informal settlements. In fact, different forms of purchase or lease of plots that
were not subject to official land subdivision and development –
and, in general, could not be approved by the norms in force – are
much more common than land squatting. Communal lands –
belonging to groups or clans, for example – are frequent instances.
In the face of urban expansion, they are donated to clan members
or sold in smaller pieces for the construction of houses. This situation is recurrent in Sub-Saharan Africa: instead of assigning a
'right of use' (the usual procedure for providing land to the
members of a tribe), the plots are sold outright. Although rarely
legal, these transactions are accepted within the social milieus of
the actors involved.[7] Communal forms of tenure can also be
temporary and serve as a kind of transition between a collective
status and individual forms. In Benin's cities and their environs,
for example, where occupants have only a contract for purchase
or a temporary occupation permit, lands are first registered to the
state, which then transmits them to a residents' association
(Association d'Intérêt Foncier) before, occasionally, registering
them as individual titles.[8]

This is also the case of Mexican *ejidos*, or communal lands
resulting from the agrarian reform beginning in the 1920s. In the
suburbs of Mexico City and other cities in Mexico, these lands
were allotted and sold to residents to construct their own houses.[9]
In both Benin and Mexico, the lands could not be subdivided
because the right that guarantees communal tenure does not allow
selling and, often, the terrains lie beyond the limit of what is
considered developable by urban perimeter plans and laws.

In these situations, we can clearly speak of a juridical pluralism:
the encounter, coexistence and, often, conflict between different
juridical orders operating on the same territory. Boaventura de
Sousa Santos developed a vast research on the theme. According
to the author:

I start from the verification – now widely recognised in Sociology of Law (and founded in multiple empirical surveys) – that, contrary to what is intended by liberal Political Philosophy and its juridical science, not one, but many forms of law or juridical modes circulate in society. The official State law – that legislated by the government or the Parliament and found in legal codes – is just one of these forms, although tendentially the most important one. These different forms vary in terms of: the field of social action or the social groups that they regulate; their durability – from the long duration of the immemorial tradition to the ephemerality of a revolutionary process; the way they prevent individual or social conflicts and solve them when they occur; the mechanisms of reproduction of legality and distribution or obscuration of juridical knowledge. I start, thus, from the idea of plurality of juridical orders or, more succinctly and coherently, from juridical pluralism.[10]

The idea of superimposed juridical orders is not only applicable to the encounter of customary law and state law, as in the situation described above. The purchase of small plots of undeveloped land on the edge of urban zones from small proprietors and farmers is one of the most common ways of producing new urban settlements in various regions of the world. These sales are generally lawful, as contracts are drawn up before witnesses and officially registered. The buyer has a document proving the validity of the purchase. However, in many cases, subdividing the land is illegal because it violates a specific zoning or subdivision statute or because the landowner did not request – or did not receive – a licence to subdivide.

This kind of legality/illegality is very common in Latin America (unregulated or clandestine land parcelling is rife in Brazil) and in Asia (such as unauthorised colonies in Indian cities).[11] In these cases, it is not a question of superposing distinct juridical layers, but of superposing distinct spheres within the same juridical and governmental field.

Government legislation is far from being an undifferentiated, consistent corpus of rules. Different sectors within it have different origins and are part of different institutions, themselves following different agendas. These sectors relate to different circumscriptions at different moments. Therefore, the state order itself is plural.[12] Legalities and illegalities of different orders frequently collide in matters of civil, urban and environmental law. As a result, grey areas emerge that are widely exploited by residents in their struggles – including legal ones – to remain where they are.

However, the notion of juridical pluralism goes beyond the plural nature of governmental juridicity and the coexistence of distinct urban orders. The coexistence of consuetudinary and statutory rights constitutes the very nature of the order, authority and power relations within autonomously produced lower-class neighbourhoods.

The work of Pedro Abramo has already shown that, in informal settlements, a 'local authority' generally emerges to mediate in any conflicts within the community, especially in relation to the contractual conditions that regulate the occupation of plots and houses by the residents. According to Abramo, such authorities are legitimised by local historical processes. This legitimacy can be religious, ethnic, cultural or political, or can arise from violence or force:

> As the literature of economic anthropology reveals in many studies, the mechanisms of communal living that ensure the local social order include some type of coercion in order to restrict and control conflictive (or deviant) behaviours. This coercion can assume the form of passive collective, representative and/or imposed coercive force. In the case of informal land markets, local authorities serve as the mediating institution for contractual conflicts and allow these contracts to be respected and/or negotiated between the parties, ensuring their intertemporal and intergenerational maintenance. Many anthropological studies of the operational form of markets and formal organisations describe coercive forms that are not restricted to their legal coercive dimension. Equally, in informal land markets, we can identify very distinct coercive forms and mechanisms, although with a similar function: to guarantee what can be called the market 'contractual pact'. The social and political history of every settlement constructs and deconstructs these coercive mechanisms.[13]

Boaventura de Sousa Santos names the set of norms and rules that regulate the management of territories in informal settlements as an internal, unofficial and fragile law,

> managed, among others, by the residents' association and applicable to the prevention and resolution of conflicts generated in the heart of the community because of the struggle for housing. This unofficial law – Pasárgada law, as I will refer to it – rules in parallel – or in conflict – with official Brazilian law. It is on this juridical duplicity that the Pasárgada juridical order feeds. Between these two laws, an extremely complex relation of juridical pluralism prevails, only revealed by a very thorough analysis. In general terms it is not an equal relationship, since Pasárgada law is, always and in multiple forms, dependent on official Brazilian law. By applying a category issued from political economy, we might call it an unequal exchange of juridicity, which reflects and replicates, in socio-juridical terms, the unequal relations between classes whose interests are based on one or on the other law.[14]

Alex Magalhães undertook a detailed analysis of the documents used in the registration of purchase contracts in Rio de Janeiro's favelas. His research shows that they are valid both from a state-juridical order perspective and from that of the concept of law devised within that specific social context. He then analyses their use in processes of land regularisation, as well as in processes of division of assets carried out in divorce or hereditary succession acts. Corroborating Sousa Santos's view, Magalhães finds that it is not a peaceful coexistence between 'laws', but a process denying juridical pacts involving the more powerless classes, which reflects and replicates class inequalities.[15]

We could stop here in our analysis of the dynamics between legality and illegality in low-income settlements and neighbourhoods. However, the superposition of legal orders – here conceptualised as juridical pluralism – does not resolve the construction of permanent transience as an essential condition for the contemporary constitution of these spaces as land reserves. Working on São Paulo's lower-income neighbourhoods, James Holston indicates the fundamental element that completes the equation: 'juridical-bureaucratic irresolution'. According to Holston,

> The urban peripheries of São Paulo developed, like most of Brazil ... as an arena of land conflict in which distinctions between legal and illegal occupation are temporary and their relations dangerously unstable. In this context, the law regularly produces irresolvable procedural and substantive complexity; this jural-bureaucratic irresolution dependably initiates extrajudicial solutions ... As such, land law promotes conflict, not resolution.[16]

The field of mediation, discretionality and arbitration is generally situated in politics, which is my next topic of reflection.

The State: Sovereignty and Exception

From the above statements, we can infer one of the most important expressions of the presence of the state in the formation and consolidation of informal neighbourhoods. Although the dominant narrative describes these localities as 'resulting from the absence of the state' or 'beyond the reach of the state', the inconsistency of these settlements' processes of formation, consolidation and eviction have been – and still are – strongly constituted and permanently mediated by the state.

This presence is the origin of many settlements on public lands where, at some point in the neighbourhood's history, its residents obtained licence to settle – documented or otherwise – from the local authorities. This situation is particularly prevalent in countries that promoted mass land nationalisation in the 1960s and 1970s, as was the case for twenty of the forty Sub-Saharan African countries.[17] Although numerous countries have lately reverted nationalisation, to this day almost all land in Ethiopia, Rwanda and Mozambique, for example, belongs to the state, which grants rights of use. In 1970s Botswana, a system for the concession of use of state land was implemented. It delivered occupation certificates, while maintaining ownership for the state.[18]

In Cambodia, after the fall of the Khmer Rouge in 1979, those who returned to Phnom Penh were selectively authorised to occupy empty buildings situated in areas near their jobs, receiving temporary permits from the authorities to establish themselves there, although ownership was still in the hands of the state. When there were no more premises available, empty peripheral areas started to be occupied, nowadays treated as 'illegal occupations'.[19]

To hold a right of occupation does not necessarily mean secure tenure. Forced and violent evictions – as in the case of Cambodia (which was previously analysed) and of residents holding rights of occupation in Nigerian cities – reveal the discretionality and instability of these temporary permits, which can be revoked at any moment without adequate reparation or compensation.[20]

Beyond its presence as owner and promoter of informal neighbourhoods – a position with clear political implications – the state has had an omnipresent role as the main mediator of consolidation in the settlements. Within democratic contexts, in which parties contend for votes in these territories, 'unblocking' the existent legal/administrative impediments in order to officialise the existence of a settlement – and, thus, to allow the provision of services and amenities – becomes a powerful political-electoral tool. This tactic has been fundamental to sustain inequality and control of cities by their elite. At the same time, it replicates political mandates, ensuring a large electoral base for the parties.

The bulk of investment in urbanisation takes place when neighbourhoods are already occupied and when this demand is difficult to address. Hence the struggle for access to investment is fierce and of major political-electoral importance. Because of the settlements' condition of informality and/or illegality, their consolidation provokes deadlocks within the bureaucracy, creating opportunities for selective and intermediated solutions. The combination of informal neighbourhoods' urban development with their precarious insertion into cities makes public goods and services into one of the most important popular demands. This leads to local mobilisation with organised campaigns for housing, transportation, health, sanitation, and so on.

The relation between the political-electoral system and these pressures is complex. On the one hand, parties whose leaders are associated with these movements bring their agendas into formal democratic institutions and into the state system. On the other, the logic of competition between political parties also penetrates these movements, transforming their cultures.

Political parties, whether on the left or the right of the spectrum, have to compete for poor people's votes. Therefore they must respond to the demand for integration into cities that comes both from organised movements and from the largest and least organised swathe of the population. This is how investments in urban development – as well as the tolerance, authorisation or even promotion of precarious settlements – become a powerful electoral tool. They offer enormous potential for political return, in the form of popular votes and/or access to campaign financing. Therefore lower-income territories receive sustained investment from politicians, who expect to collect their prize from those whom they have selectively endowed with public resources.[21]

The above line of thought – which I developed for the Brazilian context – resonates with the analysis of Partha Chatterjee for the Indian context. Chatterjee affirms that the urban poorest have not been treated as citizens with full rights, even though their demands for urban infrastructure and amenities are formulated in the language of citizenship rights. The lives and livelihoods of the urban poorest depend on 'illegal' land squatting and 'informal' productive and commercial activities. Thus, for Chatterjee, the formal-legal structure permanently hinders the extension of formal rights to the residents of such neighbourhoods, who negotiate the provision of goods and rights with the state through 'political' rather than 'civil' society. According to him, civil society is the domain of people's sovereignty that guarantees equality of rights – something denied to the majority of the world's inhabitants. Political society, on the other hand, provides services through paralegal arrangements.[22]

The practice of cut-off dates (a specific date that separates residents who can be recognised and receive benefits from those who cannot) is a clear example of the difference outlined above. The difference between rightful and non-rightful citizens ignores the universality of the residents' human condition, and the legality/illegality of the occupation. It is, in fact, a negotiation in purely political, discretionary terms, a territorial 'pact' that aims to respond to the pressures coming from the urban masses while reaffirming transience and territorial stigma.

This territorial pact signed between dominant classes and emergent social groups is based on the maintenance of an order that does not adapt to incorporate different forms of spatial occupation. Rather, it selectively tolerates exceptions to the rule. After being recognised, the exceptions are 'rewarded' with the right to remain and with public investment in urban infrastructure and services. Therefore, the 'clandestine' majority enters urban politics owing a favour to those who consider them admissible.

The political relationship established by the territorial pact has been called an 'ideology of gift' in sociological literature. In other words, the founding act of citizenship is a gift from the state to the citizen. Any donation, even if initially a voluntary, free and generous act, has in fact a double edge. The person who gives does so in recognition of a necessity. Thus, the donation also has a compulsory character, a sense of reparation. At the same time the act of giving implies another obligation, that of receiving. Every gift is only completed with its acceptance: those who give also do it out of necessity and those who receive behave in this way out of necessity. Therefore, to receive a benefit is a right, but it is also a responsibility. Because of this, the state must not only give, but also create an obligation to receive.

Finally, the term that completes and gives meaning to the relationship is *retribution*, or reciprocation. The person who receives a present creates a bond that naturally leads to an act of retribution. Consequently, the power of giving is to arouse in the recipient the consciousness of an obligation to reciprocate, as an ethical and political responsibility. It is interesting to note the difference between the requital of a donation and the payment of a debt. The requital of a donation has no deadline, nor a readily defined value: it is the acknowledgement of an obligation that transcends the utilitarian dimension. However, the established bond presupposes the ascendancy of the donor over the recipient, whose condition is that of a debtor. This implies a commitment to a return that is not previously fixed – like a bill with no set value or expiration date – and that can be demanded at any moment, under different forms.[23]

We do not speak here of what political science has designated as populism or patronage. That debate has little relevance to the objectives of this text, for it only represents one among numerous political forms of exercising these pacts. What is important here is to stress two points: the first is that these pacts result from the mobilisation power and political pressure of the settlements' residents themselves, who play fundamentally active roles within this process. The second is the effect produced by these specific forms of state action on the territories and on the nature of the relationships of sovereignty established therein.

It is in this sense that Vera Telles employs the term 'margins' to name these territories:

> They are not outlaw domains, sites of anomie, disorder, a state of nature. They are spaces produced by the modes through which the forces of order operate in these places – practices that produce the figure of *homo sacer* in situations embedded within the life and work circumstances of their inhabitants. However, they are also places where the presence of the state circumscribes a field of practices and counter-behaviours in which the subjects make (and elaborate) the experience of law, authority, order and its inverse, interacting with different modes of regulation – micro-regulations, one could say – anchored in the practical conditions of social life. The state is present in these territories produced as 'margins' and within the intricate relationships and circuits superposed therein. It is also an active part of the social ordering produced therein, in the situated, relational, contextual modes through which the criteria of order and its inverses are negotiated.[24]

Instability, irresolution and impermanence are the keys to understanding how the exceptions are politically constructed in cities, indelibly tainting informal neighbourhoods because of the ambiguity of their position as 'margins'.

In the previous sections, we analysed how the laws – here employed in a plural sense – constitute these territories while marking them out as 'illegal'. Within this set of norms, urban regulation plays a key role in articulating and defining the properly spatial attributions of this organisation. Let us examine it more closely.

Demarcating the Border Between Legal and Illegal: Urban Planning

In a previous work about the city of São Paulo, I reconstructed the history of urban regulations and their socio-political effects on the formation of a twofold city, shaped by the territorial exclusion of the poorest.[25]

The impact of urban legislation on the development of informal land markets has been studied in works of neoclassical economics, which predominantly link the increase of informality to the establishment of strict urban regulations. These studies started in the 1960s, with the works of William Alonso. It was well accepted that the prices of urban land and real estate were not solely dependent on the relation between supply and demand, since urban legislation establishes an (artificial) cap on supply. However, it was only in the 1970s that scholars began to see a relation between two other phenomena: the existence of rules to ordain the form, uses and extent of built space in cities – derived from urban planning – and the rise of house prices. Stephen Mayo and Shlomo Angel were the first to associate urban regulations with the inelasticity of supply. Although their focus was not precisely on land markets in cities where great extensions of land are occupied by unregulated neighbourhoods, their works were widely employed to 'explain' why the poor lack access to formal urbanised land and housing markets.[26]

According to this point of view, strict urban planning patterns and standards lead to the rise of land prices, making it difficult – or impossible – for the poorest to accede to housing and urban land. The outcome is the growth of a non-standardised market for land, tolerated by city authorities because, where these markets appear, there is no low-cost housing alternative. Finally, according to the same notion, a progressive public policy should strive to restrict urban regulation. This would permit the formal real-estate market to offer legal housing for the poorest.[27]

Nevertheless, if we look more closely at the functioning of urban land markets and their links to urban legislation, what appears to be its clearest failure – the existence of parallel informal markets – is, in fact, its biggest success. This informal sector is an essential element of the political economy of exclusionary urbanisation. In theory, urban planning and its resultant urban regulation should operate as a mould for the ideal or desirable city. However, urban legislation is entirely structured under the dominant economic logic. It is adapted to the rhythm and strategies of the market – especially the strategies adopted by luxury real-estate development and construction companies. Therefore, urban legislation simply defines and reserves the best urban areas for these affluent markets, avoiding 'invasion' by the poorest. Its principal function – performed even more efficiently thanks to the presence of informal land markets – is to raise invisible barriers that prevent lower-class neighbourhoods from encroaching on prime locations, leaving these exclusively for high-income real-estate development.[28]

Contrary to the rules that regulate the formation of lower-class suburbs and informal settlements – which are usually invisible on city zoning maps – the structuring of elite spaces is extremely detailed within urban legislation. Thus, in addition to solidifying into law the morphology of the city's real-estate supply, urban legislation reinforces the discriminatory *gestalt* of the city. In the exclusive neighbourhoods occupied by the elite, the main urban planning characteristic is to perpetuate the type of commercial contract established during the original real-estate development. This is essential to ensure that the substantial investment made in those areas will generate long-term profits, and to minimise the risk of depreciation. On the other hand, disobeying urban standards and rules is the best way to profit from the informal settlements: as informal land markets are usually located in devalued areas, the possibility of generating high population densities – typical of lower-income neighbourhoods – produces large returns. To enable this system, the state, as the authorising body, must provide two conditions: one, the intensity and density of construction on unregulated land must greatly exceed those permitted by urban planning; two, there must be an expectation of the arrival of urban infrastructure improvements in the area.

Additionally, central to this type of urban planning are the guarantees of exclusivity and of land profitability. The mapping of thoroughly regulated real-estate areas reserves the prime locations and best-served urban land for the elite. Simultaneously, it ignores the evolution of ultra-dense territories in areas that have not been formally developed, or are less suitable for urbanisation.

However, it is not only an economic logic that delimits the 'inside' and the 'outside' of the law in terms of urban planning. It is also a powerful machinery of ethnocultural discrimination that defines as 'prohibited' housing forms linked with certain socio-cultural practices. In previous works,[29] I sought to demonstrate how the collective housing forms practised by Afro-Brazilians – based on religious and social roots – were gradually stigmatised and banned by city building codes and zoning laws.

When one ethnic group dominates a multi-ethnic territory, the norms of urban planning, as part of the land regime, may become powerful mechanisms to control and, often, dispossess long-established communities (generally of ethnic minorities). One example is Israel and its relationship with Arab and Bedouin villages established on its territory before the creation of the Jewish state in 1947.[30] According to Oren Yiftachel and Alexandre Kedar, a set of norms, institutions and legal structures were then established by the Israeli state in order to facilitate the expansion of a Jewish nation over a territory it controlled – constructing the domination of an ethnic class, or what the authors denominate 'ethnocracy'.[31]

The institutional legal system that regulates access to land in Israel, attaching it to development projects, is founded on three pillars: a centralised planning system that defines what, when, where and how new constructions can be built; a land administration system (Israel Land Authority) that controls 93 per cent of the territory; and a complex legal system, in which queries are received, filtered and negotiated within hierarchised courts. This system of land management and planning granted access to housing for countless Israeli citizens – including Jewish migrants and refugees from anti-Semitic regimes. However, the same system enshrined ethnic-based practices that discriminate against communities or villages already established in Palestine. Some of these villages are 'recognised' and have their expansion potential 'planned'. Other villages are not. To be a non-recognised community means to be invisible in administrative terms and, thus, not to receive adequate public services. At the same time, if a territory is not planned, it cannot grow or erect new buildings. As demographic growth demands the expansion of existing structures, new buildings and extensions must be built without permission, which can cause demolition orders and evictions without compensation, as well as fines, the payment of demolition costs and eventual criminal sanctions. Small Arab towns, neighbourhoods in East Jerusalem and Bedouin villages in the Negev desert and in the West Bank are examples of this policy. The contrast between the planners' capacity to establish new Jewish settlements and their failure to expand non-Jewish villages and settlements is evident: since 1948, the Israeli state has planned and implemented more than 700 new Jewish settlements, while no new non-Jewish community was founded or even mooted – if we except the proposal to urbanise Bedouin communities by force.[32]

The situation of Bedouin communities in the Negev desert displays other components of the ethnocultural dimension of the expropriation of land and reordering of legal space undertaken by Israeli planning. Bedouin people have roamed the desert as nomad shepherds for hundreds of years. Since 1948, the Israeli state has adopted the policy of not recognising these communities' claims, instead promoting the urbanisation of their lands as 'planned towns'. Israel justifies this policy on grounds of the provision of public services. A family or clan may only gain access to these towns on condition of renouncing any demand of state recognition for their lands. Today, these planned towns are rife with unemployment, dependency, crime and social tension.[33]

The model of planning without consideration for traditional local lifestyles and forms of land occupation is one of the cogs of the ethno-classicist machine of dispossession and domination, which can also be observed in the difficult and complex situation of Romani or Roma peoples in Europe.

Today, settlements of Romani and other travelling communities in European cities represent one example of these 'others' who are invisible or 'illegal' according to urban planning norms – even when settled on lands they own. These communities have diverse origins; the Roma, who are ancestrally connected to India, arrived in Europe in the fourteenth and fifteenth centuries.[34]

Their patterns of residence and transit are not in line with European culture and are generally the source of the discrimination faced by Romani in Europe. Their territorial exclusion causes a series of problems, from intermittent access to education and work to appropriate health care or inclusion in community life. Most of their settlements are marred by infrastructural precariousness. For example, in Slovakia in 2005, 10 per cent of Romani settlements were without electricity and 81 per cent had no sewage disposal.[35] In Romania, their predicament in terms of electricity and sanitation is similar and less than 15 per cent of homes contain a bathroom.[36] In Serbia too, half of the Romani live in settlements with precarious infrastructure.[37] In Montenegro, 48 per cent of Romani residences are located near rubbish tips.[38]

As most of these settlements are deemed illegal, their residents are not allowed to register in the towns where they are situated. Their access to public services is by the same token limited. Many Romani and other traveller groups are trapped between an inadequate offer of suitable accommodation on one side, and the insecurity of unauthorised camps and constructions on the other. They also face a cycle of evictions, often successive, and violently carried out. In order to avoid evictions and to gain access to services, many families have agreed to live in permanent structures, even if reluctantly. However, they are frequently housed in highly degraded buildings and exposed to more direct and violent hostility, focused on their ethnicity and way of life.[39]

In Italy, for example, emergency legislation, adopted in 2008, constituted the legal basis for evictions and for the destruction of settlements of Romani people and other groups of travellers. Although this legislation was rescinded in 2011, violent evictions and resettlements in isolated, gated ghettos have continued in many cities.[40]

Urban planning regulations have been a powerful tool of discrimination against these groups within European urban space. In England, for example, the Green Belt planning and protection norms are often invoked by the non-traveller population – and by the authorities – as the reason to expel travellers from their sites, as happened in Dale Farm, near Basildon.[41]

Settlements self-constructed decades ago by Romani communities in cities like Istanbul and Sofia have been demolished to make way for urban renovation projects. The communities were dispersed to different areas, sometimes very distant from where they had been.[42]

In the case of Arab and Bedouin communities in Israel, as well as that of Romani people and travellers in Europe, urban planning and its regulations are what draw the border between legal and illegal. They do so through compounding an ethnically based discriminatory policy with a confrontation between different forms of occupation and the communities' relationship with the territory. Even if the discrimination is not always, or not explicitly, present, the confrontation is omnipresent in informal neighbourhoods. In addition to the general neediness and the scarcity of available resources, we find, within the territorial organisation of these neighbourhoods, morphologies, typologies and forms of use that reflect forms of organisation and economic strategies pertaining to the majoritarian sectors of the city, which are systematically blocked or not recognised by regulation.

Among the characteristic elements of informal neighbourhoods are: multifunctionality, or mixed use; 'horizontal' multi-family use, with various households sharing the same plot of land; and flexibility, or incrementalism, in the forms of construction. These are sensible strategies to maximise the space not only for housing purposes, but also for income generation – by using homes for workshop or retail activities, and letting out rooms or parts of houses. To begin with, within planning epistemology, the 'residential' category refers exclusively or predominantly to residential spaces, which automatically excludes the multifunctional nature of informal neighbourhoods' typical spaces. Moreover, the typologies generally classified as 'multi-family' are apartment buildings, not shared back yards or rooftop *lajes*.[43] This is how the restrictions mentioned above are put into action by urban regulation to underline the border between inside and outside the law.

I will use the (maybe extreme) example of the numerous kampung in Jakarta, Surabaya and Yogyakarta – major Indonesian cities – in order to problematise the statement above.

Kampung (originally villages) are urban settlements with local roots, inhabited mainly by lower- and lower-middle-class people. They are mixed-use zones, densely populated, serving as workplace and home for the great bulk of Indonesia's urban population: it is estimated that 60 per cent of Jakarta's inhabitants live in a kampung.[44] They have existed in Javanese cities since the pre-colonial era. The cities of the island of Java were constituted in the sixteenth century as ports and international commercial entrepots. Thus, the various ethnic groups involved with these activities became established, including Javanese, Malay, Buginese, Chinese, Hindu and Arab people. According to Javanese urban cultural tradition, cities were composed of a group of neighbourhoods, the kampung – communities of residency and work, some of which still exist today. Since the pre-colonial era, one of the essential functions of the kampung was to accommodate the city's newcomers. Under the Dutch, they became neighbourhoods organised by background or religious origin – such as the Chinese Pecinan and the Muslim Pekojan.

From the start, the city administration was only in charge of the area containing the palaces, the markets and the port. Each kampung was autonomous and had its own rules. In 500 years of history, kampung have not substantially changed their mixed-use characteristics. In general, commercial and productive activities occupy the ground floor while residential spaces are in the upper floors – which, today, can reach three or four stories in the densest settlements. At street level, the production of every type of food, clothes, toys, furniture, as well as electronic repair shops, spreads beyond private areas, creating semi-public spaces that are not only spaces of circulation and connection with the city, but also semi-private spaces, inviting social and economic interaction. An example is the presence of bare paved areas that may – depending on the time of the day and the day of the week – function as a place for drying laundry, a playground, a badminton court for children and teenagers or a space for parties, when they are covered by decorated fabric tents.[45]

The current relationship between urban planning and regulatory frameworks and the kampung varies from city to city. It also changes according to the political relationship that successive local and national administrations have established with each kampung.

In general, kampung are poorly served by infrastructure: there is uneven access to piped water, sanitation, drainage and flood control facilities. They also tend to have an ambiguous juridical status. However, the housing conditions in different kampung vary as, over time, some received services such as plumbed water, street paving and drainage systems. Indonesia – and Surabaya in particular – has a long history of informal settlement improvement programmes, dating back to sanitation interventions in the colonial era. The Kampung Improvement Programme (KIP), launched in 1969, is considered one of the world's largest and most successful projects for the urbanisation of informal settlements. Lately, however, this policy has lost both space and resources.[46]

The administrative and juridical integration of kampung varies from city to city. In places, at least some of the settlements are recognised by municipal plans. However, others are consensually classified by the state as 'illegal'. This is the case for kampung located near rivers, canals, railroads, green belts or parks. They are often in zones subject to flooding, in contravention of current national and local planning rules, making them entirely 'invisible' on city maps, 'illegal' and vulnerable to eviction.[47] The government abstains at every level from implementing housing policies and programmes in such settlements, and rarely invests in amenities and infrastructure. As a result, the living conditions are worse than in other kinds of kampung. These settlements clearly harbour the poorest among the urban poor, which includes undocumented internal migrants.[48]

By classifying these settlements as 'illegal', riding roughshod over pre-existent social connections, the norms of planning, construction and land occupation define these settlements' geography. It is that of invisibility in terms of urban policy, or of a constituted – but never plainly established – presence as an exception. Here, the concept of 'state of exception' may be useful. Giorgio Agamben defines 'sovereignty' as the power to determine the state of exception. For him, the paradox of sovereignty consists in the fact that the sovereign find themselves, at the same time, inside and outside of the juridical order.[49] The legal and urban planning apparatus has the power to decree the suspension of the urban order, determining what is 'illegal' and what is not, as well as which forms of 'illegality' can subsist and which must disappear.[50]

Through political mechanisms, the alternatives of expansion, consolidation, permanence or expulsion are constantly disputed and, occasionally, negotiated. However, the classification operated by planning and by land tenure systems goes beyond the territorial dimension. The expression 'We are illegals' – its semantic context linking the status of illegality to the very human condition of the inhabitants – indicates that, within the inhabitants' attitudes towards the national juridical system, it is as though the legality or otherwise of land occupation overrides all other social relations, even those that have nothing to do with land or housing.[51]

The construction of the territorial stigma is a fundamental element of the political machine that legitimises expulsion. However, alongside the state of permanent transience – a mark of the 'reserve' character of the land – and the territorial stigma, the construction of the hegemony of registered individual private property over all other forms of tenure is also clearly connected to the origin of large-scale dispossession. It is what I will analyse next.

10

Private Property, Contracts and the Globalised Language of Finance

But they [the poor] hold these resources [what the poor globally possess] in defective forms: houses built on land whose ownership rights are not adequately recorded, unincorporated businesses with undefined liability, industries located where financiers and investors cannot see them. Because the rights to these possessions are not adequately documented, these assets cannot readily be turned into capital, cannot be traded outside of narrow local circles where people know and trust each other, cannot be used as collateral for a loan and cannot be used as a share against an investment.

Hernando de Soto, *The Mystery of Capital*

In the last 250 years of the history of the social relationship between humanity and territory, a specific form of use and right over land – the individual private property – became hegemonic. This movement started with the enclosure of communal lands in Europe in the eighteenth century, through a process defined by Polanyi as 'territorial displacement' – or the separation of land and work. It advanced towards its juridical-political consecration with the construction of the liberal state. More recently, it has spread over the globe through the expansion of capitalist forms of production and consumption.[1]

According to Marx, 'if land were ... at everyone's free disposal, then a principal element for the formation of capital would be lacking ... The "production" of someone else's unpaid labour would thus become impossible and this would put an end to capitalist production altogether'.[2] When capitalism encounters situations in which the private ownership of land does not exist, it must take active steps towards its creation and, thus, guarantee the production of wage labour. The barrier raised between work and land is therefore socially necessary for the perpetuation of capitalism.

However, through creating a barrier against labour, capital also creates barriers against itself, as the landowner captures part of the produced income through the extraction of surplus value. If, on the one hand, land is liberated and transformed into an open field for capitalist operation, on the other hand, its 'enclosure' and transformation into merchandise introduces land rent and its exploiters as active agents within the process of competition. Marx defines this process as: 'rent, instead of binding man to Nature, merely bound the exploitation of the land to competition'.[3] According to Polanyi, 'To separate land from man and to organize society in such a way as to satisfy the requirements of a real-estate market was a vital part of the utopian concept of a market economy.'[4]

Private ownership of land and land appropriation through buying and selling in the market – the way land rent is extracted and the fundamental element of the capitalist accumulation regime – also have an essential political dimension. Still according to Polanyi, 'Such freedom in dealing with property, and especially property in land, formed an essential part of the Benthamite conception of individual liberty.'[5] As such, this freedom is also part of the corpus of liberal ideas that constituted the modern state in the eighteenth century. However, the freedom defended by liberals is negative freedom: freedom in the sense of not being hindered by a prohibition or obligated to perform a specific action. This meaning of freedom, formulated during the fight against monarchic despotism, coincides with Locke's conception of property – which includes life, freedom and estate – and establishes a homology between 'having rights', 'being an owner' and 'being free'.[6]

When freedom is understood in a negative form, an exclusivist vision of freedom is held: freedom is my sphere of action, in which others do not participate, and which is only limited by others' sphere of action. This is the modern definition of freedom: freedom as autonomy and, especially, as the exclusion of others from a personal sphere, the individual left in peace. Property becomes the guarantee of power over a quantity of things that excludes everyone else ... Nevertheless, these rights are not restricted to the free personal use of one's body and possessions; they extend to the human capacity – as a being endowed with reason – of giving away these rights through contract. Thus, they are capable of alienating not only their assets but also the product of their body's labour. This is the equality proclaimed by liberals: the equality of being a proprietor and of transferring properties through contract – an equality that each should have before the law. According to Norberto Bobbio, 'private law or the law of private individuals is the right derived from the state of nature, whose fundamental institutions are property and contract'.[7]

Given that, by this reasoning, freedom is dependent on private property, a government responsible for its citizens' freedom must guarantee private property as one of its fundamental obligations. At the same time, an attack against land ownership could raise considerable doubts concerning other forms of property – like that of the means of production, from which capital derives its own power and legitimacy. Therefore, the preservation (and promotion) of private property of land performs an ideological role, legitimising every other form of private property. This explains its mimesis with the full condition of citizenship.[8]

Therefore, according to liberal thinking, property, law and citizenship are interwoven. This underpins both policies for the promotion of homeownership (as seen in part one of this work), and programmes for the reform of land systems and for the registration of informal settlements – which were widely implemented on every continent since the 1980s, as central elements for the expansion of the capitalist model in its neoliberal phase.

According to this model, the characteristic of tenure systems based on registered individual property is their capacity to be investment vehicles capable of maximising its value and of cutting transaction costs. Klaus Deininger, a land policies expert highly respected by the World Bank, lists as follows the essential points for land management to fully permit the functioning of markets:

1) **Duration.** As one of the main effects of property rights is to increase incentives for investment, the duration for which such rights are awarded needs at least to match the time frame during which returns from possible investments may accrue.

2) **Modalities of Demarcation and Transfer.** Property rights to land should be defined in a way that makes them easy to identify and exchange at a cost that is low compared with the value of the underlying land.

3) **Enforcement Institutions.** The key advantage of formal, as compared with informal, property rights is that those holding formal rights can call on the power of the state to enforce their rights.[9]

Although the text is aimed at economic growth and poverty reduction, it is interesting to notice how secure tenure – understood as an essential element for the protection of human life and dignity – does not have any relevance. The focus is on economic growth, return on investments and transaction costs. Deininger's introduction spells out this position:

Property rights affect economic growth in a number of ways. First, secure property rights will increase the incentives of households and individuals to invest, and often will also provide them with better credit access, something that will not only help them make such investments, but will also provide an insurance substitute in the event of shocks ... Secure and well-defined land rights are key for households' asset ownership, productive development, and factor market functioning.

If property rights are poorly defined or cannot be enforced at low cost, individuals and entrepreneurs will be compelled to spend valuable resources on defending their land, thereby diverting effort from other purposes such as investment. Secure land tenure also facilitates the transfer of land at low cost through rentals and sales, improving the allocation of land while at the same time supporting the development of financial markets. Without secure rights, landowners are less willing to rent out their land, which may impede their ability and willingness to engage in non-agricultural employment or rural-urban migration. Poorly designed land market interventions and the regulation of such markets by large and often corrupt bureaucracies continue to hamper small enterprise start-ups and nonfarm economic development in many parts of the world. Such interventions not only limit access to land by the landless and poor in rural and urban areas of the developing world, but by discouraging renting out by landlords who are thus unable to make the most productive use of their land, they also reduce productivity and investment. High transaction costs in land markets either make it more difficult to provide credit or require costly development of collateral substitutes, both of which constrain development of the private sector.[10]

The relationship between tenure security and poverty reduction has been central since the launch of UN-Habitat's Global Campaign for Secure Tenure in 1999. 'Tenure security' was one of the elements proposed by the agency in the first version of the Millennium Development Goals in 2000, before disappearing from the adopted indicators.

The origin of the Millennium Development Goals dates back to the World Summit for Social Development in 1995, with extensive participation of NGOs and activists from all over the World. In 1996, donating countries from OECD's Development Assistance Committee (DAC) adopted a series of international development goals. Since that date, OECD countries, as well as international financial institutions, began to exert an influence over the Millennium Development Goals, particularly after the publication of the documents *Shaping the 21st Century*, by OECD, and *A Better World for All*, by the World Bank. The final list of Millennium Development Goals, adopted in 2001, did not include security of tenure; the topic was inserted into a broader context linking the 'fight against poverty' with 'economic growth'.[11]

Ever since then, the idea of defending the security of tenure of informal settlements – a historical demand of social movements and housing activists – has been translated into land reforms, registration programmes and even by settlement-eradication policies – under the motto 'Cities Without Slums', which has somehow become a synthesis of the goals, as we will see.

Long before the adoption of the Millennium Development Goals, the World Bank and regional banks from various cooperation agencies – particularly from Australia, Germany, Norway, Sweden and the United States – were already sponsoring programmes of land reform, registration and titling around the world. When a Labour government was elected in Great Britain in 1997, the British cooperation agency (Department for International Development) also launched a strategic document outlining action for poverty reduction and economic growth, and beginning to finance these initiatives.[12]

The debate around the effect of land titling on poverty reduction gained huge prominence with the publication of Hernando de Soto's 2000 book *The Mystery of Capital*. The author proposes a direct correlation between private land property and Western wealth, and argues that the persistence of poverty in poor and middle-income countries springs from their 'underdeveloped' regimes of property. According to de Soto, poor people own assets, but use them in a 'defective' way, making them 'dead capital'. What de Soto means by this is that, without formal property titles, their assets cannot be used as collateral for loans to be invested into business and entrepreneurship. Titling their lands may 'awaken' this dead capital, thus giving the poorest access to capital in order to improve their homes, start businesses and eventually leave poverty behind.[13]

Not by chance, de Soto and his ideas proved immensely popular within US and UK circles. Not by chance, either, did Bill Clinton declare to *The Observer*, in 2009, that he considered de Soto the 'world's greatest living economist'; other admirers included George Bush, Vladimir Putin and Margaret Thatcher.[14] In times of globalisation and financialisation, his theory positing a link between private property and the fight against poverty seemed like capitalism's 'philosopher's stone'. He seemed to have found the answer to the looming question: how can the financialisation of land and housing be extended to territories organised by tenure arrangements different from the 'universal' language of registered freehold?

Pedro Abramo examines the logic and nature of contracts that regulate the – mercantile – relationships within so-called informal settlements, and points to the limits of the formal market's pene-tration into these territories. According to him,

> the informal land market exists outside the framework of rights, but must have a particular institutional structure. It must guaran-tee the temporal replication of the mercantile informal practices of buying, selling and renting land and/or real estate ... These practices guarantee, in intertemporal and intergenerational terms, the contracts of implicit nature established within the market's informal transactions.
>
> In the case of the informal land market – where there are irreg-ularities (informality) in terms of both titling and urban and construction norms – the contracts of purchase, sale and rent are not protected by law, as their objects would be considered irreg-ular in terms of regulatory rights. This means that conflicts cannot be solved by instruments of legal mediation and law enforcement ... When the law does not guarantee market contractual relationships, other forms of guarantee must develop in order to re-establish a relationship of trust between the involved parties ... Otherwise, the mercantile relationship of exchange will not be accomplished due to the mutual mistrust around a potential unilateral rupture of the informal contract. In other words, without formal institutions, the informal land market must establish its own regulatory bodies, including coer-cive mechanisms in the case of unilateral contractual rupture by one of the parties ... In the case of the informal urban land market, an important base that guarantees the functioning of the market and its contractual chain is the relationship of trust and loyalty that both parties establish between themselves; therefore, buyers and sellers – as well as landlords and tenants – equally place trust upon the other, based on the expectance of reciprocity, which comes from a relationship of loyalty between the parties. The base of this informal market institution has no legal content, but depends on the enduring stability of a particular form of

social interdiction: the form trust-loyalty. This relationship of interpersonal reciprocity defines many social relations. However, in the case of mercantile relationships, it was excluded by the market's characteristic of promoting a contractual encounter between anonymous parties.

In the case of the informal and affordable land market, in which the relationship of reciprocity-trust-loyalty is one of the foundations for the potential existence of an informal mercantile exchange, it is necessary to personalise the contractual relationships.

This personalisation may not be completely transparent and may assume an opaque character. However, the personalisation – that meaning, someone sold or rented out and someone bought or rented – introduces the possibility of the relationship of trust-loyalty within the constitution of a contractual relationship. This relationship, by definition, is implicit (informal), and is not insured by the rights that regulate economic contracts. Therefore, in the informal land market, it is precisely the elimination of impersonality and the personalisation of the contractual relationship that guarantees the mechanism of trust and loyalty that supports a buy-sell agreement or an informal rent.[15]

Both land reform and land titling have been used as powerful mechanisms to eliminate ways of relating to land and housing that, for one reason or another, are not regulated by the impersonality and anonymity of contractual encounters. The previously mentioned bibliographic revision from Durand-Lasserve, Fernandes, Rakodi and Payne identified examples of land titling programmes in thirty-five countries. They also found more than 200 documents related to these programmes, all formulated within national governments or multilateral organisations. The majority of these programmes and projects are designed to create or modernise land registers, or to develop administrative institutions that can deal with land regularisation and titling.[16]

The list of land titling programmes and projects is certainly longer. At the World Bank alone, between 1995 and 2014, there were more than forty projects related to land regularisation, titling and real-estate registration. They were implemented in urban Latin America (mainly Peru and Central American countries), former socialist countries in Central Asia, the Balkans and Southeast Asian countries such as Thailand, the Philippines, Sri Lanka and Pakistan.[17] It was also not by chance that these programmes appeared 'boxed' as components of Structural Adjustment Loans (SAL), later renamed Development Policy Loans (DPL), or within projects directed to reform, create or enforce financial systems and real-estate markets.

I will now examine one of the land reform programmes that I had the opportunity of getting to know in the Maldives. Overall, they show how the land reforms of the 1990s and 2000s were primarily designed to untie the knots that still bound certain portions of the territory to traditional or lower-income communities and their tenure arrangements. The outcome was free and safe circulation of land as an asset in the market – preferably the international market.

The Maldives

The Maldives are an archipelago composed of a chain of coral atolls with 1,192 islands covering an area of more than 90,000 square kilometres, stretching 820 kilometres in length. For more than 3,000 years, the islands were traditionally inhabited by fishermen and sailors and their families. Today, only 203 of the islands (59 per cent of the total land area) are inhabited by approximately 300,000 individuals. Ninety-six per cent of the islands are smaller than one square kilometre.[18]

The distinctive geography of the Maldives plays an important role in political, economic and social issues. Around one-third of the population of the Maldives is concentrated in Malé. The remainder is dispersed among the islands, of which only three, aside from Malé, have a population greater than 5,000. Seventy-four islands have a population of less than 500. Although there are still many uninhabited islands, some specificities of the archipelago's geography and its economic model contribute to a shortage of inhabitable land. The situation of the Maldivian national territory makes the country particularly vulnerable to global phenomena such as climate change and its consequences – including an increasing number of natural disasters and rising sea levels. About 80 per cent of the islands stand less than one metre above sea level.[19]

Moreover, tourism – currently responsible for more than 30 per cent of the Maldives' GDP and employment – has been encouraged through a model of leasing entire islands to 'all-inclusive' resorts.

In 2008, the Maldives Human Rights Commission estimated that 12,000 families had no home of their own. Around 85 per cent of Malé's families shared a small apartment with other families or lived in temporary or improvised spaces. In 60 per cent of the city's dwellings are found 2.5 or more persons per bedroom, which can be defined as overcrowding.[20] In 2006, according to the Population and Housing Census, the average number of people per bedroom in Malé was 3.1.

At the same time, a boom in rent prices had been shaping the capital's real-estate market. From March to June 2008, house prices rose by up to 10 per cent.[21] The exorbitant rents have left families – especially the poorest, who migrated from rural islands – with no choice but to live in overcrowded housing units. Some families in Malé and Villingili spend up to 80 per cent of their income on rent. This leads to extreme situations, such as more than fifteen people sharing one room. Similarly, migrant workers who cannot afford adequate housing are forced to live in cramped spaces with many other people. In 2009, the total number of migrant workers was 70,000.

The country has improved its social indicators since 1997, eradicating absolute poverty (less than US$1 *per capita* per day) in 2005. But, if we take having less than US$3 a day as the poverty line, 19 per cent of the population live below it. Add to this a high unemployment rate – 16.5 per cent in 2009, reaching 23.7 per cent among women.[22]

According to the traditional system of land allocation in the Maldives, all land is public, and a plot of land is the birthright of all Maldivian citizens. This system is no longer viable, due to several factors. First, demographic growth – resulting from the fall in infant mortality and the increase of life expectancy – leads to continuous division of the land, with families inheriting progressively smaller plots and houses. At the same time, migration and the concentration of inhabitants in Malé introduced renting as the predominant form of housing, putting even more pressure on the city's housing supply. Because of these issues, land and housing became central to the country's political agenda and the government proposed a new Land Law in 2002, which was approved in 2003.

This law introduces procedures for the governmental allocation and registration of land to individuals and companies. It also regulates the opportunities for current occupants to purchase land. Moreover, it introduces mortgages and the possibility of using land as collateral for loans. After the Land Law's promulgation in 2003, a consultant from the World Bank recommended various changes to it, such as the elimination of barriers for the establishment of a financial system for housing. These changes were intended to remove the remaining obstacles to banks' repossession of houses acquired through mortgage deals, in the event of default. They also aimed to regulate more precisely the individualisation of apartments and commercial spaces in multi-family buildings and business premises through the concepts of condominium and the ideal fraction size.[23]

The press release presenting the amended law described these measures as essential in order to tackle the housing deficit:

> President Mohamed Nasheed announced the reforms that will be proposed by the government on the legislation that regulates land and its transaction in Maldives ... The president said there were a number of reforms to existing land legislation and new legislation necessary to facilitate use of land as a transferable commercial property and to ease the shortage of land in the Maldives ... In his speech today, the president underscored that the severe shortage and resulting higher cost of land prevailed in the country not because of the limited amount of land, but because of impediments to its transaction.
>
> He said the government wants to change the way land transactions are done in the Maldives to facilitate the use of land for commercial ends, as a commercially transferable asset.

The president said attaining national development and
economic growth would not be possible without freeing land
from unnecessary legal and procedural encumbrances and allowing commercial transactions of land.[24]

In the president's announcement, the 'thesis' explaining land
shortage and high rental prices is clearly laid out: land is expensive and inaccessible because of the existing limits to its free
circulation as a merchandise and financial asset. The same 'thesis'
is no less clear in an IMF report published in 2005, in response to
the Maldives' application for emergency financial aid after the
tsunami. Under the heading 'Recent Economic Development',
reforms to the financial system (including its opening to international capital flows), and land reforms introducing systems of
individual property and mortgages, are praised as positive
elements in the 'homework' the Maldives were expected to do on
the road to economic liberalisation.[25]

Nonetheless, a 2014 report from the US State Department,
analysing the economic potential of investment in the Maldives,
offers an alternative perspective. It appreciates that the mentioned
reforms imply important advances towards the consolidation of a
system of registered individual property. However, it considers that

> there is little private ownership of land, and foreign investors
> cannot own land. The Nasheed Administration drafted new legis-
> lation on land reform that could result in more trade and private
> ownership of property, but the bill is pending in Parliament.[26]

The direction of the proposed reforms – towards the provision of
land for the financialisation of real-estate markets – will certainly
increase the supply of particular kinds of products, attracting
more foreign investment. But lower-income Maldivians, unemployed people and migrant workers – the categories today
enduring the worst housing conditions – are unlikely to be benefited by the reforms. The access to land and housing for all,
regardless of social class or income, is a positive aspect of the
traditional Maldivian land allocation system – at least for
Maldivians themselves. However, this is being jettisoned without

the proposal of any substitute measure to protect the universal right to housing in the country.

The case of the Maldives, like that of Indonesia, shows how programmes of land reform which, in principle, aim to increment tenure security to the current occupants, promote economic development and fight poverty may, in fact, betray these promises. Under the aegis of a single market and the model of asset liberalisation, the conditions of access to land and housing for the poorest and most vulnerable people may be weakened instead of strengthened.

Following up this line of thought, I will now present the debate about large-scale titling policies and their effects, already well assessed worldwide.

The Mystery of Titling (and Privatisation): Who Benefits from Registered Titles?

The debate about large-scale titling policies and their effects on poor people has already produced hundreds of studies and papers around the world, including position re-evaluations from agencies promoting this strategy, such as USAID and the World Bank. We will not reproduce this whole debate.

However, it is worth summing up at least some of the 'findings' from studies that question and relativise the basic presuppositions of the utopic notion of 'capitalism for all'. This idea is based on the transformation of all bonds with land and housing into one, that of registered private property. Magical thinking about property consists in the notion that, once poor people have their land titled, the market will take care of the rest. That is, the market will provide infrastructure and services to all, offer formal credit and automatically regulate the real-estate market – which will be inflated by the entry of these new assets and clients. By this means, all families will obtain their own home and, moreover, will make money from its potential mortgage.[27] This utopia extends to rural land titling: thanks to land titles, owners will have access to agricultural credit and, through investing in mechanisation, seeds and other inputs, they will be able to increase their profits. Over the last decade, tens of studies and papers have questioned these assumptions. Here are their main arguments:[28]

1. Lack of evidence about the economic results of titling programmes

Given the intellectual and financial investments made to date in programmes for the regularisation of informal settlements based on land titling, there is a surprising dearth of independent evidence to support or challenge the application of land titling as the most appropriate policy option to promote social and economic development and reduce urban poverty. This lack of evidence is noted in the synthesis report prepared by the Land Tenure Center (LTC) for land reforms undertaken by USAID, a leading advocate of land titling programmes, when it states that

> these findings are minimal with regard to the extent that projects achieved their objectives and targets, and non-existent with regard to their long-term impact on land market development and socio-economic development. The paucity of findings is due both to the lack of project documentation, particularly end-of-project reports and final evaluations, and to the quality of information provided in the reports that were available. The lack of post-project impact evaluation studies made it impossible to determine long-term impacts.[29]

At the same time, within the rural world, and especially in Africa, it has been demonstrated that land registration had insignificant or no impact on rural investment or on its inhabitants' income.[30] Evaluations of the formalisation and registration of rural lands in former socialist countries also question if the sequence 'land reform, titling, registration, emergence of land markets, consolidation, agricultural growth and efficiency increase' did apply in every country, showing very distinct results within the different contexts in which the registration policy was uniformly applied.[31]

2. Do poor residents of informal settlements start to access credit in banks?

Studies undertaken in Peru – one of the first large-scale titling experiments *à la* de Soto, as well as in Colombia, Turkey, Mexico and South Africa – demonstrated that the presence of titles had little impact on poor people's access to formal credit. The arguments involve not only the maintenance of barriers that impede this access; they also question poor people's interest in obtaining official credit, given its implications. It requires the debtor's submission to regular payments and other conditions largely foreign to the economic strategies of lower-income groups.[32] In Mexico, for example, settlement residents avoid formal credit, preferring arrangements with relatives and friends. Borrowing money from a bank or government agency means losing flexibility, which is one of the key incentives for people to choose to live in this kind of settlement. Residents compare the payment of formal loans with monthly rent payments.[33]

3. Does formal property registration increase tenure security?

The literature on informal settlements has already pointed out that secure tenure is not necessarily related to the existence of a formal registered title. Rather, it is related to the perception, political, cultural and social, of the possibility of permanence.[34] In a study of informal settlements in Mexico, Ann Varley discusses the argument that legalisation is necessary in order to enable people to improve their housing conditions.[35] Without secure tenure provided by titling, residents would be foolish to invest in improvements to houses from which they could be later evicted. As one Mexico City *ejido* resident said in an interview with Varley: '"With the regularisation, we managed to construct [improve] the house – there is no security without title." However, he was the only person among the members of 150 interviewed families who made this explicit link.'[36]

In practical terms, the majority of residents justify their evaluation of tenure security in terms of official tolerance towards their settlements and the existence or otherwise of infrastructural improvements. Consequently, people improve their houses as and when they can pay for the work, regardless of whether they possess a formal land title.[37]

4. Do titling programmes improve the quality of life within the settlements?

Recent studies have cast doubt on the urban and socio-economic sustainability of settlements already legalised in Mexico, Peru, El Salvador and other countries that promoted titling and registration programmes.[38] Because these were limited to estate registration and were not followed by investment in infrastructure and services or by administrative and environmental regularisation, they failed to achieve the socio-spatial integration of these places into the cities.

The interest aroused by de Soto and the subsequent debate produced signs of a rethink at the heart of the international community. For example, Buckley and Kalarickal affirm that the previous consensus on this issue has changed, becoming more nuanced, as the majority of analysts and policy managers stopped simply assuming that formalisation necessarily increases tenure security and leads to collateralised lending.[39] In the same document, Buckley and Kalarickal also affirm that 'it would be dangerous to promote formal titling programmes as the sole solution necessary to solve the problems of the urban poor as some have suggested.'[40] In 2003, Klaus Deininger proposed a sort of auto-critical revision of the policy, admitting that:

> It is now widely realized that the almost exclusive focus on formal title in the 1975 paper was inappropriate, and that much greater attention to the legality and legitimacy of existing institutional arrangements will be required. Indeed, issues of governance, conflict resolution, and corruption, which were hardly recognised in the 1975 paper, are among the key reasons why land is coming to the forefront of the discussion in many countries. While there are more opportunities for win-win solutions than may often be recognised, dealing with efficiency will not automatically also resolve all equity issues.[41]

Buckley and Kalarickal also suggest that titling does not necessarily boost the assets of the poor, affirming that 'while there are good reasons to agree with the idea that improving property rights should be an essential part of the reform, there is also a range of practical problems that potentially reduce these seemingly large gains'.[42] Among these problems, they list the following:

- Titling is often a costly process. It is not just a matter of formalising informal arrangements that already exist. Very often, contradictory claims of ownership succeed the announcements of titling programmes.
- Much of the land on which informal houses are built is obtained through illegal squatting on private property, and compensation is not paid to existing owners.
- The broader web of societal contracts and constraints, as well as a wide variety of political economy issues, may well reduce the value given to property titles in isolation.
- A title is less valuable if it cannot be used as collateral. Such a result occurs whenever there is no effective formal financial system, as is the case in many developing countries.
- The anthropological perspective on tenure – that is, a continuum of tenure categories with different levels of security of tenure – applies. Across this spectrum, some may value titles much more strongly than others.[43]

There were numerous critiques of the single model of individual private property for registration and titling programmes. The Global Land Tool Network (GLTN) – a partnership between UN-Habitat and other multilateral and bilateral institutions engaged in the development of instruments for land reform programmes, with the objective of fighting poverty and increasing tenure security – proposed the concept of a 'continuum of tenure categories'. The suggestion was approved by the UN-Habitat Council in 2011. Although the word 'continuum' was intended to express the range and diversity of tenure, it is illustrated by a linear diagram: an arrow pointing from left (informal land rights) to right (formal land rights).[44] The continuum concept was rapidly adopted by circles within the World Bank and other cooperation agencies.[45]

However, the linear diagram has many implications. First, it places individual private property at the final point of the continuum (as the most formal and most secure form of tenure). This seems to suggest that registered individual private property is the ideal format, the ultimate goal, despite the fact that many other categories – in other tenure systems – also offer high levels of security, legality and legitimacy. Individual private property is not, as we have seen, an unequivocally guaranteed tenure, nor does it necessarily pave the way to economic development.

Moreover, by approaching the issue in terms of formal and informal rights, the continuum diagram reflects the binary thought that permeates the narrative about forms of tenure and bonds between people and the land they occupy: the dualities of statutory and consuetudinary tenure arrangements,[46] legal and illegal, formal and informal.

As previously noted, tenure categories are often partially formal, recognised or legal, generating legally obscure zones and combinations of legality, formality and extra-legality. The level of security offered by each of the tenure categories does not always correspond to formalist or legalist readings of the existent arrangements; on the contrary, it can vary according to the political and socioeconomic context.

The policy revision undertaken by the World Bank and organisations such as USAID is important, and directly related to pressures from both social movements and human rights organisations. However, it did not prompt clear changes in 'core' activities. Titling projects keep on being financed by the bank and other multilateral agencies, on grounds that it is the choice of national governments. Of course, changes in sectorial policies take time to reach operational and regional departments within an organisation as large as the World Bank. But it is important to point out that the critique of titling policies – expressed in 2003[47] – did not necessarily mean a retreat from the bank's economic-financial priorities. In 2006, an online discussion about property rights, organised by the World Bank's Private Sector Development (PSD) Department, posed the question: Can informal property titling programmes guarantee increase of companies' investments? From the answers, the Department concluded that while many developing countries had implemented titling programmes to ensure property rights, such programmes were often not sufficient to stimulate private sector growth. This was because these countries still offered little security for investors. Evidently, sectors of the World Bank, such as FIAS (Foreign Investment Advisory Service), are more concerned with the environment offered by countries to a foreign investment capable of stimulating the economy and using scarce land resources for 'more efficient' uses, than with solving problems related to the insecure tenure of the poorest.[48]

Even within the documents addressing the critical revision of titling and registration drives, issued by the Bank's 'experts', the evaluation is that these programmes' failure was not due to their unsuitability in transforming the land into collateral, but because there were insufficiencies:

> Nevertheless, in most developing countries, where the capital markets are undeveloped and a spectrum of ownership structures exists, titling alone will not 'unlock' capital. While such property rights may often be a necessary condition to develop a fully functional housing market, they are not a sufficient condition to unlock the trillions that are now locked up in dead assets.[49]

In the first part of this book, I set out to present several reforms of financial systems designed to develop housing markets, considering the existence of property rights as a necessary condition. Clearly, the policies of banks, multilateral and bilateral organisations can neither explain nor justify the widespread move around the world towards titling and registration of properties. In many countries, to grant titles to 'informally' settled people has not only been a response to pressures from these communities but also a way of preserving the model of territorial exclusion. We can only fully grasp the range of stakeholders involved in the matter of titling – including the potential winners and losers – by examining each situation individually.

However, this more global view – seen through the strategies of banks, multilateral and bilateral organisations – shows how a policy aiming to 'fight poverty' and combat 'insecurity of tenure of the poorest' also became a mechanism for increasing the exposure of the poorest to processes of dispossession. This happened because the policy affirmed the hegemony and the predominance of private property over all other forms of tenure and gave it preference in urban transformation processes. However, it is only possible to understand how this occurs in cities by examining the role that land – and land markets – play in the wider processes of urban transformation that have unfolded in previous decades, under the aegis of the same macroeconomic postulates. This is what we will examine next.

11

Insecure Tenure in the Era of Large Projects

Chengdu, China, 2013

Fu Liang parks his battered car in front of Golden Lakeshore, a set of luxurious villas whose sales room, decorated with chandeliers and velvet furniture, evokes the fantasy of aristocratic Tuscany. 'Here is where I used to live', he says. In 2010, after being threatened by militia and having received from the local government nine yuan per square metre of his small plot – where he kept a commercial fish-breeding tank – Fu Liang had to leave. The municipality quickly resold the plot to a real-estate development company for 640 yuan per square metre. After concluding their Tuscan fantasy project, the company will sell the villas for 6,900 yuan per square metre. Mr Fu Liang is now unemployed. He is one among tens of thousands of peasant farmers who once lived on the edges of Chengdu, Southwest China.[1]

Fu Liang's story can be repeated ad infinitum. It essentially reveals the 'saint' behind the Chinese urban miracle. The arrival of infrastructure and housing developments transform scrubby fields owned by small farmers into prosperous cities with gigantic towers. Those who visit the country and marvel at Chinese competence are probably unaware of the predominant form of financing municipal infrastructure expansion and local real-estate development. Public land is sold or leased to private real-estate development companies and to public–private partnerships (PPPs) with investors in infrastructure projects. The land is 'acquired' for much less than market value, through the expropriation of millions of farmers and urban residents. The collective farms and state lands had already been privatised in 1998, when land reforms granted property rights to their occupants for thirty years. According to a study carried out in seventeen Chinese provinces by the Landesa Rural Development Institute in 2011, the indemnities for rural land expropriations paid by the government to their owners were worth, on average, around 2 per cent of their market value. Public land expropriation has been the main source of municipal income, not only through its leasing to private investors, but also through its use as a collateral for loans. The sale and leasing of expropriated lands represented 26 per cent of total municipal budgets in 2010, according to the Ministry of Finance. In some cities, they accounted for 60 to 70 per cent of municipal income.[2]

This model can be further illustrated by the case of the construction of a ring road around Changsha, the capital of Hunan province. To build this high-speed motorway, the municipality used the Ring Road Corporation, a public–private joint venture listed on the Shanghai Stock Exchange, but whose equity is controlled by the Hunan local government. The city of Changsha transferred to the Ring Road Corporation the right to use and build on a strip of land measuring 200 metres to either side of the 33-kilometre motorway, totalling 3,300 hectares. To kick-start the project, half of the work was financed by the leasing of this land after it had been duly 'cleared' of its previous occupants. The other half was leveraged by the Ring Road Corporation through loans from China's Development Bank and commercial banks, using as security the anticipated value of the remaining land once it had been made accessible and valuable by the new infrastructure. In China, cities cannot acquire loans directly. Instead, they issue a 'comfort letter' to private banks, attesting that the public–private corporation will be able to pay their debt thanks to the future real-estate developments pledged by the city's planning authority.[3]

The same model is present in various urban infrastructure megaprojects, such as technological parks and prototypes of independent and self-governed cities in India. It frequently crops up in Bangalore, the region in which India's IT industry is concentrated. One example is the Bangalore–Mysore Infrastructure Corridor: the construction of a six-lane expressway connecting Bangalore and Mysore, the second most populated city of Karnataka. The project is operated by NICE (Nandi Infrastructure Corridor Enterprises), a trust of Indian and North American companies and investment funds. Spread over the 130km of the expressway, five new private towns will be built, each boasting a corporate centre, business park, shopping centre and museum of 'ecology and cultural patrimony' – to preserve the memory of a rural life that the project will have destroyed. After expropriating the farmers at rural land prices, the government leases the land to the trust for US$5 per acre. After twenty years, the expressway will be owned by the government, but the towns will remain private. In 2007, DLF – one of India's major real-estate development companies, which had recently concluded the country's then largest IPO – went into partnership with Dubai World, the investment and joint ventures arm of the UAE sovereign wealth fund. Together they won the bid to build and exploit one of the towns with an offer of US$15 billion. It was certainly not the highway that attracted the US and UAE investors, but the value 'unlocked' by the transformation of rural Karnataka into urban real-estate. Michael Goldman analyses the current urban transformation behind India's vaunted 'rising' as a global economic power, and designates Bangalore's urban policy 'speculative urbanism'.[4]

The scheme presented above demonstrates the new role of urban land within cities' financialised production. It is not only a question of market competition for location, or of permanent pressures in favour of a supposedly more profitable use of land. Rather, it is a new form of land agency, which combines private investment in infrastructure and real estate. This combination is promoted by corporations that bundle engineering with financial products and the management of building projects. Global investment in infrastructure has been the strategy of large sovereign wealth funds, such as the China Investment Corporation, Abu Dhabi Investment Authority and Dubai World, emulated by big pension funds.[5]

More recently, private investment funds increased their participation in this sector: in the third trimester of 2009 alone, more than US$7 billion of foreign investment migrated to India's newest speculative capital instrument – urban infrastructure funds. These funds are managed by Citigroup, Morgan Stanley, Goldman Sachs, Blackstone Group and D. E. Shaw: the very owners of the derivatives and hedge funds that sank the global economy in 2007–08.[6]

The cases of both China and Bangalore serve to proclaim the new logic of city production, particularly in terms of public infrastructure. This is composed of five elements:

- Given that local governments cannot run into debt, they appeal to 'innovative' mechanisms to finance the expansion of their infrastructure;
- Land is mobilised to leverage financing, as it ensures a future income flow;
- The investor's profit s the difference between what they paid for the land and the value that it can generate in the future;
- The necessity and the scale of the profit define the future use of the land and, thus, the content of the project;
- The fate of those who previously occupied the land is irrelevant in this model. It is the government's responsibility to deliver 'cleared' land.

We shall now examine each of these elements and their progressive transformation into cogs of the dispossession machine.

New Forms of Municipal Financing

Productive restructuring and fiscal adjustment eroded local economies and tax bases. Literature about the impact of neoliberalism on urban policies has identified the emergence of 'municipal entrepreneurship' as a response to this phenomenon. City governments abandoned the administrative view predominant in the 1960s in favour of a more 'entrepreneurial' action in the 1970s and 1980s.[7] The context in which they did so was highly complex. On one side, they faced: monetary chaos in the geo-economic environment; speculative movements of financial capital; multi-national corporations' global strategies for localisation; and intensification of the competition between localities. At the same time, the retraction of welfare-state regimes and intergovernmental transfers imposed limits on the financing of urban policies. On the other side, neoliberal programmes of deregulation, privatisation and reduction of public spending also impinged on local governments' agendas. Therefore, their urban policies became real-life laboratories. The experiments were many, including: city marketing; special zones for economic promotion; global megaprojects; and organisation of local corporations for urban development.[8]

So-called 'public–private partnerships' are among the most popular recent strategies for the management and promotion of urban development. They date back to the 1980s in North American cities, and quickly spread to the United Kingdom and Europe. They then started to feature on the agenda for technical capacity-building and knowledge dissemination pursued by the cooperation organisations' think tanks.

PPPs have been progressively mobilised in infrastructure modernisation projects directly linked to the competitiveness of urban systems. The justification is not only the shortage of resources to fund projects, but also local administrations' supposed lack of the technical know-how, agility, flexibility and management capacity required to implement very complex undertakings.[9]

In 1999, the World Bank created a specific advisory body – the Public–Private Infrastructure Advisory Facility (PPIAF) – financed by various donors, including USAID, European cooperation agencies, Japan, Australia and the Asian Development Bank. PPIAF's role was to 'provide technical assistance to governments in developing countries in support of the enabling environment conducive to private investment, including the necessary policies, laws, regulations, institutions, and government capacity. It also supports governments to develop specific infrastructure projects with private-sector participation.'[10]

The mobilisation of public land in order to finance infrastructure through PPPs is one of the pieces of 'capacity-building' provided by PPIAF. It is, in fact, one of the main suggested strategies for the promotion of urban development in developing countries. Katherine Sierra – World Bank vice president for sustainable development, the department covering the bank's urban sector – defined the advantages of this strategy as follows:

> Many cities in developing countries have underused public lands that would be more valuable if sold and converted into infra-structure assets ... As part of the overall financing mix, using land assets for infrastructure finance has several advantages. Most instruments of this type generate revenues upfront, making it easier to finance lumpy investment projects. Mobilizing finance from land transactions also generates price signals that increase the efficiency of urban land markets and help rationalize the urban development pattern.[11]

Despite all the talk of the fiscal crisis and the private sector's supe-rior capacity to attract capital, shoulder risks and introduce competitiveness and efficiency, the reality is that urban PPPs – which are generally undertaken for megaprojects of urban development – are, almost without exception, conducted and funded by the state. The risks are assumed by the taxpayer, who is also generally responsible for covering deficits when they occur.

According to Katherine Sierra's above-mentioned presentation, a beneficial side-effect of land mobilisation toward megaprojects is to 'signal' a more efficient and 'rational' allocation of urban land in the city. This would eliminate less lucrative forms of occu-pation, or forms under the control of social groups incapable of using land as a financial asset.

Public land, then, acquired through the state's power and administered by it, has a fundamental role. According to Deininger, once more in a document produced by the World Bank:

> The state, especially in developing countries, often lacks the capacity needed to manage land and bring it to its best use. Nevertheless, surprisingly large tracts of land continue to be under state ownership and management. In peri-urban areas, this can imply that unoccupied land of high potential lies idle while investment is held up by bureaucratic red-tape and

non-transparent processes of decision-making that can attract corruption. Experience demonstrates that transferring effective control of such land to the private sector could benefit local governments, increase investment, and improve equity. Where public land has been occupied by poor people in good faith for a long time and significant improvements have been made, such rights should be recognised and formalized at a nominal cost to avoid negative equity outcomes. In cases where valuable urban land owned and managed by the state lies unoccupied, auctioning it off to the highest bidder will be the option of choice, especially if the proceeds can be used to compensate original landowners or to provide land and services to the poor at the urban fringes at much lower cost.[12]

As already mentioned at the beginning of this section, the basis of speculative urbanism's success is the difference between the price paid for the occupants to 'liberate' their land and the land's expected future yield. So, the acquisition of public lands for as little as possible is crucial to this 'success'. In what way and through which mechanisms this happens in different countries will be the next focus of analysis.

Dispossession as a Strategy for Multiplying Value

The various ways of acquiring public land – as well as the juridical apparatus that sustains expropriation (or its absence) – are deeply dependent on the political relationship established between the expropriating state and the expropriated individuals or communities. In general, compulsory purchase or 'eminent domain' – the state's sovereign right to take private property for public use – are established within the laws and statutes that regulate the acquisition of public land.

In the cases of China and India – examined at the start of this chapter – we saw situations in which there was a clear asymmetry of power between those being expropriated and those promoting the project. The weakness of the former in negotiating for their lands results from a combination of elements: the urgent need for money – thus, vulnerability and propensity to accept lower compensation; ignorance concerning their rights; lack of access to specialised legal services; and clearly – in the Chinese case – authoritarianism, even the violence of paramilitary threats.

In the following examples, the main mechanisms emerge through which certain categories of landowners are 'weakened' and made into the easiest, most lucrative targets for dispossession. The forms through which indemnities are defined – as well as the reasons that can justify the deprivation of property – are the central elements of this mechanism.[13] Next, I will present a few concrete cases of expropriation processes and norms to demonstrate my point.

Indonesia

As seen in the previous chapter, parts of Indonesia's informal settlements are particularly exposed to forced eviction. They are located in the *tanah terlantar*, or public waste lands – for example under bridges, on riverbanks or alongside railways. The term appeared in 1998, during the economic recession. The 1997 Asian crisis had a heavy impact on Indonesia. At its height, the state allowed homeless people to settle in these places as a temporary solution to accommodate hundreds of unemployed from the industries that had gone bankrupt. *Tanah terlantar* would also include public lands assigned to development projects – for example, in Kemayoran, Jakarta's old airport (which closed in 1985), where residential towers, offices, golf courses and hotels from large international chains were mushrooming. Between 1998 and 1999, while waiting for investors to recover from the impact of the financial crisis, the government permitted several families to settle in certain parts of the area. A few years later (2004–05), the occupants were evicted without compensation.[14]

Some of these settlements are reasonably well-established, like other kampung – especially the oldest communities, on the banks of urban rivers and reservoirs. Those lining the Ciliwung River in Jakarta (with more than 200,000 inhabitants), the Strenkali River in Surabaya and the Code River in Yogyakarta are examples of settlements that have flourished for decades. But in 1993, national environment protection legislation defined the minimum distance between construction and the rivers as 15 metres, and these settlements started to find themselves in a position of 'illegality' ever since. When the 1997 financial crisis postponed the implementation of this rule, these and other settlements were able to remain. However, in 2007, the large floods that hit the country again transformed these communities into targets for expulsion, reinforcing their status as 'trespassers'. The distinction between these and other informal settlements is important. In the case of eviction, those kampung residents holding 'land certificates' are entitled to monetary compensation, alternative land or enrolment on *in situ* regularisation schemes. For riverbank residents, the only option is the *rusunawa* policy: low-cost rental apartments in high-rise buildings constructed by the government on the periphery of cities. There are not enough such apartments to meet the demand of hundreds of thousands of families.[15]

Therefore, this distinction has a direct impact on the eviction cost. In other words, it affects the price to be paid to 'clear' the informally occupied land and, eventually, transfer it to other uses. In the Indonesian case, although the need for eviction is consensual, there are different ideas within the government about the future use of the 'cleared' lands: on one side, some argue that they should become green spaces; on the other, the Ministry of Public Housing is intent on using part of these areas to promote their policy of large-scale house construction through market and mortgage credit. It is no coincidence that, in Indonesia's contemporary urban and housing policy, there is a convergence between the launch of titling programmes, the establishment of a policy of housing financialisation (through a secondary mortgage market and a line of mortgage credit called Liquidity Facility for Housing Finance) and the criminalisation of the occupation of certain areas of cities.

The banks of the Code, in Yogyakarta, were defined by the country's planning laws as an area of preservation of hydric resources, and thus prohibited from residential purposes. The case of families living there is representative of the issue's complexity: in 2011, more than 53 per cent of them had lived there for more than twenty-five years – since before the definition of the area as *tanah terlantar*, and before the environmental legislation, both dating from the end of the 1990s. However, only 38 per cent held a certificate of land ownership; 9 per cent held a right to use the property; 12 per cent had the status of *magersari* (authorised to stay by Yogyakarta's sultan, who today is also the governor); and 41 per cent paid rent to occupy houses or bedrooms.[16]

In the mid-1980s, the architect, theologian and writer Romo Mangunwijava led a participatory project of community rehabilitation, opening public spaces and introducing sanitation and waste collection. Residents were involved through *gotong royong* (self-governance) alongside the participation of volunteer activists and students. The project won the Aga Khan Award for Architecture in 1992.[17]

The idea of consolidating a settlement like the Code River – which was seen as a viable possibility in the 1990s – is, today, submerged under the narrative of 'protection' of the environment and, thus, of human health. This transforms any attempt to resist into an act of irresponsibility. Today, the advances and retreats of eviction actions are permeated by the environmental protection theme, the risks associated with climate change and natural disasters.

Under these circumstances, perhaps no low-cost dispossession system is more eloquent than that of the Turkish programmes for the clearance of *gecekondus*.

Turkey

Gecekondu is what informal settlements are called in Istanbul, Izmir and other major Turkish cities. *Gecekondular* appeared in the mid-twentieth century, during the country's modernisation, as homes for the large population migrating from the fields to the cities to take up the new industrial employment opportunities. Although produced by their own residents, *gecekondu* neighbourhoods' relationship with the government was marked by tolerance, ambiguity, amnesty, consolidation propositions and, on many occasions, by titling programmes for residents. However, the picture has changed since 2003. The AKP government and President Recep Erdoğan restructured production, carried out urban adjustments and implemented neoliberal policies.[18]

In Istanbul – as in Izmir and other major cities – large urban restructuring projects have been under way. These projects motivated interventions in urban areas occupied by *gecekondular*, through wholesale eviction plans or *in situ* reconstruction of apartment blocks supplied by the formal market. Toki – the agency for the promotion of housing founded in 1984 that initiated these ventures – was radically restructured in the 2000s. It became the country's most powerful real-estate development agent, responsible not only for the administration of all public land, but also for managing the urban planning and zoning of these lands. Toki was also in charge of promoting real-estate development in these areas, either directly or through partnerships with private development companies.[19] Since 2003, the agency has produced 541,000 new apartments in 1,350 locations – more than half as replacements for *gecekondular* – and plans to produce 500,000 more before 2024.[20]

Toki's intervention in the settlements was 'eased' by legal measures decreed by the government: declarations of emergency and demarcation of land were made after the 1999 earthquake, with the use of decrees established since 1978. The government identified high-risk areas and, from 2007 on, ordered the demolition of buildings or their replacement with earthquake-resistant structures. In 2004, Turkey's Penal Code labelled the construction of informal settlements a crime, punishable by five years in prison. These measures contributed to the transformation of *gecekondu* neighbourhoods' role in the urban narrative: from a place for poor workers, into a place for spongers engaged in every kind of illegal activity, including terrorism.[21]

Formally, the expropriation procedure has numerous stages, from a first proposal for the building's evaluation by municipal functionaries, to an eventual legal process if no agreement can be reached between the authorities and the resident. Compensation can be taken in cash or used to part-finance an apartment with Toki's housing programme. In some cases, especially on the periphery of cities, the new homes built by the formal market under mortgage systems may be located in the same area as the demolished settlements. In other cases, involving prime locations, the only offer to *gecekondu* evictees is an apartment miles away. In fact, the expropriations have been conducted through case-by-case negotiations, under pressure from the closure or demolition of local public amenities, threats from functionaries in charge of the negotiation and other forms of duress. These methods aim to force residents to find a solution faster and in a more advantageous way – for Toki.[22]

The new policy towards *gecekondu* neighbourhoods underlines the role of the dispossession of informal settlements as a form of low-cost land acquisition for real-estate development projects through PPPs. It also flags up another dimension of land and housing financialisation, combining the ideas in this chapter with those set out in part one of this book. In the Turkish and Indonesian cases, it is not a question of 'displacing' the poor, but of simultaneously turning the territory they occupied into saleable assets and pushing them towards the new mortgage market. Not only do their lands become commodities, therefore, but their lives – with all that they involve – are turned into mortgaged lives.[23]

The Turkish case casts light on how risks associated with natural disasters – in this case, earthquakes – can be made to serve seemingly straightforward arguments that selectively define what should be demolished and what should remain; who should be displaced and who should not. A new law governing the Transformation of Areas under Disaster Risk was proposed by the government and approved by Parliament in 2012. It grants full powers to the central government to realise expropriations 'under an emergency regime' in buildings or neighbourhoods considered at risk, allowing demolitions without negotiation with the owners. This method had already been used by the 2006 Law for the Protection and Preservation of the Historic Patrimony, supplying the legal basis for the demolition of almost all the buildings in Sulukule. This historic neighbourhood of Istanbul, largely inhabited by Romani people before, was soon gentrified. Vulnerability to earthquakes was also mobilised here as an argument for mass demolitions and evictions, even if, according to experts, the risk was no greater than in any other part of the city.[24]

The theme of 'risk' associated to low-cost land acquisition and its transfer to more lucrative projects also characterises the experience of the reconstruction of cities in the wake of natural disasters, such as floods and earthquakes.

Post-Disaster Reconstruction and Dispossession Mechanisms

'Living in risk' was how Lúcio Kowarick defined the socio-economic, political and civil vulnerability of a huge number of poor people in cities in the Northern and Southern hemispheres.[25] From this concept, I borrow the idea that the many dimensions of precariousness multiply, making the most vulnerable, such as those living in poverty or with insecure tenure, more likely to live in disaster-prone areas; they are also at greater risk of displacement and loss of livelihood in the event of a disaster; and it is they who will recover with most difficulty.

As previously analysed, the space physically and socially occupied by these populations causes (or, at the same time, results from) discrimination. This compromises the ability of individuals and communities to protect themselves, and to recover, from disasters. The discrimination against communities in disaster-response contexts may not be immediately apparent. Indeed, the term 'natural disaster' conceals the social process that constructed the area at risk and that defined how, why and under what conditions it had been occupied.

Evidence of the above statement abounds. When Hurricane Katrina struck New Orleans in 2005, African Americans and poor people (the two categories overlapping to a large extent) bore the brunt of the devastation because, for the most part, they lived in the lower-lying, more flood-prone sections of the city. In addition, because large numbers of the metropolitan area's population were poor, they lacked the means to escape the flood.[26] The particular impacts and costs of the hurricane were therefore intimately linked to pre-existing social, economic and land-use patterns, directly related to housing and urban planning policies.

Post-Katrina responses by the federal and state governments were generally found wanting when it came to supporting lower-income renters — predominantly African American — and addressing the range of obstacles that prevented them from accessing affordable housing. Despite a federal programme of housing vouchers, in practice, families with rent vouchers had difficulty in finding places to rent. The reasons included: public and rental housing shortages (due to storm damage, but also to subsequent decisions to massively cull public housing); rent increases; discrimination by landlords; the slow pace of rental housing construction; and the decision by Gulf Coast states to direct the bulk of federal funds towards repairing homeowner units rather than rental ones. With very limited renting options, many families were de facto denied return to their city and former homes, resulting in a spike in homelessness.[27]

The destruction of much of New Orleans's housing stock by Hurricane Katrina was really seen as an opportunity to fundamentally alter the housing and urban characteristics of the city. It is noticeable that the city's four largest public housing projects (the so-called Big Four), that used to shelter predominantly Afro-American residents, were demolished to make way for requalification projects, designed for mixed-income communities among other uses. Even if in some cases there was probably no alternative, due to the gravity of structural damage to the buildings, the demolitions were framed as necessary for the recovery of the city and for health and safety reasons.[28] A problematic aspect of the new housing projects was that they contained far fewer public housing units in comparison to the amount available before Hurricane Katrina.[29] The demolition was a further impediment to the return of lower-income residents to New Orleans.[30]

In Honduras, in the wake of Hurricane Mitch in 1998, the disproportionately affected groups included poor women, peasants and indigenous people, many of whom had been living under insecure tenure conditions and in vulnerable areas exposed to strong winds, flooding and landslides.[31]

In the aftermath of the Pakistan floods of 2010, it was acknowledged that the poor and vulnerable bore the brunt of the catastrophe, having no assets or safety nets. Those displaced by the floods who lost all their possessions and means of subsistence consisted mostly of landless tenants and labourers, living in non- or semi-permanent housing.[32] Similar limitations appear in the post-disaster evaluations. While conditions pertaining to tenure and land ownership may be discussed and recognised as important in principle, in practice, they are seldom addressed by policies, strategies and sectorial priorities. For instance, in the disaster needs assessment carried out by international financial institutions and the government of Pakistan following the floods, the housing proposals made no mention of land ownership or tenure issues, but focused only on the techniques and costs of reconstruction. The assessment did not consider that for those who had been most significantly affected, the problem was not the roof, but the ground.

The earthquake in Haiti exacerbated and made visible a hitherto relatively invisible problem, namely, the dire conditions of the informal settlements in which the majority of the Port-au-Prince population lived. The settlements, like many others elsewhere, had arisen spontaneously and never been formally recognised by the authorities. They had little or no basic infrastructure or services. After the earthquake, many residents moved into camps – whether because their homes or neighbourhoods had been damaged or destroyed, or in order to be able to receive food or medical assistance, to take part in cash-for-work programmes, to save on rent (in the case of renters) or in the hope of receiving a house.

Sixteen months after the earthquake, there were still 634,000 people in over 1,000 camps. Observers noted that the camp populations were declining more slowly than in 2010, suggesting that people had nowhere else to go or had decided that, however precarious their situation in the camps, it was still better than where they came from.[33] The earthquake thus highlighted long-entrenched patterns of discrimination and neglect. Disasters elsewhere have had similar effects.

The response to disasters appears to differ greatly according to whether it addresses the situation of individual, formally registered property-owners or that of people with any other type of tenure arrangement.

It has been noted that in most housing reconstruction programmes, tenure documentation and legal proof of rights are prerequisites for establishing beneficiary eligibility, with the consequence of excluding the poorest and most vulnerable, including those residing in informal settlements with temporary or informal rights of tenure. In a number of countries, displaced renters and squatters often find themselves excluded from permanent housing schemes designed to replace the assets of homeowners. The same thing is replicated in post-disaster needs assessments.

The above examples show how discrimination, as much as vulnerability, is a key factor bearing upon disaster impact and response. Discrimination based on tenure status highlights a broader problem, namely the reluctance or inability of governments, international and national organisations alike to adequately recognise and protect all forms of tenure equally.

It is often said that disasters, by creating a 'clean slate', offer precious opportunities for wholesale reform and ambitious redevelopment. Disasters do present opportunities, but also serious risks.

The 2004 Indian Ocean tsunami was seen by many as a major occasion for redevelopment, sometimes under the guise of public safety and disaster risk mitigation. In the aftermath, coastal zones where housing reconstruction was banned (buffer zones) were introduced by various countries affected by the tsunami; they ranged from 100 to 500 metres wide and, in some places, if implemented fully, would have required the relocation of over 100,000 houses.[34] The zones were purportedly declared to protect residents from future disasters. But they had major repercussions on the livelihoods of residents, especially those who relied on the sea for a living.

At the same time, ambitious plans for 'redevelopment' and luxury tourism emerged, including for those coastal areas closed off to residents for 'safety' reasons. Sri Lanka's tourism board announced at the time that the tsunami offered an opportunity to make of its country a 'world class tourism destination'.[35] It was reported that while displaced persons were forbidden from returning to their homes, the same prohibition did not apply to hotel complexes. In some places, land developers simply used the opportunity to grab land, especially from the most vulnerable communities. Luxury hotels sprang up in many coastal areas. Communities and civil-society organisations complained that the creation of buffer zones was used to arbitrarily evict poor coastal dwellers and indigenous communities, to the benefit of businesses and new tourism facilities.[36]

In Chile, following the earthquake and subsequent tsunami of February 2010, the private sector reportedly played a central role in the reconstruction of urban centres and coastal areas. Following one of the main principles of the national reconstruction plan, families could choose whether to rebuild their collapsed home on the same site or to acquire a previously existing or newly built house. However, as housing reconstruction was overwhelmingly supported by subsidies attached to individual property, private constructors preferred to rebuild housing in new areas on the outskirts of towns, rather than in the inner-city areas from which many people had been displaced, where land and house prices were much higher.

The above examples demonstrate that 'living in risk' – the condition of occupation by vulnerable populations of areas struck by disasters – can be quickly converted into an activation of new land reserves, under the pretext of 'rebuilding better'. This can be another one of the many mechanisms of dispossession.

Megaprojects, Mega-Events and Dispossession

As pointed out in the beginning of this section, it is the need for revenue from the financial capital invested in urban transformation projects that defines their content. Therefore, it is not a question of implementing urban transformations as tools for the strategies and plans of the cities' future development, based on and answering to their citizens' needs. It is, in fact, in the words of François Ascher, an 'ad hoc urbanism',[37] which privileges the negotiation over the rule and the contract over the law.

An abundance of literature on large projects and the transformation of modern urban planning in the neoliberal era has identified how essential such projects have been for the competitive repositioning of cities facing the economic transformations of post-Fordist capitalism.[38]

Nevertheless, more than reaffirming this role or bringing to light new cases for study, for the purposes of the present book it is more interesting to pose a question. Corporate towers, museums, cultural sites, luxury hotels and shopping centres become the object of these macro-projects, produced with a kind of *more-of-the-same-posing-as-a-unique-work* 'stamp'. But why these postmodern landscapes specifically? That is, what are the key elements of these operations that position them as new forms of production of built space and governance? What differentiates them from the ordinary real-estate development, valorisation and speculation that have always defined urban capitalist production?

Until now I have focused on dispossession procedures – or, in Harvey's words, procedures of 'accumulation through spoliation of the poorest's assets'.[39] I have also demonstrated the way in which land capturing became an essential mechanism for the expansion of finance capitalism. However, in the megaprojects, I will identify the 'umbilical cord that ties together accumulation by dispossession with the construction of the hegemony of finance capital, backed as ever, by state powers'.[40] Indeed, if megaprojects became one of the

> most visible and ubiquitous urban revitalization strategies pursued by city elites in search of economic growth and compet- itiveness, we also insist that it is exactly this sort of new urban policy that actively produces, enacts, embodies, and shapes the new political and economic regimes that are operative at local, regional, national, and global scales. These projects are the mate- rial expression of a developmental logic that views megaprojects and place-marketing as means for generating future growth and for waging a competitive struggle to attract investment capital. Urban projects of this kind are, therefore, not the mere result, response, or consequence of political and economic change chore- ographed elsewhere. On the contrary, we argue that such UDPs are the very catalysts of urban and political change, fuelling processes that are felt not only locally, but regionally, nationally, and internationally as well.[41]

Local studies of urban megaprojects in Italy and India have already demonstrated how their implementation was a 'lived' process of economic-political realignment for local stakeholders.

It was central for the restructuring of corporate capital, and for
the development of a new strategy of accumulation centred on the
mobilisation of land as a fictional asset.[42]

In advance of realisation, the megaprojects typically adopt
exceptional measures such as: freezing or flexibilising the traditional urban planning instruments; reshaping legal resolutions
and the responsibilities of institutional organisations; creating
agencies with special or exceptional powers of intervention and
decision-making; altering national and regional laws. Once tested,
many of these new forms of management become standard practices that gradually contaminate other territorial interventions
and policies.

The apparent justification for the adoption of these new forms
is based on the greater flexibility, efficiency and sense of opportunity that supposedly characterise the private sector in action. The
state, on the other hand, is seen as administratively paralysed and
politically colonised.

However, after observing the new types of arrangement between
public and private stakeholders, it becomes clear that

> Democratic imperatives, such as those around sustainability and
> employment rights, have been institutionally replaced and converted
> into contractual requirements on firms. This form of state-led
> privatization of the development process represents a new, and for
> some, potentially more effective mode of governance than those
> offered by traditional systems of regulation and management.[43]

Mike Raco backs up his argument by analysing the implementation of London's plan to host the 2012 Olympic Games. His
conclusions resonate with Carlos Vainer's formula, inspired by
Rio de Janeiro's preparations for the 2014 World Cup and the
2016 Olympic Games: the 'direct democracy of capital'.[44]

We seem to be facing a radicalisation of the transformation of
the city into an enterprise. This implies a change in the economic
circuits, with rent extraction playing a more active and dominant
role than production; but also a transformation of the political
model of government. Here, hegemony is constructed through the
contractual capture of public funds, via a system shielded from

social oversight by a set of regulatory procedures and management structures with massive participation from investors.[45]

On an Earth ruled into squares by the universal registration of property, it is the language of contracts that, allied with the morphology of real-estate products such as the 'corporate floor', the shopping centre and the postmodern cultural centre, allows the safe entry of international speculative capital.[46] It does not matter if we are in Dubai, Astana, Johannesburg, Mumbai or Rio de Janeiro: we speak the same language, we identify the same landscape, we step on the same floor, abstract, abstracted – and subtracted – from the territory lived and experienced by those who were there before. No *tuk-tuk* drivers navigating around cows, no mobile street vendors offering exotic food, no distinct ways of life: it is not by chance that dispossession is also a machine for the material and symbolic annihilation of lifestyles.

It is not by chance either that the preparation of cities to host mega sports events has been one of the most obvious fronts for this process. Above all because of the very nature of these events, capable of mobilising mass support, with the social cohesion and patriotism inherent in international sports competitions. Without this element, such support for megaprojects would be difficult to obtain.

It is during the period between the designation of the host city and the staging of the event that many of these transformations are accomplished. Displacements and forced evictions are common features of preparations for mega-events. The heightened demand for space to construct sports venues, accommodation and roads is channelled through urban redevelopment projects that often require the demolition of existing dwellings and the opening of space for new construction. The importance of forging a new international image for the city, as an integral part of its preparation for the Games, often entails the removal of signs of poverty and underdevelopment through re-urbanisation projects that prioritise the construction of a space composed of real-estate products that are easily identifiable and readable for the corporate world.

The city's historic agenda and needs – inscribed in its plans, rules and norms and in the daily struggle of its inhabitants for space and resources – give way to a project structured via a business model, superimposed on the territory through the suspension of existing norms and conflicts. This ensures the 'success' of the venture, in other words, assures the future revenue streams to be extracted by the investors at the term of the contractual deadlines.

When the areas designated for the projects are inhabited, their residents may face mass displacement, forced eviction and the demolition of their homes. These projects also tend to affect the residents of neighbourhoods near the hotels and stadiums, which may likewise receive 'beautification' and security enhancements: they are the scenery that decorates the projects' stages. They also constitute a protective belt, a transition between the project and the chaos and confusion of the rest of the city. Informal settlements and affordable housing projects are among the spaces considered aesthetically negative. Thus, if not removed, they may be disguised. During the Athens Olympic Games, for example, a housing project that resisted demolition was covered by a giant billboard that hid it from the road leading to the Olympic Stadium.[47]

In most cases, alternatives to evictions are not sufficiently explored, displacement is not preceded by consultation with the affected communities, and adequate compensation or alternative housing is not provided. In addition, evictions almost never allow the return of former dwellers to newly built homes. Indeed, owners, tenants and squatters are often pressured by public authorities or private developers to leave the area, their rights are seldom recognised, and they receive no guarantees of return to the redevelopment site. On many occasions, evictions are carried out in a climate of harassment and violence against the inhabitants. Time constraints are usually cited as the reason for disruptive or brutal evictions and disregard for the rights of affected communities.[48]

The situation in informal settlements is of particular concern in the run-up to mega-events. As a symbol of poverty and underdevelopment, such neighbourhoods are normally seen as ruining the image that a city seeks to project by staging the Games. Regarded as unsightly and lacking security of tenure, informal settlements are the first to be razed when a mega-event is to be held. Their precariousness in terms of urban planning, high population density and poverty are invoked to justify the eviction, and their insecure tenure enables this to be carried out at minimum cost.

The areas they once covered now become urban mobility infrastructure, sports venues, residential and hotel complexes, or simply a landscape cleansed of their presence. Local governments usually fail to adequately indemnify, let alone rehouse, the erstwhile residents of informal settlements. Entire communities are forced to relocate, generally dispersed to the outskirts of the city or to rural areas, where they find no means of subsistence and few employment opportunities, while being severed from communal ties.[49]

Examples of eviction due to urban interventions undertaken by host cities in preparation for a mega sports event:

- Seoul – 15 per cent of the population forcibly evicted and 48,000 buildings demolished in preparation for the 1988 Olympic Games;[50]
- Barcelona – 200 families evicted to make way for the construction of new city ring roads prior to the 1992 Olympic Games;[51]
- Beijing – nine projects related to venue construction, covering over one million square metres, involving relocation of residents; thirteen allegations of mass evictions, sometimes conducted by unidentified men, in the middle of the night and without prior warning, and with residents and housing activists often subject to repression, harassment and arbitrary detention;[52]
- New Delhi – 35,000 families evicted from public lands in preparation for the 2010 Commonwealth Games;[53]
- Cape Town – for N2 Gateway housing project involving the construction of rental housing for the 2010 World Cup, over 20,000 residents removed from the Joe Slovo informal settlement to impoverished areas at the edge of the city, with houses covered by metallic sheets dubbed 'microwaves'.[54]

Mass displacement in the run-up to a sports event may also result from indirect processes, such as gentrification and escalating housing costs. The sudden interest of real-estate investors in areas 'promoted' by the events in neighbourhoods previously considered of low market value raises property and rental prices. This has an impact on affordability for local residents, and often results in their de facto expulsion from the area. Tenants who lack the means to rent the new premises are forced to resettle elsewhere, and often receive no compensation, alternative housing or financial aid. In sum, gentrification and escalating prices have the effect of forcing out low-income communities in favour of middle- and upper-class residents. The community thus suffers a major change in its demographic composition.

Examples of displacement due to gentrification and escalating housing costs:

- Seoul – apartment prices increased by 20.4 per cent in the first eight months of 1988, and land prices soared by 27 per cent in 1988, the steepest rise since 1978;[55]
- Barcelona – the increase in house prices during the five-year period surrounding the Games was 131 per cent, while in the rest of the country prices increased by 83 per cent; in 1993, a year after the Olympics, house prices only rose by 2 per cent;[56]
- Atlanta – around 15,000 low-income residents were forced out of the city as the annual rent increase rose from 0.4 per cent in 1991 to 7.9 per cent in 1996, in preparation for the 1996 Olympic Games;
- Sydney – the increase in house prices during the five-year period before the Games was 50 per cent, while in the rest of the country prices increased by 39 per cent;[57]
- Beijing – around 1.5 million people were displaced from their homes to allow for urban renewal in the run-up to the 2008 Olympic Games;[58]
- London – property prices in the vicinity of the Olympic Park increased by 1.4 to 4.6 per cent as soon as the city won the bid, while in the rest of the city they were down by 0.2 per cent.[59]

The impact of redevelopment and beautification on housing accessibility and affordability is even greater when it affects neighbourhoods containing low-income dwellings and social housing. Given that many housing estates are state-owned – which spares the government from ordering expropriations – redevelopment projects tend to demolish them to open space for new developments. The availability of low-cost housing is sharply reduced, rendering low-income groups even more exposed to violations of their rights.

Examples of decreased availability of social housing:

- Atlanta – 1,200 social housing units designated for the poor were destroyed in preparation for the Olympic Games;[60]
- Sydney – reports suggest that around 6,000 people were made homeless in the run-up to the Olympics;[61]
- Vancouver – more than 1,400 low-income housing units were lost in connection to real-estate speculation generated by the 2010 Winter Olympic Games;[62]
- South Africa – the minister for housing noted that plans to build hundreds of thousands of new low-cost homes could be affected by shifting budget demands in the run-up to the 2010 World Cup;[63]
- London – the Clays Lane cooperative, a historic social housing complex on the Olympic Park site where around 400 people lived, was demolished. According to the London Development Agency, the site did not meet the government's Decent Homes Standard;[64]
- Tokyo – within the project of renovation and expansion of the sporting venues built for the 1964 Olympic Games, Tokyo 2020 requires the demolition of the housing constructed back then to resettle those who had been evicted to make way for the stadium.[65]

The situation of homeless people also deteriorates in the context of mega-events. Shortly before the events are staged, some local authorities take steps to remove homeless people from areas exposed to visitors. The homeless may be offered incentives to leave, but are more often subject to forced removal and relocation during the events. Specific legislation is introduced, criminalising acts such as sleeping in the street and begging. Similarly, street vendors and sex workers are targeted by laws that forbid them to carry out their activities in the city while the event is taking place. There are known cases of camps or large facilities being used to accommodate homeless people and other 'unsightly' groups for the duration.

Examples of the penalisation of the homeless and of certain activities due to the celebration of mega-events:

- Seoul – the 'beautification' measures prior to the 1988 Olympic Games included the detention of homeless people in facilities outside the city. In advance of the 2002 World Cup, local authorities created a list of places from which the homeless were banned;[66]
- Barcelona – homeless people were moved out of the city during the 1992 Olympic Games;[67]
- Atlanta – to wander the streets while of no fixed abode was declared an offence, for which 9,000 homeless people were indicted;[68]
- Vancouver – the city hired private security services in order to remove homeless people and anyone living in the streets of commercial zones.[69]

Despite the large number of evictees and the violation of rights in the urban restructuring procedures described above, the social cleansing during these mega-events, and during the implementation of large urban projects and post-disaster reconstruction processes, represents, in territorial and numerical terms, a drop in the ocean of precarious urban settlements around the world. It is rather a question of implanting enclaves inside cities, mapped out and governed by the international language of finance.

However, the importance of mega-events goes beyond their direct impact on the territory occupied by informal settlements. The narratives and practices established contribute to deconstruct the culture of rights that was constituted in those places, alongside the huge efforts to improve material and economic conditions over time by reinforcing the stigmatization of those territories.

All this amounts to a new form of governing urban space and politics, based on the contractual capture of public funds and implemented through a system shielded from social control and political intermediations. While 'experimenting' with this new form, the creation of privatised enclaves further weakens the capacity of the poorest to actively participate in the definition of the city's future, and complicates their struggle to hold their ground. In the cities where they are implanted, the enclaves confront

> the daily forms of subordinate contestation regarding the urban space, the daily fights of: street vendors to use the sidewalks and streets; people occupying empty buildings and spaces in order to live; subordinated people who insist in demanding and using all of the available space to build, live, inhabit, produce, commercialize. It is this 'free will' that the global agenda on governability strives to capture and utilize.[70]

In this sense, expulsions and evictions connected to large projects are only the violent and, therefore, most visible face of the current criminalisation and deepening stigmatisation of lower-income territories. Such procedures are intrinsic to the 'capitalisation' of those territories, understood as the capture of their economic, political and social logic by the logic of markets and finance.

As I have argued throughout this part of the book, land titling programmes are the most explicit form of incorporating these territories into the hegemonic forms of asset circulation, by permitting their direct inclusion into land markets. Nevertheless, subtler and more insidious forms, such as formal credit – in the shape of microcredit or the expansion of indebtedness – have also penetrated the everyday activities of these spaces, introducing so-called market skills and ultimately decapitalising some of the people who had benefited from the vast social, economic and political web that constitutes informal settlements.

The slogan 'Cities Without Slums', formulated in international cooperation circles and included in the Millennium Goals, encapsulates the statement above. The slogan reflects the emergence, within the liberal sphere, of the idea of 'ending poverty' through the promotion of inclusive, market-based growth – in other words, by the expansion of the market towards the poorest. The Millennium Development Goals express this new position – also known as 'bottom billion capitalism'.[71]

'Cities Without Slums' can carry a double meaning, understood both as an injunction to eradicate informal settlements around the world by means of evictions and resettlements, and as a proposal to 'include them' in the urban market through their regularisation and the formalisation of their economic activities. The history of this slogan lays bare the traps of a public policy that strives to combine an approach of social protection for the poor (the fight against poverty) with the idea of urban land as a financial asset, under the aegis of 'inclusive growth'.[72]

In 1999, the World Bank and UN-Habitat founded a new organisation, the Cities Alliance, with a mission to convince – and finance – governments to regularise and urbanise their informal settlements, as well as to integrate them into more general strategies of territorial planning (City Development Strategies). This initiative represented a response to one of the central points of the Habitat Agenda, drawn up by the Habitat II conference in Istanbul in 1996. Under pressure from popular movements and organisations, the Habitat Agenda called for security of tenure and the introduction of infrastructure and services for informal settlements. However, Cities Alliance was launched with the slogan 'Cities Without Slums', that appeared for the first time in the title of its inaugural publication: *Cities Alliance for Cities Without Slums: Action Plan for Moving Slum Upgrading to Scale*. In 2000, the UN General Assembly adopted Cities Alliance's objective of improving the lives of 100 million people who live in informal settlements before 2020, making it the 11th millennium development goal. The UN's adoption of a goal on informal settlements, and the mobilisation of the slogan 'Cities Without Slums' as the expression of this goal, turned the watchword 'cities without slums' into a guide for the conception of policies, projects and even legislation in many countries.[73]

The use of the word 'slum' is not naïve. It deliberately sets out to stigmatise the vast territories autonomously produced by poor people in cities and, hence, to justify their erasure. The warlike language usually employed is not naïve either: it aims to subdue territories structured under the logic of survival needs and resourcefulness in order to enable financial capital – the currency that circulates freely disembodied in any territory – to land peacefully on them.

This new form of colonisation operates via a dual system: through the occupation of the territory (by means of evictions and demolitions) and the replacement of previous ways of life; and through the daily process of constructing individuals who have entered the circuits of consumption and credit, boosting markets and global finances in both cultural and material terms.

PART III

12

Financialisation in the Tropics

May 2011, Rio de Janeiro

As I climb the steps at Morro da Providência, in Rio de Janeiro's port area, I am being followed by the eyes of the local residents, who are displayed on huge portraits pasted to their houses' walls. The work, by the acclaimed artist JR, was installed as a protest against the imminent demolition of these houses. Everyone who lives near the steps, the main access to the community for more than 100 years, will have to leave, giving way to a cable car leading to the top of the hill. There, more homes will be razed and the area will become a tourist panorama point. From up there, one has a privileged view of Porto Maravilha, the trade name of Rio de Janeiro's newest real-estate–financial complex.

As I climbed, the project was already under way under construction? through a public–private partnership (PPP), set to manage the area's services for the next fifteen years. Three-quarters of the area included in the project was originally public land, mostly old port facilities and warehouses. It was not yet possible to see the glass buildings, such as Porto Atlântico Business Square and Porto Maravilha Corporate offices. Nor could one espy the Trump Towers, which would be launched the following year, or the Museum of Tomorrow, designed by the Spanish celebrity architect, Santiago Calatrava, inaugurated during the 2016 Rio Olympic Games in the place of the old pier.

On the top of the hill, the atmosphere was one of tense apprehension. No one knew when, how or where they might go as a result of the new 'urbanisation' project. This was to be implemented by the same joint venture of contractor companies that had won the bid for Porto Maravilha, the project for renovating the port area at the base of Morro da Providência. This joint venture was the only bidder for the project, which had been designed by the consortium itself, and offered as a 'gift' to the recently elected mayor in 2013. The mayor decided to go ahead, obtaining quick approval from the city council.

For most people – especially those about to be evicted – a cable car was not the priority for the community, which had already received an upgrade less than ten years before, under the auspices of the Favela–Bairro (Slum to Neighbourhood) programme. However, as in every other favela that had been urbanised by the same programme, the municipality and the state government did not take over the management of the area. As a result, the waste was not collected, and there was no maintenance of the drainage system.

Instead, in April 2010, a Pacifying Police Unit (UPP) was set up in Morro da Providência. Launched by the state of Rio de Janeiro's government at the end of 2008, the Unit was part of a strategy to occupy and regain territories then under the control of narco-traffickers. The occupiers consisted of military police from the National Public Security Force (officers from other Brazilian states) and from Rio de Janeiro's police. With a UPP located inside the favela alongside a cable car project, Providência was on the frontline of the Rio Olímpico project – a package of works and urban interventions that were part of the city's preparations to host the 2014 World Cup and the 2016 Olympic Games.

As negotiations for the compulsory purchase of homes affected by the project were carried out with each resident individually, rumours shook the community. No one knew precisely what was going to happen. The affected families 'negotiated' their eviction with the city administration based on partial information and obscure proposals. The combination of the police occupation and a project defined and imposed from the outside, avoiding any meaningful dialogue with the community, were a reminder of similar historic cases that have afflicted Morro da Providência over its more than 100-year history.

This community was Brazil's first official favela, born when the Ministry of War permitted homeless veterans from the Canudos War (which ended in 1897) to settle there. Since then, police raids, threats of eviction, public investment, urbanisation and regularisation programmes have succeeded one another. The Porto Maravilha redevelopment project is essentially the latest chapter in a story marked by ambiguities, compromises, resistances, negotiations, porosities and conflicts.

On my way back down the steps, after walking around the community, my eye falls on a pathetic image: one of the people portrayed on the façades is a wheelchair user. The cable car is precisely the accessibility project that will expel him from the hill.

December 2013, São Paulo's south zone

On the banks of Rio Pinheiros, the landscape of office towers, shopping centres and luxury hotels announces twenty-first-century São Paulo's new 'business district'. Here, Mr Gerôncio takes me to see his apartment, one of the 252 that were built in a former favela: Jardim Edith. This community used to shelter almost 3,000 families in an area of 68,000 square metres situated between Marginal Pinheiros and Engenheiro Luís Carlos Berrini Avenues. The favela bordered the World Trade Centre, a real-estate complex developed by the WTC Association, the same developer behind the Twin Towers in New York City, destroyed in 2001. This venture includes an office tower, a five-star Meliá Hotel, a convention centre, an exhibition area, a helipad and an interior design shopping centre with 200 stores.[1] In 1996, the World Trade Centre was the newest of the developments launched in the area: most of them resulted from joint ventures, international investment funds, real-estate investment trusts or other forms of financial instruments that penetrated São Paulo's real-estate market in the 1990s.

Jardim Edith is inside the perimeter of the Operação Urbana Consorciada Água Espraiada, a PPP initiated in 1991 and modified in 2002. It was organised mainly to canalise the Água Espraiada stream and to open new avenues in the area, expanding the boundaries of São Paulo's corporate and high-income district. The funds to invest in those works were made available by the Operação Urbana through the selling of 'certificates for prospective construction' (Cepac). Jardim Edith was included in this project as one of the Zones of Special Social Interest (ZEIS), earmarked for social housing (HIS) for the displaced residents from local informal settlements. The inclusion of ZEIS Jardim Edith in the law that reviewed the PPP occurred after great pressure from the favela's residents, who occupied the city council and did not leave until the ZEIS areas were included in the project in December 2002.[2]

Jardim Edith was one of sixty-eight favelas occupying the banks of Água Espraiada stream ever since parts of the neighbourhood had been expropriated in the 1970s for the construction of the city's ring road. Up to the 1980s, the community experienced vigorous population growth.[3] Some of these favelas were removed in the beginning of the 1990s by a pool of real-estate companies which created a fund to financially support the municipal government's eviction programme. The alternatives offered to the residents were: a bus ticket back to their home town; a one-off sum of 1,500 reais per family (this amount was negotiable and could reach 11,000 reais, according to one former resident); a new apartment in Jaguaré or Jardim Educandário, on the border with the neighbouring town Taboão da Serra (and temporary accommodation until it was built), or an apartment in Cidade Tiradentes, an enormous spread of affordable housing complexes in the extreme east of the city.

Approximately 20 per cent of the evicted families were sent to housing projects situated ten, fifteen or more than thirty kilometres away from Jardim Edith. Other families accepted the cash offer and the 'free removals truck', and moved to other nearby favelas, or to *non edificandi* (building forbidden) areas near the biggest water reservoir located in the southern part of the city.[4] The first wave of evictions of the remaining families took place at the beginning of 2001, promoted by the Highway State Department (DER).

The inclusion, at the end of 2002, of the remaining favelas as ZEIS in the Law of Água Espraiada Urban Project was considered a great victory by the residents. However, Mr Gerôncio told me that the pressure for them to leave did not stop after that. Every time a family left, their shack was immediately brought down by

bulldozers that passed close to the remaining homes or 'acciden-
tally' hit a neighbouring wall. The rubble was left, degrading the
area and pressuring the families to 'quickly close the deal' and leave.

Finally, in 2008, a public civil action stopped the continuous
evictions, opening space for a judicial agreement with the city
government, who guaranteed the building of a social housing
complex in the same place.[5] In 2010, with additional intervention
from the Prosecutor's Office – which was also part of the Urban
Project Management Group – the city was ordered to start on
the construction of 252 apartments destined to accommodate the
remaining residents of Jardim Edith.

The scenes from Rio de Janeiro and São Paulo above portray the
encounter between the advance of the real-estate–financial complex
and already existing low-income territories. The sprawling, self-
built irregular settlements and favelas, where the majority of
workers and other urban poor live, were formed through a permanent process of conflicts and negotiations with the state, defining a
condition of permanent transience, a specific form of precarious
and exclusionary belonging to the city. However, these scenes
cannot by themselves make explicit the transformations that are
currently impacting on Brazilian cities. The country's experience in
this regard is just one part of the wider economic, political and
territorial changes befalling cities around the planet, under the
paradigm of neoliberalism and triumphant financialisation.

Since the end of the twentieth century and over the first decades
of the new millennium, Brazil has undergone a process of democratisation, buffeted by waves of economic recession and recovery.
It has seen in this period the rise to power – firstly locally and,
later, on the national level – of a coalition led by the Partido dos
Trabalhadores (PT, Workers' Party). This party is a political force
that emerged from trade-union struggles, social movements and
the reorganisation of left-wing groups throughout the 1980s and
1990s. Central to the PT's agenda was the construction of a
welfare state, universal access to adequate housing and the full
enjoyment of urban opportunities and amenities. On the other
hand, it was precisely during the same period that Brazil felt the
impact of both the hegemony of globalised capital and the

preponderance of the neoliberal agenda, especially in the domains of housing and urban policy. This moment was, thus, marked by ambiguities and contradictions.

After almost two decades of stagnation or recession (1980–98), Brazil embarked on a trajectory of economic growth. Between 1999 and 2009, the GDP grew at an annual rate of 3.27 per cent and employment increased by 2.29 per cent per year.[6] At the same time, the minimum wage had a nominal readjustment of 155 per cent and an increase in real terms of 73 per cent between January 2003 and March 2010.[7] After 2005 there was also a shift in economic policy, encouraging the expansion of internal consumption by roping larger portions of the Brazilian population into the formal market. Boosting consumption by the inclusion of lower-income sectors became the chief strategy for economic growth.[8]

In the realm of social policy, public measures toward the population living in extreme poverty attempted to lift them from their precarious levels of subsistence. This was done through conditional cash transfer programmes (Bolsa Família) and a set of social interventions intended to stimulate entrepreneurship and economic development opportunities.[9] The achievement in terms of work revenues, employment expansion, social security and social policy advances meant the number of poor people in Brazil dropped from 57 million in 2001 to 30 million in 2008 – or from 30 per cent to 15 per cent of the country's population.[10]

The average income per capita at the top of Brazilian income bands (the richest 10 per cent) grew, on average, by 1.6 per cent per year between 2003 and 2008. For the base of the pyramid (the poorest 10 per cent), the growth was of 9.1 per cent in the same period. This was due, initially, to real gains from the introduction of real increases in the minimum wage, which permitted an injection of 1 trillion reais into workers' income between 2003 and 2010. Another factor was the cash transfer programmes, directed to vulnerable sectors (elderly, unemployed and poor people, people with special needs, etc.) through social security and social assistance policies.[11] It is also worth noting that public banks and funds resumed providing credit and leveraged public and private investment through programmes such as PAC (Growth Acceleration Programme) and Minha Casa Minha Vida.

The former included large investments in logistics and energy infrastructure, sanitation and urbanisation of the favelas. The latter significantly increased public subsidies for the construction of residential units and the promotion of home ownership through access to credit. Finally, there were also incentives for specific economic sectors, such as automotive production and naval construction.[12] As a proportion of total GDP, credit grew from 24.2 per cent in 2002 to 45 per cent in 2009. The volume of resources invested in individuals' finance more than quadrupled between 2003 and 2009, with an important advance in housing finance, which grew from 25.7 billion reais in 2004 to 80 billion reais in 2009.[13]

The PT government therefore successfully put in practice an agenda of economic growth committed to combating poverty. It added to the market a population that was, until then, excluded from it, increasing the capacity of consumption through wage appreciation and expansion of credit for families.

In terms of urban policy, the 1980s and 1990s were marked by legal advances in the field of the right to housing and to the city. This was achieved as a result of intense mobilisation and open discussion within civil society, parties and government coalitions of the citizen's role in urban governance. The 'Urban Reform agenda' was able to insert a chapter on urban policy in the new Constitution of 1988, based on three pillars: the social function of cities and properties; the recognition of tenure rights and rights to the city for the millions living in the cities' favelas and self-built developments; and the direct incorporation of citizens into decision-making processes related to urban policies.[14]

The wider availability of subsidised housing credit provoked one of the largest-ever cycles of expansion of the real-estate sector in Brazilian cities.[15] At the same time, the decades-long great migratory flux from country to cities decreased.

On the other hand, many years of investments and consolidation of low-income territories (favelas, irregular settlements located at the urban peripheries, and housing complexes), made it impossible to define the urban development model solely by the duality of 'centre versus periphery'. On one hand, the self-built spaces formed during the years of great urban growth (1960–80) were nowadays equipped with water, electricity, public facilities and commercial spaces. On the other hand, a new, complex geography of poverty and social vulnerability defined the 'place of the poor' in cities. The 'poor' themselves were now a much more heterogeneous group than before.[16]

Nevertheless, 'periphery' and 'favela' remained strong urban and cultural categories. Despite the accumulated investments in these settlements, where basic infrastructure and social facilities were available they were still marked by precariousness, notably in the bad quality of public services. There remained, too, a persistent territorial stigma.

The period of economic growth challenged cities to improve their conditions of urbanisation in order to sustain this growth. The challenges were many. It was not merely a matter of expanding urban infrastructure to absorb future growth, although economic growth had indeed enabled the increase of public expenditure on housing and sanitation, while the constitutional City Statute (2001) promised decentralisation and the extension of the right to the city. And yet, despite these achievements and pledges, an urban crisis emerged. Why, despite so many hopes, did this happen?

Minha Casa Minha Vida and Housing Financialisation in Brazil

A residential market has been in place since the end of the 1920s in Rio de Janeiro and the end of the 1940s in São Paulo. However, it was after WWII that a specialised and professionalised real-estate development sector started to act as a true private residential market.[17] In particular, from the 1950s, real-estate developers could be either companies associated with banks, construction businesses held by families, or insurance and finance companies.[18] Nevertheless, in 1964, under the reforms launched by the military government immediately after their coup d'état, a public bank specialised in housing finance was created: the National Housing Bank (BNH). Financial instruments were also created, such as real-estate credit societies and real-estate credit bonds, making up a Housing Finance System (SFH).

In the same year legislation regulating real-estate residential development was enacted, to tweak a sector that had been running for over a decade. This law allowed the establishment of co-ops and the possibility of selling apartments, 'ideal fractions' of the buildings, which included the apartment itself and a share of the common areas.[19]

The launch of BNH resulted from a coalition of entrepreneurial interests, particularly those linked with the construction industry, which was politically close to the conservative UDN (National Democratic Union) party and its leader, Carlos Lacerda. This political proximity occurred through the Institute of Research and Social Studies (IPES), created in 1961 by private businessmen from US government donations. Its main objective was to formulate a political counteroffensive to the ascension of the left-wing President João Goulart.

Before the military coup and as part of his political campaign, according to Marcus de Mello, 'Lacerda had already announced a public commitment to create a National Bank for Social Housing, aiming to build millions of affordable housing units across the country, in order to transform every worker into a homeowner and to provide a place in the sun for the middle class'.[20] This position was reiterated by Sandra Cavalcanti, the BNH's first president: 'Homeownership turns a worker into a conservative person who defends the right to property.' Therefore she used a homeownership-based housing policy as a weapon against communist and progressive ideas in Brazil at the peak of the Cold War. However, 'it was this housing policy's economic role, dynamising the economy by generating jobs and strengthening the construction sector, that transformed it into one of the central elements of the strategy of the military government.'[21]

Therefore, since the creation of the BNH until today, a field of convergence – and, as we will see, of conflict – arose from the designation of a financial organisation as the *locus* of formulation and implementation of housing policies, and from the original ambition to make every Brazilian a homeowner. Firstly, this policy depends on and, at the same time, influences the country's monetary and fiscal strategies. Secondly, the policy is ideologically and politically fixated on the idea of combating 'housing deficit', that is, the notion that housing policy is basically the establishment of a certain number new 'private homes' to be built, which do not necessarily respond to the country's housing needs. Thirdly, the policy is an instrument to stimulate an industrial sector – the construction chain – that itself stimulates the financial sector. These three dimensions have had a greater or lesser prominence throughout SFH's history, depending on the level of influence of the various political interests surrounding the system. Its basic structure is still in force, despite the abolition of the BNH in 1986: housing policy is housing finance to support the building of new homes.

Under Sandra Cavalcanti's mandate, mass evictions were carried out in favelas, and housing complexes such as Vila Kennedy and Cidade de Deus were constructed by Cohab-GB (the Guanabara Public Housing Company), launched in 1962 by the state government with USAID financial support. The housing policy was part of the Alliance for Progress, the US programme of cooperation with Latin America launched by President Kennedy in 1961 aiming to promote development and block the spread of communism. Under Cavalcanti's administration and following the example of Cohab-GB, nineteen other Cohabs were created in the country between May 1964 and October 1965.[22]

In 1966 BNH was converted into a 'second-line' bank, as had happened to the North American Fannie Mae. With the increasing participation of private banking system representatives on the management board, it became one of the key financial instruments of the country's economy. In the same period, the government created the FGTS (Employee Indemnity Guarantee Fund), which was funded by compulsory monthly contributions from the employer on behalf of employees. FGTS functioned through the deposit of 8 per cent of the employee's salary into a private account under public management. From 1967 on, FGTS became the main funding source for BNH. The magnitude of FGTS resources lifted BNH into the position of being the country's second-largest banking institution before the end of the 1970s. To this day, FGTS is a major supplier of housing policy resources.[23]

From then on, most housing decisions were determined by the remuneration needs of the FGTS's fund, defining to whom, where, and how public funds would be available. This partially explains why, despite the BNH's claim to be an enabler of social housing, only 30 per cent of the 4.5 million housing credits conceded through BNH between 1970 and 1986 were directed to lower-income sectors.[24] It also explains the diversification of the bank's investments, as it started in the 1970s to finance large infra-structure projects and middle-class residential markets.[25]

However, it is for the political economy of housing that the existence of FGTS and its resources is most significant. In contrast to the voluntary resources of traditional savings accounts, FGTS creates compulsory savings for all registered workers, to comple-ment their retirement pensions and provide income in periods of unemployment. In that way, the workers' interests and claims for larger resources are entangled with measures that ensure the financial profitability of housing operations. There is more: as we will see further on, after 1989 the unions created during the democratic transition sat on FGTS's Administrative Council along-side representatives of employers and of the government. This picture is fundamental to understand the political intertwining of financial capital and the new union leadership, including Lula da Silva, in the 1990s and 2000s.

The role of BNH as promoter of 'affordable housing' was strengthened through the mid-1970s. This push resonated with World Bank policy and was enshrined in the economic policy established by Brazil's Second National Development Plan (II PND). II PND moved its focus from construction, automotive and consumer durable industries to those of capital goods and heavy construction.[26] In that period, Cohabs gained strength by building mass housing complexes on the fringes of major cities. For exam-ple, the José Bonifácio housing complex (Itaquera II and III) was built between 1978 and 1982. This was the largest complex produced by Cohab São Paulo: 19,600 units in a plot of more than 1 million constructed square metres, with an estimated popu-lation of 76,800 inhabitants in 1983.[27]

BNH collapsed in 1986.[28] This was not only because of economic reasons, such as the rising default rates due to recession. A more significant factor in the fall of BNH was the rupture of the coalition between corporate and political interests that had been coordinated for its creation. This rupture occurred within a wider context: the crisis of the dictatorial regime and its economic and political base. The end of the BNH system, as well as the period of economic recession and stagnation in the 1980s, signalled a retraction of real-estate activity and of housing finance.

This scenario only started to change in the mid-1990s, when reforms were implemented both in the model of housing credit regulation and in the structure and capital composition of companies involved in the residential real-estate market. In 1994, the government launched the Plano Real, aiming to control inflation. It introduced a new currency and promoted reforms to the financial system that included the opening of Brazil's market to foreign banks.

The opening of the banking system was part of a raft of measures proposed by international organisations such as the IMF and the World Bank, which exercised huge pressure on emergent countries in different ways. The theory was that the entrance of foreign banks would mean greater efficiency, modernising Brazil's banking system. At the same time, it would facilitate a larger influx of international capital. Indeed, after a cycle of mergers, acquisitions and privatisations, the participation of foreign banks in Brazil grew – though not to the point of imposing the denationalisation of the country's banking system, as was the case in Argentina, Chile and Mexico.[29]

The real-estate sector was an important target of the liberalising reforms undertaken in this period. The Brazilian Association of Mortgage and Savings (ABECIP), founded in 1968, expanded the influence of financial capital in the decision-making of BNH.[30] It also actively participated in the formulation of and negotiations over the creation of a Real-Estate Financial System on the model of the North American mortgage markets, which had been reformed in the 1970s.[31] From the 1990s on, this system introduced innovations to expand the participation of financial capital in the real-estate market, creating new financial products and constituting an environment suitable for the link between bonds and real-estate markets. Among the innovations, we may list the Certificado de Recebíveis Imobiliários – CRI [Mortgage-backed Securities]; the Fundos de Investimento Imobiliário – FII [Real

Estate Investment Funds, or REITs]; the establishment of new rules for mortgage securitisation companies; and the Fiduciary Regime, the essential tool for the establishment of chattel mortgages.[32]

This attempt to introduce a securitised mortgage market was not an immediate success in Brazil. It only gained momentum a few years later, after a first round of regulatory adjustments in the initial model, changes in the macroeconomic conditions and, above all, more public incentives through tax exemptions.[33] Nevertheless, Mortgage-Backed Securities (CRI) and the formation of Real-Estate Investment Funds FII) started to be used by commercial real-estate development companies involved with the promotion of corporate buildings and shopping centres, as we will see later.[34]

For the residential real-estate market, an important factor in the revitalisation of housing credit was the recuperation of the FGTS, due to the resumption of economic growth and the increased number of registered workers. Other regulatory measures were also responsible for this revitalisation on a new basis at the beginning of the 2000s, constituting the programmes that preceded Minha Casa Minha Vida.

Firstly, between 1995 and 1998, the individual credit bonds – *carta de crédito individual*, a programme of direct financing to the borrower, absorbed 76 per cent of FGTS resources within the SFH (Housing Finance System). In that way, the paradigm changed 'from a model centred on the financing of the production of new units and based on a network of public providers, to a model centred on financing the final borrower'.[35]

Subsequently, still under President Fernando Henrique Cardoso's administration, two programmes of social housing were launched, although smaller in scale. In one of them (Programa de Arrendamento Individual, PAR), private entrepreneurs were responsible for the whole project – from the purchase of land to the construction of the units, including the design of the project; local governments were responsible solely for the 'selection of the demand', while the federal government dealt with the direct and subsidised financing to the borrower through the Caixa Econômica Federal that had replaced the BNH. Through the Programa Social de Habitação (PSH), the second programme launched by President

Cardoso's government, the state auctioned regional subsidies, and minor banks acquired them to build houses in partnership with the municipalities. By the end of his second mandate, Cardoso was close to sealing an agreement with the World Bank to restructure Brazil's housing finance system along the lines of Mexico's.

However, in 2004, progress was halted when Lula's government adopted three new measures to expand housing credit and revitalise the housing sales circuit. With these changes, compulsory investment in housing derived from savings accounts went from less than 2 billion reais in 2002 to approximately 18 billion reais five years later. Finally, in 2005, a resolution from FGTS's Administrative Council allowed the expansion of subsidies supplied by the federal government and the doubling of the housing sector's budget for that year.[36] This was not yet a process of financialisation, as it did not involve the formation of a securitised mortgage market, nor an intense participation by financial trusts and institutions. But these were about to happen.

Since the 1990s, there had been sweeping changes in the real-estate sector, with mergers, acquisitions and the entrance of equity funds and asset management companies into the real-estate business. This intensified after the 1997–98 Asian crisis and the recovery of Latin America's economic growth.

GP Investments, for example, founded in 1993 by Jorge Lemann and his partners in Banco Garantia (an investment bank sold to Crédit Suisse in 1998), mobilised investors across the world to manage the capital and/or control fifty Latin American (mainly Brazilian) companies in real-estate, retail, logistics and telecommunications sectors. In 2005, GP brought into Gafisa (a real-estate developer incorporated by GP in 1997) one of the US's largest real-estate investment funds, Equity International Management, which acquired 32 per cent of Gafisa's capital.[37] The next year, led by GP and Equity, Gafisa made its IPO (Initial Public Offering), raising 927 million reais with the sale of 47 per cent of its stock.[38] In 2007, Gafisa raised 1,171 billion reais in a follow-on offering.[39] That same year, GP exited from Gafisa, realising a profit of approximately 6.5 times the invested capital.[40]

This process was repeated in the early 2000s by several developers and international funds. Developers sold part of the company to one or more investment funds, bought up competitors and launched IPOs. This is how the residential development sector was taken over by the financial sector.

The most explicit case of this type of arrangement was PDG (Poder de Garantir), created by a participating trust controlled by Banco Pactual's former partners in 2003, when the bank was sold to a Swiss bank. PDG progressively acquired real-estate developers and brokerages (Agra, Abyara, Klabin Segall), also bringing investment funds that had already entered into these companies, such as Enrique Bañuelos, Morgan Stanley Real Estate, Crédit Suisse and Polo Capital Management.[41] Some of those investment funds had previously participated in similar companies, like Equity International in Homex in Mexico, and brought their expertise, strategies and housing policy proposals to their new markets.

A significant proportion of the new capital was then injected into development companies and invested in land banks. In 2014, twenty-two companies were listed on São Paulo Stock and Futures Exchange (BM&F-Bovespa). Among them, nine concentrated 100 billion reais (US$37 billion) in land, which represents almost 620,000 square kilometres of urban land in various Brazilian cities. As we will see further on, this would have notable repercussions on the rise of land prices in the larger cities.[42] Giant development companies that had traditionally served the high-income residential segment now introduced new lines aimed at the 'lower middle class'.

In 2002, after three consecutive defeats, Lula finally won the presidential elections. Adopting a moderate political position, the former union leader was able to bring together the support of the historic political sectors that backed the PT in preceding contests alongside a new electorate. He obtained votes from sectors that were dissatisfied with the outcomes of the Social Democracy Party administration, and seduced by the soft reformism proposed by the PT.

If Lula's victory was full of symbolic meaning – a sense of historic triumph for workers, migrants, the poor and marginalised sectors of Brazilian society in general – it also corresponded to a widespread desire for change. It did not, however, signal the victory of an authentic left-wing political project. Rather it was a coalition of conflicting interests and purposes. Lula represented a wide and pluralistic coalition, embracing old rivals from conservative political parties, big business and other stakeholders that had stood against him in prior elections. The broadening of Lula's electorate was a response to his platform of cautious, gradual reforms, committed to the respect of market institutions and the maintenance of macroeconomic prudence.[43] His leadership, in turn, depended on pacts with conservative political parties that had joined the coalition out of expedience, resulting in a fragile political balance. In this political scenario, the actual margins for change remained very limited.[44]

One of the first initiatives taken by Lula's government was the institution of a new Ministry for Cities, a governmental board charged with formulating urban policy at the national level and providing financial and technical support for local governments. It brought together housing, sanitation and urban transportation – which had, since 1985, been spread across fourteen different ministries and secretariats. Initially run by PT members and social activists, this ministry signalled the recognition of the urban reform agenda as a political priority. Initiatives included participatory processes for policy formulation, such as councils and conferences, as well as self-management experiments for the production of housing, which gained in political scale and power among housing movements in São Paulo by the end of the PT's first term (1989–92).[45]

The government's housing policy had already been drafted during the campaign. Named Projeto Moradia (Project Housing), it was one of the pillars of development policy in a country that sought to balance social issues with economic growth and the generation of jobs.[46] For one year, Instituto Cidadania's team promoted numerous technical meetings, as well as seminars with social movements, corporate, technical and academic institutions, NGOs, unions and state sectors, in order to compile ideas and debate alternatives.

The project proposed the creation of a National Housing System that was to be supervised by the National Cities' Council and by similar bodies created at state and municipal level. They were responsible for managing funds, with a focus on subsidising housing for lower-income populations, financed by Brazil's General Budget (OGU) and FGTS.

In October 2003, the Ministry of Cities organised the first National Conference of Cities, with 2,500 delegates elected through a broad process of social mobilisation in more than 3,000 municipalities. The election of a National Housing Council resulted from this process, with 56 per cent of its representatives originating from civil society (social movements, construction industry union, professional and academic associations and NGOs) and 44 per cent coming from the government (at federal, state and municipal levels). Social movements occupied almost half of the seats allocated to civil society.[47] However, the housing policy's principal element continued to be SFH and its main funder to be FGTS, which remained subordinate to the Ministry of Finance.

In 2005, chivvied by social movements, President Lula inaugurated the Second National Conference of Cities by proclaiming his endorsement of the bill that had emerged from the people's initiative for the creation of the National Social Housing System (SNHIS), including a specific fund (FNHIS) and a council. The bill was approved. According to this law, all public resources earmarked for housing were part of SNHIS – including non-interest finances – and were to be subject to the housing plans to be formulated and approved in every municipality and state and at the national lever. Again, lower-income families were to be prioritised. Resources were to be assigned to the production of houses and urban plots, urbanisation of informal settlements, land regularisation, housing amelioration and the renovation and conversion of empty buildings into homes.

However, the implementation of SNHIS and the Ministry of Cities' urban reform agenda encountered resistance from part of the government's economic team. In addition, an internal political change in 2005 brought the fall of the minister and the resignation of a significant part of the ministerial team. After the outbreak of a big corruption scandal, dubbed the Mensalão, the government was forced to cede more space to its conservative allies in order to keep political support in Congress. As a result, the control of the

Ministry of Cities went to the right-wing Progressistas Party (PP).
In spite of the restructuring of the ministry, the Secretariat of
Housing remained under PT control, as well as the presidency of
Caixa Econômica Federal and its government vice-presidency,
tasked with running the SFH and implementing the government's
urban development programmes.

It was in this context that Dilma Rousseff, the minister of
mining and energy, assumed the position of chief of staff, the
government's top manager in effect, and politically in charge of
housing and urban infrastructure. At the same time the Ministry
of Finance changed staff and Guido Mantega, a developmental
economist from the PT's historic core and linked to the union
movements, was named minister. The government decided it was
a propitious time to focus on expanding working-class consumption, in hopes of establishing a 'new middle class'. The Minha
Casa Minha Vida programme (My House My Life) would be the
most important achievement of Dilma Rousseff's first mandate.[48]

Since the beginning of the 2000s, both housing credit and the
number of housing units produced by the market had been growing. In 2007, almost 550,000 units were financed by FGTS and
SBPE, and in mid-2008 the volume of loans reached 40 billion
reais.[49] Real-estate developers had accumulated large reserves of
land and, in that year, were poised to launch approximately 200,000
housing units.

When the subprime mortgage crisis broke in the US in 2007–
08, investors rushed to sell their stocks. By the end of 2008, land
was selling at a fraction of its value. It was a situation of international crisis with the risk of wholesale bankruptcy in the sector,
something that might contaminate the whole productive chain
and, ultimately, the Brazilian government's economic strategy. At
that moment, the affected construction and development companies, led by Gafisa and supported by the CBIC (the Brazilian
Chamber of Construction Industry), started to intensify their
lobbying of the Ministry of Finance in order to implement a 'housing package' inspired by the Mexican system – which had, in turn,
followed the Chilean model.

Through direct subsidies to buyers, the government facilitated
the purchase of the 200,000 units that the capitalised construction

companies were ready to launch in the market. Had it not been for the state's intervention, this operation would have been severely jeopardised by the crisis. The subsidies were given in the form of resources for final buyers and through easier access to mortgage credit, with the introduction of a loan guarantee fund. The 'package' was developed by the government in direct dialogue with the construction industry and investors concerned. It was originally devised to save the companies from the debacle and, at the same time, to work as a countercyclical measure furthering jobs and growth in an unfavourable international scenario.

Nevertheless, when the 'housing package' was presented to President Lula at the end of 2008, he 'politicised' its measures: instead of 200,000, he proposed the construction of 1 million houses, and increased the proportion earmarked for the lowest-income sectors, that would be subsidised 100 per cent. Governors and mayors were to be responsible for identifying the beneficiaries.

Around the end of 2008 and the beginning of 2009, social housing movements and the National Forum for Urban Reform organised several acts of protest. They were worried at the rumours of a housing policy created without their participation. The sit-ins and demonstrations in many states resulted in audiences with President Lula and his chief of staff, Dilma Rousseff, at the beginning of 2009, when the movements presented proposals to be included in the housing 'package'. The Minha Casa Minha Vida (MCMV) programme finally included the promise that a proportion of the '1 million houses' for construction would be self-managed by cooperatives formed by housing movement activists.

Initially, MCMV was designed to serve only metropolitan regions and cities with more than 100,000 inhabitants. However, during negotiations to get the relevant bill through Congress, the government agreed to extend MCMV to every municipality in the country. The programme was launched in a ceremony presided by Lula in March 2009. On that occasion, alongside the president, four more people spoke: a representative of state governors, a representative of the mayors, the president of CBIC and the president of Gafisa. In the audience, representatives of the social housing movements expressed such frustration at not being on the podium that, during the ceremony, they obtained the right to speak directly from President Lula.

Although crucial to ensure the programme's political support from social housing movements, cooperative and self-managed housing represented less than 1 per cent of the total units. More importantly MCMV offered different conditions for different income ranges, with different levels of subsidy. The first range (up to 1,600 reais in monthly household income) offers a highly subsidised product, built by private firms and 'distributed' by local governments. The beneficiaries were defined by local governments, based on their own level of demand. The takers were supposed to pay a monthly fee for twenty years, corresponding to 5 per cent of household income, with the aspiration of becoming homeowners at the end.[50] Caixa received the payments and was responsible for paying the construction company. The difference between the cost of the unit and the total amount paid by beneficiaries was covered by a public fund fed by the federal budget.

The second range (families with a monthly income of between 1,600 and 3,100 reais) also received subsidies, but to a lesser extent. When signing the contract, homebuyers in this category could access direct subsidies of up to 23,000 reais – around 20 per cent of the upper limit of a unit's price. They also benefitted from credit lines with interest set below market rates, and a guarantee extended by a public fund (FGHab). The third range only got cheaper credit and the guarantee from FGHab.

In the case of the second and third income brackets, private companies conducted the whole process of buying land, construction and marketing at their own risk. Caixa financed the production and subsidised those who wanted to buy the units, but the risks and responsibilities were assumed by private enterprise. In all cases, there was a price ceiling for the unit that had to be met in order for the housing project to be eligible for the subsidies and credit conditions: 76,000 reais for the first range, and up to 190,000 for the second.[51]

Immediately after the launch of the programme, real-estate developers recuperated the value of their shares on the bourse. Clearly, the real-estate sector and, especially, financialised developers and their investors greatly benefited from the programme, as it not only saved them from bankruptcy, but also hiked the value of their shares. After pocketing the profits, these large companies – the ones that launched the highest number of units during the first phase of MCMV – slowly left the programme in phase two, returning to more traditional market niches. In any case, propelled by the programme, housing credit went from 1.55 per cent of Brazil's GDP in 2006 to 3.48 per cent in 2010 and 6.73 per cent in 2013.[52]

MCMV's countercyclical effect on the civil construction industry was indisputable. According to data from the São Paulo Construction Companies Syndicate Review, this sector grew by 47.1 per cent between 2003 and 2013, while the country's GDP grew by 45.9 per cent in the same period. What is more, 2.23 million formal jobs were created. From 2010 on, some 1 million units financed by FGTS and SBPE have been launched per year, four times more than in 2003. The production of paint grew by 75 per cent and that of rebar by 72 per cent in the same period.[53]

However, it is not possible to understand the programme's success without closely observing its political dimensions. The centralisation of all financial resources gave a crucial role to the federal government in terms of housing policy,[54] and hence control of an important electoral capital. It was no coincidence that MCMV was launched in March 2009, eighteen months before the presidential elections. Besides mitigating the adverse political effects that an economic crisis could cast on the presidential succession, it served to strengthen the candidature of Dilma Rousseff – touted as the 'mother of Minha Casa Minha Vida', the anointed successor to Lula, who, according to the law, could not apply for re-election.

One of the programme's central devices was to overcome local government opposition. Party alignment was important in the implementation of federal government policies at a local level, generating political capital for their promoters. However, a novelty brought by MCMV was the chance to bypass the 'party' by delegating the management of housing ventures to private firms. MCMV transformed Caixa into an important actor at local level, being responsible for 'spreading' the programme and making it work as a crucial link between the parties involved – federal government, private firms, local governments and beneficiaries.[55] In that way, it reinforced the financing agent's role as the policy's main implementer.

There were electoral dividends from inaugurations of new MCMV housing complexes – always big political events, which conferred prestige on all the politicians involved.[56] They were attended not only by local executive and legislative leaders, but, often, by members of the federal executive and legislative powers. Thus, each housing unit delivered counted twice: the political capital that it generated served both the municipal and the federal government – as well as the deputies from the government's coalition.

Finally, although small in numbers, organised social movements obtained appreciable gains from MCMV: they could offer help and advice to their supporters, who were mainly families seeking a home.[57] While not participating de facto in housing policy decision-making processes, the movements were nonetheless included in debates over the share of the benefits. Making the most of their representation within councils, these groups became part of the mechanisms for controlling the distribution of the government's political assets, alongside party leaders and their support base.[58]

The ripples of MCMV's economic and political success can be seen in Dilma Rousseff's election in 2010 and re-election in 2014, after the launch of MCMV-2 (2011) and MCMV-3 (2014). According to the Ministry of Planning, in August 2014, the programme had already financed 3.5 million units and delivered approximately 1.7 million houses or apartments.[59] Thus, from a package designed to save financialised real-estate developers, MCMV grew to be the national housing policy, based solely on the model of promotion of homeownership through the market and mortgage credit. The unintended effect, however, was the end of the diversified housing policy, tailored to local needs, that social movements and urban reform activists had hoped for at the beginning of Lula's presidency and contained in the National Social Housing System (SNHIS).

The programme articulated specific patterns of coordination between public and private agents in Brazilian capitalism. If, on one hand, it was fashioned to incentivise private companies to engage in the production of housing for less affluent citizens, it remained on the other hand highly dependent on public resources, required to subsidise the acquisition of properties by low- and middle-income homebuyers. This ambivalent financial arrangement meant transferring the risks to public institutions while the eventual profits – generally amplified by indirect subsidies – went to the private sector, reiterating historical patterns of appropriation of public funds by private actors.[60]

A few years later, after the delivery of more than one million new private dwellings, collateral effects emerged. Decisions concerning the projects' location and design had been handed to private agents, and such decisions were inevitably driven by considerations of gain. Since the units' dimensions and ceiling price were pre-established, the entrepreneur's profit was based on cutting production costs. Savings were obtained through standardisation, large-scale reproduction of units, speedy approval and construction, and limited expenditure on land.[61] The result was a proliferation of indistinguishable mega housing complexes in the cities' peripheral locations.[62]

The standardisation of housing was closely related to the standardisation of the production process, which involved the uniformisation of measurements, materials, components and even forms of execution and management of the building site. This explains, for example, how a company was able to build 40,000 units in one year, following only three housing typologies in more than seventy Brazilian cities'.[63] The homogeneity of size and internal arrangement is not appropriate to families' different sizes and, above all, does not allow the flexibility to adapt to the families' changes. It is not possible to add *puxadinhos* (self-built extra rooms) to the houses so as to incorporate economic activities or to accommodate relatives.[64]

According to these construction companies, large-scale construction was a necessary condition for profitability: they argued that, with return rates of less than 15 per cent, projects for the first income range were only cost-effective at over 600 housing units. Such mass builds often had disastrous urban impacts.[65]

The issue of their location is, in turn, directly related to the effects that the growth of income and the vertiginous rise of credit availability had on land prices, mainly in big cities. Almost immediately, real-estate prices began to soar above inflation indexes, construction costs and income rise.

Given the prevalent urbanisation pattern of Brazilian cities, in which jobs, services, and economic and cultural opportunities are concentrated in pockets of middle- to high-income areas, these places experienced a price boom. Among the programme's housing complexes, those earmarked for the third income range lie closest to the cities' central and better equipped areas, while those for the first income range are relegated to the perimeters. These large-scale ventures were produced on great tracts at the fringes of cities, bleak places lacking proper infrastructure, commercial spaces, public facilities, even public transportation.

Housing policy has historically performed a key role in the consolidation of the urban model of these metropolitan regions, notably in their reproduction of socio-spatial patterns of segregation. The construction of large housing complexes in outlying areas where land is cheaper substantially contributed to urban sprawl, and the entrenchment of the territorial cleavage between rich and poor. As a result, despite the many billions of reais in public subsidies, MCMV did nothing to lessen urban segregation. Rather, this was reinforced by producing new mono-functional urban areas or adding to the population density in pre-existing ghettoised zones. This ended up generating a series of social problems that placed significant burdens on the government in the following decades.

In particular, gated communities – compulsory for the programme's vertical complexes – reproduced fortified enclaves that further fragmented and dislocated the urban social fabric. In addition, such communities required residents to pay a monthly maintenance fee. Residents in the state of São Paulo, for example, complained that such fees ate up more than 17 per cent of their income. When added to the condominium fee, this sometimes rose to almost 40 per cent of income. In time, residents started to default on such fees and conflicts emerged around management issues, often leading to the swift collapse of the project.

Housing expenses weighed even more heavily once the cost of water, electricity and gas was factored in. This impacted mainly on people who had been forcibly evicted and resettled. Their previous housing arrangements would often have included clandestine connections for water and electricity supplies, and certainly did not require payment of condominium fees.[66]

This issue is related to another effect of the programme. MCMV enabled mass evictions, for example in Campinas, where dwellers of various favelas bordering rivers and streams were moved into large complexes on the outskirts. In this case, the displacements clearly contributed to 'adjust' land values, removing lower-income families from more central districts and resettling them in homogeneous environments of very low average household income.

Eventually, some complexes became dominated by groups connected to drug trafficking and/or paramilitary groups. This came about through the control of collective spaces and also of condominium management, where leaders of residents' committees were imposed by one or another gang. Residents might even be driven from their homes in order for other families – in favour with the gangsters – to take possession. The victims' silence was ensured by threats and retaliation. Even so, 38.4 per cent of the families described their condominium as violent or dangerous, and 45.8 per cent considered them more violent or dangerous than their previous homes. Of the 494 families who had already thought about relocating, approximately 49.6 per cent cited violence as the reason.

Such data demonstrate the failure of the idea, frequently put forward to justify favela clearances, that resettling people in gated, formalised, regularised and ordered housing complexes will put an end to violence.

13

At the Frontier of the
Real-Estate–Financial Complex

The crisis that hit Brazilian cities at the end of the 1970s contributed greatly to the urban reform movement. Its advocates began to include not only the residents of cities' informal settlements, peripheries and favelas, but also middle-class sectors of liberal professionals such as architects, engineers and lawyers who, mainly through their recently created unions, supported and joined this coalition.[1] Besides demanding the recognition of informal settlements and their integration into cities, the movement proposed measures to combat 'real-estate speculation', introducing the concept of social function of the city and properties, and including forms of 'direct democracy'.

Especially in those cities most affected by the crisis, this coalition succeeded throughout the 1980s in electing local governments committed to a model of redistribution and the expansion of citizenship. Despite the extremely limited budgets available to local administrations at the time, this model set out to introduce infrastructure and public services in favelas and peripheries, and support cooperatives, business incubators, income-generation programmes and other social projects, drawing attention to the lack of national policies of this kind and counteracting national fiscal austerity policies.[2]

The new redistributive, local model also impelled a conceptual and methodological revision of urban planning and regulations – especially after the Constitution made Municipal Master Plans compulsory for municipalities with over 20,000 inhabitants.

According to this progressive agenda, the formulation of Master Plans was intended to change the model of urban development that had been followed over four decades of intense urbanisation based upon territorial exclusion of the poor. It aspired to the 'rupture of the exclusive control over access to wealth, income and opportunities generated within (and by) the use and occupation of urban land, ensuring the right to the city for all, as social wealth rather than commodification'.[3] It also set out to influence the model of urban policies concerning citizenship.[4]

As a result, the 1980–90s saw greater investment in infrastructure, especially in the more deprived areas. However, 'irregular' or 'illegal' settlements remained barred by urban and environmental planning regulations from total integration into the city. It is precisely against this background, and from a perspective of the universalisation of rights, that the first attempts to recognise favelas in urban planning and regulation came about. Recife and Belo Horizonte's pioneering experiments in the 1980s were innovative not solely for their investment in favelas, something sporadically carried out in many Brazilian cities, but because they identified and demarcated these areas as Zones of Special Social Interest (ZEIS), recognising their existence and proclaiming a public commitment to their regularisation.

In Recife's case, Prezeis (Plan for the Regularisation of the Zones of Special Social Interest) proposed rules for the implementation of urbanisation programmes and their consolidation through the development of special plans, participatory processes and the recognition of the existence of specific occupational patterns.[5] Prezeis was particularly innovative in creating a management system that involved deliberation in local Urbanisation and Legalisation Commissions (Comuls). These were formed by residents and municipal representatives, and were responsible for approving and managing each ZEIS's urbanisation plan. Moreover, a Prezeis Permanent Forum was launched to discuss and deliberate on priorities and general strategies related to the demarcated areas.

Belo Horizonte too was a pioneer, creating, in 1983, the Profavela (Municipal Programme for the Regularisation of Favelas) that developed a new zoning category in its Master Plan.

In the wake of these two experiences, there was a nationwide multiplication of programmes which directed the regularisation and urbanisation of favelas, along with new laws specifying instruments for the regularisation and recognition of tenure rights. Among Brazilian municipalities, the adoption of ZEIS accelerated between 2001 and 2009, with a significant increase after 2005, when they were incorporated into Municipal Master Plans. 'The number of municipalities whose Master Plans included ZEIS jumped from 672 in 2001 to 1,799 in 2009, which represents an increment of 168 per cent.'[6]

However, the day-to-day struggles of informal settlements and occupations in resisting violent evictions and expulsions were much more complex and contradictory. In the 1990s, the consolidation of favelas in central areas was already an object of dispute and controversy.[7] It was not a coincidence that, although approved by the National Congress, the very instrument that enabled the concession of irregularly occupied public areas to their residents – the Special Concession for Housing Purposes – was vetoed by President Cardoso. Later negotiations resulted in the promulgation of a Provisional Measure, prohibiting the application of these instruments in green spaces and environmental protection areas. The official federal system of housing finance and urban development – even under the PT coalition's administration – has never recognised anything other than fully registered property as a guarantee of security of tenure, despite its being protected by the statute books.

ZEIS were also included in some Master Plans to designate areas where affordable housing should be built, combined with innovative land policy instruments designed to curb speculation – such as progressive taxes in empty or under-utilised areas or compulsory occupation orders. These attempts faced resistance in city councils and courts, which alleged lack of federal regulation.

In 2001, the Statute of the City, a federal law, tried to provide the legal framework to solve this impasse and established a five-year deadline for all cities to approve their Master Plans. Therefore, when the team led by Olívio Dutra – an advocate of 'municipal socialism'[8] – took over the Ministry of Cities, the Ministry decided to promote the elaboration of participatory master plans as well as the incorporation of the new land policy instruments in them.

The law required master plans to consider the 'social function' of each city, through a participatory process of discussion and agreement that should take place in the public arena in each city.

Based on a proposal derived from the Technical Committee of Planning and Urban Land Management and in alliance with civil society organisations and government bodies, the ministry decided to support a campaign partnering with a network of technical and academic bodies, research institutions, state and municipal governments, social movements and, in some states, the Public Prosecutor's Office.[9] This agenda challenged the public machine, state bureaucrats and political leaders

> to produce institutions capable of generating exchanges and agreements between the various local stakeholders about the future of their society; to promote networks of stakeholders working on public problems; to establish instruments of citizens' mobilisation; to create norms to ensure the implementation of these agreements; to have a strategic capacity of political articulation; and, above all, to gain stakeholders' trust and reduce the uncertainties of the political system.[10]

From an urban planning point of view, the idea was to promote 'urban pacts' capable of promoting sustainable occupation of each city's territories, ensuring an adequate place for all its inhabitants. From a political point of view, there was a commitment to multiplying the number of actors having political representation, to allow the incorporation of new subjects into the debate and decision-making around urban policies.

After the Ministry of Cities' call, more than 4,000 Brazilian municipalities encouraged local discussion of urban development policies, either through municipal conferences, the development of participatory master plans or the participation in newly formed councils, with a variety of results. Naturally, in cities where organised social movements existed already, they used the political space opened by the debate as an additional forum to present their agendas.

In many cities, public debates on urban policy were being held for the first time. In others, it was merely a formal procedure – the

convening of a public hearing and its record in secretarial minutes –
to avoid the accusation (and possible retribution) against local
councils and mayors of non-compliance with the law. A significant proportion of local administrations went through the
motions, hoping that fulfilling the legal requirements would
make them eligible to receive federal support for urban development. Research performed by the Metropolis Observatory showed
that, despite the quantitative success of approved municipal
master plans and the presence of the Statute of the City's 'new
instruments',

> Many plans merely transcribe excerpts of the Statute; others
> incorporate instruments without assessing their pertinence to the
> territory and the municipality's management capacity; others
> incorporate fragments of concepts and ideas from the Statute
> with no connection to the urban plan itself ... This research
> exposed a generalised inadequacy of the instruments' regulation
> within master plans in terms of their auto-applicability or effec-
> tiveness, mainly in the case of instruments related to the induction
> of inclusive urban development.[11]

At the same time, the policy of growth with job generation and
wage improvement mobilised public resources to foster urban
development through large infrastructure projects, often without
any consideration of the development of housing or the effects on
urban markets. This resulted in a total disjunction between the
master plan's directives and the large investments under way or
about to be realised. According to a report on the plans developed
in Rio de Janeiro:

> large investments are imposed onto the master plan as external
> conditions, i.e., large investment definitions are decided with no
> relation to municipal master plans and plans do not dialogue as
> much as they could with existing or projected investments. Invest-
> ments in power plants, steel industries, airports, large road works
> or PAC (Growth Acceleration Programme) initiatives are not
> mentioned within master plans, and do not explicitly relate to
> any other growth strategy or directive.[12]

It is possible to say the same about Minha Casa Minha Vida's programme, which failed to include any element of land policy. Local master plans thus became law that could be enforced or not, and definitely did not direct the location choices of MCMV projects.

Meanwhile, with the defeat of the Movement for Urban Reform's agenda under the PT government at the national level, fiscal austerity measures expressed an archetypal neoliberal response to the crisis at local level. Urban policy now aimed at inciting competition between cities, demonstrating how strategic planning might become a fundamental instrument for neoliberal political administrations. Such was the case with Mayor Cesar Maia's administration, which emptied of meaning the Master Plan approved for Rio de Janeiro.[13] According to Carlos Vainer,

> It is impossible not to acknowledge the centrality of the idea of competition between cities within the theoretical and political project of urban strategic planning. It is the recognition of competition between cities that authorises the transposition of the strategic model from the entrepreneurial world to the urban universe, as it is this same recognition that authorises the sale of cities, the use of urban marketing, the authoritarian and despotic unification of citizens and, finally, the enforcement of civic patriotism.[14]

Rather than opposing 'socialist' urban policies with 'neoliberal' policies, one saw the simultaneous and contradictory presence of both ideologies inside 'left-wing' administrations. Take São Paulo. Here, the city's Master Plan, produced at the beginning of the 2000s during the administration of Mayor Marta Suplicy, incorporated various instruments from the Statute of the City for land regularisation, recognition of tenure and promotion of access to urbanised land for lower-income residents. And yet, the same plan marked out a significant part of the municipal territory as areas open to public–private partnerships and backed projects exempt from the general regulations of the city, designed to attract private capital and investment. This was a deliberate move to expand the frontiers of the real-estate–financial complex.

The first instance of bending existing zoning regulations to allow changes in land use rules, in exchange for financial compensation from real-estate developers, was on the occasion of a co-project agreement between the cities of São Paulo and Toronto at the end of the 1980s. São Paulo had recently chosen Jânio Quadros, supported by a right-wing coalition, as its first directly elected mayor (1985–88) after the military dictatorship.[15] The relaxation of regulations was proposed as a 'Law for De-Favelisation' (Law no. 10,209, 1986). The joint venture granted special authorisation for the alteration of urban patterns (area floor ratios, permitted uses, set-backs, occupation rates, etc.) in plots occupied by favelas. Authorisation to use flexible zoning rules would be granted to the owner of the plot in exchange for the obligation to build and donate social housing for the favela residents in a different location. The number of housing units to be built was calculated according to a percentage of the potential profit that the landowners would obtain with the new zoning patterns.

Two years later, interested landlords could, instead of directly building the affordable housing units, hire a municipal government body, FUNAPS (Fund for Residents of Substandard Housing), to do so: 'the payment of the compensation to FUNAPS . . . allowed the creation of a potentially huge sum, transferred from private money to a Social Fund.'[16]

For this reason, when the following elections were won by Luiza Erundina, the first PT mayor of São Paulo (1989–92), the instrument continued to be used, financing almost 4,000 of the 10,000 housing units produced during that administration. FUNAPS resources were responsible for funding projects of cooperative and self-managed housing construction, urbanisation of favelas and renovation of buildings in downtown areas. Nevertheless, during Erundina's mandate, this instrument became detached from de-favelisation and was opened to any entrepreneur. New methods of calculating and negotiating compensation were introduced, raising not only the number of projects, but also the price paid by entrepreneurs per square metre.[17]

During the following administration, under a right-wing coalition led by Paulo Maluf (1993–96), joint ventures continued, although under pressure from the city council, which demanded a say in the process of negotiation and approval.[18] The resources paid by private entrepreneurs in exchange for flexible zoning started to finance the Cingapura project – apartment buildings to replace part of the favelas neighbouring São Paulo's main avenues. Finally, in 1998, the judiciary suspended the application of the de-favelisation law. It was declared unconstitutional in 2000 and, in the following year, became the object of a Parliamentary Commission of Inquiry involving the city council, after accusations of the loss of almost US$80 million that had not been transferred to the housing fund during the administrations of Paulo Maluf and his successor, Celso Pitta.[19]

This account reveals the threads that underhandedly wove the local version of a global paradigm. Its starting point was undoubtedly the fiscal crisis. Indeed,

> since 1983, São Paulo's own investment capacity became negative. The diagnostic presented by Mário Covas's administration in 1984 indicated that, for the first time in the city's recent history, the expenditures related to the repayment of debts exceeded the level of investment.[20]

Why? Brazil's economic stagnation, combined with the galloping rise of international interest rates, hugely swelled the public debt. One recipe to confront inexorable budget deficits came from Canada, in the form of 'co-projects' between cities. Such 'co-projects' were among the new mechanisms that redrew the world of international relations, with cities and municipalities assuming more initiative and independence towards their international contacts, bent on defending their interests in the global environment. It is what is now called 'para-diplomacy', one of urban entrepreneurship's new weapons.

While Toronto 'sistered' São Paulo, the Canada Mortgage and Housing Corporation – the Canadian authority for housing and homeownership – was seeking new forms of public–private partnerships to beat the Canadian fiscal crisis. It financed the Toronto municipality's research into linkage programmes with San Francisco, in the US, and with British Columbia. These policies required corporate investors to produce housing units in their area of action, in the form of financial resources or land donations.[21]

In the same period (late 1970s to early '80s), North American cities introduced what they called 'inclusionary zoning': incentives in the form of 'density bonuses' or the possibility of increasing the construction potential in exchange for the production, by the entrepreneur, of a certain number of affordable units in the building.[22]

The 'translation' of this instrument by Jânio Quadro's administration labelled the production of houses a 'compensation', not an 'obligation', as it was in North American and Canadian linkage programmes. Under São Paulo's version of the linkage programme, both sides of the equation were interconnected: it became possible to remove favelas from cities and, at the same time, to bow to the real-estate sector's pressure to undertake construction that was currently immobilised by the rigidity of zoning regulations. By connecting the potential profits with the provision of affordable dwellings, this mechanism promoted homeownership as the solution. Within the city's political economy, the programme was presented as a fair mechanism, that helped the poorest while solving the social blight of housing precariousness. That way, it dissolved the resistance to increased liberalisation. Additionally, it gained the support of 'left-wing' parties.

The liberalisation of zoning was also a part of neoliberal ideology. It meant the creation of a less regulated working environment, with more freedom of action for the market. However, it did not mean the suspension or substitution of zoning, but the opening for potential exceptions, as described by Wilderode:

> joint ventures reveal the obsolescence of zoning. However, despite allowing the derogation of the zoning law, joint ventures do not oppose it. Conversely, the maintenance of zoning is a fundamental element for the functioning of the interconnected mechanism ... it is the creation of an exception to the previous rule, and this exception generates much more profit than is shown in the technical reports to calculate potential gains, which are produced by certified evaluators (coming from the private sector itself).[23]

In this way, practices and ideologies of different origins and objectives became interwoven, while cutting a path that progressively expanded the areas of the city to be opened up by the real-estate–financial industry.

Nonetheless, the joint ventures came to an end when their application was judicially contested by zoning regulation defenders. They were suspended, and only publicly reappeared when the city council started an inquiry into their dealings. That was when another trait of these projects' 'business' came to light: Maluf and Pitta's administrations, besides enabling earnings for the real-estate sector, did not transfer any resources resulting from joint ventures to 'affordable housing'.

While São Paulo experimented with joint ventures, it also experimented with other types of public–private partnerships. Proposed for the first time in the 1985 Master Plan project, during Mário Covas's administration, it planned to expand the supply of infrastructure, urban facilities and housing in thirty-five areas of the city – above all in the suburbs.[24] However, the proposal was shelved.

It resurfaced later, in Jânio Quadros's Master Plan, but only began to be implemented under Luiza Erundina. During his administration, Quadros had initiated a large package of roadworks (tunnels, viaducts, canals and new avenues) distributed between nine large contractor companies. The initial total value was of 330 million reais. By the end of his term, it had already risen to 416 million reais. In that way, when Erundina became mayor, she inherited an outstanding debt of 135 million reais and a total budget of 900 million reais for the completion of the works. As no external financing was obtained, the works were halted for reassessment by the new administration. It was decided to renegotiate the costs and to finish the works at Anhangabaú, due to their downtown location.[25]

The funding strategy for the new tunnel crossing the city centre was to launch a public-private partnership – Operação Urbana Centro – to sell building rights in exchange for money to finish the public works. The justification for this was the necessity of 'revitalising' the area by attracting new real-state investors. Similarly, the Faria Lima Urban Project (Operação Urbana Faria Lima), which was included in the Master Plan of 1991 and regulated only in 1995, was directly tied to a road project. The proposal for its inclusion in the city's Master Plan came from Júlio Neves's architecture office. He was involved in planning the city's new corporate district, in the south-west. Initially christened 'Boulevard Sul', the project of extending Avenue Faria Lima was presented to the city hall as 'important road works at no cost to the municipality'.[26] According to Ermínia Maricato and João Whitaker,

> the market's interest in the Marginal Pinheiros' region, along Faria Lima and Água Espraiada avenues . . . is related to the movement of private enterprise towards the creation of a new 'globalised' – and, evidently, segregated – centre in São Paulo. A powerful group was formed to put pressure on City Hall. It included renowned architects with their own interests in the project (having developed projects and urban plans for the area) . . . that is, the urban project becomes an end in itself, an element of leverage of a mega real-estate project.[27]

Faria Lima Urban Project was considered a great success, attracting the participation of developers and raising more than 2 billion reais.[28] This project also saw later on, under its first revision in the city council in 2004, the introduction of the Certificates of Additional Construction Potential, (CEPACs) – a real-estate–financial bond. CEPACs were auctioned in 'packs' and negotiated on financial markets through the Stock Exchange. The price was determined by auction and, like any other financial bond, oscillated according to the market's interests, which, in turn, depended on the appreciation of the urban spaces to which the project was linked.[29] Thus the introduction of CEPACs was another step towards the financialisation of urban development. As Paulo Sandroni notes:

> The first auction of CEPACs was made in Operação Urbana/ Urban Operation Água Espraiada in July 2004; 100,000 CEPACs were offered at the minimum price of R$300 (US$150). All of them were sold, producing revenue of R$30 million (US$15 million) . . .

In December 2004 the first CEPAC auction was held in Faria Lima Urban Operation , and 90,000 CEPACs were offered at an initial price, determined by law, of R$1,100 (US$550) each. Only 9,091 were sold, resulting in revenue of around R$10 million (US$5 million) . . .

The failure of this auction and the apparent lack of interest of developers in a very dynamic area of the city (from the real-estate business point of view) was due to many causes . . . When it became clear at the beginning of 2004 that the CEPACs law was going to be approved in urban operation Faria Lima, many developers obtained licenses to build in accordance with the former method of economic compensation . . .

Additional reasons for the huge failure of the first auction in the Faria Lima UO were a recession in the real-estate business cycle and the fact that the auction took place during the last week of the mandate of the mayor who had lost the election to the opposition . . . This caused some uncertainty about the future of urban projects in general . . . The first two public auctions in the Faria Lima UO failed . . .

The third public auction in 2007 was very successful. In this auction, 156,730 CEPACs were offered at an initial price of R$1,225, and all of them were sold for R$1,240.01, an increase of almost 13 per cent.[30]

The introduction of CEPACs in São Paulo was a step forward in weaving connections between finance, real estate and urban regulations, under both left-wing and right-wing local coalitions.

14

Real-Estate Avenues

'The Avenue Is Owned by the Funds.'

With this slogan, the Brazilian Review of Pension Funds celebrated the first business district outside of the city centre and Avenida Paulista.[1] The project took off between 1968 and 1971 with the construction of an expressway on the banks of the Pinheiros river: the Marginal Pinheiros.[2] The availability of land for sale, the presence of high-income residential neighbourhoods and the launch of the city's first shopping centre, Iguatemi, in the late 1960s (also near Marginal Pinheiros), propelled the next phase of expansion.

However, the entrance of pension funds into São Paulo's real-estate market and the shift in corporate real-estate strategy – renting floors or buildings through long-term contracts instead of building or buying them – drove the boom of corporate towers, hotels and convention and shopping centres in the region from the late 1980s onwards.[3] Between 1984 and 1999, more than 800,000 square metres of corporate buildings were completed, with the sizeable participation of Previ, Funcef, Sistel and other pension funds.[4]

Pension funds had first been introduced in Brazil in 1977 as a strategic tool for the generation of internal savings and the formation of a capital market during the military regime. Inspired by similar North American schemes, they were initially created within banks and state companies and sponsored by public companies. In 2010, there was a total of 369 funds, which, together, managed 504 billion reais – the equivalent of 17.5 per cent of Brazil's GDP. The majority were run by private companies, 64.7 per cent of the market, giving these actors considerable economic and political power. Brazil's largest funds were: Previ, fed by Banco do Brasil employees; Petros, from Petrobras; Funcef, from Caixa Econômica Federal; and Valia, from Vale (a mining and metals company that was privatised in the 1990s).[5]

Since their creation during the military dictatorship, pension funds have had strategic importance for the government and have been repeatedly mobilised for the implementation of its policies. During President Fernando Henrique Cardoso's mandate (1995–2002), they were called upon by the government, alongside the National Bank for Economic and Social Development (BNDES), to participate in state company auctions and become their minority shareholders. In that way, they formed, alongside banks and private equity funds, Special Purpose Entities (SPEs) with the sole purpose of acquiring such shares.[6] According to Sérgio Lazzarini,

> during the privatisation process, President Cardoso's government received strong criticism from left-wing opposition parties for delivering Brazil's national companies to foreign capital. At the same time, it was necessary to reassure public opinion that the auctions would be successful ... In order to attenuate this criticism and politically enable this process, state pension funds and BNDES were vigorously activated.[7]

Nonetheless, from the 1990s on, a movement led by the Bank Clerks' Union grew within the Unified Workers' Central (CUT) and other union federations to demand a say in the regulation of pension funds, aiming to expand their activities while exerting greater political control over them.[8] In 2001, a bill, strongly supported by deputies with union links, extended worker participation in the running of the funds. In October 2002, these new directors of Closed Private Pension Entities published the 'Carta de Brasília' (Brasilia Letter), supporting union leader Lula da Silva's candidature for the presidency:

> We, the undersigned, were elected by the workers to direct their pension funds, are committed to the independent and

serious management of their resources in the face of any government and manifest our support for Lula's candidature, certain
that this is the best way for the funds to develop their full potential, fulfil their commitments and contribute to the country's
development.[9]

Indeed, once elected, Lula enthusiastically mobilised the funds'
participation in PPPs and large industrial and infrastructure
projects in the country. For example, pension funds were the
main investors in high-end offices, shopping centres and holiday
resorts between the mid-1990s and mid-2000s. Thus they
worked as 'a substitute for real-estate credit in the destination of
capital flows into the real-estate sector; some funds invested up
to 20 per cent of their resources in real estate – a significant
capital flow that had important consequences for the real-estate
sector's structure at the time'.[10] However, this changed in 2002,
when the Central Bank reduced the maximum percentage of
pension fund participation in real-estate assets to 16 per cent.
From then on, this figure progressively decreased approximately
two percentage points every two years, until reaching 8 per cent
in 2009.[11]

Pension funds were important agents in the construction of
São Paulo's business district, opening a new real-estate frontier
in the city's south-west zone. In order to ensure high rates of
return, pension and real-estate funds favoured commercial
buildings classified by real-estate consultants as 'triple A', along
with shopping centres. Wherever possible, the building was situated on an axis of real-estate value appreciation: location was
everything.[12]

Nevertheless, any area's long-term value essentially relies on
public investments in infrastructure, especially roads and transportation. Public investment was decisive for setting prices and
profitability margins of real-estate investments.[13] According to
João Whitaker, 'the completion of the city's most desirable and
important real-estate front, Marginal Pinheiros's "new globalised
centrality" . . . depends almost exclusively on various investments
in the region and, thus, on the pressure of the lobby to direct
public investment according to its own interests.'[14]

At this point, another fundamental actor in the coalition emerged: the contractor.

The State and the Contractors

The state has enjoyed a strong and long-lasting relationship with the nation's contractors. It is a 'functional union' that has resulted not only in the inextricable entanglement of public and private interests, but also in the great power of contractors to influence public policies.[15]

The intimate association between the state and private capital is, in the words of Raymundo Faoro, an 'internal game of exchange of advantages, fundamentally sustained by a patrimonial network'.[16] It applies not only to the relations between state and contractors, but also to a peculiarity of capitalism in Brazil – the primacy of 'patronage'. Faoro attributes this characteristic to the specificities of Brazil's historic formation, especially in the colonial era.

During that period, in the absence of an impartial, rule-based system, the private sector's economic opportunities depended on its capacity to establish direct links with a discretionary Crown. According to Faoro, this logic dominated both the Imperial era (1822–98) and the First Republic (1898–1930), when the state became the main conductor of the economy. Sérgio Lazzarini develops the thesis that the individuals with power are those who are inserted and coordinated within a web of corporate links between public and private actors – links that are expressed through interactions across the spheres of property and company directorships.[17]

Although it is certainly possible to detect this tendency in past state–contractor relations, we must reflect upon the specificity of this sector and its role in the country in order to understand the recent transformations of the built environment, as well as the making of the Brazilian real-estate–financial complex. Contractor companies are currently the main drivers of this process, coordinating and leading the new form of infrastructure financing and governance: the PPPs – public–private partnerships.

At the end of the 1970s, due to the economic and fiscal crisis, the federal government progressively reduced its investment, cooling the market for ambitious projects. Contractor companies switched to seeking deals with state governments and metropolitan administrations. They participated in the implementation of sanitation programmes and other infrastructure sectors – for example, the construction of São Paulo's metro system.[18]

By that point, in the mid-1980s, direct elections for mayors of state capitals were already in place. As the contests for the government of states and for legislative positions grew fierce, campaign funding became a vital means of connecting political influence with big money. State and municipal elections became occasions for bargaining between candidates and their campaign sponsors. Deals were clinched directly with future members of the executive, such as mayors and governors.

São Paulo's municipal budget – the country's third largest – became increasingly attractive when the Constitution transferred resources previously reserved for the Federation to municipalities.[19] According to Szmrecsanyi and Lefèvre, the package of works proposed by Jânio Quadros in 1985 were literally a 'package', a hotchpotch of proposals presented by contractor companies, selected according to personal criteria by the then mayor. The final cut included the following projects and companies: tunnels under Ibirapuera Park (CBPO and Constran); boulevards JK I and II (Serveng-Civilsan, CBPO and Constran); tunnels under the Pinheiros river (Camargo Corrêa); a mini ring road (Andrade Gutierrez); a canalisation of the Água Espraiada creek and an avenue along its length (Mendes Jr.); the Jacu-Pêssego road complex (CR Almeida); the redevelopment of Vale do Anhangabaú's (Andrade Gutierrez).[20]

Most of the works in the 'package' launched by Mayor Quadros were directly related to the expansion and consolidation of São Paulo's southern business district. These urban projects were managed by the public company Emurb, which administered both the works themselves and the financial resources raised by the projects. Emurb was, therefore, the point of coordination between large contractor companies and the local government in São Paulo.[21]

After the return of democracy, in São Paulo and other municipalities and states, connections between contractor companies
and the government began to be made through political parties
and, more precisely, through fund-raising for electoral campaigns.
The power-brokers are generally members of the party, who occasionally also occupy positions within the government that allow
them to continue to act as links between the government and
contractor companies.

In recent decades, unsurprisingly, large contractor companies
have become the main financers of political campaigns, especially
those for executive positions, as this is the level with most power
to instigate and distribute public works contracts.[22] The companies
usually donate to several parties, betting larger sums on those who
have a better chance of winning. For contractor companies, donations work as a kind of 'insurance', to guarantee that they will be
hired by the new government, or get paid if they have ongoing
contracts. For the politicians involved, contracting and paying
those companies is a 'return' for the support received.[23] Heavy
construction has thus been politicised, as 'the condition for obtaining contracts – as well as their profits – are of a political nature,
linked to the company's ability to deploy its influence within the
state apparatus.'[24]

Ultimately, this deployment allows large and mega-contractors
not only to redirect public budgets, but also to draw up the infrastructure projects they wish to execute, 'selling' them to their
potential clients (governments and state companies).[25] This was
clearly the case for Mayor Quadros's 'package of works' (tunnels,
avenues, bridges and canals) that made up his 'urban renewal
plan'. The circle is thus closed: the 'real-estate avenues' finance the
cost of the works proposed by the contractor, simultaneously
opening new fronts for rent extraction and feeding the machine of
political campaign financing.

Moreover, throughout the 1990s, many contractors participated
in real-estate ventures as a strategy for business diversification,
joining developers and investors in building clusters of corporate towers and retail spaces. They took advantage, for
example, of previously established relations with the BNDES
(Bank for Economic and Social Development) to raise public

money to build shopping malls, defined by BNDES's lines of credit as 'urban equipment'. They also took advantage of their historic links with the public works sector to urge investment in road projects that, in turn, offered their businesses new opportunities.

But there were still bigger prizes on the horizon.

15

Real-Estate Games

2 October 2009

In the streets, you could hear the cheering. Crowds watched the big screen set up by the town hall on Copacabana Beach. Live from Copenhagen, it broadcast the announcement of Rio de Janeiro as the host city of the 2016 Olympic Games, beating Chicago and Madrid. Chief of Staff Dilma Rousseff went to Rio to add her voice to the celebration, accompanied by the minister of cities, Márcio Fortes. At the beach, many were dressed in green and yellow, responding to the call to brighten up a shoreline already decorated with a 250-metre banner that said 'Rio Loves You'.[1]

On the screen, Lula shed copious tears, while hugging Rio de Janeiro's governor, Sérgio Cabral. At the back, Henrique Meirelles, the president of Brazil's Central Bank, and Carlos Nuzman, president of the Brazilian Olympic Committee, looked on smilingly. The headline of the newspaper *O Globo* read: 'Yes, We Can: Rio Beats Chicago and Will Host the 2016 Olympic Games'. Eike Batista – then one of Brazil's richest men, the owner of mining, transportation and oil companies that had recently completed their IPOs – had donated 10 million reais to Rio's Olympic campaign and was one of those who celebrated the most.

March 2014

In Rio, the World Cup and Olympic Games People's Committee and Instituto Mais Democracia (More Democracy) publish the leaflet 'Who are the owners of Rio?' It lists the large works, with their respective values, financers and executors. The BNDES and the Caixa (National Savings Bank) together lead the financing with 10.5 billion reais. They are followed by the municipality (10.4 billion reais) and then the state of Rio de Janeiro (8.7 billion reais). Among the works planned are urbanisation projects for the favelas of Manguinhos and Alemão, the construction of the Olympic Village, the renovation of Maracanã Stadium and new transit lines such as the Light Rail, Transolímpica and Transcarioca roads and Metro Line 4, as well as the renovation of Galeão International Airport. The leaflet also lists the Porto Maravilha project.

Barring the schemes for Manguinhos and Alemão – won respectively by Andrade Gutierrez/Camargo Corrêa and Odebrecht – all the other projects on the list were PPPs, implemented by joint ventures between Odebrecht, Andrade Gutierrez, Camargo Corrêa and OAS. The renovation of Maracanã, for example, was carried out by Andrade Gutierrez and Odebrecht. The latter, alongside IMX, owned by Eike Batista, won the bid to manage the stadium. Over four years, Batista donated 80 million reais per year to equip the Pacifying Police Units (UPPs) installed in favelas surrounding the area that would host Olympic events. The UPP in the Alemão community was set up in May 2012; the one in Manguinhos, in January 2013.

Once the Rio Barra Joint Venture (CCRB), led by Odebrecht, concluded the construction of Metro Line 4, it was operated by Invepar, a joint venture that managed transportation services in partnership with OAS and the main Brazilian pension funds, Previ and Funcef. The Olympic Village in Barra da Tijuca, baptised 'Pure Island' by its constructors, has thirty-one tower blocks with 3,604 high-quality apartments that served 18,000 athletes during the Games. They were already being sold at the minimum price of 800,000 reais. This venture came under the responsibility of another joint venture composed by Odebrecht, Andrade Gutierrez and Carvalho Hosken. The latter had been one of the principal developers of the Barra da Tijuca neighbourhood since the 1970s.[2]

December 2014

I received a promotional leaflet announcing the launch of the Holiday Inn, Porto Maravilha, from Odebrecht Real Estate Developments. Besides describing Holiday Inn as the 'largest hotel chain in the world' as a hook for potential investors, the leaflet puffed Porto Maravilha itself as the city's future corporate district, with '5 million developed square metres', and Rio de Janeiro as the Brazilian city that receives the largest amounts of foreign investment. Quoting the Federation of Industries of Rio de Janeiro (Firjan), the leaflet announced that US$266 billion was to be invested in the city between 2014 and 2016. It presented Odebrecht Real Estate Developments as the pioneer in real-estate developments in Porto Maravilha, and disclosed that the Holiday Inn was to occupy the plot of Praia Formosa, the old railway station garage, which became federal property after the closing of the Federal Rail Network.

On receiving this leaflet, I remember the affordable homes project that the Ministry of Cities developed with Caixa for this piece of land in 2005. The plots of Praia Formosa, Usina do Asfalto and Pátio da Marítima had been sold to the Porto Area Real Estate Investment Trust (Fiirp), in 2013, guaranteeing the transfer of 1 billion reais to Porto Maravilha Urban Project. These resources were necessary to finance the joint venture over the second stage of the works and services.

The three scenes above introduce the main actors involved with the making of Brazil's new urban policy, founded on PPPs and strongly attached to the real-estate–financial complex. They unveil, in Carlos Vainer's words, 'the slow, complex and continuous process of the constitution of a hegemonic block, which has, since the 1970s and more so in the 1980s, set out to offer a new project to the city in crisis'.[3] In these scenarios, the protagonists are named and identified: the three levels of government (the president and the chief of staff, then the president, the governor and the mayor); Rede Globo (the leading media network, based in Rio); and 'Rio's business friends' in the figure of Eike Batista, the Federation of Industries of Rio de Janeiro [Firjan], public banks, large contractor companies, old and new real-estate developers, pension funds from public workers, and foreign investors. However, most noteworthy are the new forms of interplay between these actors, as they bind together in joint ventures and PPPs financed 100 per cent by public funds.

Mega sports events provided a favourable political environment for this transformation, 'shielding' the projects from the public administration's daily democratic-bureaucratic scrutiny. Through their network of consultants, they were also able to introduce technical-political and management devices already employed in other countries.[4] Nevertheless, the new urban regime was a local construct, designed through practices with deep roots in Brazil's history and culture, and commanded by the state. As previously seen, this construct took advantage of the experience of São Paulo's urban projects, but was also reliant on reforms of the regulatory framework for public procurement of works and services, implemented by left-wing administrations: the regulation of PPPs, changes to the concessions law, the option of public manifestations of interest (MPIs) and, finally, the adoption of the differentiated hiring regime (RDC).

The Institutionalisation of the 'Complex'

In June 2002, in the thick of the presidential campaign, the stock market seemed ready to plummet in response to the prospect of Lula's victory. This financial jolt increased the 'country risk' and depreciated Brazilian currency. It was then that Lula publicised his *Letter to the Brazilians* at a PT Congress, committing himself to the control of inflation, fiscal balance, the maintenance of the benchmark of primary surplus and the fulfilment of the country's contracts. The letter critiqued the previous government's economic policy, blaming it for the crisis, while affirming a 'responsible' agenda of growth with income redistribution. This seemed to soothe the market.

The first years of Lula's government were marked by the orthodox monetary policy laid out in the letter: high interest rates, stratospheric primary surplus and high levels of budget control. At the other end of the spectrum were the Ministry of Planning, commanded by Guido Mantega, and the chiefs of staff – first José Dirceu, then Dilma Rousseff. Constrained by the reigning economic policy, the Ministry of Planning sought alternatives to ignite the expansion of investment in infrastructure. It put forward a bill regulating public–private partnerships which was passed in December 2004.[5]

Inspired by the British model, the Brazilian PPP law was an instrument to facilitate major investments in infrastructure – mainly in transportation and energy – while bypassing the limits imposed by the then existing regulations for tenders and public procurement. The relocation of the minister of planning, Guido Mantega, into BNDES, in 2004, further ensured the availability of resources from the national bank to finance private companies willing to undertake large projects.

Although the law had been approved by Congress, and public resources had been allocated to finance the companies, the PPP solution was still hampered by a 'chronic lack of projects', according to the views expressed in the ministerial corridors of Brasília. In 2005 and 2006, during negotiations between the government and the contractor companies involved with the construction of the Santo Antônio Hydroelectric Plant, on the Madeira river, Odebrecht proposed the inclusion of a new instrument – the Public Manifestation of Interest (MPI) – into the decree that regulated PPPs.[6] Based on the European Union model, an MPI allows the private parties interested in the works that are to be done via PPP to design the project and present the partnership's technical, legal and and financial model. If their bid is not chosen by the future PPP the winners pay the MPI proponent the cost of drawing it up. Finally, once the country started preparations for the World Cup and the Olympic Games, the government instituted a new hiring regime – the Differentiated Hiring Regime (RDC) – which applied to Games-related works, airport and road infrastructure, health and education installations and new prisons. Beyond shortening deadlines and suspending certain requirements, the law introduced so-called 'integrated hiring'. Through this mechanism, contractors could be hired without submitting a detailed project, which would be developed by the contractor company after it won the bid.

Equally important, the Statute of the City also envisaged 'urban planning concessions', without defining exactly what these were. The first concession was made in 2009, as part of an attempt to renovate São Paulo's historical centre: 'Project Nova Luz'. The idea was to give the private sector the power to expropriate 400,000 square metres in one of the city's oldest neighbourhoods (Santa Ifigênia) for further private development. However, the project attracted furious protests from the affected residents and businesses, and was blocked by the courts in 2011. Due to the political mobilisation against Nova Luz, the whole topic of expropriation by the private sector gave rise to a legal debate. The issue has now been resolved, thanks to an article inserted in a 2013 Federal Law regarding construction of silos: it explicitly declares that private contractors involved in public works have the right to expropriate buildings.[7]

Thus, within less than a decade, the regulatory framework for the relations between the state and contractors of public works was transformed, chiefly by the progressive transfer to contractors of the power to plan, define and execute projects, as well as to manage spaces and services in the aftermath. This resulted in an increasing number of public spaces governed by private contractual relations, beyond state control. Contractors could now suggest and design the projects, execute the construction, and then manage the space for the lowest price. Meanwhile the state picked up the bill.

With the World Cup and the Olympic Games on the horizon, this logic was finally applied to large urban projects, through urban planning concessions and PPPs. Whole portions of cities were handed to companies to be occupied and subsequently managed by the real-estate–financial complex for as long as it took for the extraction of that area's rent. The constitution of these territories, built and controlled under the logic of rent extraction and the promotion of consumption, managed under a regime parallel to the city's general administration, expanded from residential and commercial 'enclaves' – the gated communities and malls – into wider areas of the city. In that way, private players started to exercise some of the powers of government, amplifying the indefinite zone between the public and the private and reconfiguring the political order.[8]

For Whom Is the City?

Rio de Janeiro's Olympic project was centred around the Olympic Park, at Barra da Tijuca, along with two 'clusters' around the Deodoro Sports Complex and Maracanã Stadium. In addition to these sites, in 2010 the project encompassed the port area, which was to host the Media Village and the Referees' Village. Barra da Tijuca had been the main frontier of expansion in Rio de Janeiro's real-estate market since the 1970s.[9] Barra's growth was possible due to road works implemented by Francisco Negrão de Lima's administration (1965–70). These works improved the connection between the city centre, the south zone and Barra.[10] Furthermore, in the 1980s, the different municipal administrations invested heavily in infrastructure, such as water and electricity supply.

According to Nelma Gusmão, the public notice announcing the Games included invitations to bid for the administration of services, implementation and management of the Olympic Park.[11] The winning joint venture was to assume the construction and maintenance costs of some facilities for fifteen years. Besides monetary compensation, the joint venture would receive real-estate compensation: property of an area measuring 1.8 million square metres, equivalent to 75 per cent of the land the Park is on.

According to the agreement signed after the bids were adjudicated, Rio Mais (the winning consortium, made up of Odebrecht and Andrade Gutierrez in association with Carvalho Hosken) was in charge of building a 400-bedroom hotel, the main media centre and three pavilions constituting a future Olympic Training Centre for high-performance athletes. The municipality was responsible for building various facilities in the Olympic Park that were not part of the PPP: the Aquatic Park, the Tennis Centre and the International Broadcast Centre (IBC), among others.

In addition to the public land, the real-estate compensation for the construction of Barra da Tijuca's Olympic Park also comprises the homes of the Vila do Autódromo community – a fishing community that had sprung up with the arrival of labourers building a race track nearby. These people had lived there for more than thirty years and, in the 1990s, had received from the state of Rio (the owner of the land) legal titles to occupy that land in perpetuity (a concession of real rights of use for housing purposes). Nevertheless, as the Games loomed, they became at risk of eviction.

During preparations for the Games, with their additional transportation projects, it soon became clear that expropriations and evictions would be unavoidable. The threat affected both favelas and formal neighbourhoods located outside the plots actually earmarked for the works, and the possibility emerged of selling additional building rights in those expropriated areas.

One illustration was the Plan for the Urban Restructuration of the Corridor T5/Transcarioca project, that saw the expropriation of 1,627 plots of land in a total area of 1,476,383.39 square metres.[12] According to this project, the priority was the expropriation of plots that could be reused for construction. However, the same project also stipulated the expropriation of a fifteen-metre band adjacent to the corridors in an area occupied by favelas, in order to 'reconstitute the informal urban tissue'. Therefore, the Transcarioca Corridor was intended to clear either totally or partially the following favelas: Arroio Pavuna, Comunidade São Francisco de Assis, Vila Sapê, Chácara do Tanque, Chacrinha do Mato Alto, Vila Campinho, Comendador Lisboa, Vila Santo Antônio, Uga-Uga, Avenida Teixeira de Castro and Parque União.

According to Lucas Faulhaber, a recurring problem was the affected population's total lack of information about the projects and their fate.[13] Moreover, as the new transit routes were constantly being modified, the communities suspected that such notices were only a pretext for more evictions, as was the case with Vila União in Curicica. This community was due to be urbanised under the Morar Carioca programme, but with the proposal for a BRT (rapid bus transit) system, the municipality had told 700 families that their homes were to be razed to make way for the Transolímpica Highway.[14]

Rosane Rebeca de Oliveira Santos conducted a survey of favelas undergoing, or at risk of, eviction, to reveal an 'eviction geography' directly linked to Olympic clusters and their transportation projects.[15] In October 2009, immediately after Rio's investiture as the 2016 Olympic Games host, the municipality declared that it would be necessary to resettle more than 3,500 families through the 'Plan for the Rio Olympics 2016 Urban and

Environmental Legacy'. Additional evictions came after the 2010 rains, which caused landslides in various areas. Geo-Rio's survey was contested in a counter-map commissioned by the Public Defender.[16]

Soon after, the Morar Carioca programme was launched with the goal of urbanising 100 per cent of the remaining favelas by 2020. According to Rio de Janeiro's municipality, the priority was communities in areas located within a four-kilometre radius of the Olympic facilities.[17] Despite appearances to the contrary, the municipal government dubbed these actions 'democratic evictions' – a term coined by municipal deputy Adilson Pires (PT). When announcing the plan for the reduction of the city's informal area, following the 'Olympic legacy plan', the PT congressman Jorge Bittar, then Rio's secretary of housing, declared:

> We will not evict as it has been done in the past. This process will take place without trauma. We will offer alternatives to families living in high-risk and insalubrious areas. In addition to Minha Casa Minha Vida, they can opt to buy used homes or [to receive] compensation – in this last case, in order to go back to their hometowns.[18]

This was not the residents' version of events. The methods of clearance were well rehearsed. Evictions were negotiated on a case-by-case basis. The abandonment of the debris of demolished homes, pressures and threats, and insufficient indemnity payments for the families to access alternative housing were the norm. In addition to the forms of violence described above, many dwellers learned about their imminent eviction when they discovered their homes' outer wall spray-painted with the letters SMH (the acronym for Municipal Secretary of Housing) and a number, without prior explanation or permission.[19] Moreover, cash compensation was based solely on the 'ameliorations' in the house value, not including the plot's value, even when residents had already lived in the area long enough to claim ownership, or where communities had already been granted legal titles by the government.

In a February 2014 interview, the municipal secretary for housing, Pierre Batista, admitted that 20,299 families (around 67,000 people) had been compulsorily displaced since 2009 – that is, more than ten homes per day during the full term for that administration. This number does not include buildings located in formal areas that were also expropriated to make way for infrastructure works.

Since for most residents the cash compensation was insufficient to acquire a new house, the Minha Casa Minha Vida apartments option was, in reality, the only one. According to Cardoso, Araújo, Nunes Jr. and Jaenisch, most MCMV complexes were located in Rio de Janeiro's western zone, the region most lacking in transportation, amenities, jobs and services. For example, the Ipê Amarelo housing estate at Realengo lies twenty-five kilometres away from the residents' former homes, dismantling their professional and interpersonal networks. The geography of evictions and resettlements is clear: removing from the real-estate financial complex front while at the same time creating a captive consumption market – forced resettlement – for private MCMV housing complexes in remote locations.

The Old and the New in Brazil's Urban Policy

The fictions of literature and cinema offer many plots in which a character falls deeply asleep and wakes up decades later, revealing the strangeness of the contemporary world. If someone woke up in 2014 in Brazil after a sleep of fifty years, they would be pretty surprised by the changes. The impoverished migrants so masterfully portrayed by João Cabral de Melo Neto in his play, *Morte e Vida Severina*, practically no longer exist. Nor do Rio de Janeiro's *malandros*, the charming rogues of the city's folklore.

Within that half-century Brazil's cities, once teeming with migrants in a society ruled by the agrarian world, have become large, complex and diversified metropolises. However, when exploring these cities, it is impossible to ignore the sea of affordable housing complexes that Brazilians have nicknamed 'the BNHs' (the acronym of the National Housing Bank). They are where the city centres' 'invaders' were resettled, on recently opened urban frontiers or in precariously consolidated 'non-cities'. There, we see the favelas and squatters' camps, bravely resisting, periodically hit by waves of violence or charity. There, too, we find the tunnels, viaducts and highways, always constructed by the same contractor companies, marking the latest fronts of real-estate development. There, we may also discern the links that connect these real-estate frontiers to new and old parties and political forces in the cities' governments.

Such could be the description, in 2014, of the landscapes of MCMV's popular housing, São Paulo's southern business district or the Rio Olímpico project. However, it is also possible to identify the stout roots of a state captured by private interests and shaped by a culture of racism, oppression and exclusion, stressed by a simultaneous process of struggle against poverty and inclusion by consumption, and by the seizure of urban land and housing by global finance.

Today, contractors and real-estate developers still dominate the logic of urban expansion, but now through a much more complex interweaving between them and the workers' pension funds directed by former union leaders who may also occupy city legislative and executive posts. This is the Brazilian version of the real-estate–financial complex.

In order to remain in power, political groups governing cities continue to depend both on campaign finance from those companies, and on the votes from favelas and the urban peripheries. Endeavouring to reduce the diversion of public resources involved in these balancing acts, tighter controls are applied to public administrations, making them increasingly bureaucratic and sluggish, with ever less executive capacity.

This process, along with the progressive dismantling of the state, abets the continued advance of a space removed from the democratic imperatives of social control, directly defined and managed by the real-estate–financial complex itself.

But if our fictional character should wake up in 2017 – just three years after the scene described above – she will find a very different political and economic picture. Just over a week after the closing of the Rio 2016 Olympic Games, Dilma Rousseff – re-elected in 2014 for a new four-year PT mandate – was impeached. The economy has suffered a massive recession, and contractor companies' CEOs and high-ranking government offi-cials have been arrested or are standing trial over so-called Lava Jato (Car Wash) corruption scandals. Since Michel Temer (Rousseff's former vice president) took the presidency, major fiscal austerity reforms and neoliberal economic policies have been rolled out, including drastic cuts to the subsidies of Minha Casa Minha Vida and massive privatisations. The Porto Maravilha PPP is near bankrupt: in 2016 the City of Rio was forced to inject money to keep public services running in the area, and most of the CEPACs remain unsold. What happened?

16

June 2013: Journeys and Beyond

17 June 2013

More than 100,000 people are occupying São Paulo's streets. The demonstrators are concentrated on Faria Lima Avenue, then they divide into two groups. One heads towards Paulista Avenue. The other makes for the southern business district, occupying Marginal Pinheiros, Berrini Avenue and the Ponte Estaiada that spans the Pinheiros river. Thousands of people are also occupying downtown Rio de Janeiro, in an even larger street demonstration.

Some days later, similar gatherings were sparked in different Brazilian cities, initiating what was afterwards called the 'June Journeys'. The first protests were against the increase in bus fares. They were organised via Facebook and other social media by the Movimento Passe Livre (MPL, Free Pass Movement), a decentralised group composed mostly of high-school and university students, which emerged in 2005 in different cities in response to bus fares and quality and availability of public transportation.[1] But rejection of the proposed increase in public transportation fares was not the only demand now being heard on the streets. 'It is not only for 20 cents' was the slogan written on improvised posters and banners, and shouted by the protesters. In these moments the voices of young people who refused traditional forms of representation, such as political parties and trade unions, rang out loud and clear as they defended such values as autonomy, self-management and the urban commons.

In mainstream international media, commentators were surprised at the outbreak of the massive street demonstrations. They compared the Brazilian June with other movements such as Occupy Wall Street in the United States, and with 15-M and Indignados, in Spain. The surprise came from the fact that Brazil was not experiencing an economic crisis in 2013. On the contrary, in the first years of the millennium, Brazil was part of an exclusive group of countries that had seen steady growth and that had emerged onto the international economic scene as new and thriving economies, the so-called BRICs. If the country's economy was growing, if jobs, opportunities and income were expanding in a more redistributive way, what were the reasons for the protests and who were the social actors behind them?

Reading the demands written on banners and posters, listening to what was shouted on the streets and reading the posts on Facebook and Twitter, several elements of discontent can be identified. Firstly, the quality and availability of public services, summed up in the slogan 'We want a FIFA-standard educational/health system' – alluding to the exorbitant spending in preparation for the mega-events hosted by Brazil, the World Cup and the Olympics. Secondly, the human and social rights violations that were embedded in the policies created for these events. This was also an outcry against the rise of moralistic and conservative values within the Brazilian political scene, epitomised by the appointment of an evangelical pastor who believes in the possibility of a 'gay cure' as the head of Congress's Human Rights Committee. The mood was further ignited by a more general and diffuse rejection of politicians and political parties, much like the Argentinian 'Que se vayan todos' (Away with the lot of them) in 2001.[2]

Since the protests were not organised by unions, parties or traditional social movements, the insurgency was mostly composed of young and middle-class people, as well as a very significant part of the 'new middle class'.[3] This new middle class comprised those working-class and poorer cohorts that had been roped into the consumer market and educational system thanks to the inclusionary economic and educational policies implemented by the Workers' Party (PT). This was, in effect, the first generation of working-class youth who left high school and entered university, funded by sizeable student loans. Some commentators point out the disappointment of this group with the lack of well-paid and stable jobs, despite their higher education. The fact that they finished their degrees only to become part of a precarious labour force has been put forward as one of the sources of the discontent.[4]

Although we cannot reduce the June protests solely to a youthful expression of dissatisfaction with the urban condition, this was a very important component of the June turmoil. When the Salvador city council building was occupied in July 2013, the letter to the city government presenting the protesters' claims stated: 'We are struggling for a life without turnstiles, in which citizens have the universal right to the city and to public services.'.[5]

Besides the MPL, one of the previously existing social movements that made their presence felt in June 2013 was the *Comitês Populares da Copa* (World Cup Popular Committees). In Rio, São Paulo, Fortaleza and other Brazilian cities where World Cup/ Olympics-related urban renewal works had been under way since 2011, favela dwellers threatened or affected by evictions were organising, together with NGOs and university students, to defend their right to housing – whether the right to adequate resettlement or the right to stay put. They were denouncing the way those projects were defined and designed, beyond any previous adopted planning schemes and without any public discussion.[6] The activity of the Committee demonstrators on the streets, blocking roads and the front of stadiums, did not end in 2013. They were violently repressed during the World Cup in 2014, as well.

Despite the Minha Casa Minha Vida housing programme, and in a less visible manner, the 'housing question' was also present in June's cauldron. On 19 June, for instance, MTST – Movimento dos Trabalhadores Sem Teto (Homeless Workers Movement), a housing movement that emerged in early 2000s – held street demonstrations denouncing the high cost of living and demanding housing policies.[7] According to Guilherme Boulos, MTST leader: 'What wages have given with one hand, rental and housing prices have taken away with the other.'[8] This rise in housing prices helps explain the boom of new organised squats, both of urban land and of empty buildings in São Paulo and other cities, which gained momentum after 2013.[9]

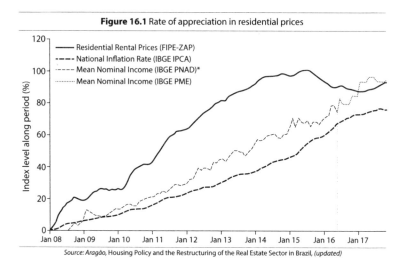

Figure 16.1 Rate of appreciation in residential prices

Source: Aragão, Housing Policy and the Restructuring of the Real Estate Sector in Brazil, *(updated)*

In any case, the different claims of the June Journeys exposed the toxic combination of the political and economic choices made in the previous years. Brazilians had more money in their pockets but were living in totally dysfunctional cities, unable to provide habitable public spaces, efficient public services or adequate housing. There was dissatisfaction with the political system and its inability to represent society's desires and voices, as increasingly it moved away from social claims and shut itself up in the business of politics.

According to the editorial of a liberal French news magazine, the events in June were

> violent riots that threw more than 1 million people into the streets of a hundred Brazilian cities, exploding like a thunderclap in an apparently tranquil sky. Nonetheless, more than protesting against the rise in transportation fares, they testify to the Brazilian miracle's collapse. After a decade of exceptional growth (5 per cent per year), which increased the income per capita from US$7,500 to US$11,800 and brought forth a middle class of 90 million people, economic activity grew only 0.9 per cent in 2012, due to Dilma Rousseff's statist and protectionist political orientation.[10]

Based on the main tenets of the neoliberal handbook, the article pointed to the high cost of labour, the heavy tax burden, state interventionism and, finally, corruption as the main causes of unrest. This vision intended to circumscribe the indignation, confining it to an ideological niche in opposition to Dilma Rousseff's 'statism'. The system was blasted as imperfect, needing correction through the successful adoption of a globalised neoliberal economy controlled by the financial system.

Indeed, one of the movements that came out of the June Journeys was the right-wing Movimento Brasil Livre [MBL, Free Brazil Movement]. MBL began with a group of former students with scholarships from Students for Liberty and the Atlas Network, a think tank funded by Koch Industries, the US fossil-fuel energy and petrochemicals giant, to promote free-market policies.[11] Together with Vem pra rua [Come to the street] and other politically and economically liberal right-wing groups (including a group rooting for the return of military dictatorship), MBL organised protests that were pro-impeachment for Rousseff and anti-PT.

This movement grew quickly with the advancement of the Operação Lava Jato, or Car Wash Operation, a judicial investigation into allegations of corruption involving contractors and politicians, starting with the state-controlled oil company Petrobras. The operation included more than 1,000 warrants for dawn raids, temporary and preventive detention and coercive measures. Led by the federal judge Sérgio Moro and the federal police, the corruption scandal grew in part because it challenged the impunity of politicians and business leaders until then, and because it was keenly supported by the media. Many high-level politicians were caught up in the investigations – present and former presidents, governors, senators and deputies from several parties, including PT, PMDB (Party of the Brazilian Democratic Movement) and PSDB (Brazilian Social Democracy Party). What with the right's increasing presence on the streets and wide support from corporate media, the investigation into the promiscuous relationship between large corporations and politicians soon evolved into an anti-corruption, anti-PT, pro-neoliberal reform movement.

But the anger with politicians and the political system was not limited to right-wing, neoliberal and opposition parties; it was also present on the left. Since the country's democratisation in the 1980's, there had been a fragmented political scene without a consistent majority in Congress. Elected presidents were forced to distribute posts in the executive and to hand out money to political allies for support in elections. This is what political scientists called '*presidencialismo de coalisão*' (coalition presidentialism) or '*pemedebismo*', in allusion to the role played by the PMDB, a centre-right party that since democratisation has taken part in every national government.

In this way, presidents found themselves the head of a conglomerate of parties and mandates, interested above all in controlling the distribution of public resources and staying in power.[12] Lula and the PT did not break with this pattern in the 2000s. The economic growth and the increase in public funds only fed the appetite of those coalitions. During his two terms in office, besides maintaining the alliance with conservative and corrupt forces, Lula also opened spaces for direct dialogue with unions and social movements; however, these spaces were not bases for decision-making, but rather 'listening' spaces, a strategy to include selected organised movements in the distribution of public benefits.[13]

Dilma Rousseff, heir to Lula's political capital but lacking his political ability, isolated herself, implementing a sort of 'technocratic developmentalism' that sought rapid results.[14] Re-elected in 2014, she promised the PT's social base to radicalise redistribution policies and to curb financial profits, putting pressure on private banks to lower interest rates. But as the signs of economic crisis became more visible, her first measures in 2015 were guided by fiscal austerity.

The anti-PT coalition that lost the presidential election in 2014 then filed for impeachment, on grounds of the dubious legality of certain fiscal accounting methods. These were called '*pedaladas*' (pedalling), that allowed the administration to fund a programme for farmers using money that was not reimbursed until several months later. But this was only a pretext: since the Brazilian Constitution does not contemplate the no-confidence vote as a device to eject a president from office, the political opposition that was gaining force resorted to impeachment to do the job.

The PMDB, via Eduardo Cunha, the Congress president, was the first to break the coalition led by PT, accepting the petition of impeachment.

Under Rousseff, on the left side of the political spectrum, spaces of direct participation became even more precarious. In the name of economic growth and development, indigenous and traditional communities' rights were increasingly bypassed, while movements like MPL, groups opposing Belo Monte (a hydroelectric dam in the Amazon), and Comitês Populares da Copa were demanding more control on the decision-making process regarding infrastructure and other investments with high impact on their territories. As a result, the PT was increasingly losing the sympathy of its traditional popular base.[15] Nonetheless, many of these groups still regarded the impeachment as a coup d'état conducted by the neoliberal coalition that had been defeated in 2014.

Rousseff's ousting in 2016 triggered the rapid implementation of massive cuts in social programmes, like Minha Casa Minha Vida. In addition, constitutional reforms were approved by Congress as part of a wholesale dismantling of the welfare state. But Brazilian civil society did not remain silent. Although it was not possible to block the impeachment and the reforms completely, polls indicated that Michel Temer, Rousseff's PMDB vice-president who stepped into her shoes, had the support of only 3 per cent of the population. And, in April 2018, six months before the presidential election, Judge Sergio Moro succeeded in imprisoning Lula. According to the polls, Lula and the PT led the electoral campaign with 40 per cent of the vote.

Despite the conservative tsunami, June was also a time of hope for the future. Here we also saw the '*ocupas*' – high-school students occupying their schools against educational reform;[16] the strengthening of an anti-racism movement fighting the genocide of black youth in Brazil, and feminist movements, among a myriad of new social organisations. In São Paulo and other Brazilian cities, hundreds of cultural and housing squats (including combinations of both) are experimenting with alternative solutions to the urban and also the political crises, self-managing their destinies while clamouring for resources and political attention.

It seems that a new coalition of social movements is starting to come together, in which the right to the city is definitely at the heart of the agenda.

Afterword

The Rental Housing Boom: New Frontiers of Housing Financialisation

9 June 2017: Carrer Leiva, Hostafrancs, Barcelona, Spain
In June 2017, I was on my way to the headquarters of the Platform for People Affected by Mortgages (Plataforma de Afectados por la Hipoteca – PAH) to take part in a debate on a housing bill to be proposed by popular initiative (filed to the Spanish Congress at the beginning of 2018), when I saw a building covered in banners that said:

> *Nos quieren echar* [They want to throw us out]
> *L'habitatge es un Dret!* [Housing is a right!]
> *No som bitxos som persones* [We are not animals we are people]
> *@Somleiva37 em lluita* [@Somleiva37 in struggle]

At PAH's headquarters, I heard many stories about the foreclosures that have been multiplying since the financial crisis of 2008. I also heard stories of victories won through the platform's actions, and through the emergence of a new housing movement in the city. I heard stories about the new faces of the housing crisis in Barcelona: people being evicted from apartments they had been renting for years, a vertiginous increase in rent prices, the proliferation of new neighbourhood organisations in districts that are being heavily impacted by those processes, and the formation of a new federation of local organisations of tenants: the Sindicat de Llogaters (tenants' union).

3 January 2017, Fulton County, Georgia, United States

On a chilly December afternoon in Atlanta, a judge told Reiton Allen that he had seven days to leave his house or the marshals would kick his belongings to the curb. In the packed courtroom, the truck driver, his beard flecked with gray, stood up, cast his eyes downward and clutched his black baseball cap.

The 44-year-old father of two had rented a single-family house from a company called HavenBrook Homes, which is controlled by one of the world's biggest money managers, Pacific Investment Management Co. Here in Fulton County, Georgia, such large institutional investors are up to twice as likely to file eviction notices as smaller owners, according to a new Atlanta Federal Reserve study.

'I've never been displaced like this,' said Allen, who said he fell behind because of unexpected childcare expenses as his rent rose above $900 a month. 'I need to go home and regroup.'[1]

The scenes described above are far from being an exception. Such scenes are visible not only in Barcelona or Atlanta, but also in Berlin, New York, Los Angeles, Dublin, Lisbon and many other cities.[2] We are facing a new wave of housing financialisation, now overwhelming rental housing. A new type of institutional, corporate landlord, usually linked to transnational financial assets management companies, has begun to control a great number of rental houses and apartments in many cities. This landlord's entry into the housing market was combined, in some global cities and tourist destinations like London, New York and Barcelona, with other dimensions of the residential real-estate–financial complex to produce this new and toxic trend, unleashing, once again, massive processes of dispossession.

Broadly speaking, large financial investors entered the rental housing market after the bursting of the real-estate bubble of 2008, seizing the opportunity to buy those so-called toxic assets on the cheap. Known as vulture investors, global financial conglomerates bought devalued assets in order to transform them into a new market frontier, infiltrating territories that had been neglected by – or protected from – them. By mobilising an enormous amount of capital via private equity funds, hedge funds, Real Estate Investment Trusts (REITs) and other financial instruments, capital obtained through shareholders or directly from loans, they were able to buy up deeply undervalued 'housing stocks' available in cities.

In the history of cities, cycles of destruction and devaluation of built space are by no means new. Such cycles generate new expansion fronts for social actors with the relevant capacity to raise capital. Despite that, there are some apparent novelties here. One is the huge scale of this process, its dimensions proportionate to the massive concentration and availability of global financial capital today; another is the velocity, directly derived from the technological revolution, of value representation, in online and real-time transactions, in increasingly abstract circuits that no longer have any connection to the social work embedded into built space, let alone to its inhabitants.[3]

These funds first entered the market by purchasing real-estate directly from the banks, a 'stock' of toxic assets composed of foreclosed or defaulting mortgages. Another way in for the funds was the acquisition of companies created after the crisis in order to 'clean' the banks' portfolios. Many funds also bought directly from indebted and desperate homeowners. But these funds have also captured part of the controlled and regulated public housing stock, buying job lots of social housing units from indebted cities asphyxiated by fiscal austerity measures.

Once the phase of wholesale buying of 'toxic' or 'rotten' stocks was over, these global corporate landlords[4] had become deeply rooted in local residential markets, controlling hundreds – sometimes thousands – of units in single districts or counties. From that point on, they started to behave like monopolies, pressing for a general increase in rents, indexing those markets towards a higher price.

Once again, the financial crisis itself ended up creating the demand for this new product – rental housing. The increased demand has been fuelled both by the expulsion of dwellers from their mortgaged houses and by the end of easy access to loans, creating a situation in which many people could no longer afford homeownership. Without access to social housing provision – destroyed in the previous cycle – and unable to become homeowners, people's only available option in residential markets is to rent.

Since 2008, in the United States, private equity funds have bought foreclosed homes repossessed from indebted families. But it was only in 2011 that some of the biggest private equity funds that invest in real estate – such as Blackstone or Colony Capital – decisively entered the business. They set up affiliates that have accumulated thousands of housing units, especially in the cities most devastated by the mortgage collapse.[5] For instance, today Blackstone owns 82,000 units in seventeen US markets.[6] According to a report published by a civil organisation in defence of the right to housing in Atlanta, the housing stock owned by private equity funds in the United States amounted to 200,000 units in 2013.[7]

At first, the purchase of toxic assets that were by-products of the financial crisis was a short-term move. The idea was to buy real-estate units at extremely low prices and sell them on: quick profits were made as a result of the difference between capital costs and the yields obtained through letting or resale. Later, there was a process of consolidation of those companies, accompanied by mergers and acquisitions. They have also entered the stock market, investing in real-estate investment funds.[8] These asset management funds operate in the United States and elsewhere. Blackstone, for example, has picked up CatalunyaCaixa's bankrupt estate stock in Spain, paying €3,6 billion for a stock valued at the time at €6,5 billion.[9]

The entry of vulture funds into collapsing housing markets was eagerly promoted by national and local governments, which have regulated and fostered the operation of these funds as a part of their post-financial-crisis measures. In addition, as part of bailout policies, asset management companies were created to segregate the toxic assets – those with little or no possibility of repayment – from the banks' portfolios. This was the case, for instance, of Ireland's National Asset Management Agency (NAMA), the UK

Asset Resolution (UKAR) and the Spanish Sociedad de Gestión de Activos Procedentes de la Reestructuración Bancaria (Sareb).[10]

Sareb had initially gathered a portfolio of 200,000 real-estate units, 56 per cent of which were housing units.[11] The entry of private equity funds – especially North American – was made through management contracts with the asset manager, as service providers in charge of negotiating foreclosures, evicting tenants and residents, with the aim of later putting those units up for sale, organised in 'packages'. US companies TPG, Apollo and Cerberus have taken part in these contracts. Through managing those services, they have gathered information on the housing stock, and were better positioned to win auctions promoted by the asset management companies. Cerberus acquired a portfolio of 118,323 securitised foreclosures that belonged to UKAR, in the United Kingdom, beating offers from Goldman Sachs, Blackstone, JP Morgan and CarVal.[12]

Besides, as happened in Ireland and in Spain, managers of toxic assets and investment funds have strongly lobbied governments to pass legislation allowing and encouraging the creation of real-estate investment funds that could buy the real-estate stock depreciated by the crisis, adopting and adapting the existing (REITs) models.

In the Spanish case, the regulatory framework of Sociedades Cotizadas de Inversión en el Mercado Inmobiliario (SOCIMIs) was codified into law in 2009, but reformulated in 2012 in order to make such firms more attractive to investors. One of these SOCIMIs is called Anticipa. The company was created with CatalunyaCaixa's 'rotten' real-estate stock, acquired by Blackstone in 2014. Other real-estate funds were also constituted through SOCIMIs. Their strategy was to empty the apartments they owned as far as possible in order to rent them out and, eventually, to sell them individually or in packages, usually to other funds or REITs.[13]

But, in Spain and in other European countries, the formation of large, institutional landlords also took place through the acquisition of public social housing, sold by municipalities and governments directly to funds and REITs. In Spain, the first SOCIMI owned by Blackstone is called Fidere. Fidere bought

1,860 public housing units in 2013 from the city of Madrid's Empresa Municipal de la Vivienda (EMV). Though this transaction created great controversy and was taken to court, the units remain with the American fund to this day.[14]

In Germany, the privatisation, but especially the financialisation, of the social housing stock has happened in many cities, above all in Berlin. In 1990, 30 per cent of Berlin's housing stock consisted of public housing; this proportion was reduced by half by 2008.[15] Unlike in the United Kingdom, for instance, where council houses were sold to their long-time tenants, in Berlin, 212,000 homes were privatised by being sold to large investment funds. This was a decision taken by the city government in view of their fiscal deficit at the end of the 1990s. Governments of different political affiliations maintained the policy for decades. Of the nineteen public housing companies in Berlin, two were sold outright to private equity funds (GSW and Gehag); others have sold part of their housing units stock.

Like Berlin, which has historically been a city of tenants, New York has also seen large investment funds enter its residential rental market. Although New York's public social housing units amount only to 6 per cent of the entire stock, since the 1970s a very significant part of its private residential rental market stock has been regulated. Every year, a Rent Guidelines Board, composed of real-estate representatives and city officials, set the maximum allowed increase in rental prices. The stabilised rental market represents, today, more than one million units, or 45 per cent of the city's total.

However, during the 1990s, new legislation began to deregulate the stabilised rental market, permitting, for instance, a specific real-estate unit to be exempt from the rental raise cap when the rental price reached US$2,000 (today, US$2,500) and the unit was vacant (vacancy decontrol). It also permitted the investment made by the landlord in improvements to the building or unit to be transferred onto the rent.[16] According to a report published in 2009 by the Association of Neighbourhood and Housing Development (ANHD), between 2005 and 2009, around 100,000 stabilised-rent units – that is, 10 per cent of New York's housing stock – were bought by private equity funds.[17]

Like the other processes, analysed in part one of this book, the financialisation of rental housing has been a result of public policies. States promote a 'regulated deregulation'[18] that enables and supports the pervasive expansion of this new urban business, strengthening a financial asset-based housing and urban policy.[19]

Even though the actual percentage of units controlled by these financialised landlords is only a minor proportion of local rental housing markets, the impacts of this process on tenants' living and housing conditions have been significant. First, this housing stock is not geographically distributed in a random or scattered manner. Whole districts collapsed with the financial and mortgage crisis, especially in the suburbs and city outskirts. There have also been radical changes in downtown areas where it was once possible to find affordable lets. Amid intense and conflictive processes of gentrification and resistance, corporate landlords owned by affiliates of globalised investment companies have now captured those units.

In the case of Barcelona, Melissa García-Lamarca's study shows the successive dispossession cycles in the city and maps their victims.[20] By georeferencing the addresses of individuals and families at risk of foreclosure who had sought help from the advisory platform PAH, and cross-referencing this data with the location and the rental prices of real-estate units owned by Blackstone's SOCIMIs, the research clearly reveals the socio-spatial dimension of this new frontier of housing financialisation. The working-class neighbourhoods in the north, northeast and south of the city were the ones that suffered the biggest devaluations during the crisis and the largest number of foreclosures afterwards. In those same neighbourhoods, 95 per cent of the rental units offered by Blackstone's affiliates charge rents above the neighbourhood average.[21]

A similar scenario prevails in Atlanta, where, as shown by some already mentioned research,[22] there is a concentration of real estate owned by funds in certain suburban areas; here, too, rental prices are above the city average. According to the same report, among the tenants of Invitation Home (Blackstone's home rental company), 45 per cent spent more than 30 per cent of their income on rent, limiting other expenditures and, often, falling into debt due to arrears and defaults. In Fulton County, on the outskirts of Atlanta's metropolitan area, more than 20 per cent of renters received eviction notices in 2015. According to a report published by the Federal Reserve Bank of Atlanta,[23] 12.2 per cent were ultimately evicted. Similar figures can be found in Los Angeles and in Riverside, California, where THR California, another one of Blackstone's affiliates, operates.[24]

The ongoing process in Fulton County reveals who are the most affected by the machinery of dispossession: the county's racial composition is largely non-white, with 44.3 per cent African Americans.[25] In New York, too, most of the evicted tenants are African American and Hispanic. With an increasing number of apartments being taken out of stabilised rent protection, evictions have multiplied. According to the data on eviction lawsuits collected by the New York City Public Advocate's Office, there were more than 450,000 lawsuits between January 2013 and June 2015, 80 per cent of them initiated by less than 10 per cent of landlords, highlighting a huge real-estate property concentration.[26] Such lawsuits are especially common in Hispanic neighbourhoods (Bronx, Washington Heights and Bushwick) or African American (Crown Heights, in Brooklyn).[27] In Berlin, the number of evictions has risen in privatised public housing projects owned by funds, mostly in those inhabited by low-income immigrant families.[28]

From the investors' viewpoint, it is necessary to maximise the profitability of the invested capital, unlocking the wealth embedded in residential built spaces. In the words of a World Bank study aiming to persuade governments of the advantages of this new frontier: 'Rental markets also play a key role in enhancing the market value of housing assets and in generating revenues from an unlocked housing wealth.'[29] 'Unlocking' means liberating these assets from any constraints that could block their immediate disposal. One way is the eviction of dwellers who can no longer afford the prices determined by funds.

The capacity to set prices is directly linked to the number of units controlled by these funds and their concentration in certain areas. But it also derives from the practices adopted by financialised landlords in order to 'unlock' those assets. Coercion and intimidation are the words most often heard in the stories told by evictees and tenants who experienced pressure to leave their homes. In Spain, Germany and the US, you hear of the same tactics being used by banks and funds to get rid of tenants: from imposed agreements to free the housing units from indebted tenants, to assaults on people living in old public rental units with stabilised rent in New York and Berlin, especially in gentrifying neighbourhoods.[30] Cutting off essential services or lowering the quality of buildings maintenance are other common tricks: winters without heating, buildings under endless repair with the tenants inside, threats to call immigration services, monthly rent cheques systematically returned, offers of cash to quit the building or not renew the contract.

In addition to those strategies, some countries and municipalities are working to facilitate evictions by making the rules more flexible. The Spanish rental law, Ley de Arrendamientos Urbanos (LAU), and the revision of stabilised rents in public housing units in Berlin and New York are some examples. The general hike in rent prices, combined with the stagnation of tenants' incomes and the absence of efficient mechanisms to protect housing affordability, generates rises in evictions and in the homeless population. The number of homeless people in large American cities like New York, Los Angeles and Seattle has skyrocketed in recent years, amounting to more than 550,000 nationwide.[31]

Lastly, despite the fact that this new wave has been detected in European and American cities, there are signs that it also impacts cities of the so-called global South. In Santiago de Chile, for instance, an asset-management company called Asset Chile is mobilizing investors' resources to buy entire residential buildings in downtown areas, launching them on the rental housing market.[32] In São Paulo, the real-estate company Vitacon has just joined up with Capital Land, an equity fund from Cingapura, to invest in 5,000 residential units to rent.[33] And, once more, just as we have already pointed out in this book, technical reports written by think tanks linked to multilateral agencies and presented in workshops for governments and business sectors are starting to circulate intensively in the countries of the capitalist periphery – arguing that now is the right time for public policies to enable rental housing.

In the UK, the presence of institutional landlords in rental residential markets has not been significant up to now; however, the government is seriously engaged in promoting their entry. In 2012 the government commissioned a study, the Montague Report, to examine the obstacles and propose measures for attracting large-scale institutional investment in new homes for private rent. This was a model of investment which is much more prevalent in other countries, and in some niche markets in the UK, like student housing.[34] In 2013, a Private Rented Sector task force was established within the Department of Communities and Local Government to enforce some of the proposed measures.[35]

The rental housing market, though, has not been restructured solely by the presence of corporate landlords. If the housing crisis has been especially acute in New York, London and Barcelona, this is also down to the tourism industry and to a global market of second homes that removes housing units from the long-term rental market.

Buying high-end houses and apartments in global, cultural or tourist cities has become a safe-deposit box for the transnational wealthy elite. It functions as a stable store of value for part of their capital, with great scope for appreciation. Many of these transactions are made via off-shore tax havens, below the radars of national and local governments.[36] London, New York and Miami are cities in which this phenomenon is conspicuous. In the last few years, Barcelona has also become a valued target for foreign investors. One of the factors that has contributed to launching Barcelona as a target was Spain's promotion of the 'Golden Visa' as one of its post-crisis recovery measures. Golden Visas are nothing less than the gift of citizenship in exchange for investments in real estate.

Furthermore, in the cases of Barcelona and New York, the popularity of sharing-economy platforms that connect people seeking to let their apartments – or apartment fractions – with people hoping to pay less than hotel rates on their next trip is another element that affects rental housing markets. Airbnb is the most notorious example of such platforms.

Although Airbnb presents itself as a 'community market', the company is, in fact, a very profitable start-up. Airbnb's market price exceeds one billion dollars and the company has not floated its capital on the stock market yet. The maths behind its profitability are very simple: the website charges a 10 per cent commission for each reservation and another 3 per cent commission for processing the payment. The 'host' pays these, but the 'guest' also pays a 6 to 12 per cent fee for the service. We are talking about a two-sided market that manages to make a profit from both sides. The platform's appeal is confirmed by its list of investors. They include venture capital companies such as Mighty Capital, Sequoia Capital, Bracket Capital; global financial services firms such as Morgan Stanley and JP Morgan Chase & Co.; banks like Citigroup, and private equity companies such as China Broadband Capital.[37]

The success of the platform has repercussions not only in the hotel industry, but also on the long-term rental housing market.[38] Due to their profitability and to flexible negotiations, Airbnb and copycat platforms have started to list premises that were formerly available on the long-term rental market, converting them into short-term lets for tourists and lodgers.

Once more, the effects of financialisation of rental housing go beyond the restructuring of rental markets, resulting in dispossession and displacement processes that hurt ethnic minorities, the poor and the vulnerable, and also young people. Once more, the financial logic of the operation – the bets and strategies to make sure that revenues from invested capital will increase – trumps city-dwellers' housing needs.

The creation and expansion of this new frontier of housing financialisation does not proceed without resistance, especially in cities where the upheaval has been particularly intense and where there is a history of organised social movements. The victims of dispossession, together with activists for the right to housing and to the city, are challenged to develop new forms of resistance in order to confront the opacity and abstraction that are intrinsic to the world of finance.[39]

In New York, resistance originated from a network of community organisations, NGOs and legal advisory groups that had existed since the struggles for adequate housing in the 1960s. Stabilized rent was one of their first conquests. This network was revived in order to confront the city's urban crisis at end of the

1970s. Rooted in the poorest communities, mainly home to African Americans and Hispanics, they were able to reactivate their capacities for mobilisation and struggle, reinventing strategies as soon as they began to detect the ominous signs of the entrance of private equity funds into the stabilized-rent housing stock in those neighbourhoods.

Local coalitions such as the Association for Neighborhood and Housing Development, along with neighbourhood organisations such as the Northwest Bronx Community and Clergy Coalition, committed to developing a critical narrative about what was going on. They mapped and developed social indicators; they engaged in advocacy, provided legal advice to tenants and designed eye-catching actions with the media.

By all these tactics, they managed to change public opinion in the city about what could be considered 'predatory equity'. In a positive reaction, the municipality began to intervene in the most egregious cases and has, more recently, started to offer free legal counselling – and other services and measures – to those threatened with eviction.[40] On the other hand, when Mayor de Blasio's administration announced measures touted as extending the offer of rental housing to the poorest – including changes to the zoning laws of whole neighbourhoods, to allow high building potentials and tax exemptions for real-estate developers – even more heated protests ensued.[41]

In the case of Barcelona, despite the emergence of a new social housing movement in 2005, Plataforma por la vivienda digna [Platform for decent housing], it was only after the outbreak of the financial and mortgage crisis that the tenants' defence bureau PAH was formed, organising those affected by foreclosures side by side with activists, housing rights campaigners and lawyers. Thanks to its wide-ranging advisory services for victims, information campaigns, proposal of legal bills and direct action – whether to stop evictions or to find shelter for those in urgent need – PAH has amplified its social base and political influence to the point that one of its leaders and founders, Ada Colau, was elected Barcelona's mayor in 2015.

Besides PAH, several organisations in the districts affected by speculation have come together in a 'tenants' union'. Their agenda includes measures to introduce rent control and collective forms of negotiation of those prices, in favour of social housing and for the protection of tenants threatened with eviction.[42] Initiatives to de-commodify housing are also springing up. Examples are social cooperatives, community land trusts and squatting of empty housing units. Direct actions like squatting are proposed both as concrete solutions for situations of urgent housing need, and as a tactic for the struggle.

Under pressure from – and committed to – those social movements, Barcelona's new city government has attempted to promote social housing, adopting measures like the introduction of rent control caps for units renovated using municipal loans. The city has embarked on building a new stock of public housing. It has confronted predatory tourism by controlling the number of housing units rented for short-term periods through online platforms. The municipality is also keeping an eye on accommodation listed on Airbnb and similar platforms that are not registered with the municipality or that violate zoning laws, fining Airbnb and HomeAway directly.[43] Given its financial and jurisdictional limitations in this matter, the local government has acted in concert with other cities to influence national housing policies, to reform the rental housing legislation and to abolish the benefits and tax incentives given for real-estate funds, REITs and through Golden Visas.[44]

Despite the fact that the new housing and urban movements emerging in New York and Barcelona were not able ultimately to reverse those financialisation processes, their practices build a link between the materiality of the victims' concrete lives – and the privations they are subjected to – and the abstraction of transnational financial flows, advancing towards a more multi-dimensional comprehension of the phenomenon.

At the same time, these struggles have begun to delineate the political confrontation between territories understood as spaces for life and its reproduction and territories understood as playgrounds for finance capital, uprooted and disconnected from human needs and desires. It is this aspect that provides the connecting point between the movements around housing and habitation in contemporary cities around the world.

The scenes that open and close this book, in Astana, Barcelona, Tel Aviv, Manchester, São Paulo and Rio de Janeiro, depict
contemporary rebellions in which space is more than the inert
setting where battles take place, being itself the object of those
battles. We are living in an era of rebellions, and occupations
often spring up simultaneously at different points on the planet.
The paradox of neoliberal economic globalisation is precisely
that it simultaneously weakens and rouses the social forces of
resistance.[45]

The occupation of public space for long periods has been one of
the tactics employed. Even in temporary occupations – for the time
of a demonstration – the occupied space carries an important
symbolism. It is what Charles Tilly calls 'symbolic geography': the
spaces become loaded with meanings, communicating the message
that the movement wants to spread.[46] Temporary occupations also
represent a type of abrupt hiatus in the cities' busy motion, bringing to the surface themes previously submerged under the avalanche
of day-to-day life.

Longer occupations – as in Tahrir Square (Cairo), Taksim
Square (Istanbul), Zuccotti Park (New York) and in empty buildings in São Paulo and other Brazilian cities – also offered the
chance to experiment and 'prefigure'. In other words, to try out
forms of organisation, decision-making, self-governance and
management of collective life, as well as to institute alternatives
today, rehearsing possible futures.[47]

Traditional forms of political representation, such as parlia-
ments, parties and unions, are being contested and there is a
proliferation of groups campaigning for autonomy, or new forms
of auto-representation and self-management. Vera Pallamin has
commented on the effect of interventions by art collectives with
reference to Edifício Prestes Maia – a building in the centre of São
Paulo that was occupied in 2002 by members of the São Paulo
Centre Homeless Movement (Movimento dos Sem Teto do
Centro – MSTC). She affirmed:

> Stamped on the urban landscape, [the image] becomes a seal
> lending substance and amplification to the actions for moral
> recognition and public subsidies taking place inside. In these

terms, we may see how forms of spatialisation and its sensitive interweavings alter the city's politico-aesthetic fabric.[48]

Finally, occupations also carry a confrontational dimension. A military occupation is the control of a space and the domination of an insurgent or enemy territory. An occupation carried out by a social movement, on the other hand, means the 'liberation' of a space so as to allow ordinary people to appropriate and intervene in it, challenging the authorities' attempt to exclude them – from a space, a project or a decision. Therefore, it also implies confrontation, but in the opposite sense to that of a police or military occupation.[49]

Against this radical appropriation of space, repressive technologies impose a militarised management of the spaces. This model invades cities and their urbanistic and housing policies, capturing territories, expelling and colonising spaces and lifestyles. The effects of this colonisation are politico-territorial, creating a new form of metropolitan government. This form has been denominated by some authors as post-political or post-democratic, in which dissent and democratic negotiation are suppressed in the name of efficiency and management technologies.[50] It is what Jacques Rancière has called a 'democratic scandal': for, despite promising equality and democracy, it produces a form of oligarchy, where political and economic power fuse perfectly.[51]

Those new forms of governance drive the expansion of the market's borders through a continuous process of accumulation through spoliation: the capitalisation of space and life. This involved the capture and encirclement of public spaces; the extension of land and housing commodification; or, simply, expulsions.

In Slavoj Žižek's words, this is the 'further expansion of the reign of the market, combined with progressive enclosure of public space, diminishing of public services (health, education, culture) and rising authoritarianism'.[52] Agamben goes even further when he describes the new forms of government in the metropolis:

we are not facing a process of growth and development of the old city, but the institution of a new paradigm ... Undoubtedly one of its main traits is that there is a shift from the model of the polis founded on a centre ... an agora, to a new metropolitan spatial-isation that is certainly invested in a process of 'de-politicisation', which results in a strange zone where it is impossible to decide what is private and what is public.[53]

The colonisation of urban land and housing by finance is a power-ful global process that, even after a crisis such as that in 2008, survives and recreates itself as a hegemonic movement, putting down roots and penetrating into different environments. Housing and urban policies cannot be considered neutral in relation to this process. On the contrary, they actively opt for the creation of material, symbolic and normative conditions that transform lived territories into abstract assets. However, at the margins, in the porosities and fissures of this process, 'ferments a new hybrid conglomerate of practices, often in the midst of deepening politi-cal exclusion and social disempowerment'.[54]

The outbursts and mass protests are seismic tremors in which the power of this ferment can be glimpsed. However, it is not only on these occasions that urban warfare takes place; it is fought on every front. It exists in every resistance against expulsion and evic-tion; in every anti-privatisation and anti-homogenisation struggle; in every appropriation of public spaces as spaces of multiplicity and freedom. It exists, thus, in the daily struggle for the right to the city:

> It is exactly these practices that urgently require attention, nurtur-ing, recognition, and valorization. They demand their own space; they require the creation of their own material and cultural land-scapes, their own emblematic geographies. These are the spaces where the post-political condition is questioned, the political re-treated, and practices of radical democratization experi-mented with.[55]

Urban planning and housing policies have been fundamental to the expansion of financialised capitalism. It will take more than imagination to protect these new geographies. Nonetheless, we need to imagine how to break with the idea that the 'highest and best use' equals the most profitable one. This logic must shift towards the universalisation of the right to housing and to the city, and towards the 'communisation' of urban spaces as the core of planning policies.

We also need a political movement to push against the current depoliticisation of urban governance – the way public–private partnerships are defined and regulated entirely in the private realm.[56] This movement must insist on the promotion of citizenship, and the recognition of dissent. Amid the current plethora of social movements and struggles, it remains impossible to agree on the design of a new utopia of political and social organisation – post-capitalist and post-socialist. It is also not yet possible to define a new model of city.

For now, it suffices to know that, in the June Journeys in Brazil, in uprisings against the evictions caused by mega-events (in Cape Town, Tokyo or Rio de Janeiro), in the Platform for People Affected by Mortgages in Spain, in demonstrations against gentrification in the Global North and South, urban struggles are in the ascendant. The Lefebvrian concept of the 'right to the city' is definitely alive and kicking in the streets.

Acknowledgements

This book is a register of what I saw – and of the reflections I developed – during and immediately after my mandate as the UN Special Rapporteur on Adequate Housing. Thanks to a sabbatical granted by the Faculty of Architecture and Urbanism of the University of São Paulo (FAU-USP), I was able to commit, for a few months, to its writing as an academic career thesis.

A Productivity Grant from the Brazilian National Council for Scientific and Technological Development (CNPq) gave me the resources that allowed me to complete several stages of the research, systematise the information collected during the years of my mandate as a rapporteur and, additionally, support the production of both the thesis and the Brazilian edition of the book.

The rapporteurs' position is part of the UN Human Rights Council's (UNHRC) 'special procedures'. They are in charge of monitoring the implementation of pacts and negotiated resolutions. All rapporteurs are specialists who act independently: they are not subject to the UNHRC nor to any government or multilateral organisation. Their mission is to listen to the voices of those who feel that their rights – in my case, to housing – are being violated and, as much as possible, to strive to understand the circumstances in which this happens in order to dialogue with the country's government, the UNHRC or the press, expressing their view on each case.

As a rapporteur, I received denouncements on a daily basis. They were accounts sent in by communities, NGOs, law clinics and other human-rights defenders, and they almost invariably involved contexts (or threats) of eviction. With the slender resources at my disposal, it was not even possible to deal with all the cases that did manage to reach me. Each year, the rapporteur has resources to realise two 'missions' – official visits to countries – as well as support to develop annual thematic reports on emergent issues within their field, with the help of one assistant from the Office of the High Commissioner (OHCHR). During the official country visits – immersions that lasted around two weeks[1] – I walked around the communities and spoke directly to those involved with housing issues: affected families and individuals, civil society organisations, academics, public authorities and representatives of all governmental levels. Despite the scarce initial resources, for each one of the observed countries and contexts, I was able to count on a vast network of collaborators willing to send material, information, articles and documents, to arrange informal conversations, public consultations and hearings during official visits, and to promote working visits in various cities, as well as online meetings and debates. It would be impossible to name here all the people who engaged in one way or another with my activities as a rapporteur.

Two international networks of housing movements, communities and NGOs for the defence of human rights have been fundamental to mobilise – within each analysed context or theme – further information and contacts: the Habitat International Coalition (HIC) and the International Alliance of Inhabitants (IAI). To their members and also to the hundreds of organisations and individuals who voluntarily collaborated with my work as a rapporteur, I register here my first acknowledgement and thanks; to all those who participated in the huge effort of making visible – and comprehensible to me – the signs of the global crisis of insecurity of tenure that is hitting the poorest and most vulnerable groups during these first decades of the third millennium.

I also want to register my gratitude to all the OHCHR staff who supported me during the six years of my mandate, organising and running all activities, thus helping me to face the tough task of producing reports, communiqués to governments and press releases, under the pressure of urgent situations, the complexities inherent in each case or theme and the diplomatic constraints to which this mechanism is subject. Special thanks go to Mara Bustelo and Jane Connors, Bahram Ghazi, Beatrice Quadranti, Denise Hauser, Brenda Vukovic, Laure-Anne Courdesse, Boris-Ephrem Tchoumavi, Marcelo Daher, Stefano Sensi, Isabel Ricupero, Lidia Rabinovich and Juana Sotomayor, with whom I have shared these challenges.

Thanks to the support of the permanent missions of Germany and Finland in Geneva (my mandate's sponsors within UNHRC), from 2010 on I could count on extra resources that allowed me to hire consultants to perform bibliographical research on specific subjects and organise meetings with specialists in certain areas, with a view to the production of reports. I register here my gratitude to these sponsors, but also and particularly to Jean du Plessis, Natalie Bugalski, David Pred, Mayra Gomez, Bret Thiele, Geoffrey Paine, Alain Durand-Lasserve, Alan Gilbert and Yves Cabannes, who collaborated as consultants in the research and writing of some reports cited in this book.

Technicians from humanitarian agencies involved with post-conflict or post-disaster emergency succour and reconstruction processes, particularly Barbara McCallin, from the Internal Displacement Monitoring Centre (IDMC), Laura Cunial, from the Norwegian Refugee Council, and Graham Saunders and Victoria Stodart, from the International Federation of the Red Cross and Red Crescent, were important interlocutors and collaborators in the effort of investigating this theme.

From 2009 on, I was fortunate to have FAU-USP's backing for the setting up of a research hub to support my mandate. Thanks to Professor Euler Sandeville's generosity and to the permanent support from the FAU-USP Design Department, the hub was set up within the Laboratory for Public Space and the Right to the City (LabCidade). It received research fellowships funded by USP and from projects financed initially by the German Ministry of International Relations, by Sida (Swedish International Development Cooperation Agency) and, from 2012 on, by Ford Foundation Brazil. I thank those people who participated in the many projects from LabCidade's Research team: Joyce Reis, Bruno Lupion, Paula Lígia Martins, Mariana Pires, Rodrigo Faria, Marília Ramos and Vitor Nisida.

I must register here my huge gratitude to Letícia Osório, responsible for convincing me to apply for the position of UN special rapporteur. She acted as the 'coordinator of my campaign', which was promoted by NGOs and international networks for the right to housing. My nomination was also endorsed before UNHRC by the Brazilian government. As Ford Foundation Brazil's human rights official, Letícia was also a great supporter of my work and a valued interlocutor throughout the mandate.

It would have been impossible to develop a critical reflexion about the processes that I observed without dialoguing with authors and researchers from all over the world, whom I also had the privilege to meet along this journey. They are cited in the book and I could not hope to mention them all here. Nevertheless, I owe particular thanks to Manuel Aalbers, with whom I have enjoyed intellectual collaboration and who generously included me in his own network of research about housing financialisation – now focused on the real-estate–financial complex, a concept widely employed in this book. I also thank my colleagues from the International Sociological Association's Research Committee on Sociology of Urban and Regional Development (RC21) and Research Committee on Housing and the Built Environment (RC43), with whom I shared fruitful sessions of intellectual exchange in seminars and encounters. I also thank my partners on the editorial board of the *International Journal of Urban and Regional Research*: as well as being understanding about my absences from the journal's activities, they sent me articles, helped with bibliography and 'obliged' me to keep up with current critical output on urban issues. My special thanks to Ananya Roy, who sent me articles and books related to these topics throughout my writing. I also thank Marcello Balbo, who had insisted for years that I should stop and write, and who repeatedly discussed the content and structure of this book with me. For writing the Afterword, updating the book, I used the information on Barcelona kindly supplied by Josep Montaner and Vanesa Valiño, from the city council, plus a huge file of news clippings and reports from the editor of Editorial Descontrol, publishers of the Spanish edition of the book. I also had articles and information from Melissa García-Lamarca and from Ana Sugranyes on Chile. Thank you!

Theses submitted for promotion to full professorship do not have supervisors. Nevertheless, without even asking if he could or would take on the role, I adopted one: David Harvey. During a conversation in Quito, after I had poured out a pile of empirical facts, he responded: 'Very well. You have shown me where and how processes of dispossession are happening. Congratulations! However, from an intellectual point of view, the interesting question is "why".' He then patiently discussed with me point by point, suggested books, gave me ideas and texts and, when my work seemed 'stuck', he answered my desperate Skype calls. I register here my profound gratitude to David Harvey.

In order to develop the third part of the book, set in Brazil, I drew on material generated by my working visits as a rapporteur to Rio de Janeiro, Salvador, Recife, Fortaleza, Porto Alegre and Belo Horizonte. I also had support from Public Defenders, the Public Ministry, NGOs, university research groups and the World Cup Popular Committees (in Rio, the World Cup and Olympic Games Popular Committee), which had been set up in 2010. Additionally, I drew on consultations and seminars held in São Paulo. I also used research material produced by LabCidade from 2009 on. With resources from FAPESP (São Paulo Research Foundation), CNPq, USP and the Lincoln Institute of Land Policy, through projects developed by the Laboratory's team or in collaboration with other universities, we were able to observe the recent evolution of housing and urban policies in Brazilian cities, especially in the state of São Paulo.[2] A significant portion of part three came directly from articles produced in collaboration with LabCidade's researchers, as well as from final reports of surveys we conducted, which are cited in the notes. I register here my gratitude to the commitment and professionalism of the team of researchers who have worked in LabCidade since 2009, including those who are still there: to Professor Paula Santoro, co-director of LabCidade, and to Professor Regina Lins, who helped to organise our 'Evictions Observatory'; to Joyce Reis, Danielle Klintowitz, Júlio Caldeira, Júlia Borrelli, Ana Paula Lopes, Fernanda Accioly, Luanda Vanucchi, Rodrigo Faria, Álvaro Pereira, Vitor Nisida, Luis Guilherme Rossi, Aluizio Marino, Pedro Lima, Pedro Rezende, Isabel Martin, Luciana

Bedeschi, Talita Gonzales, Felipe Vilela and Fernando Tulio. For some of them, I was (or am) a supervisor for their first degree, Master's or PhD theses in science. I add to this acknowledgement my gratitude to Higor Carvalho, Evaniza Rodrigues, Daniel Caldeira and Rosane Santos, former or current mentees who helped with research and Sunday emergency calls. With them – supervised mentees and LabCidade researchers – as well as with my colleagues, undergraduate and graduate students from FAU-USP, I learned more than I taught.

Dialogue with Brazilian activists and intellectuals in conversations, debates, public lectures and seminars has been fundamental for the collective effort to understand the difficult present moment and to imagine possible futures. I thank particularly my colleagues from *Le Monde Diplomatique*–Brazil's editorial board: Silvio Caccia Bava, Anna Luiza Salles Souto and Vera Telles; I also thank my friend-sister Sônia Lorenz, who, in strolls around the streets and squares of the neighbourhood where we live, shared with me the point of view of indigenous and *quilombola* communities affected by large projects in Brazil.

Two continuous dialogues were crucial for thinking about some of the questions I analyse in this book: firstly, with my professor colleagues in the Group of Urban Planning Disciplines, especially those with whom I shared (or still share) LabCidade's research – Paula Santoro, Karina Leitão and Luciana Royer; and secondly, with the members of City and Housing Research Network. A significant proportion of the book's part three has its source and empirical research base in my own experiences, during my years as part of the Movement for Urban Reform within municipal governments and the Brazilian federal government. I thank my partners in the federal government, particularly Benny Schvarsberg, Otilie Pinheiro, Celso Carvalho, Evaniza Rodrigues, Weber Sutti and Grazia de Grazia, who, sharing with me the setting up and direction of the Ministry of Cities' National Secretariat of Urban Programmes, helped me to develop a reading of the Brazilian city in the new millennium.

When writing this book, I interviewed former colleagues from various ministries and federal government institutions in order to verify information. In respect to the confidentiality that was sometimes required, I decided not to identify them, entirely assuming the responsibility for the veracity of what I have witnessed and now report.

I also thank the professorship examination committee, who problematised a preliminary version of this book. Carlos Vainer, Vera Telles, Cibele Rizek, Maria Cristina Leme and Flávio Villaça made me see (and admit) what it was that really propelled me to write this book: the ruptures and displacements that marked my intellectual and political trajectory in recent years.

Bianca Tavolari and Mariana Pires, respectively research assistant and reviser, were important partners in the process of writing this book. Bianca, a LabCidade researcher and collaborator, worked intensively on the organisation of all the material from my mandate as a rapporteur, on the development of the structure, on the setting up of the chapters and on the organisation of the bibliographic references – and then, in the research support for updating part three and writing the Afterword. She has been a firm, patient and careful interlocutor. Mariana performed the revision of this book's first versions and – even more importantly – by producing articles for my blog and for newspapers with me for five years, she taught me to be a journalist while I taught her to be an urbanist. In the updating of part three I could also count on the fruitful conversation and support of Aluizio Marino.

Finally, I found in Boitempo's publishing team the careful reading and the enthusiastic reception needed for the transformation of a thesis into a book. I particularly thank Ivana Jinkings, Kim Doria and Isabella Marcatti for their commitment, for the dozens of emails per day, for the partnership!

Translations to other languages are always complex, as it is not just a matter of language but also of culture and context. I am grateful to Felipe Hirshchorn, who, thanks to a grant from the Biblioteca Nacional, prepared an English version of the book, written originally in Portuguese. But Leo Hollis, from Verso, literally reworked the whole book with me, thinking as a British reader, but trying always to respect and understand my arguments and points of view. In order to make it more readable to a non–Brazilian audience, part three was reduced and synthesised. Thank you, Leo, and also Mark Martin and Lorna Scott Fox, copy-editors performing professional, delicate and dedicated work!

My last – and biggest – acknowledgement goes to Luiz Fernando de Almeida, my dear partner, who provides me with the necessary peace and grounding in order to navigate on my several journeys of writing, rewriting, translating and updating this book.

Notes

Introduction

1. Kenneth Gibb, 'The Multiple Policy Failures of the UK Bedroom Tax', *International Journal of Housing Policy*, vol. 15, no. 2 (June 2015).

2. Jenny Robinson, 'Postcolonialising Geography: Tactics and Pitfalls', *Singapore Journal of Tropical Geography*, vol. 24, no. 3 (2003); Achille Mbembe and Sarah Nuttall, 'Writing the World from an African Metropolis', *Public Culture*, New York, vol. 16, no. 3 (2004).

3. The first of the three reports, 'Climate Change and Housing Rights', was presented to the UN General Assembly in 2009. The other two, presented in 2011, examined processes of post-disaster reconstruction and its impacts, in concrete situations, on housing rights.

4. Ananya Roy, 'The 21st Century Metropolis: New Geographies of Theory', *Regional Studies*, vol. 43, no. 6 (2009).

5. Robinson, 'Postcolonialising Geography'; Carlos Vainer, 'Disseminating "Best Practice"? The Coloniality of Urban Knowledge and City Models', in Susan Parnell and Sophie Oldfield, *The Routledge Handbook on Cities of the Global South* (New York/Abingdon, Routledge, 2014); Andreas Wimmer and Nina Glick Schiller, 'Methodological Nationalism, the Social Sciences, and the Study of Migration: An Essay in Historical Epistemology', *International Migration Review*, New York, vol. 37, no. 3 (2003).

1. The Global Financialisation of Housing

1. Raquel Rolnik, *Report: Mission to Kazakhstan*, A/HRC/16/42/ Add.3, 2011, written in collaboration with Stefano Sensi. All mission and thematic reports that I presented to the UN and that are cited in the book are available on the UN High Commissioner for Human Rights' website: ohchr.org. The identification provided after the report's title in the Notes is the easiest way of finding the text through the website search tool.

2. Olzhas Auyezov, 'Troubled Kazakh Homeowners Protest over Foreclosures', Reuters, 18 March 2009. Available at: in.reuters. com, accessed 4 Dec. 2014.

3. Alfredo Rodríguez, Ana Sugranyes and Manuel Tironi, 'Anexo 1: Resultados de una encuesta', in Alfredo Rodríguez and Ana Sugranyes (eds), *Los con techo: Un desafío para la política de vivienda social* (Santiago, SUR, 2005), pp. 225–6.

4. Ana Sugranyes, 'La política habitacional en Chile, 1980–2000: un éxito liberal para dar techo a los pobres', in Rodríguez and Sugranyes (eds), *Los con techo*, pp. 23–33; Fernando Jiménez Cavieres, *Chilean Housing Policy: A Case of Social and Spatial Exclusion?* (doctorate thesis in Architecture, Fakultät VII, Architektur Umwelt Gesellschaft, Technische Universität Berlin, 2006).

5. Martin Roberts, 'Spanish Banks to Restrict Evictions after Suicides', *Guardian*, 12 November 2012. Available at: theguardian.com, accessed 6 Oct. 2014.

6. Ada Colau and Adrià Alemany, *Vidas hipotecadas: De la burbuja inmobiliaria al derecho a la vivienda* (Barcelona, Cuadrilátero de Libros, 2012).

7. Raúl Guillén, 'Em Madri, vidas hipotecadas', *Le Monde Diplomatique Brasil*, São Paulo, dossier n. 8, year 1 (Nov.–Dec. 2011).

8. See Friedrich Engels, *The Condition of the Working Class in England* (1845) and *The Housing Question* (1872).

9. Food banks stock farmers' surplus produce and food donated by individuals. In the UK, food banks usually donate directly to the person in need, referred by social services.

10. Soutik Biswas, 'India's Micro-Finance Suicide Epidemic', BBC, 16 Dec. 2010. Available at: bbc.co.uk, accessed 6 Oct. 2014.

11. David Harvey, *Seventeen Contradictions and the End of Capitalism* (Oxford, Oxford University Press, 2014), p. 241.

12. Manuel Aalbers, 'Corporate Financialization', in Noel Castree et al. (eds), *The International Encyclopedia of Geography: People, the Earth, Environment, and Technology* (Oxford, Wiley, 2015). Available at: academia.edu, accessed 8 Oct. 2015. See p. 3.

13. Richard Ronald, *The Ideology of Home Ownership: Homeowner Societies and the Role of Housing* (New York, Palgrave Macmillan, 2008).

14. David Harvey, *The Urban Experience* (Oxford, Blackwell, 1989); Ugo Rossi, 'On Life as a Fictitious Commodity: Cities and the Biopolitics of Late Neoliberalism', *International Journal of Urban and Regional Research*, vol. 37, no. 3 (May 2013).

15. Leda Maria Paulani, 'O Brasil na crise da acumulação financeirizada', IV Encuentro Internacional de Economía Política y Derechos Humanos, 2010, p. 5. Available at: madres.org, accessed 6 Oct. 2014.

16. Manuel Aalbers and Rodrigo Fernandez, *Housing and the Variations of Financialized Capitalism*, international seminar, The Real Estate/Financial Complex (Refcom), Leuven, 2014, mimeo, p. 1.

17. International Monetary Fund, *Long-Term Investors and Their Asset Allocation: Where Are They Now?* (Washington, DC, IMF, 2011), cited in Aalbers and Fernandez, *Housing and the Variations of Financialized Capitalism*, p. 13.

18. Aalbers and Fernandez, *Housing and the Variations of Financialized Capitalism*, p. 14.

19. Ibid.

20. Herman M. Schwartz and Leonard Seabrooke, 'Conclusion: Residential Capitalism and the International Political Economy', in Schwartz and Seabrooke (eds), *The Politics of Housing Booms and Busts* (London, Palgrave Macmillan, 2009), p. 210.

21. Ibid. p. 209.

22. Aalbers and Fernandez, *Housing and the Variations of Financialized Capitalism*, p. 4.

23. The concept of real-estate/financial complex was presented to me by Manuel Aalbers. He leads research focused on the relationship between real estate, finance and the state, drawing a parallel with the US military–industrial complex. See: ees.kuleuven.be /geography, accessed 10 Aug. 2015.

24. Mariana Fix, *Financeirização e transformações recentes no circuito imobiliário no Brasil* (PhD thesis in Economic Development, Campinas, IE-Unicamp, 2011); Rossi, 'On Life as a Fictitious Commodity'.

25. Schwartz and Seabrooke, 'Conclusion', p. 210; Philippe Zivkovic, 'Financiarisation de l'immobilier: La réponse innovante du groupe BNP Paribas', 2006, cited in Higor Rafael de Souza Carvalho, *A cidade como um canteiro de negócios* (Undergraduate Final Work in Architecture and Urban Planning FAU-USP, São Paulo, 2011), p. 155.

26. Neil Brenner and Nik Theodore, 'Cities and the Geographies of "Actually Existing Neoliberalism"', in Brenner and Theodore (eds), *Spaces of Neoliberalism: Urban Restructuring in North America and Western Europe* (Oxford, Blackwell, 2002).

27. World Bank, *Housing: Enabling Markets to Work* (Washington, DC, World Bank, 1993).

28. Herman M. Schwartz and Leonard Seabrooke, 'Varieties of Residential Capitalism in the International Political Economy: Old Welfare States and the New Politics of Housing', in Schwartz and Seabrooke (eds), *The Politics of Housing Booms and Busts*, p. 16.

29. Loïc Chiquier and Michael Lea (eds), *Housing Finance Policy in Emerging Markets* (Washington, DC, World Bank, 2009), pp. xxxi–ii.

30. Robert M. Buckley and Jerry Kalarickal (eds), *Thirty Years of World Bank Shelter Lending: What Have We Learned?* (Washington, DC, World Bank, 2006), p. 41.

31. David Harvey, *Limits to Capital* (London and New York, Verso, 2007); *A Companion to Marx's Capital*, 2 vols (London and New York, Verso, 2013).

32. Brenner and Theodore, 'Cities and the Geographies of "Actually Existing Neoliberalism"'.

33. Ibid.

34. World Bank, *Housing: Enabling Markets to Work*.

35. Raquel Rolnik, *Thematic Report about the Impact of Financialization on the Right to Adequate Housing*, A/67/286, 2012, in collaboration with Lidia Rabinovich.

2. The Mortgage System

1. In Great Britain and Northern Ireland, for example, around 5.5 million social housing units were built between the end of World War II and 1981. See Michael Harloe, *The People's Home? Social Rented Housing in Europe and America* (Hoboken, NJ, Wiley-Blackwell, 1995); and David Fée, 'Le logement social en Angleterre: trente ans de déclin', *Informations Sociales*, no. 159 (2010).

2. Claire Lévy-Vroelant and Christian Tutin (eds), *Le logement social en Europe au début du XXIe siècle* (Rennes, Presses Universitaires de Rennes, 2010), p. 15.

3. Ibid., p. 18.

4. Raquel Rolnik, *Thematic Report about Rental and Collective Housing*, A/68/289, 2013, in collaboration with Lidia Rabinovich.

5. World Bank, *Housing: Enabling Markets to Work*, p. 6.

6. Joe Doherty et al., *The Changing Role of the State: Welfare Delivery in the Neoliberal Era* (Brussels, Feantsa, 2005).

7. UN-Habitat, *Affordable Land and Housing in Europe and North America* (Nairobi, UN-Habitat, 2011), p. 9.

8. Raquel Rolnik, 'Late Neoliberalism: The Financialization of Home-ownership and Housing Rights', *International Journal of Urban and Regional Research*, vol. 37, no. 3 (2013).

9. Hugo Priemus and Frans Dieleman, 'Social Housing Policy in the European Union: Past, Present and Perspectives', *Urban Studies*, vol. 39, no. 2, 2002.

10. Darinka Czischke and Alice Pittini, *Housing Europe 2007: Review of Social, Co-operative and Public Housing in the 27 EU Member States* (Brussels, Cecodhas European Social Housing Observatory, 2007), p. 49.

11. Estonia's and Slovenia's answers to a questionnaire sent by the UN special rapporteur on adequate housing on 5 April 2012. All answers can be found at: ohchr.org/EN/Issues/Housing/Pages/HousingFinancingForThePoorAnswerstoQuestionnaire.aspx.

12. Julie Lawson, Tony Gilmour and Vivienne Milligan, *International Measures to Channel Investment towards Affordable Rental Housing* (Research report, Australian Housing and Urban Research Institute, Melbourne, May 2010). Available at: apo.ed.au, accessed 6 Jan. 2015.

13. Mikael Atterhög and Han-Suck Song, 'A Survey of Policies that May Increase Access to Home Ownership for Low-Income Households', *Housing, Theory and Society*, vol. 26, no. 4 (2009), pp. 248–9.

14. Dan Andrews and Aida Caldera Sánchez, 'Drivers of Homeownership Rates in Selected OECD Countries', *OECD Economics Department Working Papers*, no. 849 (2011), p. 9.

15. Jim Kemeny, '"The Really Big Trade-Off" between Home Ownership and Welfare: Castles' Evaluation of the 1980 Thesis, and a Reformulation 25 Years on', *Housing, Theory and Society*, vol. 22, no. 2 (2005); Janneke Toussaint and Marja Elsinga, 'Exploring "Housing Asset-Based Welfare": Can the UK be Held Up as an Example for Europe?', *Housing Studies*, vol. 24, no. 5 (2009), cited in Aalbers and Fernandez, *Housing and the Variations of Financialized Capitalism*.

16. Ewald Engelen, 'The Logic of Funding European Pension Restructuring and the Dangers of Financialisation', *Environment and Planning A*, vol. 35, no. 8 (2003); Greta Krippner, *Capitalizing on Crisis: The Political Origins of the Rise of Finance* (Cambridge, MA, Harvard University Press, 2011); Randy Martin, *Financialization of Daily Life* (Philadelphia, Temple University Press, 2002), cited in Aalbers and Fernandez, *Housing and the Variations of Financialized Capitalism*.

17. UNCTAD, *Trade and Development Report: Adjusting to the Changing Dynamics of the World Economy*, 13 Sept. 2013, cited in Aalbers and Fernandez, *Housing and the Variations of Financialized Capitalism*.

18. Colin Crouch, 'Privatised Keynesianism: An Unacknowledged Policy Regime', *The British Journal of Politics and International Relations*, vol. 11, no. 3 (2009), cited in Aalbers and Fernandez, *Housing and the Variations of Financialized Capitalism*.

19. UN-Habitat, *Financing Urban Shelter: Global Report on Human Settlements* (Nairobi, UN-Habitat, 2005), p. 1.

20. Maria Kaika and Melissa García Lamarca, '"Mortgaged Lives": The Biopolitics of Debt and Homeownership in Spain', 2014. Available at: escholar.manchester.ac.uk, accessed 6 Jan. 2015.

21. Western Regional Advocacy Project, *2012 HUD Budget Fact Sheet*, 2011. Available at: docsrush.net, accessed 12 Jan. 2015.

22. Raquel Rolnik, *Report: Mission to the USA*, A/HRC/13/20/Add.4, 2010, in collaboration with Denise Hauser.

23. Slovakia's answers to a 2012 questionnaire.

24. UN-Habitat, *A Policy Guide to Rental Housing in Developing Countries* (Nairobi, UN-Habitat, 2011), p. 1; *Rental Housing: An Essential Option for the Urban Poor in Developing Countries* (Nairobi, UN-Habitat, 2003), p. 1.

25. Raquel Rolnik and Lidia Rabinovich, 'Late-Neoliberalism: The Financialization of Homeownership and the Housing Rights of the Poor', in Aoife Nolan (ed.), *Economic and Social Rights after the Global Financial Crisis* (Cambridge, Cambridge University Press, 2014).

26. Duncan Bowie, *The Politics of Housing Development in an Age of Austerity* (London, Chartist, 2011), p. 19. Available at: researchgate.net, accessed 5 Jan. 2015.

27. *Betterment* can be defined as 'improvement contribution'. *Planning gains* correspond to the participation of private promoters in funding the provision of the infrastructure needed for urban development.

28. United Kingdom, *Town and Country Planning Act*, London, 1990. Available at: legislation.gov.uk, accessed 18 Aug. 2015.

29. Matt Griffith and Pete Jefferys, *Solutions for the Housing Shortage* (London, Shelter, 2013), p. 13.

30. Doherty et al., *The Changing Role of the State*; Rolnik, *Thematic Report about the Impact of Financialization*.

31. United Kingdom, *Housing Act*, London, 1980. Available at: legislation.gov.uk, accessed 12 Jan. 2015.

32. Department for Communities and Local Government (DCLG), *Live Tables on Social Housing Sales*, Table 678, London, DCLG, 2012. Available at: gov.uk, accessed 12 Jan. 2015.

33. Eoin Rooney and Mira Dutschke, 'Case Study: Right to Housing in Northern Ireland', in Rory O'Connell et al., *Applying an International Human Rights Framework to State Budget Allocations: Rights and Resources* (London, Routledge, 2014).

34. Michael E. Stone, *Social Housing in the UK and US: Evolution, Issues and Prospects*, May 2003, p. 21. Available at: gold.ac.uk, accessed 6 Jan. 2015.

35. HM Revenue & Customs, *Regulatory Impact Assessment: Withdrawal of Mortgage Interest Relief and Miras* (London, HMRC,

2000). Available at: webarchive.nationalarchives.gov.uk, accessed 6 Jan. 2014.

36. Rolnik, *Thematic Report about the Impact of Financialization*, paragraph 11.

37. Matthew Watson, 'Planning for a Future of Asset-Based Welfare? New Labour, Financialized Economic Agency and the Housing Market', *Planning, Practice and Research*, vol. 24, no. 1 (2009), p. 43, cited in Mary Robertson, 'What Goes Up Mustn't Come Down: The Contradictions of the Government's Response to the UK Housing Crisis', *RC43 Pre-conference PhD Workshop*, July 2013, mimeo. Available at: academia.edu, accessed 6 Jan. 2015.

38. DCLG, *Live Tables on Dwelling Stock*, Table 104, London, DCLG, 2012. Available at: gov.uk, accessed 18 Aug. 2015.

39. DCLG, *Kick-Starting a New Private Rented Sector*. Informative material for the special rapporteur's visit, 2013. Available at: selondonhousing.org, accessed 18 Aug. 2015.

40. Scottish Government, *Housing Statistics for Scotland 2013: Key Trends Summary*, 2013, p. 9. Available at: scotland.gov.uk, accessed 16 Nov. 2014.

41. DCLG, *Live Tables on Housing Market and House Prices*, table 586, London, DCLG, 2012. Available at: gov.uk, accessed 12 Jan. 2015.

42. Griffith and Jefferys, *Solutions for the Housing Shortage*, p. 13.

43. DCLG, *Live Tables on Housing Market and House Prices*, Table 244, London, DCLG, 2012. Available at: gov.uk, accessed 18 Aug. 2015.

44. Steve Wilcox and John Perry, *UK Housing Review 2013 Briefing Paper* (Coventry, Chartered Institute of Housing/Orbit Group, 2013), p. 9. Available at mycih.cih.org, accessed 15 Nov. 2014.

45. DCLG, *Live Tables on Rents, Lettings and Tenancies*, table 600, London, DCLG, 2012. Available at: gov.uk, accessed 12 Jan. 2015.

46. Tenant Participation Advisory Service (TPAS), *Written Submission to the All-Party Parliamentary Group for the Private Rented Sector: How the Sector Should Be Regulated*, 2013, mimeo, paragraph 2.2. Available at: tpas.ed.uk, accessed 18 Aug. 2015.

47. Graeme Cooke and Andy Hull, *Together at Home: A New Strategy for Housing* (London, Institute for Public Policy Research, 2012), pp. 7–75. Available at: ippr.org, accessed 6 Jan. 2015.

48. Kate Barker, 'Delivering Stability: Securing Our Future Housing Needs', *Review of Housing Supply* (London, HM Treasury, 2004), p. 3. Available at: image.guardian.co.uk, accessed 15 Nov. 2014.

49. National Housing Federation, *The Bedroom Tax in Merseyside: 100 Days On* (London, NHF, 2013). Available at: housing.ed.uk, accessed 16 Nov. 2014.

50. Barker, 'Delivering Stability'.

51. Robertson, 'What Goes Up Mustn't Come Down', p. 1.

52. Northern Ireland, *Mortgages: Actions for Possession*, Jul.– Sep. 2013 (provisional data). Available at: courtsni.gov.uk, accessed 6 Jan. 2015.

53. DCLG, *English Housing Survey: Households 2011–2012* (London, DCLG, 2013), p. 11, image 1.1. Available at: gov.uk, accessed 15 Nov. 2014.

54. England and Scotland indicated that legislation to regulate this sector is in process of development.

55. Guy Lynn and Ed Davey, 'London Letting Agents "Refuse Black Tenants"', BBC News, 14 Oct. 2013. Available at: bbc.com, accessed 15 Nov. 2014.

56. Greater London Authority (GLA), 'Rent Reform: Making London's Private Rented Sector Fit for Purpose', *London.co.uk*, 9 June 2013, p. 23. Available at: london.gov.uk, accessed 12 Jan. 2015.

57. DCLG, *A Plain English Guide to the Localism Act*, London, DCLG, Nov. 2011. Available at: gov.uk, accessed 12 Jan. 2015.

58. Kathleen Kelly, 'Taxing Question', *Inside Housing*, London, 7 Nov. 2013. Available at: insidehousing.co.uk, accessed 16 Nov. 2014.

59. DCLG, *Accelerating the Release of Public Sector Land: Update, Overview and Next Steps*, London, DCLG, Oct. 2011. Available at: gov.uk, accessed 12 Jan. 2015.

60. United Kingdom, 'Affordable Home Ownership Schemes', last update 7 Oct. 2015. Available at: gov.uk, accessed 9 Oct. 2015.

61. Scottish Government, *The Future of Right to Buy in Scotland: Consultation Report*, 2013, paragraph 3.1. Available at: scotland.gov.uk, accessed 16 Nov. 2014.

62. Oxfam, 'A Cautionary Tale: The True Cost of Austerity and Inequality in Europe', *Oxfam Briefing Paper*, no. 174, Oxford, Sept. 2013, p. 8. Available at: oxfam.org, accessed 16 Nov. 2014.

63. Tom McInnes et al., *Monitoring Poverty and Social Exclusion 2013* (York, Joseph Rowntree Foundation, 2013), p. 26. Available at: jrf.ed.uk, accessed 16 Nov. 2014.

64. United Kingdom, *Housing Benefit: Under Occupation of Social Housing*, London, Department for Work and Pensions, 28 Jun. 2012. Available at: gov.uk, accessed 16 Nov. 2014.

65. Scotland, *The 'Bedroom Tax' in Scotland*, Edinburgh, 19 Oct. 2013, paragraph 1. Available at: scottish.parliament.uk, accessed 12 Jan. 2015.

66. National Housing Federation, *Briefing – Welfare Reform Act 2012: Size Criteria*, London, NHF, March 2012, p. 7. Available at: democracy.york.gov.uk, accessed 16 Nov. 2014.

67. See NHF declaration on the six-month anniversary of the bedroom tax, on 30 September 2013. See also Suzanne Fitzpatrick et al., *The Homelessness Monitor: England 2013*, London, Crisis Head Office, Dec. 2013. Available at: crisis.ed.uk, accessed 16 Nov. 2014.

68. Office for National Statistics, *Index of Private Housing Rental Prices*, United Kingdom, ONS, 26 June 2013. Available at: ons.gov.uk, accessed 13 Jan. 2015.

69. Patrick Butler, 'Heat or Eat? Or Take Out a Loan. Do Both, and Hope for the Best?', *Guardian*, 1 Oct. 2013. Available at: theguardian.com, accessed 15 Nov. 2014.

70. National Housing Federation, *The Bedroom Tax in Merseyside*, p. 5.

71. DCLG, *Live Tables on Housing Market and House Prices*.

72. Marshall W. Dennis and Thomas Pinkowish, *Residential Mortgage Lending: Principles and Practices* (Mason, NH, Thomson/South -Western, 2004), cited in Manuel Aalbers, *Place, Exclusion, and Mortgage Markets* (Oxford, Wiley-Blackwell, 2011), p. 83.

73. Larry Bennett, Janet L. Smith and Patricia A. Wright (eds), *Where Are Poor People to Live? Transforming Public Housing Communities* (Armonk, NY, M. E. Sharpe, 2006).

74. Lawrence J. Vale, *Purging the Poorest: Public Housing and the Design Politics of Twice-Cleared Communities* (Chicago, University of Chicago Press, 2013), p. 11.

75. Nowadays, 69 per cent of public housing residents belong to racial minorities: 46 per cent are Afro-descendants and 20 per cent are Latin Americans. Cf. US Housing Scholars and Research Advocacy

Organizations, *Residential Segregation and Housing Discrimination in the United States: Violations of the International Convention on the Elimination of All Forms of Racial Discrimination* (Washington, DC, Poverty and Race Research Action Council/National Fair Housing Alliance, 2008). Available at: prrac.org, accessed 16 Nov. 2014.

76. John Atlas and Peter Dreier, 'Public Housing: What Went Wrong?', *Shelter Force*, National Housing Institute, no. 74 (Sept.–Oct. 1994).

77. Vale, *Purging the Poorest*, p. 16.

78. National Fair Housing Association, *The Future of Fair Housing: Report of the National Commission on Fair Housing and Equal Opportunity*, Dec. 2008, p. 9. Available at: nationalfairhousing. org, accessed 16 Nov. 2014.

79. Aalbers, *Place, Exclusion, and Mortgage Markets*.

80. Janet L. Smith, 'Public Housing Transformation: Evolving National Policy', in Bennett, Smith and Wright (eds), *Where Are Poor People to Live?*, p. 30.

81. Ibid., p. 31.

82. Barbara Sard and Will Fischer, *Preserving Safe, High Quality Public Housing Should Be a Priority of Federal Housing Policy*, Washington, DC, Center on Budget and Policy Priorities, 8 Oct. 2008, p. 12. Available at: cbpp.org, accessed 6 Jan. 2015.

83. Department of Housing and Urban Development (HUD), *HOPE VI: Best Practices and Lessons Learned 1992–2002* (Washington, DC, HUD, 2002).

84. Susan J. Popkin et al., *A Decade of HOPE VI: Research Findings and Policy Challenges*, Washington, DC, The Urban Institute, 18 May 2004. Available at: urban.org, accessed 18 Aug. 2015.

85. Ibid., p. 20.

86. Interview with the executive director of the Coalition to Protect Public Housing. I did not have access to official data on the total number of demolished or constructed units within Chicago's Plan for Transformation.

87. For more data on how much banks were forced to offer 'risky' loans, see Peter Marcuse, 'The Deceptive Consensus on Redlining: Definitions Do Matter', *Journal of the American Planning Association*, vol. 45, no. 4 (Oct. 1979).

88. Joint Center for Housing Studies, 'Executive Summary', in *The State of the Nation's Housing 2007*, Cambridge, MA, Harvard University, 11 June 2007. Available at: jchs.harvard.edu, accessed 12 Jan. 2015.

89. Martha Poon, 'Aux origines était la bulle: La mécanique des fluides des subprimes', *Mouvements*, no. 58 (2009).

90. Kevin Fox Gotham, 'The Secondary Circuit of Capital Reconsidered: Globalization and the U.S. Real Estate Sector', *American Journal of Sociology*, vol. 112, no. 1 (July 2006).

91. HUD, *FY 2010 Budget: Road Map for Transformation* (Washington, DC, HUD, 2010), p. 5. Available at: hud.gov, accessed 12 Jan. 2015.

92. See National Coalition for the Homeless et. al., *Foreclosure to Homelessness 2009: The Forgotten Victims of the Subprime Crisis* (Washington, DC, National Coalition for the Homeless, 2009), p. 2. Available at: nationalhomeless.org, accessed 6 Jan. 2015. As reported by Los Angeles County, there has been a significant growth in home foreclosures in the last few years: from 12,469 in 2007 to 35,058 in 2008.

93. Danilo Pelletiere and Keith Wardrip, 'Renters and the Housing Credit Crisis', *Poverty and Race*, vol. 17, no. 4 (July–Aug. 2008), pp. 3–7.

94. New York State Division of Housing & Community Renewal, *History of Rent Regulation: Rent Regulation after 50 Years – An Overview of New York State's Rent Regulated Housing*, 1993. Available at: tenant.net, accessed 4 Dec. 2014.

95. Pratt Center for Community Development and New York Immigrant Housing Collaborative, *Confronting the Housing Squeeze: Challenges Facing Immigrant Tenants, and What New York Can Do*, New York, Pratt Center for Community Development, 16 Oct. 2008, p. 16. Available at: prattcenter.net, accessed 6 Jan. 2015.

96. Policy Link, *Expiring Use: Retention of Subsidized Housing* (Oakland, CA, Policy Link, 2014). Available at: policylink.info, accessed 4 Dec. 2014.

97. Douglas Rice and Barbara Sard, *The Effects of the Federal Budget Squeeze on Low-Income Housing Assistance* (Washington, DC, Center on Budget and Policy Priorities, Feb. 2007), p. 5.

98. Ibid., p. 10.

99. The United States Conference of Mayors, *Hunger and Homelessness Survey: A Status Report on Hunger and Homelessness in America's Cities* (Washington, DC, The United States Conference of Mayors, 2008), p. 23. Available at: usmayors.org, accessed 18 Aug. 2015.

100. HUD, *FY 2010 Budget*, p. 9.

101. Rice and Sard, *Effects of the Federal Budget Squeeze*, p. 2.

102. Joint Center for Housing Studies, 'Executive Summary', in *The State of the Nation's Housing 2008*, Cambridge, MA, Harvard University, 23 June 2008, p. 28. Available at: jchs.harvard.edu, accessed 12 Jan. 2015.

103. Manuel Aalbers, 'The Financialization of Home and the Mortgage Market Crisis', *Competition & Change*, vol. 12, no. 2 (June 2008).

104. European Economic and Social Committee, 'Opinion of the European Economic and Social Committee on "Issues with Defining Social Housing as a Service of General Economic Interest" (Own-Initiative Opinion)', *Official Journal of the European Union*, Brussels, 15 Feb. 2013. Available at: eur-lex.europa.eu, accessed 4 Dec. 2014.

105. Peter Boelhouwer and Hugo Priemus, 'Dutch Housing Policy Realigned', *The Netherlands Journal of Housing and Environmental Research*, vol. 5, n. 1, 1990, p. 115.

106. Ibid., p. 110.

107. Susan Fainstein, 'Cities and Diversity: Should We Want It? Can We Plan for It?', *Urban Affairs Review*, vol. 41, (Sep. 2005), cited in Justin Kadi and Richard Ronald, 'Market-Based Housing Reforms and the "Right to the City": The Variegated Experiences of New York, Amsterdam, and Tokyo', *International Journal of Housing Policy*, vol. 14, no. 3 (2014).

108. Marja Elsinga and Frank Wassenberg, 'L'exception néerlandaise', in Lévy-Vroelant and Tutin (eds), *Le logement social en Europe*, p. 52.

109. Aalbers, 'The Financialization of Home'.

110. De Nederlandsche Bank (DNB), *Het bancaire hypotheekbedrijf onder de loep. Rapport over de ontwikkelingen op de hypotheek-markt in de periode 1994–1999* (Amsterdam, De Nederlandsche Bank, 2000), cited in Aalbers, 'The Financialization of Home'.

111. Kadi and Ronald, 'Market-Based Housing Reforms and the "Right to the City"'.

112. Karin Hedin et al., 'Neoliberalization of Housing in Sweden: Gentrification, Filtering, and Social Polarization', *Annals of the Association of American Geographers*, vol. 102, no. 2 (2012).

113. Ibid., p. 444.

114. Ibid.

115. Julie Pollard, 'Political Framing in National Housing Systems: Lessons from Real-Estate Developers in France and Spain', in Schwartz and Seabrooke (eds), *The Politics of Housing Booms and Busts*.

116. Jaime Palomera, 'How Did Finance Capital Infiltrate the World of the Urban Poor? Homeownership and Social Fragmentation in a Spanish Neighborhood', *International Journal of Urban and Regional Research*, vol. 38, no. 1 (Jan. 2014).

117. Melissa García Lamarca, 'Resisting Evictions Spanish Style', *New Internationalist* (April 2013). Available at: newint.org, accessed 12 Jan. 2015.

118. Colau and Alemany, *Vidas hipotecadas*, p. 35.

119. Pollard, 'Political Framing in National Housing Systems'.

120. Colau and Alemany, *Vidas hipotecadas*, p. 56.

121. Josep Roca Cladera and Malcom C. Burns, 'The Liberalization of the Land Market in Spain: The 1998 Reform of Urban Planning Legislation', *European Planning Studies*, vol. 8, no. 5 (July 2000).

122. Ibid., p. 46.

123. Colau and Alemany, *Vidas hipotecadas*, pp. 51–6.

124. Ibid., p. 66.

125. Ibid.

126. Guillén, 'Em Madri, vidas hipotecadas', p. 46.

127. Observatori Drets Econòmics Socials i Culturals and Plataforma de Afectados por la Hipoteca, *Emergencia habitacional en el Estado español: la crisis de las ejecuciones hipotecarias y los desalojos desde una perspectiva de derechos humanos*, 2013, pp. 106–8. Available at: afectadosporlahipoteca.com, accessed 15 Oct. 2014.

128. Instituto Nacional de Estadística, *Censos de Población y Viviendas 2011*. Available at: ine.es, accessed 4 Dec. 2014.

3. Exporting the Model

1. World Bank, *Housing: Enabling Markets to Work*, p. 3.
2. Buckley and Kalarickal (eds), *Thirty Years of World Bank Shelter Lending*.
3. Ibid., pp. 60–3.
4. Ibid.
5. World Bank, *Housing: Enabling Markets to Work*, pp. 35–6.
6. Buckley and Kalarickal (eds), *Thirty Years of World Bank Shelter Lending*, pp. 18–19.
7. Ibid.
8. World Bank, *Housing: Enabling Markets to Work*, p. 6.
9. Ibid., p. 5.
10. Ibid., pp. 37–8.
11. Buckley and Kalarickal (eds), *Thirty Years of World Bank Shelter Lending*.
12. World Bank, *Housing: Enabling Markets to Work*, pp. 37–8.
13. Council of Europe Development Bank (CEB), *Housing in South Eastern Europe: Solving a Puzzle of Challenges* (Paris, CEB, 2004).
14. David Donnison and Clare Ungerson, *Housing Policy* (Harmondsworth, Penguin, 1982), p. 107, cited in Mark Stephens, 'A Critical Analysis of Housing Finance Reform in a "Super" Home-Ownership State: The Case of Armenia', *Urban Studies*, vol. 42, no. 10 (Sep. 2005).
15. József Hegedüs, Stephen E. Mayo and Iván Tosics, 'Transition of the Housing Sector in the East Central European Countries', *Review of Urban & Regional Development Studies*, vol. 8, no. 2 (July 1996).
16. Mark Stephens, 'A Critical Analysis of Housing Finance Reform in a "Super" Home-Ownership State', pp. 1795–7.
17. Mark Stephens, 'Locating Chinese Urban Housing Policy in an International Context', *Urban Studies*, vol. 47, no. 14 (Dec. 2010).
18. Slovakia's answers to a 2012 questionnaire.
19. Ibid.
20. Estonia's answers to a 2012 questionnaire.
21. József Hegedüs, Martin Lux and Petr Sunega, 'Decline and Depression: The Impact of the Global Economic Crisis on Housing Markets in Two Post-Socialist States', *Journal of Housing and the Built Environment*, vol. 26, no. 3 (Sep. 2011).

22. See Eurostat, epp.eurostat.ec.europa.eu, accessed 4 Dec. 2014.

23. Stephens, 'Locating Chinese Urban Housing Policy in an International Context'.

24. UN Economic Commission for Europe (UNECE), *Housing Finance Systems for Countries in Transition: Principles and Examples* (New York/Geneva, UNECE, 2005). Available at: unece.org, accessed 12 Jan. 2015.

25. UN-Habitat, *Affordable Land and Housing in Europe and North America*, p. 62.

26. Council of Europe, *Housing Policy and Vulnerable Social Groups: Report and Guidelines* (Strasbourg, Council of Europe Publishing, 2008), p. 53.

27. Slovakia's answers to a 2012 questionnaire; Scott Leckie, *Regional Housing Issues Profile: Implementing Housing Rights in South East Europe*, Regional Consultation on Making Cities Inclusive, Belgrade, 2002.

28. Sasha Tsenkova, *Housing Policy Reforms in Post-Socialist Europe: Lost in Transition* (Heidelberg, Physica, 2009).

29. Jian-Ping Ye, Jia-Ning Song and Chen-Guang Tian, 'An Analysis of Housing Policy During Economic Transition in China', *International Journal of Housing Policy*, vol. 10, no. 3 (Sep. 2010), pp. 273–5.

30. Ya Pin Wang, *Urban Poverty, Housing and Social Change in China* (London, Routledge, 2004), cited in Stephens, 'A Critical Analysis of Housing Finance'.

31. Yuqin Huang, *Where Is Home? Hukou, Non-Local Young People and New Inequalities in Relation to Housing in Contemporary Shanghai*, China, XVIII ISA World Congress of Sociology, Yokohama, 2014, mimeo.

32. UN-Habitat, *Affordable Land and Housing in Europe and North America*.

33. Tsenkova, *Housing Policy Reforms in Post-Socialist Europe*, pp. 160–1.

34. Hegedüs, Lux and Sunega, 'Decline and Depression', p. 319.

35. European Bank for Reconstruction and Development (EBRD), *Crisis and Transition: The People's Perspective* (London, EBRD, 2011), p. 56. Available at: ebrd.com, accessed 20 Aug. 2015.

36. Ibid., pp. 55–6. See also: Eurostat, *Housing Statistics*, available at: ec.europa.eu, accessed 20 Aug. 2015.

37. Wallace Kaufman and Ilya Lipkovich, *Housing in Kazakhstan: Recent Statistics and Trends* (Almaty, International City/County Management Association, 1995). Available at: pdf.usaid.gov, accessed 6 Jan. 2015.

38. In part two of this book, I will delve more deeply into the nature of urban megaprojects.

39. Alima Bissenova, 'Construction Boom and Banking Crisis in Kazakhstan', Central Asia-Caucasus Institute Analyst, March 2009. Available at: old.cacianalyst.org, accessed 17 Oct. 2014.

40. Ibid.

41. Raquel Rolnik, *Report: Mission to Kazakhstan*, A/HRC/16/42/ Add.3, 2011, in collaboration with Stefano Sensi.

42. See the report on the activities of the Commissioner for Human Rights in the Republic of Kazakhstan. Available at: ombudsman. kz, accessed 4 Dec. 2014.

4. Post-Crisis Measures

1. Manuel Aalbers, 'Debate on Neoliberalism in and after the Neoliberal Crisis', *Debates and Development. International Journal of Urban and Regional Research*, vol. 37, no. 3 (May 2013), p. 1054.

2. Observatori Drets Econòmics Socials i Culturals and Plataforma de Afectados por la Hipoteca, *Emergencia habitacional en el Estado español*, p. 13.

3. This was the assessment of Joseph Stiglitz, cited by the economist Michael Hudson in an interview for *Democracy Now!*. See 'New $600B Fed Stimulus Fuels Fears of US Currency War', *Democracy Now!*, 5 Nov. 2010. Available at: democracynow.org, accessed 10 Nov. 2014.

4. The White House, *Fact Sheet: President Obama's Plan to Help Responsible Homeowners and Heal the Housing Market*, 1 Feb. 2012. Available at: whitehouse.gov, accessed 10 Nov. 2014.

5. Ibid.

6. Peter S. Goodman, 'U.S. Will Push Mortgage Firms to Reduce More Loan Payments', *New York Times*, 28 Nov. 2009. Available at: nytimes.com, accessed 10 Nov. 2014.

7. IMF, *Global Financial Stability Report: Durable Financial Stability: Getting There from Here* (Washington, DC, IMF, April 2011), pp. 115–16.

8. Robertson, 'What Goes Up Mustn't Come Down', p. 1.

9. See United Kingdom, 'Affordable Home Ownership Schemes'.

10. Montenegro's answers to a 2012 questionnaire.

11. Andorra's answers to a 2012 questionnaire.

12. IMF, *Global Financial Stability Report*, pp. 115–16.

13. The White House, *Fact Sheet*.

14. Greece's answers to a 2012 questionnaire.

15. David Harvey, 'Globalization and the "Spatial Fix"', *Geographische Revue – Zeitschrift für Literatur und Diskussion*, vol 3, no. 2 (2001).

5. The Demand-Side Subsidies Model

1. There is an important distinction between subsidies that operate through the financial system and those that do not. For example, the construction and management of rental housing units or the concession of aid to help tenants pay the rent are not part of financialised circuits. In this chapter, we will only examine demand-side subsidies, which aim to promote home-purchase through the financial market. See UN-Habitat, *Guide to Preparing a Housing Finance Strategy* (Nairobi, UN-Habitat, 2009), p. 45.

2. Harold M. Katsura and Clare T. Romanik, *Ensuring Access to Essential Services: Demand-Side House Subsidies*, Social Protection Discussion Paper Series no. 0232 (Washington, DC, World Bank, 2002), p. 6. Available at: documents.worldbank.org, accessed 6 Jan. 2015. Canada's answers to a 2012 questionnaire; Australia's answers to a 2012 questionnaire.

3. France's answers to a 2012 questionnaire.

4. Chiquier and Lea (eds), *Housing Finance Policy in Emerging Markets*, p. 436.

5. Ibid.

6. UN-Habitat, *The Role of Government in the Housing Market: The Experiences from Asia* (Nairobi, UN-Habitat, 2008), pp. 39–40.

7. Jesús Leal, 'La política de vivienda en España', *Documentación Social*, vol. 138 (2005), pp. 63–80, cited in Palomera, 'How Did Finance Capital Infiltrate the World of the Urban Poor?'

8. Council of Europe, *Housing Policy and Vulnerable Social Groups*, p. 31.

9. Alan Gilbert, 'Power, Ideology and the Washington Consensus: The Development and Spread of Chilean Housing Policy', *Housing Studies*, vol. 17, no. 2 (July 2002).

10. UN-Habitat, *Quick Guide 2*, p. 57.

11. According to El Salvador's, Guatemala's, Mexico's and Venezuela's answers to a questionnaire. Approximately 20 per cent of the Inter-American Development Bank's (IBD) loans to housing were allocated through grant subsidy programmes. See Eduardo Rojas, *Sharpening the Bank's Capacity to Support the Housing Sector in Latin America and the Caribbean: Background Paper for the Implementation of the Social Development Strategy* (Washington, DC, IBD, 2006).

12. Financial and Fiscal Commission of South Africa, *Building an Inclusionary Housing Market: Shift the Paradigm for Housing Delivery in South Africa* (Midrand, FFC, 2012). Available at: housingfinanceafrica.org, accessed 5 Jan. 2015.

13. Ben Richards, 'Poverty and Housing in Chile: The Development of a Neo-liberal Welfare State', *Habitat International*, vol. 19, no. 4 (1995); Tomás Moulian, *Chile actual: Anatomía de un mito* (Santiago, LOM Editores/Universidad Arcis, 1997), cited in Cavieres, *Chilean Housing Policy*.

14. According to Cavieres, 'Many of the ministers under Pinochet that took key positions in this period were postgraduate students of the Chicago school where one of the most influential professors was the Nobel Prize laureate economist Milton Friedman, widely known as a fierce promoter of a neo-liberal free-market economy.' Cavieres, *Chilean Housing Policy*, p. 76, fn. 18.

15. Manuel Castells, *The City and the Grassroots: A Cross-Cultural Theory of Urban Social Movements* (Berkeley, University of California Press, 1983), p. 200, cited in Paul Posner, 'Targeted Assistance and Social Capital: Housing Policy in Chile's Neoliberal Democracy', *International Journal of Urban and Regional Research*, vol. 36, no. 1 (Jan. 2012).

16. José Miguel Simian, *Eigentumsorientierte Wohnungspolitik in Deutschland und Chile. Kooperations- und Genossenschaftswissenschaftliche Beiträge* series (Münster, Institut für Genossenschaftswesen der Universität Münster, 2000), pp. 153–6, cited in Rodríguez and Sugranyes (eds), *Los con techo*, pp. 23–33.

17. A. R. Ferraz, *Economic Adjustment and Housing Policy: General Trends and the Chilean Case*, Primer Congreso Virtual de Arquitectura, 1999, mimeo; Claudio Adrián Pardo, *Housing Finance in Chile: The Experience in Primary and Secondary Mortgage Financing* (Washington, DC, BID, 2000); Eduardo Rojas, *The Long Road to Housing Reform. Lessons from the Chilean Experience* (Washington, DC, BID, 1999), cited in Cavieres, *Chilean Housing Policy*.

18. Sugranyes, 'La política habitacional en Chile', p. 29.

19. Ibid., pp. 23–33.

20. Arnold Harberger, 'Notas sobre los problemas de vivienda y planificación de la ciudad', *Auca*, no. 37 (1979); Carlos A. de Mattos, 'Santiago de Chile, globalización y expansión metropolitana: lo que existía sigue existiendo', in Alfredo Rodríguez and Paula Rodríguez (eds), *Santiago, una ciudad neoliberal* (Quito, OLAC-CHI, 2009); Martim Smolka and Francisco Sabatini, 'The Land Market Deregulation Debate in Chile', *Land Lines*, vol. 12, no. 1 (Jan. 2000). Available at: lincolninst.edu, accessed 12 Nov. 2014, cited in Cavieres, *Chilean Housing Policy*.

21. Alfredo Rodríguez and Ana María Icaza, 'Chile: The Eviction of Low-Income Residents from Central Santiago de Chile', in Antonio Azuela de la Cueva, Emilio Duhau and Enrique Ortiz (eds), *Evictions and the Right to Housing: Experience from Canada, Chile, the Dominican Republic, South Africa, and South Korea* (Ottawa: International Development Research Centre, 1998). Available at: idrc.ca, accessed 6 Jan. 2015. Cited in Cavieres, *Chilean Housing Policy*.

22. Fernando Kusnetzoff, 'The State and Housing in Chile: Regime Types and Policy Choices', in Gil Shidlo (ed.), *Housing Policy in Developing Countries* (London, Routledge, 1990), cited in Cavieres, *Chilean Housing Policy*.

23. Rodríguez and Sugranyes (eds), *Los con techo*.

24. Pablo Trivelli, 'Sobre la evolución de la política urbana y la política de suelo en el Gran Santiago en el período 1979–2008', and Carlos

A. de Mattos, 'Santiago de Chile, globalización y expansión metropolitana: lo que existía sigue existiendo', both in Rodríguez and Rodríguez (eds), *Santiago, una ciudad neoliberal.*

25. Alfredo Rodríguez and Ana Sugranyes, 'El traje nuevo del emperador: las políticas de financiamiento de vivienda social en Santiago de Chile', in Rodríguez and Rodríguez (eds), *Santiago, una ciudad neoliberal.*

26. Sugranyes, 'La política habitacional en Chile', pp. 23–33.

27. Elena Ducci, 'Chile: The Dark Side of a Successful Housing Policy', in Joseph S. Tulchin and Allison M. Garland (eds), *Social Development in Latin America: The Politics of Reform* (Washington, DC/ Boulder, Woodrow Wilson Center/Lynne Rienner Publishers, 2000), pp. 149–74.

28. Rodríguez and Sugranyes, 'El traje nuevo del emperador', p. 303.

29. Pablo Trivelli et al., *Urban Structure, Land Markets and Social Housing in Santiago, Chile*, Jan. 2010, mimeo. Available at: cafedelasciudades.com.ar, accessed 16 Nov. 2014.

30. Gilbert, 'Power, Ideology and the Washington Consensus'.

31. World Bank, *World Bank Housing Mission to South Africa, August 1994* (Washington, DC, World Bank, 1994), mimeo, cited in Gilbert, 'Power, Ideology and the Washington Consensus'.

32. Javier Corral, *La vivienda social en México: pasado, presente y futuro* (Mexico City, JSA, 2012), p. 34, cited in Higor Carvalho, *Social Housing Policies in the Era of Financial Accumulation: A Comparative Analysis between Agents and Impacts in Brazil and Mexico*, report presented at the Latin American Studies Association (LASA) meeting, Puerto Rico, 2015.

33. Ibid.

34. Edith Jiménez Huerta, *Renting and Sharing: Housing Options for the Poor*, report presented in the XIII International Sociology Association World Congress, 2014 (RC21-43 joint session: 'Unequal cities and political economy of housing').

35. Corral, *La vivienda social en México: pasado, presente y futuro.*

36. Victoria Burnett, 'They Built It. People Came. Now They Go', *New York Times*, 8 Sep. 2014. Available at: nytimes.com, accessed 6 Jan. 2015.

37. Gilbert, 'Power, Ideology and the Washington Consensus', p. 29.

38. UN-Habitat, *Financing Urban Shelter.*

39. Gilbert, 'Power, Ideology and the Washington Consensus', pp. 31–2.

40. Chiquier and Lea (eds), *Housing Finance Policy in Emerging Markets*, pp. 405–6. Microcredit is the theme of my next chapter.

6. Microfinance

1. Ananya Roy, *Poverty Capital: Microfinance and the Making of Development* (New York, Routledge, 2010), p. 89.

2. UN-Habitat, *Financing Urban Shelter*.

3. UN-Habitat, *Housing for All: The Challenges of Affordability, Accessibility and Sustainability – The Experiences and Instruments from the Developing and Developed Worlds* (Nairobi, UN-Habitat, 2008), p. 11; UN-Habitat, *Financing Urban Shelter*, pp. 99–100.

4. Don Johnston Jr. and Jonathan Morduch, 'The Unbanked: Evidence from Indonesia', *World Bank Economic Review*, vol. 22, no. 3 (2008), p. 517.

5. Bruce Ferguson and Peer Smets, 'Finance for Incremental Housing: Current Status and Prospects for Expansion', *Habitat International*, vol. 34, no. 3 (2010), pp. 288–9; Chiquier and Lea (eds), *Housing Finance Policy in Emerging Markets*, p. 395.

6. David Bornstein, *The Price of a Dream: The Story of the Grameen Bank* (New York, Simon and Schuster, 1996), p. 331, cited in Roy, *Poverty Capital*.

7. C. K. Prahalad and Stuart L. Hart, 'The Fortune at the Bottom of the Pyramid', *Strategy and Business*, no. 26 (2002), p. 1. Available at: cs.berkeley.edu, accessed 6 Jan. 2014; Raquel Rolnik, *Thematic Report on the Financial Crisis*, A/HRC/10/7, 2009, in collaboration with Bahram Ghazi.

8. Roy, *Poverty Capital*, p. 5.

9. C. K. Prahalad, *The Fortune at the Bottom of the Pyramid: Eradicating Poverty through Profits* (Upper Saddle River, NJ, Wharton School of Publishing, 2004).

10. Center for Urban Development Studies, *Housing Microfinance Initiatives: Synthesis and Regional Summary – Asia, Latin America and Sub-Saharan Africa with Selected Case Studies* (Bethesda, MD,

Microenterprise Best Practices/Development Alternatives Inc., 2000).

11. Chiquier and Lea (eds), *Housing Finance Policy in Emerging Markets*, p. 399; Bruce Ferguson, 'Housing Microfinance: A Key to Improving Habitat and the Sustainability of Microfinance Institutions', *Small Enterprise Development*, vol. 14, no. 1 (2003), p. 21.

12. UN-Habitat, *Financing Urban Shelter*, pp. 106–12; Doris Köhn and J. D. von Pischke (eds), *Housing Finance in Emerging Markets: Connecting Low-Income Groups to Markets* (Berlin, Springer, 2011), pp. 33–5.

13. Chiquier and Lea (eds), *Housing Finance Policy in Emerging Markets*, pp. 395–7.

14. Gruffydd Jones, '"Cities Without Slums"? Global Architectures of Power and the African City', in Karel A. Bakker (ed.), *African Perspectives 2009 – The African Inner City: [Re]sourced* (Pretoria, University of Pretoria, 2010), pp. 769–70. Available at: lirias. kuleuven.be, accessed 6 Jan. 2015.

15. UN-Habitat, 'An Approach to Financial Action Planning for Slum Upgrading and New Low-Income Residential Neighbourhoods', *The SUF Handbook – Design Phase* vol. 1 (Vancouver, Jun. 2006). Available at: mirror.unhabitat.org, accessed 6 Jan. 2015.

16. Ibid., p. 771.

17. UN-Habitat, 'Housing for All', p. 22; *Financing Urban Shelter*, p. 106.

18. Michael Kihato, *Scoping the Demand for Housing Microfinance in Africa: Status, Opportunities and Challenges* (Johannesburg, Centre for Affordable Housing Finance in Africa, 2009), mimeo. Available at: finmark.ed.za, accessed 5 Jan. 2015.

19. Annika Nilsson, 'Overview of Financial Systems for Slum Upgrading and Housing', *Housing Finance International*, vol. 23, no. 2 (Dec. 2008), pp. 20–1; Sally Merrill and Nino Mesarina, 'Expanding Microfinance for Housing', *Housing Finance International*, vol. 21, no. 2 (Dec. 2006), p. 21.

20. See: grameeninfo.org, accessed 4 Dec. 2014.

21. Chiquier and Lea (eds), *Housing Finance Policy in Emerging Markets*, p. 398.

22. UN-Habitat, *Housing for All*, p. 20; Sally Merrill, *Microfinance for Housing: Assisting the 'Bottom Billion' and the 'Missing Middle'*

(Washington, DC, Urban Institute Center on International Development and Governance, Jun. 2009), mimeo, p. 4.

23. UN-Habitat, *Enabling Shelter Strategies: Review of Experience from Two Decades of Implementation* (Nairobi, UN-Habitat, 2006), p. 91.

24. UN-Habitat, *Financing Urban Shelter*, p. 114.

25. UN-Habitat, *Housing for All*, p. 19.

26. Chiquier and Lea (eds), *Housing Finance Policy in Emerging Markets*, p. 410.

27. See: compartamos.com, accessed 4 Dec. 2014.

28. UN-Habitat, *Housing for All*, pp. 24–5.

29. P. K. Manoj, 'Prospects and Problems of Housing Microfinance in India: Evidence from "Bhavanashree" Project in Kerala State', *European Journal of Economics, Finance and Administrative Sciences*, no. 19 (April 2010), p. 178.

30. UN-Habitat, *Housing for All*, p. 23.

31. Chiquier and Lea (eds), *Housing Finance Policy in Emerging Markets*, pp. 36–7.

32. Center for Urban Development Studies, *Housing Microfinance Initiatives* (Bethesda, MD, Microenterprise Best Practices/Development Alternatives Inc., 2000), p. 24.

33. Nilsson, 'Overview', p. 19.

34. Erlend Sigvaldsen, *Key Issues in Housing Microfinance* (Oslo, Nordic Consulting Group, 2010), pp. 16–17.

35. UN-Habitat, *Financing Urban Shelter*, p. 99.

36. Ferguson and Smets, 'Finance for Incremental Housing', pp. 293–4; UN-Habitat, *Housing for All*, pp. 88–9; Somsook Boonyabancha, 'Baan Mankong: Going to Scale with "Slum" and Squatter Upgrading in Thailand', *Environment and Urbanization*, vol. 17, no. 1 (April 2005).

37. By January 2011, 1,546 communities and 90,000 residents were involved in or had benefited from Baan Mankong projects. See UN-Habitat, *Affordable Land and Housing in Asia* (Nairobi, UN-Habitat, 2011).

38. UN-Habitat, *Financing Urban Shelter*, p. 120.

39. This is the case with the Community Mortgage Programme, in the Philippines.

40. Rolnik and Rabinovich, 'Late-Neoliberalism'; Rolnik, *Thematic Report on the Financial Crisis*.

41. Roy, *Poverty Capital*.

42. See: brac.net, accessed 17 Dec. 2006.

43. Roy, *Poverty Capital*, p. 203.

44. Consultative Group to Assist the Poor (CGAP), *The Global Financial Crisis and Its Impacts on Microfinance*, 2009, p. 5. Available at: cgap.org, accessed 12 Oct. 2016.

45. Jones, '"Cities Without Slums"?', p. 785.

46. Roy, *Poverty Capital*, p. 218.

7. Tenure Insecurity

1. Seth Mydans, 'In Cambodia, Land Seizures Push Thousands of the Poor into Homelessness', *New York Times*, 27 July 2008. Available at: nytimes.com, accessed 17 Nov. 2014.

2. Ciro Barros, 'Altair enfrenta a terceira remoção da vida pelas Olimpíadas', *Pública: Agência de Reportagem e Jornalismo Investigativo*, 21 June 2013. Available at: apublica.org, accessed 26 Dec. 2014.

3. See the *Economist*'s interactive guide of global house prices, available at: economist.com, accessed 26 Dec. 2014.

4. Mentioned by UN-Habitat and in the document *Losing Your Home: Assessing the Impact of Eviction*, from UN Human Rights High Commissioner's Office (2011, p. 1). For further data and testimonies of cases, see, for example, the Habitat International Coalition's *Land and Housing Rights Web 2012 Annual Report* (HIC, 2012).

5. Michael Cernea, 'IRR: An Operational Risks Reduction Model for Population Resettlement', *Hydro Nepal: Journal of Water, Energy and Environment*, vol. 1, no. 1 (2007), p. 36.

6. Raquel Rolnik, *Thematic Report on the Impact of Mega-Events on the Realization of the Right to Adequate Housing*, A/HRC/13/20, 2009, in collaboration with Brenda Vukovic.

7. Internal Displacement Monitoring Centre, *Global Overview 2011: People Internally Displaced by Conflict and Violence* (Geneva, IDMC, 2012), p. 8. Available at: unhcr.org, accessed 6 Jan. 2015. Internal Displacement Monitoring Centre, *Global Estimates 2011: People Displaced by Natural Hazard-Induced Disasters* (Geneva,

IDMC, 2012), p. 4. Available at: internal-displacement.org, accessed 6 Jan. 2015. See also: Raquel Rolnik, *Thematic Report on Security of Tenure*, A/HRC/22/46, 2013, in collaboration with Laure-Anne Courdesse.

8. UN-Habitat, *Handbook on Best Practices, Security of Tenure and Access to Land* (Nairobi, UN-Habitat, 2003).

9. Some initiatives to measure tenure insecurity are under way. See, for example, Remy Stiechiping et al., *Monitoring Tenure Security within the Continuum of Land Rights: Methods and Practices*, World Bank annual Conference on Land and Poverty, Washington DC, 2012, available at landandpoverty.com/agenda/pdfs/paper/ sietchiping_full_paper.pdf, accessed 6 January 2015.

10. UN-Habitat, *The Challenge of Slums: Global Report on Human Settlements 2003* (Nairobi, UN-Habitat, 2003).

11. UN-Habitat, *Slums of the World: The Face of Urban Poverty in the New Millennium?* (Nairobi, UN-Habitat, 2003), p. 24.

12. UN-Habitat, *State of the World's Cities 2010-2011: Bridging the Urban Divide* (Nairobi, UN-Habitat, 2011), p. 33.

13. Ibid. See also: UN-Habitat, *Slums of the World*.

14. World Bank, *Investigation Report – Cambodia: Land Management and Administration Project* (Washington, DC, World Bank, 2010). Available at: wds.worldbank.org, accessed 18 Nov. 2014. Raquel Rolnik, *Thematic Report on the Mission to the World Bank*, A/ HRC/22/46/Add.3, 2013, in collaboration with Beatrice Quadranti, Natalie Bugalski and David Pred.

15. David Palmer, Szilard Fricska and Babette Wehrmann, *Towards Improved Land Governance: Land Tenure Working Paper 11* (Rome/ Nairobi, FAO/UN-Habitat, 2009), p. 2. Available at: fao.org, accessed 6 Jan. 2015.

16. Daniel Adler and Sokbunthoeun So, 'Toward Equity in Development when the Law Is Not the Law: Reflections on Legal Pluralism in Practice', in Brian Tamanaha, Caroline Sage and Michael Woolcock (eds), *Legal Pluralism and Development: Scholars and Practitioners in Dialogue* (Cambridge, Cambridge University Press, 2012); Klaus Deininger and Derek Byerlee, *Rising Global Interest in Farmland: Can It Yield Sustainable and Equitable Benefits?* (Washington, DC, World Bank, 2011). Available at: elibrary.world bank.org, accessed 18 Nov. 2014.

17. David Harvey, *Seventeen Contradictions and the End of Capitalism* (Oxford, Oxford University Press, 2014), p. 241.

18. COHRE et al, *Untitled: Tenure Insecurity and Inequality in the Cambodian Land Sector* (Genebra/Phnom Penh, COHRE/Bridges Across Borders/Jesuit Refugee Service, 2009). Available at babcambodia.org/untitled/untitled.pdf, accessed 18 nov. 2014.

8. From Enclosures to Foreclosures

1. Centro para el Desarrollo Económico y Social de América Latina (Desal), *Marginalidad en América Latina: un ensayo de diagnóstico* (Barcelona, Herder, 1969), in Samuel Jaramillo Gonzalez, 'Urbanización informal: diagnósticos y políticas – una revisión al debate latinoamericano para pensar líneas de acción actuales', in Clara Eugenia Salazar (ed.), *Irregular: suelo y mercado en América Latina* (Mexico City, Colegio de México, 2012).

2. George Martine and Gordon McGranahan (eds), *Urban Growth in Emerging Economies: Lessons from the BRICs* (Abingdon/New York, Routledge, 2014).

3. Mike Davis, *Planet of Slums* (London/New York, Verso, 2006), p. 21.

4. Loïc Wacquant, 'Urban Outcasts: Stigma and Division in the Black American Ghetto and the French Urban Periphery', *International Journal of Urban and Regional Research*, vol. 17, no. 3 (Sept. 1993).

5. Francisco de Oliveira, 'A economia brasileira: crítica à razão dualista', *Estudos Cebrap*, no. 2, 1972; Lúcio Kowarick, *Capitalismo e marginalidade na América Latina* (Rio de Janeiro, Paz e Terra, 1975).

6. Davis, *Planet of Slums*, p. 16.

7. Josef Gugler, 'Introduction: Rural–Urban Migration', in *Cities in the Developing World: Issues, Theory, and Policy* (Oxford, Oxford University Press, 1997); Davis, *Planet of Slums*, p. 14.

8. Neil Brenner and Nik Theodore (eds), *Spaces of Neoliberalism: Urban Restructuring in North America and Western Europe* (Oxford, Blackwell, 2002).

9. Minurvi, *Instrumentos financieros para mejorar el acceso a la vivienda de los sectores de menores ingresos en America Latina y*

el Caribe, XV General Assembly of Ministers and High Authorities on Housing and Urbanism in Latin American and the Caribbean, Montevideo, 2005, mimeo.

10. Davis, *Planet of Slums*, p. 14.

11. Ibid., p. 15.

12. Ibid., pp. 16–17.

13. Karl Marx, *Capital: A Critique of Political Economy*, Volume I, *The Process of Production of Capital*.

14. Harvey, *Seventeen Contradictions*, p. 240.

15. Mark Tran, 'Land Deals in Africa Have Led to a Wild West: Bring on the Sheriff, Says FAO', *Guardian*, 29 Oct. 2012. Available at: theguardian.com, accessed 18 Nov. 2014.

16. Harvey, *Seventeen Contradictions*, p. 222.

17. Manuel Aalbers and Rodrigo Fernandez, *Housing and the Variations of Financialized Capitalism*, The Real Estate/Financial Complex (Refcom) International Seminar, Leuven, 2014, mimeo, pp. 7–8.

18. Keith Clifford Bell, Shivakumar Srinivas and Juan Martinez, *Reforming Indonesia's Complex Legal Environment for Land Governance: Complementary Top-Down and Bottom-Up Approaches*, Annual World Bank Conference on Land and Poverty, Washington, DC, 2013, mimeo, p. 6.

19. World Bank (2013). Information provided by BPN to the special rapporteur on adequate housing on 3 June 2013 in Jakarta.

20. Information provided by BPN on 3 June 2013, and by the Indonesian government on 11 October 2013.

21. Bell, Srinivas and Martinez, *Reforming Indonesia's Complex Legal Environment*, pp. 8–12.

22. Maharani Hapsari, 'The Political Economy of Forest Governance in Post-Suharto Indonesia', in Hirotsune Kimura et al. (eds), *Limits of Good Governance in Developing Countries* (Yogyakarta, Gadjah Mada University Press, 2011), pp. 103–37.

23. Timothy Lindsey, 'Square Pegs & Round Holes: Fitting Modern Title into Traditional Societies in Indonesia', *Pacific Rim Law and Policy Journal*, vol. 7 (1998), pp. 699–719; Daniel Fitzpatrick, 'Disputes and Pluralism in Modern Indonesian Land Law', *Yale Journal of International Law*, vol. 22 (1997), pp. 171–212.

24. Oxfam, ' "Our Land, Our Lives": Time out on the Global Land Rush', *Oxfam Briefing Paper*, Oxford, Oct. 2012. Available at: oxfam.org, accessed 18 Nov. 2014.

25. Vincent Basserie and Hubert M. G. Ouedraogo, 'La Sécurisation foncière: un des défis majeurs pour le nouveau siècle', *Grain de sel*, nos. 41–2 (Dec. 2007–May 2008), p. 13.

26. Harvey, *Seventeen Contradictions*, p. 244.

27. Harvey, *Seventeen Contradictions*, p. 240.

28. Deininger and Byerlee, *Rising Global Interest in Farmland*.

29. Rolnik, *Thematic Report on Security of Tenure*.

30. I would like to thank David Harvey, who debated this chapter's empirical content with me, suggesting the conceptual framework adopted above.

9. Informal, Illegal, Ambiguous

1. F. L. J., *Diário de uma invasora* (Rio de Janeiro, Livre Expressão, 2012), pp. 5–15. Flavia gave me her book as a present, with a dedication written in tiny letters, on 3 May 2013. It was at a public event, where she tried to defend – as she had done countless times before – Horto's residents' right to remain there.

2. Vera da Silva Telles, *As cidades na fronteira do legal e do ilegal* (Belo Horizonte, Argumentum, 2010), p. 29.

3. Lisa Björkman, 'Becoming a Slum: From Municipal Colony to Illegal Settlement in Liberalization-Era Mumbai', in Gavin Shatkin (ed.), *Contesting the Indian City: Global Visions and the Politics of the Local* (Oxford, Wiley-Blackwell, 2013).

4. Davis, *Planet of Slums*, p. 26.

5. Ibid., pp. 34–41.

6. Alain Durand-Lasserve and Geoffrey Payne, *Holding On: Security of Tenure – Types, Policies, Practices and Challenges*, research paper for an expert meeting on security of tenure convened by the UN special rapporteur on adequate housing, 2012, mimeo. Available at: ohchr.org, accessed 20 Nov. 2014.

7. Jean-François Tribillon, 'Afrique de l'Ouest: consolider les droits fonciers urbains populaires', in AITEC (ed.), *La Terre est à nous. Pour la fonction sociale du logement et du foncier, résistances et*

alternatives (Paris, Passerelle, 2014), p. 48; Durand-Lasserve and Payne, *Holding On*.

8. Durand-Lasserve and Payne, *Holding On*.

9. Antonio Azuela de la Cueva, 'Los asentamientos populares y el orden jurídico en la urbanización periférica de América Latina', *Revista Mexicana de Sociología*, vol. 55, no. 3 (July–Sept. 1993); Ann Varley, 'Urbanization and Agrarian Law: The Case of Mexico City', *Bulletin of Latin American Research*, vol. 4, no. 1 (1985).

10. Boaventura de Sousa Santos, 'Uma cartografia simbólica das representações sociais', *Revista Crítica de Ciências Sociais*, no. 24 (March 1988).

11. Durand-Lasserve and Payne, *Holding On*.

12. Omar Razzaz, 'Land Disputes in the Absence of Ownership Rights: Insights from Jordan', in Edésio Fernandes and Ann Varley (eds), *Illegal Cities: Law and Urban Change in Developing Countries* (London, ZED, 1998), p. 86.

13. Pedro Abramo, 'A cidade comfusa: a mão inoxidável do mercado e a produção da estrutura urbana nas grandes cidades latinoamericanas', *Revista Brasileira de Estudos Urbanos e Regionais*, vol. 9, no. 2 (2007).

14. Boaventura de Sousa Santos, 'Notas sobre a história jurídico-social de Pasárgada', in Cláudio Souto and Joaquim Falcão (eds), *Sociologia jurídica* (São Paulo, Pioneira, 1980).

15. Alex Ferreira Magalhães, *O direito das favelas* (Rio de Janeiro, Letra Capital/Faperj, 2013); Alex Ferreira Magalhães, 'O "Galo cantou", mas não foi para os moradores das favelas: problematizando a política estadual de titulação de favelas', *Cadernos do Desenvolvimento Fluminense*, no. 1 (Feb. 2013).

16. James Holston, *Insurgent Citizenship: Disjunctions of Democracy and Modernity in Brazil* (Princeton and Oxford, Princeton University Press, 2008), *p. 204*.

17. Akin L. Mabogunje, *Perspective on Urban Land and Urban Management Policies in Sub-Saharan Africa* (Washington, DC, World Bank, 1992). Available at: documents.worldbank.org, accessed 25 Aug. 2015. Durand-Lasserve and Payne, *Holding On*.

18. Saad Yahya, 'The Certificate of Rights Story in Botswana', in Geoffrey Payne (ed.), *Land, Rights and Innovation: Improving Tenure*

Security for the Urban Poor (London, ITDG, 2002), in Durand-Lasserve and Payne, *Holding On*.

19. Pierre Fallavier, *Understanding Slums: The Case of Phnom Penh (A Case Study for the Global Report on Human Settlements)* (Nairobi, UN-Habitat, 2003), in Durand-Lasserve and Payne, *Holding On*.

20. COHRE, Serac, *The Myth of the Abuja Master Plan: Forced Evictions as Urban Planning in Abuja, Nigeria* (Geneva/Lagos, COHRE/Serac, 2008). Available at: abahlali.org, accessed 20 Nov. 2014.

21. George Avelino Filho, 'Clientelismo e política no Brasil: revisitando velhos problemas', *Novos Estudos – Cebrap*, no. 38 (1994); José Murilo de Carvalho, 'Mandonismo, coronelismo, clientelismo: uma discussão conceitual', *Dados*, vol. 40, no. 2 (1997); Raquel Rolnik, 'Democracia no fio da navalha: limites e possibilidades para a implementação de uma agenda de reforma urbana no Brasil', *Revista Brasileira de Estudos Urbanos e Regionais*, vol. 11, no. 2 (2009).

22. Partha Chatterjee, *Politics of the Governed: Reflections on Popular Politics in Most of the World* (New York, Columbia University Press, 2004), in Björkman, 'Becoming a Slum'.

23. Raquel Rolnik, *A cidade e a lei: legislação, política urbana e territórios na cidade de São Paulo* (São Paulo, Studio Nobel, 1997).

24. Da Silva Telles, *As cidades na fronteira do legal e do ilegal*, p. 29.

25. Rolnik, *A cidade e a lei*.

26. Ciro Biderman, *La informalidad en Brasil: ¿Tienen importancia las reglamentaciones sobre el uso de la tierra y la edificación?* (Cambridge, MA, Lincoln Institute of Land Policy, 2008), p. 2. Available at: lincolninst.edu, accessed 20 Nov. 2014.

27. World Bank, *Housing: Enabling Markets to Work* (Washington, DC, World Bank, 1993).

28. Raquel Rolnik, 'Legislación urbana y mercados informales de tierra: el vínculo perfecto', in Edésio Fernandes (ed.), *Derecho, espacio urbano y medio ambiente* (Madrid, Dykinson, 2000).

29. Rolnik, *A cidade e a lei*; Raquel Rolnik, 'Territórios negros nas cidades brasileiras: etnicidade e cidade em São Paulo e no Rio de Janeiro', *Revista de Estudos Afroasiáticos*, no. 17 (1989).

30. Raquel Rolnik, *Mission Report on Israel and the Occupied Palestinian Territories*, A/HRC/22/46/Add.1, 2012, in collaboration with Marcelo Daher and Isabel Recupero, paragraph 24.

31. Alexandre Kedar and Oren Yiftachel, 'Land Regime and Social Relations in Israel', in Hernando de Soto and Francis Cheneval (eds), *Realizing Property Rights: Swiss Human Rights Book – Volume 1* (Zürich, Ruffer & Rub, 2006).

32. Rolnik, *Mission Report on Israel and the Occupied Palestinian Territories*.

33. Ibid.

34. Claude Cahn, *Social Control and Human Rights: A Case Study of the Roma in Europe* (Versoix, ICHRP, 2009).

35. Alliance of Women in Slovakia et al., *Joint Submission: Shadow Report to the Committee on the Elimination of Discrimination against Women for the Slovak Republic*, Bratislava, 2008, p. 52. Available at: iwraw-ap.org, accessed 5 Jan. 2015.

36. Open Society Institute, *Broadening the Agenda: The Status of Romani Women in Romania* (New York, Open Society Institute, 2006), pp. 66–7. Available at: soros.org, accessed 6 Jan. 2015.

37. UNDP, *At Risk: The Social Vulnerability of Roma, Refugees and Internally Displaced Persons in Serbia* (Belgrade, UNDP, 2006), p. 29. Available at: policy.hu, accessed 6 Jan. 2015.

38. UNDP, *At Risk: The Social Vulnerability of Roma, Refugees and Internally Displaced Persons in Montenegro* (Podgorica, UNDP, 2006), p. 35. Available at: policy.hu, accessed 6 Jan. 2015.

39. UNDP, *At Risk: The Social Vulnerability of Roma, Refugees and Internally Displaced Persons in Montenegro* (Podgorica, UNDP, 2006), p. 35. Available at: policy.hu, accessed 6 Jan. 2015.

40. Raquel Rolnik, *Mission Report to the United Kingdom*, A/HRC/25/54/Add.2, 2014, in collaboration with Juana Sotomayor.

41. Ibid.

42. Rolnik, *Thematic Report on the Financial Crisis*, paragraphs 86–7; Raquel Rolnik, *Mission Report to Rwanda*, A/HRC/22/46/Add.2, 2012, in collaboration with Boris-Ephrem Tchoumavi, paragraphs 39–40.

43. A *laje* is a flat concrete roof, commonly regarded in Brazil as an extension of the house, used for leisure, drying clothes or as a basis for potential extra floors to the building.

44. Jieming Zhu, *Symmetric Development of Informal Settlements and Gated Communities: Capacity of the State. The Case of Jakarta, Indonesia* (Singapore, Asia Research Institute, 2010), p. 9; Paul

McCarthy, 'Urban Slums Report: The Case of Jakarta, Indonesia', in UN-Habitat, *Understanding Slums: Case Studies for the Global Report on Human Settlements 2003* (Nairobi, UN-Habitat, 2003). Available at: ucl.ac.uk, accessed 6 Jan. 2015.

45. Jo Santoso, *The Fifth Layer of Jakarta* (Jakarta, Centropolis, 2009).

46. World Bank, *Indonesia: Urban Poverty and Program Review*, p. 6.

47. Ibid., p. 5.

48. As UN special rapporteur, I could verify that some settlements had been urbanised by their own residents throughout time.

49. Giorgio Agamben, *Homo Sacer: Sovereign Power and Bare Life* (Stanford, CA, Stanford University Press, 1998).

50. Ananya Roy, 'Urban Informality: Toward an Epistemology of Planning', *Journal of the American Planning Association*, vol. 71, no. 2 (2005), p. 149.

51. Sousa Santos, 'Notas sobre a história jurídico-social de Pasárgada'.

10. Private Property, Contracts and Language

1. Rosa Congost, *Tierras, leyes, historia. Estudios sobre 'la gran obra de la propiedad'* (Barcelona, Crítica, 1997); Karl Polanyi, *The Great Transformation: The Origins of Our Time* (New York, Farrar and Rinehart, 1944), pp. 43–4; Raúl Wagner, 'La construcción social de la propiedad privada en la evolución histórica reciente del país y la región', in Susana Aravena et al., *La vivienda, entre el derecho y la mercancía: Las formas de propiedad en América Latina* (Montevideo, Trilce, 2014).

2. Karl Marx, *Theories of Surplus Value* (London, Lawrence and Wishart, 1969), Part 2, pp. 43–4; David Harvey, *The Limits to Capital* (London and New York, Verso, 1999), p. 359.

3. Harvey, *The Limits to Capital*, p. 361.

4. Polanyi, *The Great Transformation*, p. 187.

5. Ibid., p. 189.

6. Letícia Marques Osório, *The Social Function of Property and the Human Right to Security of Tenure in Latin America, with a Particular Focus on Brazil* (PhD thesis, Essex University School of Law, 2013).

7. Paulo Baptista Caruso MacDonald, 'Propriedade e direitos humanos: os limites do individualismo possessivo', *Revista da*

Associação dos Juízes do Rio Grande do Sul, vol. 33, no. 101 (2006).

8. Holston, *Insurgent Citizenship*, p. 113; Harvey, *The Limits to Capital*.

9. Klaus Deininger, *Land Policies for Growth and Poverty Reduction* (Washington, DC/Oxford, World Bank/Oxford University Press, 2003), p. xxiii. Available at: documents.worldbank.org, accessed 5 Jan. 2015.

10. Ibid., p. xix.

11. Marie Huchzermeyer, ' "Slum" Upgrading or "Slum" Eradication? The Mixed Message of the MDGs', in Malcolm Langford, Andy Summer and Alicia Ely Yamin (eds), *The Millennium Development Goals and Human Rights: Past, Present and Future* (New York, Cambridge University Press, 2013), p. 300.

12. Julian Quan, *Reflections on the Development Policy Environment for Land and Property Rights, 1997–2003*, International Workshop on Fundamental Rights in the Balance: New Ideas on the Rights to Land, Housing & Property, Sussex, 2003, mimeo; Alain Durand-Lasserve et al., *Social and Economic Impacts of Land Titling Programmes in Urban and Peri-Urban Areas: A Review of the Literature*, 2007, mimeo. Available at: birmingham.ac.uk, accessed 5 Jan. 2014.

13. Durand-Lasserve et al., *Social and Economic Impacts of Land Titling Programmes*, pp. 4–5.

14. Geoffrey Payne, Alain Durand-Lasserve and Carole Rakodi, 'The Limits of Land Titling and Home Ownership', *Environment and Urbanization*, vol. 21, no. 2 (Oct. 2009), p. 445.

15. Pedro Abramo, 'La ciudad informal com-fusa: El mercado y la producción de la territorialidad urbana popular', in Claudia Eugenia Salazar (ed.), *Irregular: Suelo y mercado en América Latina* (Mexico City, El Colégio de México, 2012), pp. 30–1, translator's rendering.

16. Durand-Lasserve et al., *Social and Economic Impacts of Land Titling Programmes*.

17. To access this list, enter 'land reform' into the search toolbox of the World Bank's website: worldbank.org, accessed 13 Jan. 2015.

18. Maldivas, *Maldives Submission under Human Rights Council Resolution 7/23*, Sept. 2008. Available at: ohchr.org, accessed 12 Jan. 2015.

19. Maldivas, *Maldives Submission under Human Rights Council resolution 7/23*, set. 2008. Available at: ohchr.org, accessed 12 Jan. 2015.

20. Raquel Rolnik, *Mission Report to the Maldives,* A/HRC/13/20/ Add.3, 2009, in collaboration with Bahram Ghazi.

21. Maldives, *Maldives Submission.*

22. UNDP, *Rapid Economic/Poverty Assessment of the Maldives* (UNDP, Colombo, 2009).

23. Rolnik, *Mission Report to the Maldives.*

24. Maldives, *President Announces Land Reform Measures (Press Release)*, Malé, 8 June 2011. Available at: presidencymaldives.gov.mv, accessed 28 Aug. 2015.

25. IMF, *Maldives: Use of Fund Resources – Request for Emergency Assistance* (Washington, DC, IMF, 2005). Available at: imf.org, accessed 28 Aug. 2015.

26. United States, *2014 Investment Climate Statement – Maldives* (Washington, DC, US Department of State, June 2014). Available at: state.gov, accessed 6 Jan. 2015.

27. Alan Gilbert, *On the Mystery of Capital and the Myths of Hernando de Soto: What Difference Does Legal Title Make?* 2001, mimeo. Available at: ucl.ac.uk, accessed 22 Dec. 2014.

28. For a wide revision of the literature and documents on the theme, see Durand-Lasserve et al., *Social and Economic Impacts of Land Titling Programmes*, where some of the mentioned arguments are raised.

29. Land Tenure Center (LTC), *Guidelines for Analysis of USAID's Land Market Projects: Documents Annex 3 Assessment Guidelines* (Madison, University of Wisconsin, 2002), pp. 7–8, in Durand-Lasserve et al., *Social and Economic Impacts of Land Titling Programmes.*

30. Thomas Pinckney and Peter Kimuyu, 'Land Tenure Reform in East Africa: Good, Bad or Unimportant?', *Journal of African Economies*, vol. 3, no. 1 (1994); David A. Atwood, 'Land Registration in Africa: The Impact on Agricultural Production', *World Development*, vol. 18, no. 5 (May 1990).

31. Peter Ho and Max Spoor, 'Whose Land? The Political Economy of Land Titling in Transitional Economies', *Land Use Policy*, vol. 23, no. 4(Oct. 2006).

32. Gustavo Riofrio, *Why Have Families Mortgaged So Little?* Lincoln Institute Workshop on Comparative Policy Perspectives on Urban Land Market Reform in Latin America, Southern Africa and Eastern Europe, Cambridge, MA, July 1998, mimeo; Julio A. Calderón Cockburn, 'Comparative Analysis of the Benefited and Non-Benefited Population by the National Formalization Plan', in Instituto Nacional de Estadística e Informática (INEI), *Has the Well-Being of the Population Improved? A Balance of the Main Social Policies and Programs* (Lima, INEI, 2001); Sule Özüekren, 'Informal and Formal Housing Construction in Turkey: Blurred Boundaries and Regulations', in Reino Hjerppe e Pii Elina Berghäll (eds), *Urbanization: Its Global Trends, Economics and Governance* (Helsinki, Vatt-Government Institute for Economic Research, 1998); Patrick Bond and Angela Tait, 'The Failure of Housing Policy in Post-Apartheid South Africa', *Urban Forum*, vol. 8, no. 1 (March 1997); Robina Goodlad, 'The Housing Challenge in South Africa', *Urban Studies*, vol. 33, no. 9 (Nov. 1996); Mary R. Tomlinson, 'South Africa's New Housing Policy: An Assessment of the First Two Years, 1994–1996', *International Journal of Urban and Regional Research*, vol. 22, no. 1 (1998), in Gilbert, *On the Mystery of Capital*; Edésio Fernandes, 'La influencia de *El misterio del capital* de Hernando de Soto', *Land Lines*, vol. 14, no. 1 (Jan. 2002), available at: cepal.org, accessed 22 Dec. 2014.

33. Ann Varley, 'Private or Public: Debating the Meaning of Tenure Legalization', *International Journal of Urban and Regional Research*, vol. 26, no. 3 (Sept. 2002).

34. Alain Durand-Lasserve, *L'Exclusion des pauvres dans les villes du Tiers-Monde* (Paris, L'Harmattan, 1986); Patrick McAuslan, *Urban Land and Shelter for the Poor* (London, Earthscan, 1985); Magalhães, 'O "Galo cantou"', in Gilbert, *On the Mystery of Capital*.

35. Varley, 'Private or Public'.

36. Varley, 'Urbanization and Agrarian Law'.

37. Varley, 'Private or Public'.

38. Emilio Duhau, *Impacts of Regularization Programs: Notes on the Mexican Experience*, and Aída Zeledón, *De Facto and Legal Regularization Programs in El Salvador*, both presented at Lincoln

Institute Workshop on Informal Land Markets: Land Tenure Regularization and Urban Upgrading Programs, Cambridge, MA, Oct. 2001; Ayako Kagawa, *Policy Effects and Tenure Security Perceptions of Peruvian Urban Land Tenure Regularization Policy in the 1990s*, N-AERUS Workshop, Leuven, June 2001, in Fernandes, 'La influencia de *El misterio del capital*'.

39. Robert M. Buckley and Jerry Kalarickal (eds), *Thirty Years of World Bank Shelter Lending: What Have We Learned?* (Washington, DC, World Bank, 2006).

40. Ibid., p. 23.

41. Deininger, *Land Policies for Growth and Poverty Reduction*, p. xv.

42. Buckley and Kalarickal (eds), *Thirty Years of World Bank Shelter Lending*, pp. 30–1.

43. Ibid.; Durand-Lasserve et al., *Social and Economic Impacts of Land Titling Programmes*, p. 7.

44. UN-Habitat and GLTN, *Secure Land Rights for All* (Nairobi, UN-Habitat, 2008), p. 8.

45. Deutsche Gesellschaft für Internationale Zusammenarbeit (GIZ), *Securing Land Rights, Briefing Note*, Bonn, 2011, mimeo.

46. World Resources Institute, *World Resources Report – The Wealth of the Poor: Managing Ecosystems to Fight Poverty* (Washington, DC, World Resources Institute, 2005), pp. 60–1.

47. World Bank, *Land Policy for Pro-Poor Development* (Washington, DC, World Bank, 2003).

48. Durand-Lasserve et al., *Social and Economic Impacts of Land Titling Programmes*.

49. Buckley and Kalarickal (eds), *Thirty Years of World Bank Shelter Lending*, p. 23.

11. Insecure Tenure in the Era of Large Projects

1. Tom Orlik, 'Tensions Mount as China Snatches Farms for Homes', *Wall Street Journal*, 14 Feb. 2013. Available at: online.wsj.com, accessed 24 Nov. 2014.

2. See landesa.org/where-we-work/china, accessed 10 Nov. 2014.

3. George E. Peterson, *Unlocking Land Values to Finance Urban Infrastructure* (Washington, DC, World Bank, 2009), pp. 66–7.

4. Michael Goldman, 'Speculative Urbanism and the Making of the Next World City', *International Journal of Urban and Regional Research*, vol. 35, no. 3 (May 2011).

5. Confederation of British Industry, *An Offer They Shouldn't Refuse: Attracting Investment to UK Infrastructure* (London, CBI, 2011), p. 33. Available at: cbi.ed.uk, accessed 5 Jan. 2015.

6. Goldman, 'Speculative Urbanism', p. 565.

7. David Harvey, 'From Managerialism to Entrepreneurialism: The Transformation in Urban Governance in Late Capitalism', *Geografiska Annaler (B)*, vol. 71, no. 1 (1989), p. 4.

8. Brenner and Theodore (eds), *Spaces of Neoliberalism*.

9. Rose Compans, *Empreendedorismo urbano: entre o discurso e a prática* (São Paulo, Editora Unesp, 2004), pp. 114–16.

10. See ppiaf.org, accessed 26 Dec. 2014.

11. Cited in Peterson, *Unlocking Land Values*, p. x.

12. Deininger, *Land Policies for Growth and Poverty Reduction*, p. xii.

13. Antonio Azuela de la Cueva (ed.), *Expropiación y conflicto social en cinco metrópolis latinoamericanas* (Mexico City/Cambridge, MA, UNAM/Lincoln Institute of Land Policy, 2013), p. 19. Available at: ru.iis.sociales.unam.mx, accessed 5 Jan. 2015.

14. Abidin Kusno, 'Housing the Margin: Perumahan Rakyat and the Future Urban Form of Jakarta', *Indonesia*, vol. 94, Oct. 2012, p. 43–4.

15. Raquel Rolnik, *Mission Report to Indonesia*, A/HRC/25/54/Add.1, 2014, in collaboration with Lidia Rabinovich.

16. Parwoko's Weblog, *Landscape Analysis to the Informal Settlement on the Code Riverfront in Yogyakarta – Indonesia*, 2012. Available at: parwoko.wordpress.com, accessed 12 Feb. 2015.

17. Muhammad Kamil, 'Participatory Design: The Social Role of Architects and Architecture in Kampung Upgrading', *Inside Indonesia*, no. 118 (Oct.–Dec. 2014). Available at: insideindonesia.org, accessed 12 Jan. 2015.

18. Çağlar Keyder, 'Globalization and Social Exclusion in Istanbul', *International Journal of Urban and Regional Research*, vol. 29, no. 1 (March 2005); Neslihan Demirtaş-Milz, 'The Regime of Informality in Neoliberal Times in Turkey: The Case of the Kadifekale Urban Transformation Project', *International Journal of Urban and Regional Research*, vol. 37, no. 2 (March 2013); Ozan

Karaman, 'Urban Renewal in Istanbul: Reconfigured Spaces, Robotic Lives', *International Journal of Urban and Regional Research*, vol. 37, no. 2 (March 2013).

19. Tuna Kuyucu and Özlem Ünsal, ' "Urban Transformation" as State -Led Property Transfer: An Analysis of Two Cases of Urban Renewal in Istanbul', *Urban Studies*, vol. 47, no. 7 (June 2010), in Demirtaş-Milz, 'The Regime of Informality in Neoliberal Times'.

20. Official answer sent by Turkey in 2012 to the author's questionnaire.

21. Ozan Karaman, 'Urban Renewal in Istanbul', p. 719.

22. Demirtaş-Milz, 'The Regime of Informality in Neoliberal Times', pp. 701–8.

23. Karaman, 'Urban Renewal in Istanbul', p. 730.

24. European Roma Rights Centre, *European Roma Rights Centre Submission to the European Commission on Turkey* (Budapest, ERRC, May 2012). Available at: errc.org, accessed 12 Jan. 2015.

25. Lúcio Kowarick, *Viver em risco: Sobre a vulnerabilidade socio-econômica e civil* (São Paulo, Editora 34, 2009).

26. The Brookings Institution, *New Orleans after the Storm: Lessons from the Past, a Plan for the Future* (Washington, DC, 2005), p. 6. Available at: brookings.edu, accessed 6 Jan. 2015.

27. Elizabeth Ferris and Daniel Petz, *A Year of Living Dangerously: A Review of Natural Disasters in 2010* (Washington, DC/London, The Brookings Institution/London School of Economics, 2011); Raquel Rolnik, *Mission Report to the United States*, A/HRC/13/20/ Add.4, 2010, written in collaboration with Denise Hauser; Advisory Group on Forced Evictions (AGFE), *Mission report to New Orleans*, 2009, mimeo. Available at: morror.unhabitat.org /downloads/docs/10009_1_593996.pdf. accessed 20 Oct. 2015.

28. Julia Cass and Peter Whoriskey, 'New Orleans to Raze Public Housing', *Washington Post*, 8 Dec. 2006. Available at: washington-post.com, accessed 12 Jan. 2015.

29. Amnesty International, *Un-natural Disaster: Human Rights in the Gulf Coast* (Washington, DC, Amnesty International, 2010), p. 6. Available at: amnestyusa.org, accessed 5 Jan. 2015.

30. Rolnik, *Mission Report to the United States*, paragraph 30.

31. Raquel Rolnik, *Thematic Report on Post-Conflict and Post-Disaster Reconstruction and the Right to Adequate Housing*, A/HRC/16 /42, 2011, in collaboration with Jean du Plessis, paragraph 32.

32. Pakistan, Asian Development Bank and World Bank, *Pakistan Floods 2010: Preliminary Damage and Needs Assessment* (Islamabad, Nov. 2010), p. 68. Available at: siteresources.worldbank.org, accessed 12 Jan. 2015. Azmat Budhani and Haris Gazdar, *Land Rights and the Indus Flood, 2010–2011: Rapid Assessment and Policy Review* (Oxford, Oxfam, June 2011). Available at: oxfam.org, accessed 12 Feb. 2015.

33. International Organization on Migration, *Displacement Tracking Matrix*, 2011. Available at: eshelter-cccmhaiti.info, accessed 13 Jan. 2015.

34. Oli Brown and Alec Crawford, *Addressing Land Ownership after Natural Disasters: An Agency Survey* (Winnipeg, International Institute for Sustainable Development, 2006), p. 6. Available at: iisd.org, accessed 5 Jan. 2015. Human Rights Watch, 'After the Deluge: India's Reconstruction Following the 2004 Tsunami', *Human Rights Watch*, vol. 17, no. 3 (May 2005), p. 41. Available at: hrw.org, accessed 6 Jan. 2015.

35. Tourism Concern, *Post-Tsunami Reconstruction and Tourism: A Second Disaster?* (London, Tourism Concern, 2005). Available at: naomiklein.org, accessed 6 Jan. 2015.

36. Malcolm Langford and Jean du Plessis, *Dignity in the Rubble? Forced Evictions and Human Rights Law* (Geneva, COHRE, 2006).

37. François Ascher, *Les Nouveaux principes de l'urbanisme* (Avignon, L'Aube, 2004), pp. 83–4.

38. Susan Fainstein, 'Mega-Projects in New York, London and Amsterdam', *International Journal of Urban and Regional Research*, vol. 32, no. 4 (Dec. 2008); Peter Newman and Andy Thornley, *Urban Planning in Europe: International Competition, National Systems, and Planning Projects* (London, Routledge, 1996).

39. David Harvey, *O novo imperialismo* (São Paulo, Loyola, 2003), p. 115–33, author's translation.

40. Ibid., p. 126.

41. Erik Swyngedouw, Frank Moulaert and Arantxa Rodriguez, 'Neoliberal Urbanization in Europe', *Antipode*, vol. 34, no. 3 (July 2002), p. 546.

42. Maria Kaika and Luca Ruggiero, 'Land Financialization as a "Lived" Process: The Transformation of Milan's Bicocca by Pirelli',

European Urban and Regional Studies, June 2013; Llerena Guiu Searle, 'Conflict and Commensuration: Contested Market Making in India's Private Real Estate Development Sector', *International Journal of Urban and Regional Research*, vol. 38, no. 1 (Jan. 2014).

43. Mike Raco, 'Delivering Flagship Projects in an Era of Regulatory Capitalism: State-led Privatization and the London Olympics 2012', *International Journal of Urban and Regional Research*, vol. 38, no. 1 (Jan. 2014), p. 176.

44. Carlos Vainer, 'Cidade de exceção: reflexões a partir do Rio de Janeiro', *Anais do XIV Encontro Nacional da Anpur*, Rio de Janeiro, 2011. Available at: br.boell.org, accessed 6 Jan. 2015.

45. Ibid.

46. Pedro Fiori Arantes, *Arquitetura na era digital-financeira: desenho, canteiro e renda da forma* (São Paulo, Editora 34, 2012).

47. Stavros Stavrides, 'Urban Identities: Beyond the Regional and the Global: The Case of Athens', in Jamal Al-Qawasmi, Abdesselem Mahmoud and Ali Djerbi (eds), *Regional Architecture and Identity in the Age of Globalization* (Tunis, CSAAR Press, 2008).

48. Rolnik, *Thematic Report on the Impact of Mega-Events*.

49. Ibid.

50. Solomon J. Greene, 'Staged Cities: Mega-Events, Slum Clearance, and Global Capital', *Yale Human Rights and Development Law Journal*, vol. 6, no. 1 (2003).

51. COHRE, *Fair Play for Housing Rights. Mega-events, Olympic Games and Evictions* (Geneva, COHRE, 2007), p. 197.

52. Human Rights Watch, 'Demolished: Forced Evictions and the Tenant's Rights Movement in China', *Human Rights Watch*, vol. 16, no. 4 (March 2004). Available at: hrw.org, accessed 6 Jan. 2015.

53. COHRE, *Fair Play for Housing Rights*, p. 28.

54. Caroline Newton, 'The Reverse Side of the Medal: About the 2010 Fifa World Cup and the Beautification of the N2 in Cape Town', *Urban Forum*, vol. 20, no. 1 (Feb. 2009), p. 9.

55. Greene, 'Staged Cities', p. 172.

56. COHRE, *Barcelona 1992 – International Events and Housing Rights: A Focus on the Olympic Games* (Geneva, COHRE, 2007).

57. East Thames Group, *Home Games: A Study of the Housing and Regeneration Legacies of Recent Olympic and Paralympic Games*

and the Implications for Residents of East London (London, East Thames Group, 2012), p. 14. Available at: east-thames.co.uk, accessed 15 Jan. 2014.

58. COHRE, *One World, Whose Dream? Housing Rights Violations and the Beijing Olympic Games* (Geneva, COHRE, 2008).

59. Rolnik, *Report on the Impact of Mega-Events*.

60. East Thames Group, *Home Games*, p. 13.

61. Ibid., p. 16.

62. Pivot Legal Society, *Cracks in the Foundation: Solving the Housing Crisis in Canada's Poorest Neighbourhood* (Vancouver, Pivot Legal Society, Sept. 2006), pp. 1–3. Available at: pivotlegal.org, accessed 15 Jan. 2015.

63. Miloon Kothari, *Relatório de Missão à África do Sul*, A/HRC/7/16 /Add.3, 2007.

64. Rolnik, *Report on the Impact of Mega-Events*.

65. The information about Tokyo was obtained during my visit to the country and to this housing project in particular.

66. COHRE, *Fair Play for Housing Rights*, p. 198.

67. East Thames Group, *Home Games*, p. 15.

68. COHRE, *Fair Play for Housing Rights*, p. 198.

69. Rolnik, *Report on the Impact of Mega-Events*.

70. Jones, ' "Cities Without Slums"?'

71. Roy, *Poverty Capital*, p. 140.

72. Ananya Roy, 'Slum-free Cities of the Asian Century: Postcolonial Government and the Project of Inclusive Growth', *Singapore Journal of Tropical Geography*, vol. 35, no. 1 (March 2014).

73. Huchzermeyer, ' "Slum" Upgrading or "Slum" Eradication?'

12. Financialisation in the Tropics

1. Mariana Fix, *Parceiros da exclusão: duas histórias da construção de uma 'nova cidade' em São Paulo: Faria Lima e Água Espraiada* (São Paulo, Boitempo, 2001), pp. 19, 37.

2. Mariana Fix, *São Paulo cidade global: fundamentos financeiros de uma miragem* (São Paulo, Boitempo, 2007), p. 104.

3. Ibid.

4. Ibid, pp. 98–101; Fix, *Parceiros da exclusão*.

5. Paulo Somlanyi Romeiro, *Zonas Especiais de Interesse Social: materialização de um novo paradigma no tratamento de assentamentos informais ocupados por população de baixa renda* (Master's Degree Dissertation in Law, PUC-SP Law School, São Paulo, 2010), p. 77.

6. Raquel Rolnik and Jeroen Klink, 'Crescimento econômico e desenvolvimento urbano: por que nossas cidades continuam tão precárias?', *Novos Estudos Cebrap*, no. 89 (Mar. 2011), p. 89.

7. Ermínia Maricato, *O impasse da política urbana no Brasil* (Petrópolis, Vozes, 2011), p. 34.

8. Tagore Villarim de Siqueira, 'Competitividade sistêmica: desafios para o desenvolvimento econômico brasileiro', *Revista do BNDES*, vol. 16, no. 31 (June 2009), p. 141.

9. Maria Hermínia Tavares de Almeida, 'A política social no governo Lula', *Novos Estudos Cebrap*, no. 70 (Nov. 2004).

10. Maricato, *O impasse da política urbana no Brasil*, p. 35.

11. Marcio Pochmann, 'Políticas sociais e padrão de mudanças no Brasil durante o governo Lula', *SER Social*, vol. 13, no. 28 (Jan.–June 2011), pp. 26–7.

12. André A. Sant'Anna, Gilberto R. Borça Jr. and Pedro Q. de Araújo, 'Mercado de crédito no Brasil: evolução recente e o papel do BNDES (2004–2008)', *Revista do BNDES*, vol. 16, no. 31 (June 2009), pp. 43–8.

13. Pochmann, 'Políticas sociais e padrão de mudanças'.

14. Raquel Rolnik, 'Democracy on the Edge: Limits and Possibilities in the Implementation of an Urban Reform Agenda in Brazil', *International Journal of Urban and Regional Research*, vol. 35 (2011), pp. 239–55.

15. Rosana Denaldi, Karina Leitão and Silvana Zioni, 'Nota técnica: infraestrutura e desenvolvimento urbano', in Tânia B. Araújo (ed.), *Trajetórias do Brasil frente aos compromissos assumidos pelo governo Lula 2003–2009, dimensão melhoria da qualidade de vida* (Brasilia, CGEE, 2010), mimeo.

16. Haroldo da Gama Torres and Eduardo Marques, 'Reflexões sobre a hiperperiferia: novas e velhas faces da pobreza no entorno municipal', *Revista Brasileira de Estudos Regionais e Urbanos*, no. 4 (2001); Suzana Pasternak Taschner and Lucia Bógus, 'A cidade dos anéis', in Luiz Cesar de Queiroz Ribeiro (ed.), *O futuro das*

metrópoles: desigualdades e governabilidade (Rio de Janeiro, Revan, 2000).

17. Rossella Rossetto, *Produção imobiliária e tipologias residenciais modernas: São Paulo, 1945–1964* (PhD thesis in Architecture and Urbanism, FAU-USP, São Paulo, 2002).

18. Ibid.

19. Luciana de Oliveira Royer, *Financeirização da política habitacional: limites e perspectivas* (São Paulo, Annablume, 2014), p. 51.

20. Marcus A. B. C. de Mello, 'Classe, burocracia e intermediação de interesses na formação da política de habitação', *Espaço e Debates*, no. 24, year VIII (1988), p. 76.

21. Nabil Bonduki, 'Política habitacional e inclusão social no Brasil: revisão histórica e novas perspectivas no governo Lula', *Arquitectura Urbana*, no. 1(2008). Available at: usjt.br, accessed 12 Dec. 2014.

22. De Oliveira Royer, *Financeirização da política habitacional*, p. 53; Marcelo Burgos, 'Dos parques proletários ao Favela-Bairro: as políticas públicas nas favelas do Rio de Janeiro', in Zaluar and Alvito (eds), *Um século de favela*.

23. De Oliveira Royer, *Financeirização da política habitacional*, p. 55.

24. Ibid., p. 67.

25. Ermínia Maricato, 'Autoconstrução, a arquitetura possível', in *A produção capitalista da casa (e da cidade) no Brasil industrial* (2nd ed., São Paulo, Alfa-Ômega, 1982), p. 80.

26. De Mello, 'Classe, burocracia e intermediação de interesses'.

27. Mariana Fix, *Financeirização e transformações recentes no circuito imobiliário no Brasil* (PhD thesis in Economic Development, IE-Unicamp, Campinas, 2011), p. 102.

28. Marta Arretche, 'Intervenção do Estado e setor privado: o modelo brasileiro de política habitacional', *Espaço & Debates*, vol. 10, no. 31, 1990; Sérgio de Azevedo, 'Vinte e dois anos de habitação popular (1964–1986): criação, trajetória e extinção do BNH', *Revista de Administração Pública*, vol. 4, no. 22 (Oct.–Dec. 1988); Gabriel Bolaffi, *Aspectos socioeconômicos do Plano Nacional de Habitação* (PhD thesis in Architecture and Urbanism, FAU-USP, São Paulo, 1972); Ermínia Maricato, *Política habitacional no regime militar: do milagre brasileiro à crise econômica* (Petropolis, Vozes, 1987); de Mello, 'Classe, burocracia e intermediação de interesses'. For a

review of the literature, see De Oliveira Royer, *Financeirização da política habitacional*, p. 52 et seq.

29. Patricia Olga Camargo, *A evolução recente do setor bancário no Brasil* (São Paulo, Cultura Acadêmica, 2009).

30. De Mello, 'Classe, burocracia e intermediação de interesses', p. 81.

31. Peter Marcuse, *Subprime Housing Crisis*, 2008, mimeo. Available at: hic-gs.org, accessed 4 Sept. 2015.

32. De Oliveira Royer, *Financeirização da política habitacional*; Thêmis Amorim Aragão, *Housing Policy and the Restructuring of the Real Estate Sector in Brazil*, international seminar, The Real Estate/Financial Complex (Refcom), Leuven, 2014, mimeo.

33. Álvaro Luis dos Santos Pereira, Luciana de Oliveira Royer and Aline Viotto Gomes, 'Mercado de capitais e mercado imobiliário: a crescente importância dos títulos de base imobiliária', *Anais do XV Encontro Nacional da Anpur*, Recife, 2013. Available at: unuhospedagem.com.br, accessed 4 Sept. 2015.

34. Fix, *Financeirização e transformações recentes no circuito imobiliário*.

35. Ibid., p. 123.

36. Ibid., p. 134.

37. Higor Rafael de Souza Carvalho and Daniel Ávila Caldeira, *Housing Under Finance Influence: The Case of São Paulo, Brazil*, International Sociological Association Forum, Amsterdam, 2013, mimeo.

38. Data from the company's financial report. See: gafisa.com.br, accessed 13 Dec. 2014.

39. According to the announcement of completion of primary and secondary public distributions of common stock issued by São Paulo Stock and Futures Exchange. See: bmfbovespa.com.br, accessed 13 Dec. 2014.

40. Souza Carvalho and Ávila Caldeira, *Housing Under Finance Influence*.

41. Fix, *Financeirização e transformações recentes no circuito imobiliário*, pp. 158–61.

42. Aragão, *Housing Policy and the Restructuring of the Real Estate Sector*.

43. André Singer, *Os sentidos do lulismo: Reforma gradual e pacto conservador* (São Paulo, Companhia das Letras, 2012).

44. Rolnik and dos Santos Pereira, *The Financialization of Housing and Spatial Segregation*.

45. Bonduki, *Habitação e autogestão*.

46. Under Lula's supervision and the general coordination of Clara Ant (architect, former PT congresswoman and Lula's advisor), Projeto Moradia's coordination board was formed by: André de Souza, the Unified Workers' Central (CUT) representative at the FGTS Curator Council; Ermínia Maricato; Evaniza Rodrigues (leader of the Housing Movements' Union); Iara Bernardi (then a PT congresswoman); Lúcio Kowarick; Nabil Bonduki, and Pedro Paulo Martoni Branco.

47. In the council's first line-up, social movements held nineteen seats, while corporate institutions held seven.

48. Rolnik and dos Santos Pereira, *The Financialization of Housing and Spatial Segregation*.

49. Fix, *Financeirização e transformações recentes no circuito imobiliário*, p. 135.

50. The fee was later fixed at 50 reais per month for this range.

51. There are different price ceilings for different categories of cities and regions, São Paulo, Rio and other metropolitan regions being the highest, and small cities in the hinterland the lowest.

52. Sinduscon/FGV, *Conjuntura da Construção, ano XII*, no. 3 (Oct. 2014), p. 6. Available at: sindusconsp.com.br, accessed 6 Jan. 2015.

53. Ibid., pp. 4, 6–7.

54. Marta Arretche, *Capacidades administrativas dos municípios brasileiros para a política habitacional* (Brasilia/São Paulo, Ministério das Cidades/Cebrap, 2012), p. 164.

55. Raquel Rolnik, Rodrigo Iacovini and Danielle Klintowitz, 'Habitação em municípios paulistas: construir políticas ou "rodar" programas?', *Revista Brasileira de Estudos Urbanos e Regionais*, vol. 16, no. 2 (Nov. 2014).

56. Regina Coeli Moreira Camargos, *Estado e empreiteiros no Brasil: uma análise setorial* (Master's thesis in Political Science, IFCH-Unicamp, Campinas, 1993).

57. Evaniza Lopes Rodrigues, *A estratégia fundiária dos movimentos populares na produção autogestionária da moradia*, Master's dissertation in architecutre and urban studies at São Paulo 2013.

58. Rolnik, Iacovini and Klintowitz, 'Habitação em municípios paulistas'.

59. See Ministry of Planning, *Governo federal responde editorial do jornal O Estado de S. Paulo*, 8 Aug. 2014. Available at: planejamento.gov.br, accessed 7 Dec. 2014.

60. Rolnik and dos Santos Pereira, *The Financialization of Housing and Spatial Segregation*.

61. Zanin Shimbo, *Habitação social de mercado*.

62. See LabCidade's research report at: labcidade.fau.usp.br. accessed 15 Dec. 2014.

63. Zanin Shimbo, *Habitação social de mercado*, p. 211.

64. Among the people interviewed by LabCidade's survey, 68.8 per cent miss a space or ambience that they had in their previous home. This absence is more strongly felt by resettled dwellers (74.5 per cent), who became part of the programme not by voluntary subscription or lottery, but because they had been forcebly evicted by the government and resettled in a MCMV housing complex. Among those who claimed to miss a space or surrounding, 70.5 per cent missed having a yard.

65. Raquel Rolnik et al., 'O programa Minha Casa Minha Vida nas regiões metropolitanas de São Paulo e Campinas: aspectos socio-espaciais e segregação', *Cadernos Metrópole*, vol. 17, no. 33 (May 2015).

66. This group corresponds to 329 (35.4 per cent) of the 930 interviewed families. Within this group, 83 per cent did not pay rent before, 96 per cent did not pay condominium fees, 37 per cent had no electricity expense and 33 per cent had no water expense.

13. At the Frontier of the Real-Estate–Financial Complex

1. Margaret E. Keck, *The Workers' Party and Democratization in Brazil* (New Haven, Yale University Press, 1992), pp. 190–3.

2. The lack of resources meant greater participation of beneficiaries themselves. In many instances of collective neighbourhood urbanisation, the municipality provided the machinery and materials and the residents constituted the workforce. See Raquel Rolnik, 'Urbanização a conta-gotas', *Versus: Revista de Ciências Sociais Aplicadas do CCJE/UFRJ*, vol. 2 (2009).

3. Orlando Alves dos Santos Jr., 'Cidade, cidadania e planejamento urbano: desafios na perspectiva da reforma urbana', in Sarah Feldman and Ana Fernandes (eds), *O urbano e o regional no Brasil contemporâneo: mutações, tensões, desafios* (Salvador, Edufba, 2007), p. 297.

4. Maria Celia Paoli, 'Movimentos sociais no Brasil: em busca de um estatuto político', in Michaela Hellmann (ed.), *Movimentos sociais e democracia no Brasil: 'sem a gente não tem jeito'* (São Paulo, Marco Zero, 1995), p. 376.

5. Milton Botler and Geraldo Marinho, 'O Recife e a regularização dos assentamentos populares', *Revista Pólis*, no. 29 (1997); João Sette Whitaker Ferreira and Daniela Motisuke, 'A efetividade da implementação de Zonas Especiais de Interesse Social no quadro habitacional brasileiro: uma avaliação inicial', in Laura Machado de Mello Bueno and Renato Cymbalista (eds), *Planos Diretores Municipais: novos conceitos de planejamento territorial* (São Paulo, Annablume/Instituto Pólis/Puccamp, 2007); Lívia Miranda and Demóstenes Moraes, 'O Plano de Regularização das Zonas Especiais de Interesse Social (Prezeis) do Recife: democratização da gestão e planejamento participativo', in Adauto Lúcio Cardoso (ed.), *Habitação social nas metrópoles brasileiras: uma avaliação das políticas habitacionais em Belém, Belo Horizonte, Porto Alegre, Recife, Rio de Janeiro e São Paulo no final do século XX* (Porto Alegre, Antac, 2007); Demóstenes Moraes, *Por uma política de habitação de interesse social para o Recife: apontamentos sobre o Prezeis* (Recife, URB, 2005). Available at: habitare.org.br, accessed 5 Sept. 2015.

6. Orlando Alves dos Santos Jr. and Daniel Todtmann Montandon (eds), *Os planos diretores municipais pós-Estatuto da Cidade: balanço crítico e perspectivas* (Rio de Janeiro, Letra Capital, 2011), p. 31.

7. Jacqueline Severo da Silva, 'Regularização fundiária, exercitando um novo paradigma: um conflito também ideológico – apresentação de casos', *Planejamento e Políticas Públicas*, no. 34 (Jan.–June 2010). Available at: ipea.gov.br, accessed 6 Jan. 2015.

8. Benjamin Goldfrank and Andrew Schrank, 'Municipal Neoliberalism and Municipal Socialism: Urban Political Economy in Latin America', *International Journal of Urban and Regional Research*, vol. 33, no. 2, June 2009.

9. The Ministry provided support through the production of educational material – the 'Master Plan Kit' – with video-guidebooks and technical reference material, and also supported promoters of capacity building workshops across the country.

10. Carlos Roberto Sanchez Milani, 'Les paradoxes du "principe participatif" dans la gestion publique locale', in Daniel van Eeuwen (ed.), *Le nouveau Brésil de Lula: dynamique des paradoxes* (La Tour d'Aigues, L'Aube, 2006), p. 232.

11. Alves dos Santos Jr. and Todtmann Montandon (eds), *Os planos diretores municipais*, pp. 31–4.

12. Pedro Manuel Rivaben de Sales, 'Operações Urbanas Consorciadas', in Alves dos Santos Jr. and Todtmann Montandon (eds), *Os planos diretores municipais*, p. 7.

13. Pedro Novais Lima Jr., *Uma estratégia chamada 'planejamento estratégico': deslocamentos espaciais e atribuições de sentido na teoria do planejamento urbano* (PhD thesis in Urban and Regional Planning, Ippur-UFRJ, Rio de Janeiro, 2003); Carlos Vainer, 'Pátria, empresa e mercadoria: notas sobre a estratégia discursiva do Planejamento Estratégico Urbano', in Otilia Arantes, Erminia Maricato, Carlos Vainer (eds) *A cidade do Pensamento único:desmanchando consensos* (Petrópolis Vozes, 2000).

14. Vainer, 'Pátria, empresa e mercadoria', p. 99.

15. In the first direct election to choose São Paulo's mayor, Jânio Quadros, leading the PTB/PFL coalition, defeated Fernando Henrique Cardoso, standing for the PMDB (the opposition party during the dictatorship), and Eduardo Suplicy, of the PT (a party formally created in 1981).

16. Adauto Lúcio Cardoso et al., 'Flexibilização da legislação urbanística no Rio de Janeiro: uma avaliação das operações interligadas', *Anais do VIII Encontro Nacional da Anpur*, Porto Alegre, 1999.

17. Daniel Julien van Wilderode, 'Operações interligadas: engessando a perna de pau', in Raquel Rolnik and Renato Cymbalista (eds), *Instrumentos urbanísticos contra a exclusão social* (São Paulo, Pólis, 1997).

18. Paulo Maluf initiated his political career as part of Arena, the military dictatorship party, and was São Paulo city mayor and São Paulo state governor during that period. He was convicted of

corruption many times, generating, within the political vocabulary, the verb 'to maluf', a synonym of 'to divert public resources'.

19. Luiz Guilherme Rivera de Castro, *Operações Urbanas em São Paulo: interesse público ou construção especulativa do lugar* (PhD thesis in Architecture and Urbanism, FAU-USP, São Paulo, 2006).

20. Van Wilderode, 'Operações interligadas', p. 53.

21. See: cmhcschl.gc.ca, accessed 29 Oct. 2015.

22. Nico Calavita and Kenneth Grimes, 'Inclusionary Housing in California: The Experience of Two Decades', *Journal of the American Planning Association*, vol. 64, no. 2 (1998).

23. Van Wilderode, 'Operações interligadas', p. 54.

24. Rivera de Castro, *Operações Urbanas em São Paulo*.

25. Maria Irene Q. F. Szmrecsanyi and José Eduardo de Assis Lefèvre, 'Grandes empreiteiras, Estado e reestruturação urbanística da cidade de São Paulo, 1970–1996', *Anais do IV Seminário de História da Cidade e do Urbanismo*, vol. 4, Rio de Janeiro (1996). Available at: unuhospedagem.com.br, accessed 6 Jan. 2015.

26. Mariana Fix, 'A "fórmula mágica" da parceria público-privada: operações urbanas em São Paulo', *Cadernos de Urbanismo*, year 1, no. 3 (2000).

27. Ermínia Maricato and João Sette Whitaker Ferreira, 'Operação consorciada: diversificação urbanística participativa ou aprofundamento da desigualdade?', in Letícia Marques Osório (ed.), *Estatuto da Cidade e reforma urbana: novas perspectivas para as cidades brasileiras* (Porto Alegre, Sergio Fabris Editor, 2002), p. 10.

28. See the summary of movements of Urban Project Faria Lima, developed by SP-Urbanismo on 25 Nov. 2014. Available at: prefeitura.sp.gov.br, accessed 17 Dec. 2014.

29. Fix, *Financeirização e transformações recentes no circuito imobiliário*, pp. 181–2.

30. Paulo Sandroni, 'CEPACs: Certificates of Additional Construction Potential: A New Financial Instrument of Value Capture in São Paulo', in Gregory Ingram and Yu-Hung Hong (eds), *Municipal Revenues and Land Policies*, Lincoln Institute of Land Policy, Cambridge, 2010. Available at: sandroni.com.br, accessed 6 Jan. 2015.

14. Real-Estate Avenues

1. Fix, *São Paulo cidade global*; Eduardo Alberto Cusce Nobre, *Reestruturação econômica e território*.

2. When Light&Power's electricity sector was nationalised by the federal government in 1978, the rest of the company was reorganised as Brascan Holdings, operating in the areas of mining, energy, agribusiness and real estate (new developments, shopping centres, hotels). Brascan – later named Brookfield – opened an investment bank in 1989 and became a powerful developer in Barra da Tijuca, Rio de Janeiro, and in São Paulo's southern industrial district, having participated in one of the first residential real-estate investment funds to be set up: Panamby.

3. Eduardo Alberto Cusce Nobre, *Reestruturação econômica e território*; Mariana Fix, *São Paulo cidade global*.

4. Eduardo Alberto Cusce Nobre, *Reestruturação econômica e território*, p. 523.

5. Maria Chaves Jardim, *Observatório de investimentos na Amazônia: fundos de pensão* (Brasília, Inesc, 2010).

6. Ibid.

7. Sérgio Lazzarini, *Capitalismo de laços: os donos do Brasil e suas conexões* (Rio de Janeiro, Campus/Elsevier, 2011), p. 11.

8. An example was the conference of leaders representing pension fund holders which took place in Brasilia in 2001, with the collaboration of the National Union of Closed Private Pension Entities (Sindapp). In a document sent to President Cardoso, the participants demanded the expansion of the complementary pension sector by giving permission to other sectors to establish their own pension funds. They also demanded increased participation of workers' representatives in the management of these funds. The document requested 'the plurality of public functionaries' complementary pension entities' (Carta de Brasília, 17 Oct. 2002). Among the signatories of the document, it is important to highlight the names of Luiz Gushiken, Ricardo Berzoini and José Pimentel, who, during Lula's first term, were in commanding positions and actively involved with the proposal for social security reform sent to the government in 2003. See Maria Chaves Jardim, ' "Nova" elite no Brasil? Sindicalistas e ex-sindicalistas no mercado financeiro', *Sociedade e Estado*, v. 24, n. 2, May–Aug. 2009.

9. Maria Chaves Jardim, *Observatório de investimentos na Amazônia.*

10. Mariana Fix, *Financeirização e transformações recentes no circuito imobiliário no Brasil*, p. 179.

11. Adriano Botelho, *O urbano em fragmentos: a produção do espaço e da moradia pelas práticas do setor imobiliário* (São Paulo, Annablume/Fapesp, 2007), p. 175.

12. Mariana Fix, *Financeirização e transformações recentes no circuito imobiliário no Brasil.*

13. Flávio Villaça, *Espaço intraurbano no Brasil* (São Paulo, Studio Nobel/Fapesp, 1998).

14. João Sette Whitaker Ferreira, *O mito da cidade-global: o papel da ideologia na produção do espaço urbano* (São Paulo/Petrópolis/ Salvador, Editora Unesp/Vozes/Anpur, 2007), pp. 188–9.

15. Regina Coeli Moreira Camargos, *Estado e empreiteiros no Brasil*, cited in Rodrigo Faria Gonçalves Iacovini, *Rodoanel Mário Covas: atores, arenas e processos* (Masters thesis in Architecture and Urbanism, FAU-USP, São Paulo, 2013).

16. Raymundo Faoro, *Os donos do poder: formação do patronato político brasileiro* (3rd ed., São Paulo, Globo, 2001), p. 447.

17. Sérgio Lazzarini, *Capitalismo de laços*, p. 13.

18. Szmrecsanyi et al., 'Grandes empreiteiras, Estado e reestruturação urbanística da cidade de São Paulo, 1970–1996', p. 1023.

19. Ibid., p. 1025.

20. Ibid.

21. Nowadays, Emurb is divided into two state companies: SP Urbanismo still manages urban projects, while SP Obras manages larger projects. They still are, thus, the aforementioned point of coordination.

22. Pedro Henrique Pedreira Campos, *A ditadura dos empreiteiros.*

23. Rodrigo Faria Gonçalves Iacovini, *Rodoanel Mário Covas*, p. 189.

24. Regina Coeli Moreira Camargos, *Estado e empreiteiros no Brasil*, p. 54.

25. Ibid.

15. Real-Estate Games

1. Isabela Vieira, 'Cem mil pessoas devem acompanhar em Copacabana anúncio da sede das Olimpí- adas', *Agência Brasil*, 1 Oct. 2009. Available at memoria.ebc.com.br, accessed on: 6 Jan. 2015.

2. Samantha Lima, 'Empresário terá de construir e vender 3.600 apartamentos da vila dos atletas', *Folha de S.Paulo*, 7 Dec. 2014. Available at www1.folha.uol.com.br, accessed on 7 Jan. 2015.

3. Carlos Vainer, 'Cidade de exceção'.

4. Nelma Gusmão de Oliveira, 'Força-de-lei: rupturas e realinhamentos institucionais na busca do "sonho olímpico" carioca', *Anais do XIV Encontro Nacional da Anpur*, Rio de Janeiro, 2011, available at unuhospedagem.com.br, accessed on 12 Jan. 2015.

5. Law n. 11.079/2004.

6. Decree n. 5.977/2006.

7. Law n. 12.873/2013.

8. Erik Swyngedouw, 'The Post-Political City', in Bavo (ed.), *Urban Politics Now: Re-imagining Democracy in the Neoliberal City* (Rotterdam, NAI Publishers, 2007).

9. Luiz Cesar de Queiroz Ribeiro, *Dos cortiços aos condomínios fechados: as formas de produção da moradia na cidade do Rio de Janeiro* (Rio de Janeiro, Civilização Brasileira/Ippur-UFRJ/Fase, 1997), p. 308.

10. Adauto Lúcio Cardoso, 'O espaço do capital: a Barra da Tijuca e a grande promoção imobiliária', *Anais do III Encontro Nacional da Anpur*, Águas de São Pedro, 1989.

11. Nelma Gusmão de Oliveira, 'Força-de-lei'.

12. Municipal Law n. 32.576, from 28 Jan 2010. The contract, public notice and attachments are available at: portomaravilha.com.br, accessed on 19 Dec. 2014.

13. Ibid.

14. CCR – a company which administers several tolled motorways – is part of the Camargo Corrêa group and also participates in the implementation of Porto Maravilha's Lightrail system.

15. Rosane Rebeca de Oliveira Santos, *O planejamento da cidade é o planejamento dos jogos?*

16. Ibid., p. 98.

17. Ibid.

18. Jorge Bittar, cited in Isabela Bastos and Selma Schmidt, 'Plano Estratégico: Paes quer reduzir em 3,5% total da área de favelas até 2012', *Extra*, Rio de Janeiro, 5 Dec. 2009, available at extra.globo. com, accessed on 12 Jan. 2015.

19. Rio de Janeiro's World Cup and Olympic Games Popular Committee, *Megaeventos e violações dos direitos humanos no Rio de Janeiro* (Rio de Janeiro, Rio de Janeiro's World Cup and Olympic Games Popular Committee, 2013), p.27, available at comitepopulario.files.wordpress.com, accessed on 7 Jan. 2015.

16. June 2013

1. Jonas Medeiros, 'Junho de 2013 no Brasil e movimentos sociais em rede pelo mundo', in José Rodrigo Rodriguez and Felipe Gonçalves Silva (eds.), *Manual de Sociologia Jurídica* (2nd ed., São Paulo, Saraiva, 2017).

2. André Singer, 'Brasil, junho de 2013: Classes e ideologias cruzadas', *Novos Estudos*, no. 97 (Nov. 2013); Marcos Nobre, '1988 + 30', *Novos Estudos*, no. 105 (July 2016); Jean Tible, 'Selvagem Junho', in Gerardo Silva and Leonora Corsini (eds), *Democracia x Regimes de pacificação: a insistente recusa do controle exercido em nome da segurança* (São Paulo, Annablume, 2015).

3. Michael Hardt and Antonio Negri, *Multitude: War and Democracy in the Age of Empire* (London, Penguin, 2005).

4. Ruy Braga, 'Sob a sombra do precariado', in Ermínia Maricato et al. (eds.). *Cidades Rebeldes* (São Paulo, Boitempo, 2013), p. 82.

5. Bianca Tavolari, 'Direito à cidade: uma trajetória conceitual', *Novos Estudos*, no.104 (March 2016), p. 93.

6. ANCOP, *Dossiê Megaeventos e violações dos direitos humanos*, 2014. Available at: comitepopulario.files.wordpress.com, accessed 5 March 2018; Carlos Vainer, 'Quando a cidade vai às ruas', in Maricato et al. (eds.), *Cidades Rebeldes*, p.39.

7. Singer, 'Brasil, junho de 2013', p. 15;, Guilherme Simões, Marcos Campos and Rud Rafael, *MTST: 20 anos de história – Luta, organisação e esperança nas periferias do Brasil* (São Paulo, Autonómia Literária, 2017).

8. Guilherme Boulos was interviewed by the author on 20 Feb. 2018.

9. Jonathan Watts, 'Resistance! São Paulo Homeless Seize the City', *Guardian*, 27 Nov. 2017. Available at: theguardian.com, accessed 6 March 2018.

10. Nicolas Baverez, 'Le grand basculement vers le Sud', *Le Point*, 27 June 2013. Available at: lepoint.fr, accessed 12 Jan. 2015. Quoted in Raquel Rolnik, 'Apresentação – As vozes das ruas: as revoltas de junho e suas interpretações', in Maricato et al., *Cidades rebeldes*.

11. Dom Phillips, 'Brazil's right on the rise as anger grows over scandal and corruption', *Guardian*, 26 July 2017. Available at: theguardian.com, accessed 6 March 2018.

12. Nobre, '1988 + 30', pp. 138–9; G. Baiocchi, E. Braathen and A. C. Teixeira, 'Transformation Institutionalized? Making Sense of Participatory Democracy in the Lula Era', in C. Stokke and O. Thornquist (eds), *Democratization in the Global South: The Importance of Transformative Politics* (London, Palgrave Macmillan, 2012).

13. Raquel Rolnik, 'Ten years of City Statute in Brazil: From the struggle for urban reform to the World Cup cities', *International Journal of Urban Sustainable Development*, vol. 5 (2013).

14. Nobre, '1988 + 30'.

15. Tible, 'Selvagem Junho', p. 116.

16. Antonia Campos, Jonas Medeiros and Márcio Ribeiro, *Escolas de luta* (São Paulo, Veneta, 2016).

Afterword

1. Prashant Gopal, 'Wall Street, America's New Landlord, Kicks Tenants to the Curb', Bloomberg News, 1 March 2017. Available at: bloomberg.com, accessed 22 Jan. 2018.

2. Desiree Fields and Sabina Uffer, 'The Financialisation of Rental Housing: A Comparative Analysis of New York City and Berlin', *Urban Studies* (2014); M. Byrne, '"Asset Price Urbanism" and Financialization after the Crisis: Ireland's National Asset Management Agency', *International Journal of Urban and Regional Research*, vol. 40, no. 1 (2016), pp. 31–45; Gertjan Wijburg, Manuel Aalbers and Susanne Heeg, 'The Financialization of Rental Housing 2.0: Releasing Housing into the Privatized Mainstream of Capital Accumulation', mimeo, 2017; S. Soederberg, 'The Rental

Housing Question: Exploitation, Eviction and Erasures', *Geoforum*, vol. 1, no. 10 (2017); Melissa García-Lamarca, 'From Mortgage Securitisation to REITs: Dispossession and Financialised Housing 2.0 in Spain?' Working paper, under revision.

3. Harvey, *Seventeen Contradictions*, p. 241.

4. Joe Beswick, Georgia Alexandri, Michael Byrne, Sònia Vives-Miró, Desiree Fields, Stuart Hodgkinson and Michael Janoschka, 'Speculating on London's housing future', *City*, vol. 20, no. 2 (2016), pp. 321–41.

5. Ibid., p. 324. Rob Call, Denechia Powell and Sarah Heck, *Blackstone: Atlanta's newest landlord – The new face of rental market*, Homes for All, 2014. Available at: homesforall.org, accessed 22 Jan. 2018.

6. See invitationhomes.com, accessed 30 Jan. 2018.

7. Call et al., *Blackstone: Atlanta's newest landlord*, p. 6; Jade Rahmanai, Bose George and Ryan O'Steen, *Single-Family REO: An Emerging Asset Class* (3rd edition, Keefe, Bruyette and Woods, 2013).

8. Matthew Goldstein, 'Major Rental-Home Companies Set to Merge as U.S. House Prices Recover', *New York Times*, 10 Aug. 2017. Available at: nytimes.com, accessed 22 Jan. 2018.

9. Beswick et al., 'Speculating on London's housing future', p. 325.

10. Michael Byrne, 'Bad banks: The urban implications of asset management companies', *Urban Research and Practice* (2015).

11. García-Lamarca, 'From mortgage securitisation to REITs'; Michael Byrne, '"Asset price urbanism" and financialization after the crisis: Ireland's National Asset Management Agency', *International Journal of Urban and Regional Research* (2016).

12. Beswick et al., 'Speculating on London's housing future', p. 332.

13. Alba Brualla, 'Anticipa, filial de Blackstone, quiere ser la mayor gestora de pisos en alquiler', *eleconomista.es*, 30 March 2017. Available at: eleconomista.es, accessed 22 Jan. 2018.

14. Alfonso Simón Ruiz, 'Blackstone construye un gigante de viviendas para el alquiler en España', *Cinco Días*, 15 May 2017. Available at: cincodias.elpais.com, accessed 22 Jan. 2018.

15. Manuel Aalbers, *The Financialization of Housing: A Political Economy Approach* (Abingdon, Routledge, 2016), p. 121.

16. Benjamin F. Teresa, 'Managing fictitious capital: The legal geography of investment and political struggle in rental housing in New

York City', *Environment and Planning A*, vol. 48, no. 3 (2016), p. 472. Desiree Fields, 'Contesting the financialization of urban space: Community organizations and the struggle to preserve affordable rental housing in New York City', *Journal of Urban Affairs*, vol. 37, no. 2 (2014), p. 149.

17. Teresa, 'Managing fictitious capital', p. 142.

18. Aalbers, *Financialization of housing*, p. 117.

19. Byrne, '"Asset Price Urbanism"', pp. 31–45.

20. García-Lamarca, 'From mortgage securitisation to REITs'.

21. Ibid., pp. 9–10.

22. Call et al., *Blackstone: Atlanta's newest landlord.*

23. Elora Raymond, Richard Duckworth, Ben Miller, Michael Lucas and Shiraj Pokharel, 'Corporate Landlords, Institutional Investors, and Displacement: Eviction Rates in Single-Family Rentals', Federal Reserve Bank of Atlanta Community and Economic Development Discussion Paper Series, no. 04–16, 2016, p. 14.

24. Strategic Actions for a Just Economy and Right to the City Alliance, *Renting from Wall Street: Blackstone's Invitation Homes in Los Angeles and Riverside,* 2014.

25. United States Census Bureau, DP-1, 'Profile of General Population and Housing Characteristics: 2010 Demographic Profile Data', 29 Dec. 2015. Available at: factfinder.census.gov, accessed 23 Jan. 2018.

26. Marcelo Rochabrun and Cezary Podkul, 'The Fateful Vote That Made New York City Rents So High', *ProPublica*, 15 Dec. 2016. Available at: propublica.org, accessed 23 Jan. 2018.

27. See statisticalatlas.com, accessed 23 Jan. 2018.

28. Soederberg, 'The rental housing question', p. 4.

29. Ira Gary Peppercorn and Claude Taffin, *Rental Housing: Lessons from International Experience and Policies for Emerging Market*, Washington, DC, World Bank, 2013, p. x. Available at: documents. worldbank.org, accessed 22 Jan. 2018.

30. Fields, 'Contesting the financialization of urban space'; Fields and Uffer, 'The financialisation of rental housing'; Soederburg, S. 'The rental housing question: Exploitation, eviction and erasures', *Geoforum* 1–10, 2017.

31. US Department of Housing and Urban Development, *The 2017 Annual Homeless Assessment Report (AHAR) to Congress*, December 2017.

32. Juan Manuel Villagrán, 'Asset Chile afina compra de nuevos edifícios y eleva fondo de renta inmobiliaria residencial', *Economía y Negocios*, 20 Jan. 2018. Available at: economiaynegocios.cl, accessed 22 Jan. 2018; María de los Ángeles Pattillo, 'Edificios con un solo dueño y destinados 100% a renta residencial se concentran en Santiago e Independencia', *El Mercurio*, 3 Sept. 2016.

33. Interview with Alexandre Frankel, Vitacon CEO, on 'Moeda forte', Istoé Dinheiro, 6 March 2018.

34. Department of Communities and Local Government, 'Review of the Barriers to Institutional Investment in Private Rented Homes', 2012.

35. Beswick et al., 'Speculating on London's housing future'.

36. Rodrigo Fernández, Annelore Hofman and Manuel Aalbers, 'London and New York as a safe deposit box for the transnational wealth elite', *Environment and Planning A*, vol.48, n.12, 2016.

37. For the complete list of investor companies, see crunchbase.com/organisation/airbnb, accessed 18 Jan. 2017.

38. Bianca Tavolari, 'AirBnB e os impasses regulatórios do compartilhamento de moradia', in Rafael Zanatta, Pedro C. B. de Paula and Beatriz Kira (eds), *Economias do compartilhamento e o direito* (Curitiba, Juruá, 2017). Available at: internetlab.org.br, accessed 30 Jan. 2018.

39. Fields, 'Contesting the financialization of urban space'.

40. Teresa, 'Managing fictitious capital', p. 472; Fields, 'Contesting the financialization of urban space'.

41. Michael Greenberg, 'Tenants Under Siege: Inside New York City's Housing Crisis', *New York Review of Books*, 17 Aug. 2017. Available at: nybooks.com, accessed 30 Jan. 2018.

42. See sindicatdellogateres.org, accessed 23 Jan. 2018.

43. Tavolari, 'AirBnB e os impasses regulatórios', p. 269. In July 2014, Mayor Colau fined Airbnb and other homestay platforms €30,000: A. Kassam, 'Airbnb fined €30,000 for illegal tourist lets in Barcelona', *Guardian*, 7 July 2014. Available at: theguardian.com, accessed 18 Jan. 2016. In December 2015, the fine was even bigger: I. Gutiérrez, 'Colau multa a Airbnb y Homeaway por anunciar pisos sin licencia turística', El Economista, 22 Dec. 2015. Available at: eleconomista.es, accessed 1 Feb. 2016.

44. Stephen Burgen, 'Airbnb faces crackdown on illegal apartment rentals in Barcelona', *Guardian*, 2 June 2017. Available at: theguardian.com, accessed 23 Jan. 2018.

45. Barry K. Gills and Kevin Gray, 'People Power in the Era of Global Crisis: Rebellion, Resistance and Liberation', *Third World Quarterly*, vol. 33, no. 2 (April 2012).

46. Charles Tilly, 'Spaces of Contention', *Mobilization*, vol. 5, no. 2 (Sept. 2000), p. 137.

47. Peter Marcuse, 'Keeping Space in Its Place, in the Occupy Movements', *Progressive Planning*, vol. 191 (April 2012).

48. Vera Pallamin, 'Do lugar-comum ao espaço incisivo: dobras do gesto estético no espaço urbano', in Maria Beatriz de Medeiros e Marianna Monteiro (eds), *Espaço e performance* (Brasilia, Editora da Pós-Graduação em Arte da UnB, 2007), p. 192.

49. John Hammond, 'The Significance of Space in Occupy Wall Street', *Interface*, vol. 5, no. 2 (Nov. 2013).

50. Erik Swyngedouw, *Post-Democratic Cities: For Whom and for What?*, Regional Studies Association Annual Conference, Pecs, Budapest, 2010. Available at: variant.org.uk, accessed 12 Jan. 2015.

51. Jacques Rancière, *La Haine de la démocratie* (Paris, La Fabrique, 2005).

52. Slavoj Žižek, 'Problemas no paraíso', Ermínia Maricato et al. (eds), *Cidades rebeldes*, p. 186, author's translation.

53. Giorgio Agamben, 'Metropolis', Seminar, 16 Nov 2006, available at thefunambulist.net, accessed 11 April 2018.

54. Swyngedouw, *Post-Democratic Cities*, p. 13.

55. Ibid.

56. Raco, 'Delivering Flagship Projects'.

Acknowledgements

1. The shortest missions I carried out lasted ten days (Maldives, Argentina and Algeria); the longest, eighteen days (United States).

2. I particularly highlight: Rede Cidade e Moradia, who, with CNPq and Ministry of Cities' resources, developed surveys about the program Minha Casa Minha Vida; surveys developed in collaboration with the Observatório das Metrópoles, coordinated by myself and Orlando Jr., from IPPUR; and the set of research papers on urban and housing regulation, supported by resources from FAPESP and the Lincoln Institute of Land Policy, developed in LabCidade.

Index

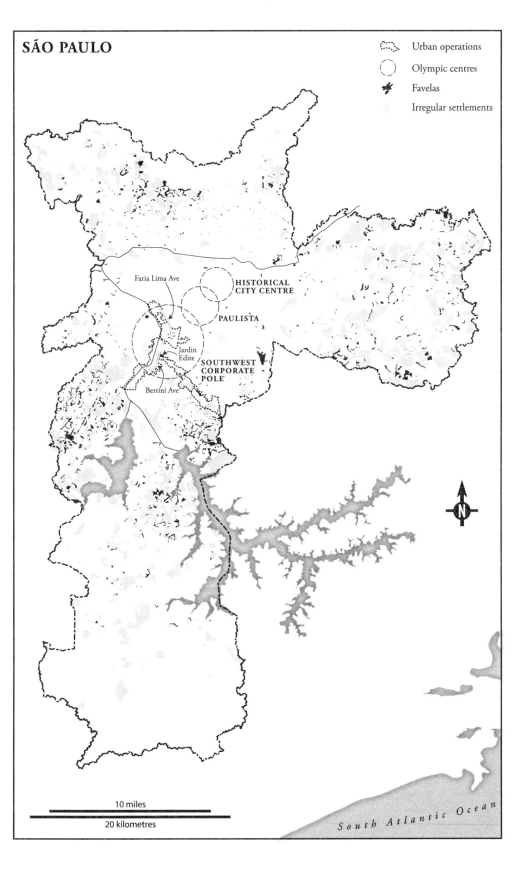

SÃO PAULO

Urban operations

Olympic centres

Favelas

Irregular settlements

HISTORICAL
CITY CENTRE

PAULISTA

Faria Lima Ave

Jardin
Edite

SOUTHWEST
CORPORATE
POLE

Berrini Ave

N

10 miles

20 kilometres

South Atlantic Ocean

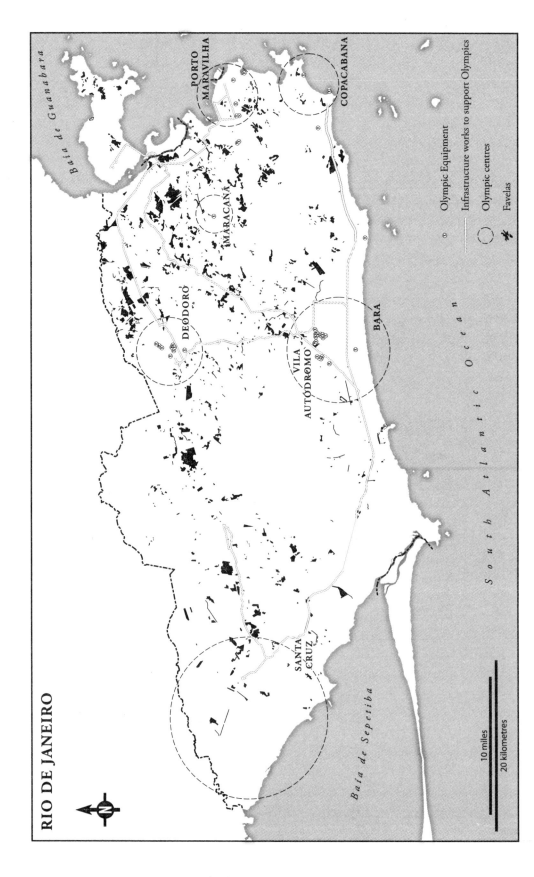

RIO DE JANEIRO

Baía de Guanabara

PORTO MARAVILHA

COPACABANA

MARACANÁ

DEÓDORO

VILA AUTÓDROMO

BARRA

SANTA CRUZ

Baía de Sepetiba

South Atlantic Ocean

Olympic Equipment
Infrastructure works to support Olympics
Olympic centres
Favelas

10 miles
20 kilometres